George Sale, Elwood Morris Wherry

A Comprehensive Commentary on the Qurán

Vol. 2

George Sale, Elwood Morris Wherry

A Comprehensive Commentary on the Qurán
Vol. 2

ISBN/EAN: 9783337817619

Printed in Europe, USA, Canada, Australia, Japan

Cover: Foto ©Lupo / pixelio.de

More available books at **www.hansebooks.com**

A COMPREHENSIVE COMMENTARY

ON

THE QURÁN:

COMPRISING SALE'S TRANSLATION

AND

PRELIMINARY DISCOURSE,

WITH ADDITIONAL NOTES AND EMENDATIONS.

TOGETHER WITH

A Complete Index to the Text, Preliminary Discourse, and Notes,

BY THE REV. E. M. WHERRY, M.A.

VOL. II.

BOSTON:
HOUGHTON, MIFFLIN AND COMPANY.
NEW YORK: 11 EAST SEVENTEENTH STREET.
The Riverside Press, Cambridge.
1884.

CONTENTS.

CHAP.		PAGE
III.—Entitled Sur ál Imran (The Family of Imrán)		1
IV.—Entitled Surat un Nisa (Women)	. . .	64
V.—Entitled Surat ul Máida (The Table)	. .	118
VI.—Entitled Surat al Anám (Cattle)	. . .	159
VII.—Entitled Surat al Aráf (The Partition Wall)		201
VIII.—Entitled Surat al Aufál (The Spoils)	. .	248
IX.—Entitled Surat al Tauba (Repentance, Immunity)		273
X.—Entitled Surat al Yunas (Jonah)	. . .	321
XI.—Entitled Surat al Húd		342
XII.—Entitled Surat al Yasuf (Joseph)	. . .	368
XIII.—Entitled Surat al Raad (Thunder)	. . .	396

THE QURÁN.

CHAPTER III.

ENTITLED SURAT ÁL IMRÁN (THE FAMILY OF IMRÁN).

Revealed at Madína.

INTRODUCTION.

THIS chapter contains a variety of passages belonging to different periods. The *revelations* are, however, all of Madína origin, excepting verses 26 and 27, which seem to be the remnant of a lost Makkan Sura.

As to matter, the chapter may be divided into two portions. The first, extending to verse 120, relates to various matters of instruction and warning, suited to the circumstances of the Muslims during the period of prosperity intervening between the victory at Badr and the defeat at Ohod. The remainder of the chapter was intended to counteract the evils consequent upon the misfortunes of the Muslims at Ohod.

Probable Date of the Revelations.

Verses 1–25, 28–57, 66–94, and 98–120, belong to the period intervening between Ramadhán of A.H. 2 (Badr) and Shawwál of A.H. 3 (Ohod).

Verses 26 and 27 are Makkan, but their date cannot be ascertained. Verses 58–65 allude to the visit of the Christians of Najrán to Madína in A.H. 9. They probably belong to that year.

Verses 95–97, referring to the rites of pilgrimage as fully established, must be referred to the later years of Muhammad's life, say A.H. 10.

The remaining verses, 121–200, belong to a period immediately succeeding the battle of Ohod, and must therefore be referred to the latter part of A.H. 3 or the beginning of A.H. 4.

Principal Subjects.

God one and self-existent . . . . . verses	1, 2
The Qurán to be believed . . . . . ,,	3, 4
God omniscient . . . . ,,	5, 6
Plain and obscure verses of the Qurán . . ,,	7
The prayer of those versed in Quránic mystery . ,,	8, 9
The punishment of Pharaoh a warning to infidels . ,,	10, 12
The victory at Badr alluded to . . . . ,,	13
The faithful, their character and reward . . ,,	14–18
Islám the true religion . . . . . . ,,	19, 20
The punishment of unbelievers eternal . . . ,,	21–25
God omnipotent and sovereign . . . . ,,	26, 27
Obedience to God enjoined . . . . . ,,	28–34
The Virgin Mary—her conception—nurtured by Zacharias . . . . ,,	35–38
John Baptist, his birth . . . . . . ,,	39–41
Christ announced to the Virgin—his miracles—apostles, &c. . . . . ,,	42–57
Muhammad's dispute with the Christians of Najrán ,,	58–65
The hypocritical Jews reproached . . . . ,,	66–77
Prophets not to be worshipped . . . . ,,	78–83
God's curse on infidels . . . . . . ,,	84–91
Almsgiving enjoined . . . . . . ,,	92
The Jews unlawfully forbid certain meats . . ,,	93–95
The Kaabah founded . . . . . . ,,	96, 97
Muslims are warned against the friendship of Jews, &c. . . . . ,,	98–105
The lot of infidels and believers contrasted . . ,,	106–109
Muslims safe from the enmity of Jews and Christians . . . . ,,	110–112
Certain believing Jews commended for their faith . ,,	113–115
Muslims not to make friends of Jews and Christians ,,	116–120
The battle of Ohod alluded to . . . . ,,	121, 122
Disheartened Muslims encouraged . . . ,,	123–129
Usury forbidden . . . . ,,	130–136
The doom of calumniators of the apostles . . ,,	137, 138
Islám not dependent on Muhammad for success . ,,	139–144
The former prophets are examples of perseverance . ,,	145–148
Unbelievers to be avoided . . . . . ,,	149–151
Certain Muslims disobedient at Ohod . . . ,,	152–154

The hypocrites rebuked	verses 155-157
Muslims slain at Ohod to enter paradise	„ 158, 159
Mild treatment of vacillating Muslims	„ 160, 161
The spoils of war to be honestly divided	„ 162-165
The faithful sifted by defeat at Ohod	„ 166-169
The joy of the Ohod martyrs in paradise	„ 170-172
Certain Muslims commended for faithfulness	„ 173-176
The fate of unbelievers	„ 177-180
The miser's doom	„ 181
Scoffing Jews denounced—they charge Muhammad with imposture	„ 182-190
Meditations and prayers of the pious	„ 191-195
God's answer to the prayers of the pious	„ 196-198
Certain believing Jews and Christians commended	„ 199
Exhortation to patience and perseverance	„ 200

IN THE NAME OF THE MOST MERCIFUL GOD.

|| (1) A. L. M. (2) There is no GOD but GOD, the living, R ¼. the self-subsisting: (3) he hath sent down unto thee the

(1) *A. L. M.* See note on chap. ii. ver. 1, and Prelim. Disc., p. 100.

(2) *There is no God but God, &c.* These words express one half of the Muslim creed; they are said to have been delivered on the occasion of a visit to the Prophet by certain Christians from Najrán. On being invited to join Islám, they professed their faith in Jesus the Son of God. To this Muhammad replied that they were unable to receive the true religion because of their having attributed to the Deity the human relationships of wife and son. The Christians declared their belief in the Sonship of Jesus, saying, "If God were not his father, who was?" To this Muhammad replied, that, according to their own religion, God was immortal, and yet they believed that Jesus would taste of death; that he ate and drank, slept and awoke, went and came, &c. This, he averred, could not be predicated of divinity. See *Tafsír-i-Husainí in loco.*

According to the *Tafsír-i-Raufi*, this verse contains a distinct rejection of the Christian doctrine of the Divinity of Christ as well as of the Trinity. The tradition handed down to the present generation by these commentators, and, so far as I know, by all commentators of the Qurán, confirms our interpretation of chap. ii. vers. 86, 116. Muhammad knew of no Trinity save that of God, Mary, and Jesus, and Muhammadan commentators know of no other Trinity, unless it be that of God, Jesus, and Gabriel—see *Tafsír-i-Raufi in loco*—probably a modern gloss of the Bible language, "Father, Son, and Holy Ghost," the term Holy Spirit, as found in the Qurán, being

book *of the Qurán* with truth, confirming that which was *revealed* before it; for he had formerly sent down the law, and the gospel a direction unto men; and he had also sent down the distinction *between good and evil.* (4) Verily those who believe not the signs of GOD shall suffer a grievous punishment; for GOD is mighty, able to revenge. (5) Surely nothing is hidden from GOD, *of that which is* on

---

always understood to refer to the Angel Gabriel: see chap. ii. 253. No Christian would object to the statement upon which we are now commenting. It is a statement clearly set forth in our Scriptures. But if this statement is intended to refute the *Christian* doctrine concerning the person of Christ and the Trinity, what becomes of the claims set up for the Qurán in this same verse as "confirming that which was revealed before it"? What are we to say of the inspiration of a prophet who seems to have been ignorant of the teaching of the Scriptures he professed to confirm? If he were not ignorant of these doctrines, then what becomes of his character for integrity? How he could be so ignorant of them, after personal intercourse with Christians as testified by tradition, as to attribute to them views never held by any sect however heretical, I confess myself unable to show.

(3) *He had formerly sent down the law, &c.* The Muslim commentators understand the reference to be to all the Scriptures of the Old and New Testament, and that these were "a direction" unto the Jews that they should not call Ezra the Son of God, and "a direction" to the Christians that they should not call Christ "God, the Son of God, or one of three persons of a Trinity."—*Tafsír-i-Raufi.*

The distinction. The original word is *Al Furqán*, a word usually translated in the Persian and Urdú versions of the Qurán, "miracles." It is applied to the Qurán in the sense of the text, as the distinguisher "between good and evil," especially between the false and true in religion. This name, say the Muslims, is intended to point to the miraculous character of the Qurán. But if so, the same character must be credited to the Christian and Jewish Scriptures, for the commentators admit that what is referred to in the first part of this verse *in detail* is here referred to *in general* (*Tafsír-i-Raufi in loco*). The word therefore probably points to the *seal of miracles* which God set upon all his prophets and his word as revealed by them. In the case of the Qurán, the verses ($Ayát$ = signs) are the miraculous seal of inspiration.

(4) *Those who believe not the signs, i.e.,* who reject the teaching of the Qurán. If our view of the latter clause of the preceding verse be correct, allusion may be had to the teaching of former Scriptures as well.

(5) *Nothing is hidden from God, &c.* A distinct recognition of the omniscience of God. The commentators see in this statement a refutation of the Christian doctrine of the Divinity of Christ. The Son

earth, or in heaven : (6) it is he who formeth you in the wombs, as he pleaseth; there is no GOD but he, the mighty, the wise. (7) It is he who hath sent down unto thee the book, wherein are some verses clear to be understood, they are the foundation of the book; and others are parabolical. But they whose hearts are perverse will follow that which is parabolical therein, out of love of schism, and a desire of the interpretation thereof; yet none knoweth the interpretation thereof, except God. But they who are well

---

of Mary did not know everything, therefore he could not be divine. Here again we see that the Muslim conception of Christ's divinity is that his humanity was divine.

(6) *He that formeth you, &c., i.e.,* "tall or short, male or female, black or white, deformed or perfect, beautiful or ugly, good and fortunate, or wretched and miserable."—*Tafsír-i-Raufí.*

(7) *Some verses clear, ... others are parabolical.* "This passage is translated according to the exposition of al Zamakhsharí and Baidháwi, which seems to be the truest.

"The contents of the Qurán are here distinguished into such passages as are to be taken in the literal sense, and such as require a figurative acceptation. The former, being plain and obvious to be understood, compose the fundamental part, or, as the original expresses it, *the mother* of the book, and contain the principal doctrines and precepts, agreeably to and consistently with which, those passages which are wrapt up in metaphors and delivered in enigmatical, allegorical style are always to be interpreted." See Prelim. Disc., p. 113.—*Sale.*

On this subject, Hughes, in his *Notes on Muhammadanism,* pp. 32-34, second edition, writes as follows :—"The sentences (*'Ibárat*) of the Qurán are either *Záhir* or *Khafí, i.e.,* either obvious or hidden.

"Obvious sentences are of four classes : *záhir, nass, mufassar, muhkam.*

"*Záhir* = those sentences the meaning of which is *obvious* or clear without any assistance from the context, &c.

"Hidden sentences are either *khafí, mushkil, mujmal,* or *mutashabih," i.e.,* "hidden," "ambiguous," "compendious," or "intricate."

We have therefore in this passage the foundation principle of Muslim exegesis. See also the *Tafsír-i-Raufí in loco.*

None knoweth the interpretation, &c. Sale has followed the interpretation of the Sunní or orthodox sect in this translation. The Shiáh sect, however, dissents from an interpretation which makes God say that he has revealed what is not after all a revelation. They, therefore, understand this sentence as being closely connected with the one following, as the original will very well allow, and render the passage thus : " *None knoweth the interpretation thereof except God* AND *those who are well grounded in the knowledge which*

grounded in the knowledge say, We believe therein, the whole is from our LORD; and none will consider except the prudent. (8) O LORD, cause not our hearts to swerve *from truth,* after thou hast directed us: and give us from thee mercy, for thou art he who giveth. (9) O LORD, thou shalt surely gather mankind together, unto a day *of resurrection:* there is no doubt of it, for GOD will not be contrary to the promise.

‖ (10) As for the infidels, their wealth shall not profit them anything, nor their children, against GOD: they shall be the fuel of *hell* fire. (11) According to the wont of the people of Pharaoh, and of those who went before them, they charged our signs with a lie; but GOD caught them in their wickedness, and GOD is severe in punishing. (12) Say unto those who believe not, Ye shall be overcome, and thrown together into hell; and an unhappy couch *shall it be.* (13) Ye have already had a miracle *shown you* in two armies,

---

say, &c. By "those who are well grounded in the knowledge," they understand the Imáms of their own sect. This interpretation, however, does not avail them much, inasmuch as they are dependent on the fallible testimony of the traditionists for a knowledge of the dictum of the Imáms; and, amidst the conflict of witnesses, most men would be ready to say with the text, "None knoweth the interpretation thereof except God."

The *principle* enunciated in this verse should not be forgotten by Christians when called upon by Muslims to explain some of the obscure passages of the Bible or the mysteries of our religion.

(8) *O Lord, &c.* Muslims understand all prayers of this kind found in the Qurán as introduced by the word "say." See notes in chap. i. This prayer is dictated by the third clause of the preceding verse, and is connected with that passage thus: "They who are well grounded, say . . . O Lord," &c.

(9) *A day, &c.* Rodwell gives the correct rendering of this passage thus: "For the day of whose coming there is not a doubt, thou wilt surely gather mankind together." So too the Urdú and Persian translations.

(11) *They charged our signs with a lie.* Muhammad again likens himself to Moses and other prophets, whose message had been treated with contempt by infidels like unto the Jews and Quraish of his time.

(12) *Ye shall be overcome.* These defiant words, addressed to the enemies of Islám, and to the Quraish in particular, were inspired by the Muslim victory at Badr, A.H. 2.

(13) *Ye have already had a miracle shown you.* "The sign or

which attacked each other: one army fought for GOD's true religion, but the other were infidels; they saw *the faithful* twice as many as themselves in *their* eyesight; for GOD strengthened with his help whom he pleaseth. Surely herein was an example unto men of understanding. (14)

---

miracle here meant was the victory by Muhammad in the second year of the Hijra over the idolatrous Makkans ... in the valley of Badr.... Muhammad's forces consisted of no more than three hundred and nineteen men, but the enemy's army of near a thousand, notwithstanding which odds he put them to flight, having killed seventy of the principal Quraish" (forty-nine, see *Muir's Life of Mahomet*, vol. iii. p. 107, note), "and taken as many prisoners, with the loss of only fourteen of his own men. This was the first victory obtained by the Prophet; and though it may seem no very considerable action, yet it was of great advantage to him, and the foundation of all his future power and success. For which reason it is famous in the Arabian history, and more than once vaunted in the Qurán (chap. viii. 45, 46) as an effect of the divine assistance. The miracle, it is said, consisted in three things: 1. Muhammad, by the direction of the Angel Gabriel, took a handful of gravel and threw it towards the enemy in the attack, saying, *May their faces be confounded;* whereupon they immediately turned their backs and fled. But though the Prophet seemingly threw the gravel himself, yet it is told in the Qurán (chap. viii. 17) that it was not he, but God, who threw it, that is to say, by the ministry of his angel. 2. The Muhammadan troops seemed to the infidels to be twice as many in number as themselves, which greatly discouraged them. And 3. God sent down to their assistance first a thousand, and afterwards three thousand angels, led by Gabriel, mounted on his horse Haizúm; and, according to the Qurán (chap. viii. 17), these celestial auxiliaries really did all the execution, though Muhammad's men imagined themselves did it, and fought stoutly at the same time."—*Sale*.

There is a discrepancy between the statement of this verse and that of chap. viii. 46. Here the *miracle* consists in the dismay wrought among the Quraish by magnifying the number of Muslims in *their* eyes; but there it is recorded that "when he caused them to appear unto you when ye met to be few in your eyes, *and* diminished your number in their eyes." In this verse the *miracle* consisted in encouraging the Muslims by diminishing the number of those of Makkah and in luring on the Quraish to destruction by making the number of their adversaries appear even less than it really was. The commentators reconcile these statements by making the former to succeed the latter in time. Considering the number of angels called in to assist the Muslims on this occasion, one would infer that the angelic hosts of Islám were not highly gifted in the art of war. Compare Isa. xxxvii. 36, but see below, ver. 123, note, and on chap. viii. 45, 46.

The love and eager desire of wives, and children, and sums heaped up of gold and silver, and excellent horses, and cattle, and land, is prepared for men: this is the provision of the present life; but unto GOD shall be the most excellent return. (15) Say, Shall I declare unto you better *things* than this? For those who are devout *are prepared* with their LORD gardens through which rivers flow; therein shall they continue for ever: and *they shall enjoy* wives free from impurity, and the favour of GOD; for GOD regardeth *his* servants, (16) who say, O LORD, we do sincerely believe; forgive us therefore our sins, and deliver us from the pain of *hell* fire: (17) the patient, and the lovers of truth, and the devout, and the almsgivers, and those who ask pardon *early* in the morning. (18) GOD hath borne witness that there is no GOD but he; and the angels, and *those who are* endowed with wisdom, *profess the same;* who executeth righteousness; there is no GOD but he; the mighty, the wise.

‖ (19) Verily the *true* religion in the sight of GOD is

---

(15) *Shall I declare unto you better things than this?* This verse, taken in connection with the preceding, clearly shows that the joys of the Muslim heaven are carnal. "The provision of the present life," viz., women, gold and silver, horses, cattle, and land, were such as could alone gratify the "eager desire" of an Arab in this life. All these are to be infinitely multiplied amid the pavilions and gardens of paradise. See also notes on chap. ii. 25.

The attempt to explain these passages as figurative and symbolical of spiritual blessing, while sanctioned by the teaching of some Muslim writers, does violence to the language of the Qurán as well as to the faith of the orthodox in all ages of Islám. It is unfair to quote in evidence the dreamy statements of the Súfis or the rationalistic pleading of modern free-thinkers. These are alike regarded as infidels by the orthodox Muhammadan. There cannot be a shadow of a doubt that the heaven of Muslims is a place of sensual delights. No orthodox Muslim commentator takes any other view, "and it is impossible for any candid mind to read the Qurán and the traditions and arrive at any other conclusion on the subject." See *Hughes's Notes on Muhammadanism*, 2d ed., pp. 91–95.

God regardeth his servants who say, &c. The ground of forgiveness, as here stated, is faith in Islám and obedience to its precepts.

(19) *The true religion . . . is Islám.* "The proper name of the Muhammadan religion, which signifies the *resigning* or *devoting one's self* entirely to God and his service. This they say is the religion

Islám: and they who had received the scriptures dissented not *therefrom*, until after the knowledge *of God's unity* had come unto them, out of envy among themselves; but whosoever believeth not in the signs of GOD, verily GOD will be swift in *bringing him to* account. (20) If they dispute with thee, say, I have resigned myself unto GOD, and he who followeth me *doth the same;* and say unto them who have received the scriptures, and to the ignorant, Do ye profess *the religion of* Islám? now if they embrace Islám, they are surely directed; but if they turn their backs, verily unto thee *belongeth* preaching *only;* for GOD regardeth his servants.

‖ (21) And unto those who believe not in the signs of GOD, and slay the prophets without a cause, and put those men to death who teach justice; denounce unto them a painful punishment. (22) These are they whose works perish in this world, and in that which is to come; and they shall have none to help them. (23) Hast thou not observed those unto whom part of the scripture was

---

which all the prophets were sent to teach, being founded on the unity of God."—*Sale, Jaláluddín.*

See also below, on vers. 83, 84.

They who had received the Scriptures dissented, &c. The meaning of this passage seems to be that Jews and Christians belonged to this true religion of Islám *until* the revelation of the Qurán came. They were then filled with envy, and on this account dissented from the truth.

Muhammad, therefore, again attests the truth of Judaism and Christianity, and in this passage seems clearly to state that the Jews and Christians were the followers of the true religion up to the date of his prophetic claim. If so, a comparison of the religions will show how far Islám falls short of being the true religion taught by the prophets and Jesus, and also how far the charge of *envy* is justified.

(20) *Do ye profess Islám?* See Rodwell's note on this passage. The mission of Muhammad thus far was that of a *preacher* only. Although the enemies of Islám were threatened, the policy of Muhammad was as yet purely defensive.

(21, 22) The Jews are referred to in these verses. The intensity of the opposition is very marked.

(23) *Part of the Scripture, i.e.,* the Scriptures given to the Jews. This verse shows clearly that these Jews possessed copies of the Scriptures attested as the word of God by the Qurán. Some com-

given? They were called unto the book of GOD, that it might judge between them; then some of them turned their backs, and retired afar off. (24) This *they did* because they said, the fire *of hell* shall by no means touch

---

mentators regard the word *nasiban=part*, as designating only a portion of the Pentateuch, but "the book of God" in the following sentence is evidently the equivalent of "part of the Scriptures" here, and that undoubtedly refers to the volume of the Jewish Scriptures.

They were called unto the book of God. The following is Sale's note on this passage :—

"This passage was revealed on occasion of a dispute Muhammad had with some Jews, which is differently related by the commentators.

"Al Baidháwi says that Muhammad, going one day into a Jewish synagogue, Náim Ibn Amr and al Hárith Ibn Zaid asked him what religion he was of. To which he answering, 'Of the religion of Abraham,' they replied, 'Abraham was a Jew;' but on Muhammad's proposing that the Pentateuch might decide the question, they would by no means agree to it.

"But Jaláluddín tells us that two persons of the Jewish religion having committed adultery, their punishment was referred to Muhammad, who gave sentence that they should be stoned, according to the law of Moses. This the Jews refused to submit to, alleging there was no such command in the Pentateuch; but on Muhammad's appealing to the book, the said law was found therein. Whereupon the criminals were stoned, to the great mortification of the Jews.

"It is very remarkable that this law of Moses concerning the stoning of adulterers is mentioned in the New Testament [John viii. 5], (though I know some dispute the authenticity of that whole passage), but it is not now to be found either in the Hebrew or Samaritan Pentateuch, or in the Septuagint; it being only said that such *shall be put to death* [Lev. xx. 10]. This omission is insisted on by the Muhammadans as one instance of the corruption of the law of Moses by the Jews.

"It is also observable that there was a verse once extant in the Qurán commanding adulterers to be stoned; and the commentators say the words only are abrogated, the sense of the law still remaining in force."

On the question of the law relating to *stoning* raised here, see Alford's Greek Testament, notes on John viii. 5. Stoning was the *ordinary* mode of execution among the Jews (Exod. xvii. 4; Luke xx. 6; John x. 31; and Acts xiv. 5), and therefore the general statement of Lev. xx. 10 would designate this mode, *unless some other mode were distinctly commanded.* Besides, Deut. xxii. 21–24 very clearly appoints this as the mode of punishment. This suggests a sufficient reply to the Muslim claim referred to by Sale in the note just quoted.

us, but for a *certain* number of days; and that which they had falsely devised hath deceived them in their religion. (25) *How then will it be with them*, when we shall gather them together at the day *of judgment*, of which there is no doubt; and every soul shall be paid that which it hath gained, neither shall they be treated unjustly? (26) Say, O GOD, who possessest the kingdom; thou givest the kingdom unto whom thou wilt, and thou takest away the kingdom from whom thou wilt: thou exaltest whom thou wilt, and thou humblest whom thou wilt: in thy hand is good, for thou art almighty. (27) Thou makest the night to succeed the day: thou bringest forth the living out of the dead, and thou bringest forth the dead out of the living; and providest food for whom thou wilt without measure. (28) Let not the faithful take the infidels for their protectors, rather than the faithful: he who doth this shall not be *protected* of GOD at all; unless ye fear any

---

(24) *A certain number of days.* The number, according to the commentators, is *forty* or *seven* or *four*. It is worth noting the fact that this claim ascribed here to the presumption of the Jews is precisely the claim of all Muhammadans who believe that all believers in God and Muhammad will certainly reach the joys of paradise. Some may have to undergo purgatorial sufferings, but only for "a certain number of days."

That which they have falsely devised, *i.e.*, their imagining that their sins would be lightly punished through the intercession of their fathers (*Tafsír-i-Raufí*).

(25) *How then will it be*, &c. Sale gives a tradition on the authority of Baidháwi, " that the first banner of the infidels that shall be set up on the day of judgment will be that of the Jews, and that God will first reproach them with their wickedness over the heads of those who are present, and then order them to hell."

(26, 27) Rodwell regards these verses as misplaced here. They are probably the fragment of some Makkan chapter.

(28) *Unless ye fear any danger from them.* There shall be no friendship between Muslims and unbelievers, unless fear of the enmity of the infidels should make it *necessary*. Here we find a divine sanction to that duplicity so prevalent among Muslims. Taken in connection with the preceding context, this passage would seem to sanction apparent estrangement from Islám, provided expediency should demand it. Under such circumstances a Muslim may *appear to be more friendly* towards the unbelievers than he is towards his co-religionists.

danger from them: but GOD warneth ye to beware of himself: for unto GOD must ye return. (29) Say, Whether ye conceal that which is in your breasts, or whether ye declare it, GOD knoweth it; for he knoweth whatever is in heaven, and whatever is on earth: GOD is almighty. (30) On the *last* day every soul shall find the good which it hath wrought, present; and the evil which it hath wrought, it shall wish that between itself and that were a wide distance: but GOD warneth you to beware of himself; for GOD is gracious unto his servants.

‖ (31) Say, if ye love GOD, follow me: *then* God shall

---

(29) *Whether ye conceal, &c., i.e.,* God knows the faith of your hearts. If, therefore, you should find it necessary to dissemble so as *apparently* to deny the faith, be of good cheer—God knows your *heart-faith*—"God knowest whatever is in heaven, whatever is in earth."

(31) *Say, if ye love God, follow me.* Passages inculcating the duty of love to God are of rare occurrence in the Qurán. Here it is made the ground or reason of acceptance with God and of the pardon of sin. In other places salvation is made to depend on *faith and good works* (chap. ii. 3-5. 37, 38; chap. iii. 194; chap. iv. 55, 121-123, &c.), on *repentance* (chap. ii. 161; chap. xxv. 69-76, &c.), on *pilgrimage and warring for the faith* (chap. ii. 217; chap. iii. 196; chap. lxi. 12, &c.), on *almsgiving* (chap. ii. 271-274), on *the grace of God* (chap. xxxvii. 39, 55), &c. Everywhere the plan of salvation by atonement, as clearly taught in the Christian Scriptures, is ignored. It is in reference to *this fact* that missionaries have been led to make the statement, controverted by Mr. Bosworth Smith ("Muhammad and Muhammadanism," 2d ed. p. 332), that "even the religious creed of Muhammadanism is further removed from the truth than is that of the heathen." We think there can be scarcely any doubt as to the truth of this statement. All heathen forms of religion have relics of truth bound up in their doctrines and rites, handed down, probably, by tradition from ancient times, which afford to the Christian evangelist some kind of common ground in his endeavour to lead them to accept Christ as their substitute, and to believe in him as their Saviour, because he alone satisfies the conditions of their own religion and the cravings of their souls for a Divine Helper. But Muhammadanism strikes at this most important doctrine—this very heart of Christianity. It sweeps away almost every vestige of Bible truth as to the way of pardon. It fills the mind of its votaries with complacent pride and self-satisfaction. It destroys the last workings of a guilty conscience. In short, it imports all the evils of that form of Judaism against which our Lord hurled his "woes," saying, among other things, "Ye compass sea and land to make one prose-

love you, and forgive you your sins; for GOD is gracious and merciful. (32) Say, Obey GOD, and *his* apostle; but if ye go back, verily GOD loveth not the unbelievers. (33) GOD hath surely chosen Adam, and Noah, and the family of Abraham, and the family of Imrán above the *rest of the* world; (34) a race *descending* the one from the other: GOD is he who heareth and knoweth. (35) *Remember* when the wife of Imrán said, LORD, verily I

---

lyte; and when he is made, ye make him twofold more a child of hell than yourselves." Does Mr. Smith deny the justice of this declaration of our Lord? If not, does he infer that our Lord himself thought "polytheism better than monotheism, and idolatry than a sublime spiritualism"?

(33) *The family of Abraham.* This expression, say the commentators, includes a number of prophets descended from Abraham, including Muhammad. It probably is intended to include all the prophets from Abraham to Moses. See *Tafsír-i-Raufi* and *Abdul Qádir.*

Family of Imrán. This expression, like the one just noted, also includes all prophets descended from Imrán, *e.g.*, Moses, Aaron, Zacharias, John, and Jesus. Mary, the mother of Jesus, is said to have been "the daughter of the son of Imrán" (*Tafsír-i-Raufi*, &c.)

(34) *A race descending the one from the other.* This seems to show that Muhammad regarded the prophets as either lineally descended one from another, or that they were successors to each other in office, both of which ideas are incorrect.

(35) *When the wife of Imrán said, &c.* According to the commentators her name was Anna or Hannah. In the Apocryphal Gospels the parents of Mary are called Joachim and Anna. The name was probably derived from Christian tradition (see Arnold, *Islám and Christianity*, p. 150), but the "wife of Imrán" in this verse looks very like the wife of Elkanah in 1 Sam. i. 11. All the stories related by the commentators confirm this impression.

Again, the statement here, that the Virgin Mary was the "daughter of Imrán," coupled with that of chap. xix. 29, that she was "the sister of Aaron," certainly looks as if the Virgin Mary were confounded with the sister of Moses and Aaron. That there is in this passage a medley of Jewish and Christian traditionary fiction and Bible story, learned from hearsay, I think indisputable. I will quote briefly the views of several writers, giving both sides of the question, and leave the reader to draw his own inference :—

"From her (Mary) being called the sister of Aaron and the daughter of Amran, it has been justly concluded that Muhammad considered the Virgin Mary and Miriam, the sister of Moses and Aaron, as identical; and no sophistry on the part of Muhammadan

have vowed unto thee that which is in my womb, to be dedicated *to thy service;* accept *it* therefore of me;

---

divines or European writers can remove this impression."—*Arnold, Islám and Christianity,* p. 149.

"It is concluded by some that Mahomet confounded Mary (Maryam) with the sister of Moses. The confusion of names is the more suspicious, as it is not favoured by Christian authority of any description—the traditional names of Mary's parents being Joachim and Anna."

"Gerock combats this idea at some length (p. 24), showing that Imrán is never named in the Coran as the father of Moses, nor Mary (Maryam) as his sister, and that Mahomet is seen elsewhere to be well aware of the interval between Jesus and Moses. The latter fact cannot, of course, be doubted; Mahomet could never have imagined that Mary, the mother of Jesus, was the sister of Moses and Aaron. But it is still extremely probable that the confusion of this mis-nomenclature originated in the notions of Jewish informants, amongst whom the only notorious Mary (Maryam) was the daughter of Imrán and sister of Moses; and they could ordinarily give the name of *Maryam* those accompaniments; that is, they would speak of 'Mary the daughter of Imrán.' Mahomet adopted the phraseology (for his informants were mainly, if not solely, Jews) probably through inadvertence and without perceiving the anachronism it involved."—*Muir, Life of Mahomet,* vol. ii. pp. 281, 282, note.

The following is Sale's note on this passage, in which he combats the charge of anachronism brought by Reland, Marracci, and Prideaux; his Muslim authorities are, as usual, Baidháwi and Zamakhsharí:—

"Amrán is the name of two several persons, according to the Muhammadan tradition. One was the father of Moses and Aaron, and the other was the father of the Virgin Mary; but he is called by some Christian writers Joachim. The commentators suppose the first, or rather both of them, to be meant in this place; however, the person intended in the next passage, it is agreed, was the latter, who, besides Mary the mother of Jesus, had also a son named Aaron, and another sister named Ishá (or Elizabeth), who married Zacharias, and was the mother of John the Baptist; whence that prophet and Jesus are usually called by the Muhammadans, *The two sons of the aunt,* or the cousins-german.

"From the identity of names it has been generally imagined by Christian writers that the Qurán here confounds Mary the mother of Jesus with Mary or Miriam the sister of Moses and Aaron; which intolerable anachronism, if it were certain, is sufficient of itself to destroy the pretended authority of this book. But though Muhammad may be supposed to have been ignorant enough in ancient history and chronology to have committed so gross a blunder, yet I do not see how it can be made out from the words of the Qurán. For it does not follow, because two persons have the same name, and have each a father and brother who bear the

for ¦thou art he who heareth and knoweth. (36) And when she was delivered of it, she said, LORD, verily I have brought forth a female (and GOD well knew what she had brought forth), and a male is not as a female.

---

same names, that they must therefore necessarily be the same person : besides, such a mistake is inconsistent with a number of other places in the Qurán, whereby it manifestly appears that Muhammad well knew and asserted that Moses preceded Jesus several ages. And the commentators accordingly fail not to tell us that there had passed about one thousand eight hundred years between Amrán the father of Moses and Amrán the father of the Virgin Mary : they also make them the sons of different persons ; the first, they say, was the son of Yeshar, or Izhar (though he was really his brother), the son of Káhath, the son of Levi ; and the other was the son of Mathán, whose genealogy they trace, but in a very corrupt and imperfect manner, up to David, and thence to Adam.

"It must be observed that though the Virgin Mary is called in the Qurán the sister of Aaron, yet she is nowhere called the sister of Moses ; however, some Muhammadan writers have imagined that the same individual Mary, the sister of Moses, was miraculously preserved alive from his time till that of Jesus Christ, purposely to become the mother of the latter."

To be dedicated. " The Arabic word is *free,* but here signifies particularly one that is *free* or detached from all worldly desires and occupations, and wholly devoted to God's service."—*Sale, Jaláluddín.*

(36) *I have brought forth a female.* Hannah prayed for a son (1 Sam. i. 11 ; see note on ver. 35). The birth of a female seemed to be a disappointment, as such would not be suitable for the service of the Temple. For extracts from the spurious Gospels containing the traditions which are here incorporated in the Qurán, see Arnold's *Islám and Christianity* (pp. 150-155) and Muir's *Life of Muhomet* (vol. ii. pp. 282, 283). These both draw from the *Christologie des Koran,* by Gerock, 1839, pp. 30-47.

I have called her Mary, &c. " This expression alludes to a tradition that Abraham, when the devil tempted him to disobey God in not sacrificing his son, drove the fiend away by throwing stones at him ; in memory of which, the Muhammadans, at the pilgrimage of Makkah, throw a certain number of stones at the devil, with certain ceremonies, in the valley of Miná. (See Prelim. Disc., p. 188.)

"It is not improbable that the pretended immaculate conception of the Virgin Mary is intimated in this passage; for according to a tradition of Muhammad, every person that comes into the world is touched at his birth by the devil, and therefore cries out : Mary and her son only excepted, between whom and the evil spirit God placed a veil, so that his touch did not reach them. And for this reason, they say, neither of them were guilty of any sin, like the rest of the children of Adam : which peculiar grace they obtained

I have called her MARY; and I commend her to thy protection, and *also* her issue; against Satan driven away with stones. (37) Therefore the LORD accepted her with a gracious acceptance, and caused her to bear an excellent offspring. (38) And Zacharias took care of *the child;* whenever Zacharias went into the chamber to her, he found provisions with her: *and* he said, O Mary whence hadst thou this? she answered, This is from GOD: for GOD provideth for whom he pleaseth without measure. There Zacharias called on his LORD, *and* said, LORD, give me from thee a good offspring, for thou art the hearer of prayer. (39) And the angels called to him, while

---

by virtue of this recommendation of them by Hannah to God's protection."—*Sale, Jaláluddín, and Baidháwi.*

(37) *The Lord accepted her,* i.e., though a female, she was received into the Temple as one dedicated to God. Zacharias became her guardian and cared for her.

(38) *He found provisions with her.* "The commentators say that none went into Mary's apartment but Zacharias himself, and that he locked seven doors upon her; yet he found she had always winter fruits in summer and summer fruits in winter."—*Sale.*

This story owes its origin to Christian tradition. See *Historia de Nativ. Marie et de Infan. Salv.* (chap. vi.) and *Protev. Jacob.* (chap. viii.), quoted in Muir's *Life of Mahomet* (p. 283) and in Arnold's *Islám and Christianity* (pp. 150, 151).

There Zacharias called on his Lord. The prayer would seem to have been offered in the inner chamber of the Temple assigned, according to the story, to Mary. The commentators think the prayer was suggested by the miraculous supply of food furnished to Mary. Zacharias was at this time ninety-nine years old, and his wife ninety-eight (*Tafsír-i-Raufi*). Abdul Qádir says Zacharias prayed in secret, because, at this age, to have prayed openly for *offspring* would have exposed him to ridicule.

Offspring. In chap. xix. 5, "a successor," from which Gerock would infer that Zacharias did not pray for a son, but for an *heir* only. But in the ninth verse of that same chapter he says, "How shall I have *a son?*" &c. This decides clearly in favour of that interpretation which makes offspring to mean an heir from his own body.

(39) *The angels.* In chap. xix. 17 it is said that a "spirit" (Gabriel) came to Mary. The commentators interpret "angels" to be equivalent to "spirit," and understand Gabriel to be meant. They account discrepancies of this sort as of little moment.

The word which cometh from God. See notes on chap. ii. 86. The Muslim interpretation, that Jesus is here called the WORD because

he stood praying in the chamber, *saying*, Verily GOD promiseth thee *a son named* John, who shall bear witness to the Word *which cometh* from GOD; an honourable person, chaste, and one of the righteous prophets. (40) He

---

he was conceived by the word or command of God is, to say the least, unsatisfactory.

The "witness" of John concerning the WORD was very different from that of Muhammad. Is it possible that he should have learned so much of John and Jesus from tradition, and not have known more of the character of the latter, as witnessed by John and Jesus himself? In answer to this question, I venture to give the following: —(1.) Muhammad *heard* more than he *believed*. This is evident from the effort he made to refute the doctrine of the Trinity, the Sonship of Christ, and the doctrine of Christ's death and resurrection. (2.) What he learned concerning these and other doctrines he learned from *hearsay*, and usually from unreliable sources. Hence the indiscriminate mixing up of statements obtained originally from the Bible and tradition—Jewish and Christian. (3.) He seems to have learned most of what he knew of Christianity, and perhaps of Judaism also, after his arrival in Madína, and consequently after his claim to be a prophet had been assumed. His most definite and extended statements regarding Bible story are found in the Madína chapters. (4.) The criterion by which he decided the true and false as to what he heard was *his own prophetic claims and the character of his religion*. Whatever would exalt Jesus over himself was rejected. Hence Jesus is only "the son of Mary;" he is born miraculously, but is not divine; he wrought miracles, but always by "the permission of God" (ver. 48), &c. Again, whatever was contrary to the religion he promulgated was either refuted or ignored; the character of the prophets is always moulded after his own; the character of all infidels in former ages is like that of the unbelieving Quraish and Jews of Arabia.

Making every reasonable allowance for the Arabian prophet on the score of ignorance and on the score of misrepresentations to which he was no doubt subjected, still enough remains to substantiate the charge of imposture, however displeasing this charge may be to his admirers and friends. The facts in this matter are against them. Muhammad put these statements concerning matters of history into the mouth of God, and so promulgated them as his infallible word, confirming the Scriptures of the Old and New Testaments—Scriptures of whose teaching he was personally ignorant. Make out half as strong a case against any one of the inspired writers of the Bible, and who among these apologists for Islám would defend him? Truly the glory of this hero-god seems to have dazzled their eyes.

Chaste. Sale says, "The original word signifies one who refrains not only from women, but from all other worldly delights and desires."

(40) *How shall I have a son?* See note on ver. 38. Sale states, on

answered, LORD, how shall I have a son, when old age hath overtaken me, and my wife is barren? *The angel said,* So GOD doth that which he pleaseth. (41) *Zacharias answered,* LORD, *give me a sign. The angel said,* Thy sign shall be, that thou shalt speak unto no man for three days, otherwise than by gesture: remember thy LORD often, and praise *him* evening and morning.

‖ (42) And when the angels said, O Mary, verily GOD hath chosen thee, and hath purified thee, and hath chosen thee above *all* the women of the world: (43) O Mary, be devout towards thy LORD, and worship, and bow down with those who bow down. (44) This is a secret history: we reveal it unto thee, although thou wast not present with them when they threw in their rods *to cast lots* which of them should have the education of Mary;

---

the authority of Jaláluddín, that the wife of Zacharias was eighty-nine.

(41) *Thy sign shall be, &c.* This statement disagrees with that of Luke in two particulars—(1) In duration of Zacharias's dumbness; and (2) in regarding this dumbness as merely a sign given in answer to prayer, and in no way a punishment for unbelief. The "three days," say the commentators, began with John's being conceived in his mother's womb.

Remember thy Lord often. Zacharias's tongue was only free to speak the praise of God.

(42) *The angels.* Gabriel. Compare Luke i. 28.

(43) *Be devout, &c.* This passage is also based on Christian tradition. See Rodwell's note.

Bow down, &c. The forms of worship ascribed to Jews in the Qurán are, as here, distinctively Muslim.

(44) *When they threw in their rods.* "When Mary was first brought to the Temple, the priests, because she was the daughter of one of their chiefs, disputed among themselves who should have the education of her. Zacharias insisted that he ought to be preferred because he had married her aunt; but the others not consenting that it should be so, they agreed to decide the matter by casting of lots; whereupon twenty-seven of them went to the river Jordan, and threw in their rods (or arrows without heads or feathers, such as the Arabs used for the same purpose), on which they had written some passages of the law, but they all sunk except that of Zacharias, which floated on the water; and he had thereupon the care of the child committed to him."—*Sale, Jaláluddín.*

The casting of lots, attributed here to the Jewish priests, is the same in spirit as that forbidden in chap. ii. 218.

neither wast thou with them when they strove among themselves. (45) When the angels said: O Mary, verily GOD sendeth thee good tidings, *that thou shalt bear* the Word *proceeding* from himself; (46) his name shall be CHRIST JESUS the son of Mary, honourable in this world and in the world to come, and *one* of those who approach near *to the presence of* GOD; and he shall speak unto men in the cradle, and when he is grown up; and he shall be *one* of the righteous: (47) she answered, LORD, how shall I have a son, since a man hath not touched me? *the angel* said, So GOD createth that which he pleaseth: when he decreeth a thing, he only saith unto it, Be, and it is: (48) GOD shall teach him the scripture, and wisdom, and the law, and the gospel; and *shall appoint him his*

---

(45) *The son of Mary.* See note on ver. 39. The phrase "Jesus, son of Mary," had become so stereotyped in Muhammad's mind, that he here puts it in the mouth of the angels when addressing Mary herself.

Christ Jesus. The Messiah Jesus. He is honourable in this world as a prophet, and in the next as an intercessor. Muslims, however, only regard him as the intercessor of his own followers, *i.e.*, of those who lived during the period intervening between the times of Jesus and Muhammad.

(46) *He shall speak . . . in the cradle.* For his words see chap. xix. 28-34. The commentators tell many stories to illustrate this text. In regard to these Sale says:—"These seem all to have been taken from some fabulous traditions of the Eastern Christians, one of which is preserved to us in the spurious Gospel of the *Infancy of Christ*, where we read that Jesus spoke while yet in the cradle, and said to his mother, 'Verily I am Jesus the Son of God, the Word which thou hast brought forth, as the Angel Gabriel did declare unto thee; and my Father hath sent me to save the world.'"

When he is grown up. The original word (*káhlan*) describes a person of between thirty and fifty years of age.

(47) Compare with Luke i. 34, &c., to see how far this comes short of attesting the former Scriptures.

(48) *Scripture . . . wisdom . . . law . . . gospel.* The last two expressions describe more clearly the meaning of the first two. Jesus is said to have acquired a perfect knowledge of the law without any course of human instruction (*Abdul Qádir*).

A bird. "Some say it was a bat (*Jaláluddín*), though others suppose Jesus made several birds of different sorts (*Al Thálabi*).

"This circumstance is also taken from the following fabulous tradition, which may be found in the spurious Gospel above men-

apostle to the children of Israel; *and he shall say,* Verily I come unto you with a sign from your LORD; for I will make before you, of clay, as it were the figure of a bird; then I will breathe thereon, and it shall become a bird, by the permission of GOD; and I will heal him that hath been blind from his birth; and the leper: and I will raise the dead by the permission of GOD: and I will prophesy unto you what ye eat, and what ye lay up for store in your houses. Verily herein will be a sign unto you, if ye believe. And (49) *I come* to confirm the law which was *revealed* before me, and to allow unto you as lawful part of that which hath been forbidden you: and I come unto you with a sign from your LORD; therefore fear GOD, and obey me. (50) Verily GOD is my LORD, and your LORD; therefore serve him. This is

---

tioned. Jesus being seven years old, and at play with several children of his age, they made several figures of birds and beasts, for their diversion, of clay; and each preferring his own workmanship, Jesus told them that he would make his walk and leap; which accordingly, at his command, they did. He made also several figures of sparrows and other birds, which flew about or stood on his hands as he ordered them, and also ate and drank when he offered them meat and drink. The children telling this to their parents, were forbidden to play any more with Jesus, whom they held to be a sorcerer" (*Evang. Infant.*)—*Sale.*

By the permission of God. See note on ver. 39. The commentators, Baidhāwi, &c., understand this phrase to have been added lest any one should suppose Jesus to be divine. See *Sale.*

What ye eat, &c. This would furnish evidence of the power of Jesus to reveal secrets. These miracles were the seal of prophecy to Jesus, as were the verses (*ayát* = signs) of the Qurán to the prophetic claim of Muhammad.

(49) *To confirm the law, i.e.,* Jesus attested the genuineness and credibility of the Jewish Scriptures. The language implies the presence of these Scriptures in the time of Jesus, as does similar language imply that the Christian Scriptures were present in the days of Muhammad.

Part of that . . . forbidden you. "Such as the eating of fish that have neither fins nor scales, the caul and fat of animals, and camels' flesh, and to work on the Sabbath. These things, say the commentators, being arbitrary institutions in the law of Moses, were abrogated by Jesus, as several of the same kind instituted by the latter have been since abrogated by Muhammad."—*Sale, Jalāluddin.*

the right way. (51) But when Jesus perceived their unbelief, he said, Who *will be* my helpers towards GOD? The apostles answered, We *will be* the helpers of GOD; we believe in GOD, and do thou bear witness that we are true believers. (52) O LORD, we believe in that which thou hast sent down, and we have followed thy apostle; write us down therefore with those who bear witness *of him.* (53) And *the Jews* devised a stratagem

---

As intimated in note on ver. 39, we here see that Muhammad's endeavour is to make Christ appear to be a prophet *like himself.* The mission, character, authority, and experience of all the prophets were none other than those assumed by Muhammad for himself.

(51) *The apostles.* The twelve disciples of Jesus are here likened to the companions and helpers of Muhammad.

"In Arabic *al Hawáriyún*, which word they derive from *Hára, to be white*, and suppose the apostles were so called either from the *candour* and *sincerity* of their minds, or because they were princes and wore white garments, or else because they were by trade *fullers* (*Jaláluddín*) According to which last opinion, their vocation is thus related: That as Jesus passed by the seaside, he saw some fullers at work, and accosting them, said, 'Ye cleanse these cloths, but cleanse not your hearts;' upon which they believed on him. But the true etymology seems to be from the Ethiopic verb *Hawyra, to go;* whence *Hawárya* signifies *one that is sent*, a *messenger* or *apostle."—Sale.*

The *Tafsír-i-Raufi* relates a story current among Muslims as to the calling of these disciples, to the effect that Jesus, being persecuted by the Jews, fled to Egypt. On the banks of the river Nile he found some fishermen, whom he invited to accept Islám and to become his followers, which they did.

(52) *We believe* on the gospel. *We have followed the apostle, i.e.,* Jesus.

(53) *Stratagem.* This is better translated by Rodwell, *plot.* The plotting of the Jews was to kill Jesus; God plotted for his delivery. Sale remarks on this as follows:—"This stratagem of God's was the taking of Jesus up into heaven, and stamping his likeness on another person, who was apprehended and crucified in his stead. For it is the constant doctrine of the Muhammadans that it was not Jesus himself who underwent that ignominious death, but somebody else in his shape and resemblance (chap. iv. 156, 157). The person crucified some will have to be a spy that was sent to entrap him; others that it was one Titian, who by the direction of Judas entered in at a window of the house where Jesus was, to kill him; and others that it was Judas himself, who agreed with the rulers of the Jews to betray him for thirty pieces of silver, and led those who were sent to take him.

"They add, that Jesus, after his crucifixion in *effigy*, was sent

against him; but GOD devised a stratagem *against them;* and GOD is the best deviser of stratagems.

---

down again to the earth to comfort his mother and disciples, and acquaint them how the Jews were deceived; and was then taken up a second time into heaven.

"It is supposed by several that this story was an original invention of Muhammad's; but they are certainly mistaken; for several sectaries held the same opinion long before his time. The Basilidians, in the very beginning of Christianity, denied that Christ himself suffered, but that Simon the Cyrenean was crucified in his place. The Cerinthians before them, and the Carpocratians next (to name no more of those who affirmed Jesus to have been a mere man), did believe the same thing; that it was not himself, but one of his followers very like him that was crucified. Photius tells us that he read a book entitled, *The Journeys of the Apostles,* relating the acts of Peter, John, Andrew, Thomas, and Paul; and among other things contained therein, this was one, *that Christ was not crucified, but another in his stead,* and that therefore *he laughed at his crucifiers,* or those who thought they had crucified him.

"I have in another place mentioned an apocryphal Gospel of Barnabas, a forgery originally of some nominal Christians, but interpolated since by Muhammadans, which gives this part of the history of Jesus with circumstances too curious to be omitted. It is therein related, that the moment the Jews were going to apprehend Jesus in the garden, he was snatched up into the third heaven by the ministry of four angels, Gabriel, Michael, Raphael, and Uriel; that he will not die till the end of the world, and that it was Judas who was crucified in his stead, God having permitted that traitor to appear so like his master in the eyes of the Jews that they took and delivered him to Pilate; that this resemblance was so great that it deceived the Virgin Mary and the apostles themselves; but that Jesus Christ afterwards obtained leave of God to go and comfort them; that Barnabas having then asked him why the Divine Goodness had suffered the mother and disciples of so holy a prophet to believe even for one moment that he had died in so ignominious a manner, Jesus returned the following answer: 'O Barnabas, believe me that every sin, how small soever, is punished by God with great torment, because God is offended with sin. My mother therefore and faithful disciples, having loved me with a mixture of earthly love, the just God has been pleased to punish this love with their present grief, that they might not be punished for it hereafter in the flames of hell. And as for me, though I have myself been blameless in the world, yet other men having called me God and the son of God, therefore God, that I might not be mocked by the devils at the day of judgment, has been pleased that in this world I should be mocked by men with the death of Judas, making everybody believe that I died upon the cross. And hence it is that this mocking is still to continue till the coming of Muhammad, the messenger of God, who, coming into the world, will undeceive every one who shall believe in the law of God from this mistake.'"

‖ (54) When GOD said, O Jesus, verily I will cause SULS.
thee to die, and I will take thee up unto me, and I will R. 6/14.
deliver thee from the unbelievers; and I will place those
who follow thee above the unbelievers, until the day of
resurrection: then unto me shall ye return, and I will
judge between you of that concerning which ye disagree.
(55) Moreover, as for the infidels, I will punish them
with a grievous punishment in this world, and in that
which is to come; and there shall be none to help them.
(56) But they who believe, and do that which is right, he
shall give them their reward: for GOD loveth not the
wicked doers. (57) These signs and this prudent admonition do we rehearse unto thee. (58) Verily the likeness
of Jesus in the sight of GOD is as the likeness of Adam;
he created him out of the dust, and then said unto him,
Be; and he was. (59) *This is* the truth from thy LORD;

---

(54) *I will cause thee to die, &c.* These words are a source of great difficulty to the commentators, as they seem clearly to contradict the statement of chap. iv. 156. All Muslims agree that Jesus was taken up to heaven. This verse, however, taken as a chronological state-ment of events, would make it necessary to believe he had died *before* he "was taken up" into heaven. The same is true of chap. v. 117. To evade this, some deny the chronological arrangement demanded by the copulative *and*. Others admit the order, and either claim that Jesus did die a natural death—remaining under its power for three hours—or explain the death spoken of here in a figurative manner, regarding it as a promise that God would cause him "to die a spiritual death to all worldly desires." (See notes by Rodwell and Sale *in loco*.) Others refer the passage to the time when Jesus will come to destroy *Dajjál;* when, say the commentators, Jesus will die and be buried in the empty tomb prepared for him at Madína, and afterwards arise at the judgment day.

These interpretations are manifestly mere attempts at evasion. But for chap. iv. 156, no Muslim would have any difficulty in accepting the plain common-sense import of this verse.

I will place those . . . above unbelievers. By unbelievers Muslims understand the *Jews* to be meant. This is, however, a limitation no way justified by the Qurán. The term is general, and fairly indi-cates all who reject the gospel of Jesus "until the judgment day." The allusion is, therefore, to the final and constant victory of Islám, and the followers of Jesus are here regarded as true Muslims.

(58) *The likeness of Jesus, &c.*, *i.e.*, both were brought into being miraculously, neither having a human father. "Jaláluddín says the resemblance consists in this—both were created by the word of

be not therefore *one* of those who doubt; (60) and whoever shall dispute with thee concerning him, after the knowledge which hath been given thee, say *unto them,* Come, let us call together our sons and your sons and our wives and your wives, and ourselves and yourselves; then let us make imprecations, and lay the curse of GOD on those who lie. (61) Verily this is a true history: and there is no GOD but GOD; and GOD is most mighty and wise. (62) If they turn back, GOD well knoweth the evil-doers.

‖ (63) Say, O ye who have received the scripture, come to a just determination between us and you; that we wor-

---

God (compare the verses in 1 Cor. xv.) Adam made from the dust, Christ took flesh from the Virgin; Adam sinned, Christ sinned not; Adam a man, Christ a spirit proceeding from God, according to Muhammad."—*Brinckman in Notes on Islám.*

(60) *Come let us call together our sons, &c.* This passage refers to a visit paid to Muhammad at Madína by Abu Hárith, bishop of Najrán, with other Christians, who came to make a treaty of peace with the prophet of Arabia, now rapidly growing in political power. A controversy having arisen between them and Muhammad, the latter proposed to settle it in the strange manner proposed in the text. The Christians very consistently declined the test proposed. The spirit of the two religions is well illustrated by the conduct of Muhammad and Jesus under similar circumstances. See also notes of *Rodwell in loco,* and of *Muir's Life of Mahomet,* vol. ii. pp. 302, 303.

Sale gives the story of the commentators Jaláluddín and Baidháwi as follows:—" Some Christians, with their bishop, named Abu Hárith, coming to Muhammad as ambassadors from the inhabitants of Najrán, and entering into some disputes with him touching religion and the history of Jesus Christ, they agreed the next morning to abide the trial here mentioned, as a quick way of deciding which of them were in the wrong. Muhammad met them accordingly, accompanied by his daughter Fátima, his son-in-law Ali, and his two grandsons, Hasan and Husain, and desired them to wait till he had said his prayers. But when they saw him kneel down, their resolution failed them, and they durst not venture to curse him, but submitted to pay him tribute.

(63) *Ye who have received the Scriptures, i.e.,* Jews and Christians.

A just determination. The proposal here, though carrying great pretension of liberality and reason, really means out-and-out acceptance of Islám.

Lords. This expression has special reference to the dignity accorded by Jews and Christians to their religious guides. None are

ship not *any* except GOD, and associate no creature with him; and that the one of us take not the other for lords, beside GOD. But if they turn back, say, Bear witness that we are true believers. (64) O ye to whom the scriptures have been given, why do ye dispute concerning Abraham, since the Law and the Gospel were not sent down until after him? (65) Do ye not therefore understand? Behold ye are they who dispute concerning that which ye have some knowledge in; why therefore do you dispute concerning that which ye have no knowledge of? GOD knoweth, but ye know not. (66) Abraham was neither a Jew nor a Christian; but he was of the true religion, one resigned *unto God*, and was not of the *number of the* idolaters. (67) Verily the men who are the nearest *of kin*

---

more addicted to the practice here condemned than the Muslims themselves. The worship of *Walís* and *Pírs* is of a kind with the worship of saints among certain sects of Christians.

(64) *Why do ye dispute?* The commentators say both Jews and Christians claimed that Abraham belonged to their religion; Muhammad here decides that he belongs to neither. He, however, thereby contradicts his oft-repeated claim that every new revelation confirmed that which had preceded it; that the prophets belonged to a common "race" or class (ver. 34, and note); and that all true believers in *every* dispensation were true Muslims, professing the "religion of Abraham the orthodox." See also notes on chap. ii. 135-140.

This passage implies that the Jews and Christians were in possession of the Scriptures of the Old and New Testament current in his day. The same is implied in Baidháwi's note on the next verse, quoted by Sale:—" Ye perversely dispute even concerning those things which ye find in the Law and the Gospel, whereby it appears that they were both sent down long after Abraham's time: why then will ye offer to dispute concerning such points of Abraham's religion of which your Scriptures say nothing, and of which ye consequently can have no knowledge?"

(66) See notes on chap. ii. 135-140. It would seem that Muhammad was ignorant of the national relationship existing between Abraham and the Jews. The term *Jew* was probably understood by him in an ecclesiastical sense only. Yet this is the teaching of God and his prophet! See also Rodwell's note on chap. xvi. 121.

(67) *Nearest of kin.* The relationship here spoken of is not necessarily one of kindred; the words *of kin* do not belong to the original Arabic. The *nearness* spoken of here should rather refer to nearness in point of religious faith and practice. See vers. 64-66, and *Tafsír-i-Raufí in loco.*

unto Abraham are they who follow him: and this prophet, and they who believed *on him:* GOD is the patron of the faithful. (68) Some of those who have received the scriptures desire to seduce you; but they seduce themselves only, and they perceive *it* not. (69) O ye who have received the scriptures, why do ye not believe in the signs of GOD, since ye are witnesses *of them?*

‖ (70) O ye who have received the scriptures, why do you clothe truth with vanity, and knowingly hide the truth? (71) And some of those to whom the scriptures were given say, Believe in that which hath been sent down unto those who believe, in the beginning of the day; and deny *it* in the end thereof; that they may go back *from their faith*; (72) and believe him only who followeth your religion. Say, Verily the *true* direction is the direc-

---

And this prophet, i.e., Muhammad. The meaning is that Muhammad, and those who believe on him, are most nearly related to Abraham.

(68) *Some . . . desire to seduce you.* Sale, on the authority of Baidháwi, refers this passage to the time when certain Jews endeavoured to pervert Hudhaifa, Amár, and Muádh to their religion. So too *Tafsír-i-Raufí.*

(69) *Why not believe?* The *signs* to be believed were the incomparable verses of the Qurán. The argument of the prophet was certainly not convincing.

(70) *Clothe truth with vanity, &c.* See note on chap. ii. 41.

(71) *Deny it in the end thereof.* "The commentators, to explain this passage, say that Qáb Ibn al Ashraf and Málík Ibn al Saif (two Jews of Madína) advised their companions, when the Qibla was changed (chap. ii. 142), to make as if they believed it was done by the divine direction, and to pray towards the Kaabah in the morning, but that in the evening they should pray as formerly towards the Temple of Jerusalem, that Muhammad's followers, imagining that the Jews were better judges of this matter than themselves, might imitate their example. But others say these were certain Jewish priests of Khaibar, who directed some of their people to pretend in the morning that they had embraced Muhammadanism, but in the close of the day to say that they had looked into their books of Scripture and consulted their Rabbins, and could not find that Muhammad was the person described and intended in the law; by which trick they hoped to raise doubts in the minds of the Muhammadans."—*Sale, Baidháwi.*

(72) *Your religion, i.e.,* Judaism.

That there may be given, &c. This passage is very obscure, but the idea seems to be that if the Jews are directed by God, they should bring forth verses like unto those of the Qurán.

tion of GOD, that there may be given unto some other *a revelation* like unto what hath been given unto you. Will they dispute with you before your Lord? Say, Surely excellence is in the hand of GOD, he giveth it unto whom he pleaseth; GOD is bounteous and wise: (73) he will confer peculiar mercy on whom he pleaseth; for GOD is endued with great beneficence. (74) There is of those who have received the scriptures, unto whom if thou trust a talent he will restore it unto thee; and *there is also* of them, unto whom if thou trust a dinár, he will not restore it unto thee, unless thou stand over him continually *with great urgency*. This *they do*, because they say, We are not obliged to observe justice with the heathen: but they utter a lie against GOD, knowingly. (75) Yea, whoso keepeth his covenant, and feareth *God*, GOD surely loveth those who fear *him*. (76) But they who make merchandise of GOD'S covenant, and of their oaths, for a small price, shall have no portion in the next life, neither shall GOD speak to them or regard them on the day of resurrection, nor shall he cleanse them; but they shall suffer a grievous punishment. (77) And there are certainly some of them who read the scriptures perversely, that ye may think

---

(74) *A talent . . . a dinár.* As usual, the commentators have a story to illustrate the text. A Jew, by name Abdullah Ibn Salám, having borrowed twelve hundred ounces of gold from a Quraishite, paid it back punctually at the time appointed. Another Jew, Phineas Ibn Azúra, borrowed a dinár, and afterwards denied having received it! The followers of the Arabian prophet must have been very simple-minded indeed to make this *revelation* necessary.

Sale thinks the person especially intended was Qáb Ibn Ashraf, a Jew, who finally became so inimical that Muhammad proscribed him and caused him to be slain.

Some commentators (Baidháwi, &c.) think the trustworthy persons referred to here are Christians and the dishonest ones Jews. This view agrees very well with the sentiments of contempt for the heathen attributed to these covenant-breakers in the latter portion of this verse.

(75) *Whoso keepeth his covenant, &c.* Muslims showing the spirit attributed to Jews in the preceding verse cannot quote this precept of Muhammad in justification of their conduct.

(77) *Some . . . read the Scriptures perversely.* The charge here is

what they read to be really in the scriptures, yet it is not in the scripture; and they say, This is from GOD; but it is not from GOD: and they speak that which is false concerning GOD, against their own knowledge. (78) It is not *fit* for a man that GOD should give him a book of *revelations*, and wisdom, and prophecy; and then he should say unto men, Be ye worshippers of me, besides GOD; but *he ought to say,* Be ye perfect in knowledge and in works, since ye know the scriptures, and exercise yourselves therein. (79) GOD hath not commanded *you* to take the angels and the prophets for *your* lords: Will he command *you* to become infidels after ye have been true believers?

‖ (80) And *remember* when GOD accepted the covenant of the prophets, *saying, This* verily *is* the scripture and

---

that Jews and Christians misrepresent the teaching of their own Scriptures. The author of the notes on the Roman Urdú Qurán thinks this passage and others like it show the eagerness of Muhammad to find a sanction for his prophetic claims in the Scriptures of the Old and New Testament. When, however, the Jews frankly told him what their Scriptures taught, he charged them with wicked concealment of the prophecies concerning himself. It is possible that Muhammad was himself the victim of misrepresentation on this subject by interested parties.

This passage, too, shows beyond dispute that Muhammad regarded the Scriptures in the hands of the Jews and Christians as credible. No charge is ever brought against the Scriptures, but invariably against the interpreters.

(78) *It is not fit, &c.* This verse is evidently directed against Christians, who worship Jesus.

Sale says, "This passage was revealed, say the commentators, in answer to the Christians, who insisted that Jesus had commanded them to worship him as God."

Worshippers of me besides God. Here again we see that Muhammad's conception of Christian theology was all wrong.

(79) *The angels.* The idolaters of Makkah worshipped angels.

The prophets for your lords, e.g., the Jews worship Ezra and the Christians worship Jesus.—*Tafsir-i-Raufi.*

(80) *The covenant of the prophets.* "Some commentators interpret this of the children of Israel themselves, of whose race the prophets were. But others say the souls of all the prophets, even of those who were not then born, were present on Mount Sinai when God gave the law to Moses, and that they entered into the covenant here mentioned with him. A story borrowed by Muhammad from the

the wisdom which I have given you: hereafter shall an apostle come unto you, confirming the truth of that *scripture* which is with you; ye shall surely believe in him, and ye shall assist him. GOD said, Are ye firmly resolved, and do ye accept my covenant on this *condition?* They answered, We are firmly resolved: *God* said, Be ye therefore witnesses; and I also bear witness with you: (81) and whosoever turneth back after this, they are surely the transgressors. (82) Do they therefore seek any other religion but GOD'S? since to him is resigned whosoever is in heaven or on earth, voluntarily or of force: and to him shall they return. (83) Say, We believe in GOD,

---

Talmudists, and therefore most probably his true meaning in this place."—*Sale.*

The prophecy alluded to here is probably the general promise of the Messiah contained in such passages as Deut. xviii. 15-18, and which constituted the *spirit of prophecy.* The only direct statement in the Qurán giving the very words of prophecy is found in chap. lxi. 6, where the allusion is to the Paraclete. In either case the prophet of Arabia made a serious mistake. The desperation of his followers to find the prophecies of the Bible relating to him is manifested at one time by their attempts to disprove the genuineness of the same, at another time by their endeavours to show that Deut. xviii. 15-18, John xiv. 16, 26, and xvi. 13, &c., really refer to their prophet. For a specimen of the latter the reader is referred to *Essays on the Life of Mohammad* by Sayd Ahmad Khan, Bahadur, C.S.I.

(82) *Resigned . . . voluntarily or of force.* The idea of converting men by force is here said to have belonged to the covenant of Sinai. The verse, however, conveys a threat against unbelieving Arabs.

(83) This verse very well illustrates the kind of attestation borne to the former Scriptures and to the prophetic character of the prophets by whom they were revealed. An array of names and a general statement declaring their truly prophetic character is given, but everywhere their doctrine is ignored or rejected when conceived of as in conflict with the Qurán and the Arabian prophet. Now, Muhammad must be regarded as either making *a statement of fact* as to the oneness of his faith with that of the persons he mentions, or he was ignorant of what he here states as a fact. In either case he seems to me fairly chargeable with imposture. For even if he were ignorant of what he pretends to know, his pretence is a deception, and no reasonable apology can be offered for his putting a statement of this character in the mouth of God. How, then, Mr. Smith (*Muhammad and Muhammadanism,* p. 25) can so positively assert the impossibility of any longer regarding Muhammad as an impostor,

and that which hath been sent down unto us, and that which was sent down unto Abraham, and Ismaíl, and Isaac, and Jacob, and the tribes, and that which was delivered to Moses, and Jesus, and the prophets from their LORD; we make no distinction between any of them; and to him are we resigned. (84) Whoever followeth any other religion than Islám, it shall not be accepted of him: and in the next life he shall be of those who perish. (85) How shall GOD direct men who have become infidels after they had believed, and borne witness that the apostle was true, and manifest declarations *of the divine will* had come unto them? for GOD directeth not the ungodly people. (86) Their reward shall be, that on them *shall fall* the curse of GOD, and of angels, and of all mankind: (87) they shall remain under the same for ever; their torment shall not be mitigated, neither shall they be regarded; (88) except those who repent after this and amend; for GOD is gracious and merciful. (89) Moreover they who become infidels after they have believed, and yet increase in infidelity, their repentance shall in nowise be accepted, and they are those who go astray. (90) Verily they who

---

I can only understand by supposing him to be blinded to the faults of his hero by the glory of his own ideal. See also notes on chap. ii. 61.

Whosoever . . . any other religion. Islám is here contemplated by the prophet as equivalent, or rather as identical with, the true religion of Abraham, Moses, and Jesus. Were Islám so identified with the one true religion of God, then all might assent to the statement of the text; but as a matter of fact there never was any such recognition of Judaism or Christianity in practice among Muslims. They have never been the preservers of the Scriptures herein attested as the Word of God; and any man preferring either religion to Islám is thereby stigmatised as an infidel.

(85–89) *How shall God direct . . . infidels, &c.* This passage seems to teach that apostasy from Islám can never be repented of. Such a person is a reprobate. See *Tafsír-i-Raufi in loco.* God is merciful to forgive those who repent in time, but for those who "yet increase in infidelity," *i.e.*, go on in an obstinate course of apostasy, there is no forgiveness.

(90) *For his ransom.* The punishment of infidels is eternal and without remedy. The idea of a *ransom* for a sinner is recognised

believe not, and die in their unbelief, the world full of gold shall in nowise be accepted from any of them, even though he should give it for his ransom; they shall suffer a grievous punishment, (91) and they shall have none to help them.

|| (92) Ye will never attain unto righteousness until ye give in alms of that which ye love : and whatever ye give, God knoweth it. (93) All food was permitted unto

FOURTH SIPARA. R 10.

---

here only to be rejected. Yet this passage obscurely recognises the infinite value of the soul.

(92) *Alms.* See notes on chap. ii. 42, and Prelim. Disc., p. 172.

(93) *Except what Israel forbade, &c.* Sale says :—"This passage was revealed on the Jews reproaching Muhammad and his followers with their eating of the flesh and milk of camels (Lev. xi. 4, Deut. xiv.), which they said was forbidden Abraham, whose religion Muhammad pretended to follow. In answer to which he tells them, that God ordained no distinction of meats before he gave the law to Moses, though Jacob voluntarily abstained from the flesh and milk of camels; which some commentators say was in consequence of a vow, made by that patriarch when afflicted with the *sciatica,* that if he were cured he would eat no more of that meat which he liked best, and that was camel's flesh; but others (Baidháwi, Jaláluddín) suppose he abstained from it by the advice of physicians only.

"This exposition seems to be taken from the children of Israel's not eating of the sinew on the hollow of the thigh, because the angel with whom Jacob wrestled at Peniel touched *the hollow of his thigh in the sinew that shrank* (Gen. xxxii. 32)."

Bring hither the Pentateuch and read it. This is a clear acknowledgment that the Pentateuch, which the Qurán attests as the Word of God, was in the possession of the Jews in the time of Muhammad. Yet, while the Prophet was ever ready to challenge Jews and Christians to bring their Scriptures that he might therewith prove to them his apostleship, it is a remarkable fact that he never permitted his own followers to read or hear those Scriptures. The *Mishqát-ul-Masábih* (Book i. chap. vi. part 2, Matthews' translation, vol. i. p. 53) contains the following tradition, on the authority of JÁBIR :—" Jábir said, Verily OMAR IBN-AL-KHATTÁB brought a copy of the Pentateuch to the Prophet, and said, 'This is a copy of the Pentateuch.' Muhammad was silent, and Omar was very near reading part of it, and the face of the Prophet changed; when Abu Baqr said : 'Your mother weeps for you. Do you not look on the Prophet's face?' Then Omar looked and said, 'God protect me from the anger of God and his Prophet. I am satisfied with this, that God is my cherisher, and Islám my religion, and Muhammad my prophet.' Then Muhammad said, 'If Moses were alive and found my prophecy, he would follow me.'"

the children of Israel, except what Israel forbade unto himself before the Pentateuch was sent down. Say *unto the Jews*, Bring hither the Pentateuch and read it, if ye speak truth. (94) Whoever therefore contriveth a lie against GOD after this, they will be evil-doers. (95) Say, GOD is true: follow ye therefore the religion of Abraham the orthodox; for he was no idolater. (96) Verily the first house appointed unto men *to worship in* was that which was in Bakkah; blessed, and a direction to all creatures. (97) Therein are manifest signs: the place where Abraham

---

Matthews gives another tradition of similar import in vol. i. p. 50. A remarkable tradition, on the authority of ABU HURÁIRAH, states that the Jews and Christians had translated the Scriptures from the *Hebrew*, for the benefit of "the people of Islám." It is as follows:— "Abu Huráirah said there were people of the book who read the *Bible* in *Hebrew* and translated it into *Arabic* for the people of Islám. And the Prophet said, 'Do not consider them liars or tellers of truth; but say to them, We believe in God and that which is sent to us, and what was sent to Moses and Jesus.'"—*Mishqát-ul-Masábih*, book i. chap. vi. part 1.

From these traditions it is quite clear that Muhammad was not sincere in his claim that the former Scriptures testified concerning his apostleship. Had he been sincere, how very easy it would have been *to confirm the faith of his own disciples* as well as to convince all sincere Jews and Christians that he was the prophet of God foretold by Moses and Jesus! Instead of this, however, he forbade his disciples investigating this matter for themselves, *even in his presence;* and when Jews and Christians declared what was written in their Scriptures, he charged them with dishonesty in translation. Controversy from the Jewish or Christian standpoint was, therefore, quite out of the question.

(95) *Abraham the orthodox.* In Arabic, *Hanif.* There seems to have been a sect of deistic Arabs before Muhammad declared himself a prophet, who called themselves by this title, and claimed to be the followers of the religion of Abraham. Sprenger gives the names of four of these, viz., Waraqa, Othmán, Obaid, and Zaid (R. B. Smith's *Muhammad and Muhammadanism,* pp. 108, 109). This is one of Sprenger's arguments to prove that Muhammadanism existed prior to Muhammad, as the Reformation existed prior to Luther.

(96) *The first house . . . in Bakkah, i.e.,* Makkah. Baidháwi says *m* and *b* are frequently interchanged (Sale *in loco*). The *first house* was the Kaabah. See notes on chap. ii. 125, 142–146.

(97) *Manifest signs.* "Such as the stone wherein they show the print of Abraham's feet, and the inviolable security of the place, immediately mentioned; that the birds light not on the roof of the

stood; and whoever entereth therein shall be safe. And *it is a duty* towards GOD, *incumbent* on those who are able to go thither, to visit this house; but whosoever disbelieveth, verily GOD needeth not *the service* of any creature. (98) Say, O ye who have received the scriptures, why do ye not believe in the signs of GOD? (99) Say, O ye who have received the scriptures, why do ye keep back from the way of GOD him who believeth? Ye seek to make it crooked, and yet are witnesses *that it is the right:* but GOD will not be unmindful of what ye do. (100) O true believers, if ye obey some of those who have received the scripture, they will render you infidels, after ye have believed; (101) and how can ye be infidels, when

---

Kaabah, and wild beasts put off their fierceness there; that none who came against it in a hostile manner ever prospered, as appeared particularly in the unfortunate expedition of Abraha al Ashram (chap. cv.); and other fables of the same stamp which the Muhammadans are taught to believe."

The place of Abraham. See note on chap. ii. 125; also Rodwell *in loco.*

Those who are able. "According to an exposition of this passage attributed to Muhammad, he is supposed to be able to perform the pilgrimage who can supply himself with provisions for the journey and a beast to ride upon. Al Sháfa'í has decided that those who have money enough, if they cannot go themselves, must hire some other to go in their room. Málik Ibn Ans thinks he is to be reckoned *able* who is strong and healthy, and can bear the fatigue of the journey on foot, if he has no beast to ride, and can also earn his living by the way. But Abu Hanífah is of opinion that both money sufficient and health of body are requisite to make the pilgrimage a duty."—*Sale, Baidháwi.*

(99) *Him who believeth.* The person alluded to here is said to be 'Amár or Sarhán, whom the Jews endeavoured to pervert from the way of Islám (*Tafsír-i-Raufi*).

(100-109) *If ye obey, &c.* "This passage was revealed on occasion of a quarrel excited between the tribes of al Aus and al Khazraj by one Shás Ibn Qais, a Jew, who, passing by some of both tribes as they were sitting discoursing familiarly together, and being inwardly vexed at the friendship and harmony which reigned among them on their embracing Muhammadanism, whereas they had been for 120 years before most inveterate and mortal enemies, though descendants of two brothers, in order to set them at variance sent a young man to sit down by them, directing him to relate the story of the battle of Buáth (a place near Madína), wherein, after a bloody fight, al Aus had the better of al Khazraj, and to repeat some verses

the signs of GOD are read unto you, and his apostle is among you? But he who cleaveth firmly unto GOD is already directed in the right way.

R ½.

|| (102) O believers, fear GOD with his true fear; and die not unless ye also be true believers. (103) And cleave all *of you* unto the covenant of GOD, and depart not *from it*, and remember the favour of GOD towards you: since ye were enemies, and he reconciled your hearts, and ye became companions and brethren by his favour: and ye were on the brink of a pit of fire, and he delivered you thence. Thus GOD declareth unto you his signs, that ye may be directed. (104) Let there be people among you who invite to the best *religion;* and command

---

on that subject. The young man executed his orders; whereupon those of each tribe began to magnify themselves, and to reflect on and irritate the other, till at length they called to arms, and great numbers getting together on each side, a dangerous battle had ensued if Muhammad had not stepped in and reconciled them by representing to them how much they would be to blame if they returned to paganism and revived those animosities which Islám had composed, and telling them that what had happened was a trick of the devil to disturb their present tranquillity."—*Sale, Baidháwi, Tafsír-i-Raufi.*

The incident here related shows the powerful influence Muhammad had acquired over these fiery young men. Spirits aroused to a frenzy of excitement are calmed in a moment by the presence of the prophet and the voice of the oracle giving expression to the words of this verse.

(102) *Fear God with his true fear.* The *Tafsír-i-Raufi* says most commentators regard this verse as abrogated, on the ground that it is impossible for man to fear God as he ought to be feared. It is more likely that the passage was addressed to certain *adherents* of the tribes of Aus and Khazraj at Madína; these are here exhorted to remain steadfast in the faith even unto death.

(103) *And cleave . . . unto the covenant.* In Arabic, *Hold fast by the cord of God.* The allusion may be either to the Qurán, sometimes called by Muhammad *Habl Allíh al matán, i.e.,* the sure cord of God (*Sale, on authority of Baidháwi*), or to Islám, as the means of salvation.

Since ye were enemies. The tribes of Aus and Khazraj are here reminded of what Islám had done for them.

(104) *A people who invite, &c.* Abdul Qádir thinks this verse required that a body of men should be kept for religious warfare (Jihád), which should extirpate all heresy, as well as propagate the true faith. This view certainly accords with the spirit of Islám. The sword is its strong argument, and the end of all controversy.

that which is just, and forbid that which is evil; and they shall be happy. (105) And be not as they who are divided, and disagree *in matters of religion*, after manifest proofs have been brought unto them: they shall suffer a great torment. (106) On the day of *resurrection* some faces shall become white, and *other* faces shall become black. And unto them whose faces shall become black *God will say*, Have you returned unto *your* unbelief after ye had believed? therefore taste the punishment for that ye have been unbelievers: (107) but they whose faces shall become white *shall be* in the mercy of GOD, therein shall they remain for ever. (108) These are the signs of GOD: we recite them unto thee with truth. GOD will not deal unjustly with *his* creatures. (109) And to GOD *belongeth* whatever is in heaven and on earth; and to GOD shall *all* things return.

|| (110) Ye are the best nation that hath been raised up R $\frac{1\,2}{3}$. unto mankind: ye command that which is just, and ye forbid that which is unjust, and ye believe in GOD. And if they who have received the scriptures had believed, it had surely been the better for them: there are believers

---

(105) *They who are divided, i.e.*, Jews and Christians. Nevertheless Muslims are as thoroughly divided in matters of religion as ever Christians were.

(106) *Faces ... white ... and black.* See Prelim. Disc., pp. 149, 150.

(109) This verse ends the passage said to have been revealed on the occasion of the threatened outbreak between the tribes of Aus and Khazraj. See note on ver. 101.

(110) *Ye are the best nation.* The Muslims are now regarded as the chosen people of God. The word *ummat* is here translated "nation," and by Rodwell "folk." It is, however, used to describe the followers of the prophets, *e.g.*, the *ummat* of Moses (Jews), the *ummat* of Jesus (Christians), the *ummat* of Muhammad (Muslims). This statement is hardly reconcilable with the claim that the *ummat* of every true prophet belongs to Islám. The comparison is probably drawn between the Jews, Christians, and Muslims of Muhammad's day. It must be observed that the reason given for their superiority is not very convincing, and the high claim set up here for Muslim integrity is not borne out by historical evidence.

There are believers. "As Abdullah Ibn Salám and his companions, and those of the tribes of al Aus and al Khazraj, who had embraced Muhammadanism."—*Sale.*

among them, but the greater part of them are transgressors. (111) They shall not hurt you, unless with a *slight* hurt; and if they fight against you, they shall turn their backs to you; and they shall not be helped. (112) They are smitten with vileness wheresoever they are found; unless *they obtain security* by *entering into* a treaty with GOD, and a treaty with men: and they draw on themselves indignation from GOD, and they are afflicted with poverty. This *they suffer* because they disbelieved the signs of GOD and slew the prophets unjustly; this, because they were rebellious and transgressed. (113) *Yet* they are not *all* alike: there are of those who have received the scriptures, upright people; they meditate on the signs of GOD in the night season, and worship; (114) they believe in GOD, and the last day; and command that which is just, and forbid that which is unjust, and zealously strive *to excel* in good works; these are of the righteous. (115) And ye shall not be denied *the reward*

---

(111) *They shall not be helped.* "This verse, al Baidháwi says, is one of those whose meaning is mysterious, and relates to something future; intimating the low condition to which the Jewish tribes of Quraidha, Nadír, Bani Qáinuqáa, and those who dwelt at Khaibar, were afterwards reduced by Muhammad."—*Sale.*

(112) *They are smitten.* The past tense used for the future, meaning that they *shall certainly* be smitten, &c. The passage indicates the change of policy in respect to the Jews of Madína and the vicinity. They are now to submit to be plundered and exiled as the Bani Nadhír, or be slaughtered as the Bani Quraidha, as the only alternative to their accepting Islám. The fate of these tribes at the hands of Muhammad sadly illustrates Matt. xxvii. 25. It is remarkable that the reason given here for the punishment of the Jews accords with the denunciations of the Bible, and this notwithstanding the selfish and cruel designs of the Arabian prophet. "They slew the prophets, . . . were rebellious and transgressed."

(113) *They are not all alike.* Some had become Muslims. These meditate on the "signs of God," *i.e.,* the Qurán. Whether any were good or bad, just or unjust, depended now upon their being Muslims or unbelievers. Compare our Lord's words, Matt. vii. 22, 23.

Night-season. Night devotions, especially those performed between midnight and morning, are regarded as peculiarly meritorious. See *Mishqát ul Masábíh,* book iv. chap. xxxvi.

(115) *And ye shall not be denied, &c.* Rodwell also translates "ye shall not be denied," &c. Sale says, "Some copies have a different

of the good which ye do; for GOD knoweth the pious. (116) As for the unbelievers, their wealth shall not profit them at all, neither their children, against GOD: they *shall be* the companions of *hell* fire; they shall continue therein for ever. (117) The likeness of that which they lay out in this present life is as a wind wherein there is a scorching cold: it falleth on the standing corn of those men who have injured their own souls, and destroyeth it. And GOD dealeth not unjustly with them; but they injure their own souls. (118) O true believers, contract not an intimate friendship *with any* besides yourselves; they will not fail to corrupt you. They wish for that which may cause you to perish: their hatred hath already appeared

---

reading," viz., *they shall not be denied*. This reading, in the *third* person instead of the second, is that of all Arabic copies I have seen. The reading of the text is contrary to the analogy of the previous context. I think, therefore, the reading of Fluegel, though doubtless sanctioned by good authority, is in error. A careful collation of any considerable number of ancient MSS. would no doubt bring to light many such various readings.

(117) Savary translates, "Their alms are like unto an icy wind, which bloweth on the fields of the perverse and destroyeth their productions." The idea seems to be, that while the alms (*good*, ver. 115) of the faithful will bring back a certain reward, those of the unbelievers will be as a drain on their wealth, a blight on their crops. Good works without faith in Islám are of no avail.

(118) *Contract not . . . friendship, &c.* Muhammad was exceedingly jealous of counter-influences. Such friendships were sure to result in apostasy from Islám. The sentiment of chap. v. 104 seems to be the reverse of this. There he says, "He who erreth shall not hurt you while you are directed." The consistency of these statements is to be found in the circumstances of the new religion. Before the political power of the Prophet was secured, it was his policy to preserve his people from the contaminating influences of the unbelievers. They were to be avoided, no friendships were to be formed with them. In argument no reply was to be made beyond a declaration of adherence to Islám. Afterwards, however, when the power of the Muslims was supreme, they could afford to defy opposition. Success had rendered the chances of apostasy from Islám almost nil. The erring ones had therefore little power to injure. Yet, with all the power of Islám, it has been, and is still, the most intolerant of all religions.

Their hatred. See the suspicious fears of Muhammad illustrated by his treatment of the Bani Nadhír in Muir's *Life of Mahomet*, vol. iii. pp. 209, 210.

from out of their mouths; but what their breasts conceal is yet more inveterate. We have already shown you signs *of their ill-will towards you*, if ye understand. (119) Behold, ye love them, and they do not love you: ye believe in all the scriptures, and when they meet you, they say, We believe; but when they assemble privately together, they bite their fingers' ends out of wrath against you. Say *unto them*, Die in your wrath: verily GOD knoweth the innermost part of *your* breasts. (120) If good happen unto you, it grieveth them; and if evil befall you, they rejoice at it. But if ye be patient and fear *God*, their subtlety shall not hurt you at all; for GOD comprehendeth whatever they do. (121) *Call to mind* when thou wentest forth early from thy family, that thou

---

(119) *Ye love them.* The spirit of the prophet's love is shown in the last clause of this verse—" Die in your wrath !" The evident purpose of the exhortation here is to eradicate every vestige of natural affection for unbelieving friends and neighbours from the hearts of his followers. Nothing was too heartless or cruel for Muhammad to counsel or perform, provided his interest or his revenge could thereby be satisfied—to wit, the assassination of Asma, Abu Afaq, and Káb Ibn Ashraf, the exile of the Jewish tribes of Nadhír and Qainuqáa, and the inhuman slaughter of eight hundred prisoners of the Bani Quraidha, and many other instances of a similar nature.

Ye believe in all the Scriptures. This is no doubt what Muhammad intended they should do, but in the sense of simply acknowledging them to be the Word of God, and not in the sense that they should read them or hear them read (see note on ver. 93). This is the practice of Muslims still, showing how well they understand their prophet. They profess to accept the Pentateuch, Psalms, and Gospels as the Word of God, but the moment these are produced and made to testify against Islám, they declare they have been corrupted. All arguments are set aside by the claim that whatever is in accord with Islám is true, and whatever is not in accord therewith is either false, or, if true, abrogated.

(121) *When thou wentest forth, &c.* "This was at the battle of Ohod, a mountain about four miles to the north of Madína. The Quraish, to revenge their loss at Badr (ver. 13, note), the next year, being the third of the Hijra, got together an army of 3000 men, among whom there were 200 horse and 700 armed with coats of mail. These forces marched under the conduct of Abu Sufián and sat down at Dhu'l Hulaifa, a village about six miles from Madína. Muhammad, being much inferior to his enemies in numbers, at first determined to keep himself within the town, and receive them there; but afterwards, the advice of some of his companions prevailing, he

mightest prepare the faithful a camp for war; and GOD heard and knew *it ;* (122) when two companies of you were anxiously thoughtful, so that ye became faint-hearted,

---

marched out against them at the head of 1000 men (some say he had 1050 men, others but 900), of whom 100 were armed with coats of mail, but he had no more than one horse, besides his own, in his whole army. With these forces he formed a camp in a village near Ohod, which mountain he contrived to have on his back; and the better to secure his men from being surrounded, he placed fifty archers in the rear, with strict orders not to quit their post. When they came to engage, Muhammad had the better at first, but afterwards, by the fault of his archers, who left their ranks for the sake of the plunder, and suffered the enemy's horse to encompass the Muhammadans and attack them in the rear, he lost the day, and was very near losing his life, being struck down by a shower of stones, and wounded in the face with two arrows, on pulling out of which his two foreteeth dropped out. Of the Muslims seventy men were slain, and among them Hamza, the uncle of Muhammad, and of the infidels twenty-two. To excuse the ill success of this battle and to raise the drooping courage of his followers is Muhammad's drift in the remaining part of this chapter."—*Sale.*

Muir gives a wonderfully vivid description of the crisis through which Muhammad was called to pass after the defeat at Ohod. "The scoffs and taunts of infidels and Jews well-nigh overthrew the faith of the Muslims. 'How can Mahomet pretend now,' they asked, 'to be anything more than an aspirant to the *kingly* office? No true claimant of the *prophetic* dignity hath ever been beaten in the field, or suffered loss in his own person and that of his followers, as he hath.' Under these circumstances it required all the address of Mahomet to avert the dangerous imputation, sustain the credit of his cause, and reanimate his followers. This he did mainly by means of that portion of the Qurán which appears in the latter half of the third Sura."—*Life of Mahomet,* vol. iii. p. 189.

Students of the Qurán will not fail to notice here that every device of the Prophet to encourage his crestfallen people is clothed in the garb of inspiration. Every exhortation to steadfastness in the cause of Islám, every rebuke for unfaithfulness, every plaudit bestowed upon the brave, is presented as coming from the mouth of God.

(122) *Two companies.* "These were some of the families of Bani Salma of the tribe of al Khazraj, and Bani ul Hárith of the tribe of al Aus, who composed the two wings of Muhammad's army. Some ill impression had been made on them by Abdullah Ibn Ubai Sulúl, then an infidel, who having drawn off 300 men, told them that they were going to certain death, and advised them to return back with him; but he could prevail on but a few, the others being kept firm by the divine influence, as the following words intimate." —*Sale, Baidháwi.*

Muir expresses the belief that "the *two companies*" were the

but GOD was the supporter of them both; and in GOD let the faithful trust.

R 13/4. ‖ (123) And GOD had already given you the victory at Badr, when ye were inferior *in number;* therefore fear GOD, that ye may be thankful. (124) When thou saidst unto the faithful, Is it not enough for you that your LORD should assist you with three thousand angels sent down *from heaven?* (125) Verily if ye persevere and fear *God,* and *your enemies* come upon you suddenly, your LORD will assist you with five thousand angels, distinguished *by their horses and attire.*

RUFA. ‖ (126) And this GOD designed only as good tidings for

---

refugees and citizens. The flight was caused by their losing heart in the midst of the battle (*Life of Mahomet,* vol. iii. p. 191, note).

(123) *Victory at Badr.* See note on ver. 113. The word translated *victory* here means *help.* The angels, say the commentators, did not do the fighting, but rendered miraculous assistance by warding off the blows of the enemy and by appearing to them in human form, thus working dismay in their ranks by multiplying the number of Muslims in their sight.

(124) *Three thousand angels.* Muhammadan tradition gives numerous instances of similar interference of angels on behalf of the Muslims. See references at p. lxiv., Muir's *Life of Mahomet,* vol. i., *Introduction.*

(125) *Angels, distinguished.* The word *musawwamína* is the same as that translated *excellent horses* in ver. 14. The primary reference is to horses distinguished by white feet and a streak of white on the face, a sign of special excellence in horses. The passage may therefore mean that the angels rode on horses distinguished by the marks of excellence.

"The angels who assisted the Muhammadans at Badr rode, say the commentators, on black and white horses, and had on their heads white and yellow sashes, the ends of which hung down between their shoulders."—*Sale, Baidháwi.*

(126) *Good tidings.* Muhammad very adroitly argues that the question of victory or defeat does not rest with the Muslims. It is God's war against the infidels, and he cannot be defeated. If Muslims suffer defeat, it is for their discipline, to teach them to trust God and his prophet.

The commentators tell a story to the effect that when at the battle of Badr seventy Quraish fell into the hands of the Muslims as prisoners, Muhammad advised their summary execution, but the Muslims preferred to let them go on condition of a ransom price being paid. Muhammad yielded, but at the same time foretold that seventy Muslims would lose their lives in lieu of the seventy ransomed infidels. This prophecy was fulfilled in the defeat of Ohod.

you, that your hearts might rest secure; for victory is from GOD alone, the mighty, the wise. (127) That he should cut off the uttermost part of the unbelievers, or cast them down, or that they should be overthrown and unsuccessful, *is nothing to thee.* (128) It is no business of thine; whether *God* be turned unto them, or whether he punish them; they are surely unjust doers. (129) To GOD belongeth whatsoever is in heaven and on earth; he spareth whom he pleaseth, and he punisheth whom he pleaseth; for GOD is merciful.

|| (130) O true believers, devour not usury, doubling it twofold, but fear GOD, that ye may prosper: (131) and fear the fire which is prepared for the unbelievers; (132) and obey GOD and *his* apostle, that ye may obtain mercy. (133) And run with emulation *to obtain* remission from your LORD, and paradise, whose breadth *equalleth* the

R $\frac{14}{5}$.

This story was invented in order to cover up the disgrace of the ignominious defeat of the Muslims. This defeat was due to the disobedience of the followers of Muhammad (see note on ver. 122). This fact the prophet keeps in the background. The interests of Islám require that the Muslims should rather be encouraged than rebuked. They are therefore exhorted to trust God, and to look for certain victory in the future.

(127) This verse should be connected with the one preceding, and should depend upon the words "And this God designed." To connect it with the following verse, as Sale does, destroys the main point of the exhortation, which promises certain victory over the unbelievers.

(128) *They are surely unjust doers.* "This passage was revealed when Muhammad received the wounds above mentioned at the battle of Ohod, and cried out, 'How shall that people prosper who have stained their prophet's face with blood, while he called them to their Lord?' The person who wounded him was Otha the son of Abbu Wakkás."—*Sale, Baidháwi.*

(129) *He spareth.* In original *he pardoneth. He is merciful.* The original would better be rendered *He is forgiving, kind.* Every exhortation of the Prophet ends with a doxology of this sort, the sentiment being in accord with the character of the revelation preceding.

(130) *Devour not usury.* See note on chap. ii. 275. Abdul Qádir conjectures that the subject of usury is here spoken of because of the previous mention of cowardice, which is usually produced by habits of extortion. The passage seems to be misplaced, the sentiment having no perceptible connection with that of ver. 129, which is closely connected with ver. 139.

heavens and the earth, which is prepared for the godly; (134) who give alms in prosperity and adversity; who bridle their anger and forgive men; for GOD loveth the beneficent. (135) And who, after they have committed a crime, or dealt unjustly with their own souls, remember GOD, and ask pardon for their sins (for who forgiveth sins except GOD ?), and persevere not in what they have done knowingly; (136) their reward shall be pardon from their LORD, and gardens wherein rivers flow; they shall remain therein forever: and how excellent is the reward of those who labour! (137) There have already been before you examples of punishment *of infidels*, therefore go through the earth, and behold what hath been the end of those who accuse *God's apostles* of imposture. (138) This *book*

---

(134) "It is related of Hasan the son of Ali, that a slave having once thrown a dish on him boiling hot as he sat at table, and fearing his master's resentment, fell on his knees and repeated these words, 'Paradise is for those who bridle their anger:' Hasan answered, 'I am not angry.' The slave proceeded—'and for those who forgive men.' 'I forgive you,' said Hasan. The slave, however, finished the verse, adding, 'for God loveth the beneficent.' 'Since it is so,' replied Hasan, 'I give you your liberty, and four hundred pieces of silver.' A noble instance of moderation and generosity."—*Sale, Tafsír-i-Raufi.*

Forgive men. "The best kind of forgiveness is to pardon those who have injured you."—*Tafsír-i-Raufi.*

(135) *What they have done knowingly, i.e.*, the pious do not sin deliberately. The duty of repentance for known sin is here clearly enjoined, and the test of true repentance is also given.

(136) *Their reward.* This statement contradicts the teaching of the former Scriptures. However sincere repentance, its *reward* cannot be pardon. Repentance can affect the conduct of the *future*, but it has no power to atone for the crimes of the *past* (see note on ver. 31).

(137) *Those who accuse of imposture.* This passage gives another illustration of the constant and strained effort of Muhammad to refute the charge of imposture. In reply to his accusers, he says others were accused of like imposture, and the end of their accusers was dreadful. But the author of the notes on the Roman Urdú Qurán points out the fact that *no true prophet ever showed the anxiety of Muhammad to establish his claim to the prophetic office.* We may therefore fairly conclude that Muhammad's imposture was not, in the first instance at least, unconscious.

(138) See note, chap. ii. 2.

is a declaration unto men, and a direction and an admonition to the pious. (139) And be not dismayed, neither be ye grieved; for ye shall be superior *to the unbelievers* if ye believe. (140) If a wound hath happened unto you *in war*, a like wound hath already happened unto the *unbelieving* people: and we cause these days *of different success* interchangeably to succeed each other among men; that GOD may know those who believe, and may have martyrs from among you: (GOD loveth not the workers of iniquity;) (141) and that GOD might prove those who believe, and destroy the infidels. (142) Did ye imagine that ye should enter paradise, when as yet GOD knew not those among you who fought strenuously *in his cause*, nor knew those who persevered with patience? (143) Moreover ye did sometimes wish for death before that ye

---

(139) The thread of discourse dropped at ver. 129 is here taken up again. This verse reveals something of the demoralization of Muhammad's followers after the defeat of Ohod, and he uses every effort to inspire courage for a new conflict. Muhammad's high moral courage, strong will, and capability as a leader are well illustrated here.

(140) *A like wound, i.e.*, at Badr, where forty-nine of the Quraish were killed and an equal number wounded. Muslim accounts say seventy were killed and seventy wounded. Muir says, "The number *seventy* has originated in the supposition of a correspondence between the *fault* of Mahomet in taking (and not slaying) the prisoners of Badr and the retributive reverse at Ohod; hence it is assumed that seventy Meccans were taken prisoners at Badr."—*Life of Mahomet*, vol. iii. p. 107, note.

We cause these days, &c. The idea here is that God, by this reverse, intended to sift the true from the false among the number of those who professed themselves Muslims, and, so far as the slain were concerned, he desired to have them be martyrs. Thus comfort is bestowed upon the faithful, both for the disgrace of defeat and the loss of relatives in battle.

(142) *God knew not.* This is translated by Rodwell, *God had taken knowledge*. So also Abdul Qádir and others. This is certainly the *meaning* of the original. Those who catch at the form of the words (notes on Roman Urdú Qurán) to raise an objection lay themselves open to a charge of cavilling. The same cavil could be raised against Gen. xxii. 12.

(143) *Ye did ... wish for death.* "Several of Muhammad's followers who were not present at Badr wished for an opportunity of obtaining, in another action, the like honour as those had gained

met it; but ye have now seen it, and ye looked on, *but retreated from it.*

R $\frac{15}{6}$.
∥ (144) Muhammad is no more than an apostle; the *other* apostles have already deceased before him : if he die, therefore, or be slain, will ye turn back on your heels ? but he who turneth back on his heels will not hurt GOD at all; and GOD will surely reward the thankful. (145) No soul can

---

who fell martyrs in that battle, yet were discouraged on seeing the superior numbers of the idolaters in the expedition of Ohod. On which occasion this passage was revealed."—*Sale, Baidháwi.*

But retreated. The succeeding context justifies these words as necessary to fill in the ellipsis.

(144) *Muhammad is no more than an apostle.* In this passage Muhammad declares himself mortal, and these words were repeated by Abu Baqr at the death of Muhammad to convince Omar and other Muslims that their prophet was actually dead.

Arnold holds (on the authority of an ancient writer, Al Kindy) that Muhammad had prophesied that he would rise from the dead within three days. He thinks this prophecy—carefully suppressed by Muslim writers, however—alone accounts for the conduct of Omar at Muhammad's death, and that this alone explains why "Muhammad's body was buried *unwashed,* without the burial linen, but with the red scarf around his waist which he had worn during his last illness" (*Islám and Christianity,* p. 351, note). Were the statement of Al Kindy well founded, we could still accept this verse as genuine, for it does not deny the possibility of Muhammad's *rising from the dead,* but only implies that he would *die.* But, granting that Muhammad ever did prophesy his resurrection after three days, and that, according to the story of Al Kindy, the Muslims had waited three days for his resuscitation, how would the invention of this verse or the repetition of it if genuine—a verse which does not give a shadow of a hope of a resurrection in three days—account for the sudden acquiescence of the Muslims in the view of Abu Baqr that he was dead, and acquiesce at the same time in his conduct in having *during these very three days* assumed the authority of the caliphate ? The fact is, that Omar was not looking for the resurrection of Muhammad, but he could not believe him *dead;* and, as Muir clearly points out, the power of these words to persuade the people "was solely due to *their being at once recognised as a part of the Coran*" (*Life of Mahomet,* vol. i. Introd., p. xx., and vol. iv. p. 284, notes).

Will not hurt God, i.e., the cause of Islám will prosper in spite of the defection of unbelievers. Sale says, "It was reported in the battle of Ohod that Muhammad was slain : whereupon the idolaters cried out to his followers, 'Since your prophet is slain, return to your ancient religion, and to your friends; if Muhammad had been a prophet he had not been slain.'"

(145) *No soul can die, &c.* "Muhammad, the more effectually to

die unless by the permission of GOD, according to *what is written in* the book containing the determinations of things. And whoso chooseth the reward of this world, we will give him thereof: but whoso chooseth the reward of the world to come, we will give him thereof: and we will surely reward the thankful. (146) How many prophets have encountered those who had many myriads *of troops:* and yet they desponded not in their mind for what had befallen them in fighting for the religion of GOD; and were not weakened, neither behaved themselves in an abject manner? GOD loveth those who persevere patiently.

---

still the murmurs of his party on their defeat, represents to them that the time of every man's death is decreed and predetermined by God, and that those who fell in the battle could not have avoided their fate had they stayed at home; whereas they had now obtained the glorious advantage of dying martyrs for the faith."—*Sale.*
See also Prelim. Disc., p. 164.

The book. Rodwell tells us that the Rabbins teach a similar doctrine; see his note *in loco.* The *Tafsir-i-Raufi* says that this verse was revealed to incite the Muslims to acts of daring. Since the hour of death is fixed for every man, every one is immortal until that hour arrive.

Whoso chooseth. These words seem clearly to recognise the free agency of men, and the statement is the more remarkable, coming as it does immediately after another which clearly teaches the absolute predestination of all things. The meaning of the whole passage is, I think, that the hour of death is fixed. Whether in the battlefield or in the quiet of domestic surroundings, each man must die at the appointed hour. Those, therefore, who choose ease and freedom from danger in this life will be permitted to secure them, though they will not thereby avert death for a moment beyond the time written in the book, while those who choose martyrdom will yet live out their appointed time, and receive the martyr's reward beside. It would be very easy to raise an objection to the Qurán on the ground of contradiction between the doctrine of God's sovereignty and man's free will; but we consider this difficult ground for a Christian to take, for while there is a strong element of fatalism permeating Islám, it is no easy task to fasten that doctrine upon the Qurán without laying Christianity open to a countercharge from the Muslim side.

(146) *How many of the prophets.* Muhammad again likens himself, even in his misfortune, to the former prophets; many of them had reverses in fighting for the religion of God. Why should he then behave himself in an abject manner? The plain inference from this passage is that in Muhammad's mind many of the prophets were warriors like himself, "fighting for the religion of God."

(147) And their speech was no other than what they said, Our LORD forgive us our offences, and our transgressions in our business; and confirm our feet, and help us against the unbelieving people. (148) And GOD gave them the reward of this world, and a glorious reward in the life to come; for GOD loveth the well-doers.

R $\frac{16}{7}$. ‖ (149) O ye who believe, if you obey the infidels, they will cause you to turn back on your heels, and ye will be turned back and perish: (150) but GOD is your LORD; and he is the best helper. (151) We will surely cast a dread into the hearts of the unbelievers, because they have associated with GOD that concerning which he sent them down no power: their dwelling shall be the fire *of hell*: and the receptacle of the wicked shall be miserable. (152) GOD

---

(147) *Forgive us our offences.* This verse clearly disproves the popular doctrine that the prophets were *sinless.*

(148) *The reward of this world, i.e.,* victory over the infidels (*Tafsír-i-Raufi*). The marked difference between the teaching of the Qurán and the Bible as to the condition of the people of the Lord in this world is worthy of note. The Qurán everywhere teaches that though they had trials similar to those endured by Muhammad and the Muslims of Makkah and Madína, yet *in the end* they were manifestly triumphant over the infidels in this world. The Christian need not be told that this is very far from the teaching of the Bible. Final triumph is certain, but it may be wrought out on the cross or amidst the faggots and instruments of persecution and death.

(149) "This passage was occasioned by the endeavours of the Quraish to seduce the Muhammadans to their old idolatry as they fled in the battle of Ohod."—*Sale.*

Turn back on your heels, i.e., to relapse into idolatry.

(151) *We will surely cast a dread,* &c. "To this Muhammad attributed the sudden retreat of Abu Sufián and his troops, without making any farther advantage of their success, only giving Muhammad a challenge to meet them next year at Badr, which he accepted. Others say that as they were on their march home, they repented that they had not utterly extirpated the Muhammadans, and began to think of going back to Madína for that purpose, but were prevented by a sudden consternation or panic fear, which fell on them from God."—*Sale, Baidháwi.*

Associated with God. This formula, oft-repeated, expresses the Muslim idea of idolatry. It correctly describes it as bestowing upon the creature the worship belonging solely to the Creator.

No power should be translated *no authority.*

(152) *When ye destroyed them,* &c., *i.e.,* in the beginning of the battle at Ohod.

had already made good unto you his promise, when ye destroyed them by his permission, until ye became faint-hearted, and disputed concerning the command *of the apostle,* and were rebellious; after *God* had shown you what ye desired. (153) Some of you chose this present world, and others of you chose the world to come. Then he turned you *to flight* from before them, that he might make trial of you : (but he hath now pardoned you: for GOD is endued with beneficence towards the faithful;) (154) when ye went up *as ye fled,* and looked not back on any: while the apostle called you, in the uttermost

---

Were rebellious. "That is, till the bowmen, who were placed behind to prevent their being surrounded, seeing the enemy fly, quitted their post, contrary to Muhammad's express orders, and dispersed themselves to seize the plunder ; whereupon Khâlid Ibn al Walîd perceiving their disorder, fell on their rear with the horse which he commanded, and turned the fortune of the day. It is related that though Abdullah Ibn Jubair, their captain, did all he could to make them keep their ranks, he had not ten that stayed with him out of the whole fifty."—*Sale, Baidhâwi.*

What ye desired, i.e., victory and spoils. This is a very characteristic confession, pointing to the motive that really inspired the courage of the Muslims. And yet throughout this discourse the prophet offers the rewards of piety to all who fought *in the way of God,* and declares that those who lost their lives received the crown of martyrdom. The purpose to plunder and destroy their enemies is sanctified by executing it in "the way of the Lord," and in obedience to the command of the prophet. How far this permission to plunder comes short of confirming the former Scriptures may be seen by comparing therewith the regulations made by Moses, Joshua, and Samuel to check this disposition of all invaders (Num. xxxi., Josh. vi. and vii., and 1 Sam. xv.)

(153) *Some . . . and others, i.e.,* some sought the spoil in disobedience to the command of Muhammad, others stood firm at the post of duty. See note on ver. 152.

The faithful=Muslims. Their conduct had been very *unfaithful,* but they were now pardoned—not because they had repented, for they were murmuring, and almost ready to apostatise, but because it was now *politic* to show clemency rather than severity. See ver. 160.

(154) *While the apostle called,* "Crying aloud, *Come hither to me, O servants of God! I am the apostle of God; he who returneth back shall enter paradise.* But notwithstanding all his endeavours to rally his men, he could not get above thirty of them about him."—*Sale.*

Rodwell's translation is much more graphic: *When ye came up the*

part of you. Therefore *God* rewarded you with affliction on affliction, that ye be not grieved *hereafter* for the *spoils* which ye fail of, nor for that which befalleth you, for GOD is well acquainted with whatever ye do. (155) Then he sent down upon you after affliction security; a soft sleep which fell on some part of you; but *other* part were troubled by their own souls; falsely thinking of GOD, a foolish imagination, saying, Will anything of the matter *happen* unto us? Say, Verily, the matter *belongeth* wholly unto GOD. They concealed in their minds what they declared not unto thee; saying, If anything of the matter had happened unto us, we had not been slain here. Answer, If ye had been in your houses, verily they would have gone forth to fight, whose slaughter was decreed, to the places where they died, and *this came to pass* that GOD might try what was in your breasts, and might discern what was in your hearts; for GOD knoweth the innermost parts of the breasts *of men*.

---

height, and took no heed of any one, while the prophet in your rear was calling to the fight.

Therefore God rewarded, &c., i.e., " God punished your avarice and disobedience by suffering you to be beaten by your enemies, and to be discouraged by the report of your prophet's death, that ye might be inured to patience under adverse fortune, and not repine at any loss or disappointment for the future."—*Sale.*

(155) *He sent down . . . security.* After the battle of Ohod the Muslims fell asleep. Some slept soundly and were refreshed, others were excited, indulging in wild imaginations, supposing themselves to be on the verge of destruction. So the commentators generally.

We had not been slain. The meaning is that they considered God to be against them because they had not secured any gain in the battle. They therefore said to themselves or one to another, "If God had assisted us according to his promise;" or, as others interpret the words, "If we had taken the advice of Abdullah Ibn Ubai Sulúl, and had kept within the town of Madína, our companions had not lost their lives."—*Sale, Jaláluddín.*

Answer, if ye had been in your houses. See note on ver. 145. The teaching of this verse is decidedly fatalistic, and, *taking it by itself,* the only conclusion one could logically draw would be that Muhammad was a fatalist. But there are many passages asserting the freedom of the will. We regard Muhammad as having been strongly inclined to fatalism, owing to the emphasis which he laid upon the doctrine of God's absolute sovereignty. But *being a man,* his own

‖ (156) Verily they among you who turned their backs NISF. on the day whereon the two armies met each other *at Ohod*, Satan caused them to slip for some *crime* which they had committed: but now hath God forgiven them; for GOD is gracious and merciful.

‖ (157) O true believers, be not as they who believed R $\frac{17}{8}$. not, and said of their brethren when they had journeyed in the land or had been at war, If they had been with us, those had not died, nor had these been slain: *whereas what befell them was so ordained* that GOD might take it *matter of* sighing in their hearts. GOD giveth life and causeth to die: and GOD seeth that which ye do. (158) Moreover if ye be slain, or die in defence of the religion

---

consciousness of freedom asserted itself, and so he was saved from that "belief in an absolute predestination, which turns men into mere puppets, and all human life into a grim game of chess, wherein men are the pieces, moved by the invisible hand of but a single player, and which is now so general in Muhammadan countries" (R. B. Smith's *Muhammad and Muhammadanism*, pp. 191, 192.) And yet, while believing Muhammad much less a fatalist than his disciples, whose wild fanaticism is described so eloquently by Gibbon, yet we can by no means go the length of saying with Mr. Smith, that "there is little doubt that Muhammad himself, if the alternative had been clearly presented to him, would have had more in common with Pelagius than with Augustine, with Arminius than with Calvin." Muhammad was not a "consistent fatalist"— *no man ever was*. Yet, notwithstanding his having "made prayer one of the four practical duties enjoined upon the faithful," and his constant use of language freely asserting the freedom of the will, there is such a multitude of passages in the Qurán which clearly make God the author of sin (chap. vii. 155, 179, 180; xv. 39-43; xvi. 95; xvii. 14-16, &c.), so many which assert the doctrine of absolute predestination, and all this so constantly confirmed by tradition, that the conclusion is irresistibly forced upon us that Muhammad is responsible for the fatalism of Islám.

(156) *Satan caused them to slip, i.e.*, by tempting them to disobedience. *For some crime, &c.*—" For their covetousness in quitting their post to seize the plunder."

(157) *Who believed not, i.e.*, the hypocrites of Madína who declined to fight at Ohod. *Had journeyed*, with a view to merchandise, or *been at war* for the cause of religion (*Tafsir-i-Raufi*). The sentiment of this and the two following verses is like that of vers. 139-143; the hour of death is fixed for every man in the eternal decree of God, and those who die fighting for Islám shall be pardoned and accepted of God, and be made partakers of the joys of paradise.

of GOD; verily pardon from GOD, and mercy, is better than what they heap together *of worldly riches.* (159) And if ye die or be slain, verily unto GOD shall ye be gathered. (160) And as to the mercy *granted unto the disobedient* from GOD, thou, *O Muhammad,* hast been mild towards them; but if thou hadst been severe and hardhearted, they had surely separated themselves from about thee. Therefore forgive them, and ask pardon for them: and consult them in the affair *of war;* and after thou hast deliberated, trust in GOD; for GOD loveth those who trust *in him.* (161) If GOD help you, none shall conquer you; but if he desert you, who is it that will help you after him? Therefore in GOD let the faithful trust. (162) It is not *the part* of a prophet to defraud, for he who

---

(160) *If thou hadst been severe, &c.* The *policy* of Muhammad in dealing with his followers is here distinctly announced. They had certainly merited severe punishment. But there were powerful adversaries in Madína who would have taken advantage of any attempt to enforce punishment of a severe nature. Besides, no slight shock to the new faith had been felt owing to the defeat, and it became a matter of the utmost importance to establish that faith. Hence the *mild* words, and the forgiveness so freely bestowed.

Let it be observed that all these mild words and expressions of forgiveness are set forth as coming from the mouth of God, and yet the same Divinity commends the mildness of the Prophet! Surely there is more of the politician than of the prophet here.

(162) *It is not the part of a prophet to defraud.* Sale says, on the authority of Baidháwi and Jaláluddín, that "this passage was revealed, as some say, on the division of the spoil at Badr, when some of the soldiers suspected Muhammad of having privately taken a scarlet carpet, made all of silk and very rich, which was missing. Others suppose the archers, who occasioned the loss of the battle of Ohod, left their station because they imagined Muhammad would not give them their share of the plunder; because, as it is related, he once sent out a party as an advanced guard, and in the meantime attacking the enemy, took some spoils which he divided among those who were with him in the action, and gave nothing to the party that was absent on duty."

The *Tafsír-i-Raufi* says the passage was occasioned by certain of the companions desiring a larger share of the booty than their weaker brethren. God here signifies that all are to be treated alike, and that partiality in the division of booty would be dishonest. This passage is regarded as vindicating the prophet from every charge of dishonesty.

defraudeth shall bring with him what he hath defrauded *any one of,* on the day of the resurrection. Then shall every soul be paid what he hath gained; and they shall not be treated unjustly. (163) Shall he therefore who followeth that which is well-pleasing unto GOD be as he who bringeth on himself wrath from GOD, and whose receptacle is hell? an evil journey shall it be *thither.* (164) There shall be degrees *of rewards and punishments* with GOD, for GOD seeth what they do. (165) Now hath GOD been gracious unto the believers when he raised up among them an apostle of their own nation, who should recite his signs unto them, and purify them, and teach them the book *of the Qurán* and wisdom: whereas they were before in manifest error. (166) After a misfortune had befallen you *at Ohod* (ye had already obtained two equal advantages), do ye say, Whence

---

He who defraudeth shall bring, &c. "According to a tradition of Muhammad, whoever cheateth another will, on the day of judgment, carry his fraudulent purchase publicly on his neck."—*Sale.*

(164) *There shall be degrees, &c.* This explains the purport of ver. 163. God will reward his servants in accordance with their works. The brave companions (note, ver. 162) need not be troubled by an equal division of the booty. God will reward, for "God seeth what ye do." As indicated by Sale in his translation, this principle applies to *punishments* as well as to *rewards.*

(165) *An apostle of their own nation.* Sale, on the authority of Baidháwi, says some manuscripts have *min anfasihim* instead of *min anfusihim,* whence it would read, *An apostle of the noblest among them,* meaning the Quraish, of which tribe Muhammad was descended. I have not been able to find any copy of the Qurán containing this reading. It is not likely that the spirit of Muhammad's inspiration would have made, *at this time,* any such invidious distinction between the tribes of Arabia, especially when as yet the Quraish were the mortal enemies of Muhammad. The expression is better understood as having reference to the Arabs in general.

Purify them, i.e., from idolatry and evil customs, such as infanticide, &c.

And wisdom. Baidháwi understands this expression to refer to the *Sunnat,* or Book of Traditions.

(166) *Two equal advantages.* ";In the battle of Badr, where he slew seventy of the enemy, equalling the number of those who lost their lives at Ohod, and also took as many prisoners."—*Sale.* See notes on vers. 13 and 152.

cometh this? Answer, This is from yourselves: for GOD is almighty. (167) And what happened unto you, on the day whereon the two armies met, was certainly by the permission of GOD; (168) and that he might know the ungodly. It was said unto them, Come, fight for the religion of GOD, or drive back *the enemy:* they answered, If we had known *ye went out* to fight, we had certainly followed you. They were on that day nearer unto unbelief than they were to faith; they spake with their mouths what was not in their hearts: but GOD perfectly knew what they concealed; (169) who said of their brethren, *while themselves* stayed *at home,* If they had obeyed us, they had not been slain. Say, Then keep back death from yourselves, if ye say truth. (170) Thou shalt in nowise reckon those who have been slain *at Ohod,* in the cause of GOD, dead; nay, they are sustained alive

---

God is almighty, i.e., he could not suffer defeat, wherefore your reverse has been a punishment for your disobedience.

(168) *That he might know the ungodly.* See note on ver. 142.

If we had known, &c. "That is, if we had conceived the least hope of success when ye marched out of Madína to encounter the infidels, and had not known that ye went rather to certain destruction than to battle, we had gone with you. But this Muhammad here tells them was only a feigned excuse; the true reason of their staying behind being their want of faith and firmness in their religion."—*Sale, Baidháwi.*

Rodwell translates this phrase, *Had we known how to fight.* This agrees with the various translations in Persian and Urdú. The meaning is, that the *hypocrites* feigned not to have known the Muslims were going out *to fight.* To this Muhammad replies in the remainder of the verse by telling them plainly that they lied.

(169) This verse gives the reason for the charge against the hypocrites in the previous verse. They are judged out of their own mouths.

Keep back death. See notes on vers. 145 and 155.

(170) *Thou shalt in nowise reckon, &c.* See note on chap. ii. 155. The crown of martyrdom was easily won. Even those slain because of their disobedience and covetousness (vers. 3, 122, 152, and 153, &c.) are now to be regarded as "alive with their God," and "rejoicing for what God of his favour hath granted them" (next verse). There is here a striking contrast between the teaching of the Qurán and the Word of God. It is the contrast between a counterfeit and the genuine article.

with their LORD, (171) rejoicing for what GOD of his favour hath granted them; and being glad for those who, coming after them, have not as yet overtaken them; because there shall no fear come on them, neither shall they be grieved. (172) They are filled with joy for the favour *which they have received* from GOD and *his* bounty; and for that GOD suffereth not the reward of the faithful to perish.

|| (173) They who hearkened unto GOD and *his* apostle, R $\frac{18}{9}$. after a wound had befallen them *at Ohod*, such of them as do good works, and fear *God*, shall have a great reward; (174) unto whom *certain* men said, Verily the men *of Makkah* have already gathered *forces* against you, be ye therefore afraid of them: but *this* increased their faith, and they

---

(171) *Those who, coming after them, i.e.*, who are yet destined to suffer martyrdom.

(173) *They who hearkened.* "The commentators differ a little as to the occasion of this passage. When news was brought to Muhammad, after the battle of Ohod, that the enemy, repenting of their retreat, were returning towards Madína, he called about him those who had stood by him in the battle, and marched out to meet the enemy as far as Humará al Asad, about eight miles from that town, notwithstanding that several of his men were so ill of their wounds that they were forced to be carried; but a panic fear having seized the army of the Quraish, they changed their resolution, and continued their march home; of which Muhammad having received intelligence, he also went back to Madína: and according to some commentators the Qurán here approves the faith and courage of those who attended the prophet on this occasion. Others say the persons intended in this passage were those who went with Muhammad the next year to meet Abu Sufián and the Quraish, according to their challenge, at Badr, where they waited some time for the enemy, and then returned home; for the Quraish, though they set out from Makkah, yet never came so far as the place of appointment, their hearts failing them on their march; which Muhammad attributed to their being struck with a terror from God. This expedition the Arabian histories call the *second* or *lesser expedition of Badr.*"—*Sale, Baidháwi.*

Muir, in his *Life of Mahomet*, vol. iii. p. 222, refers this passage to Muhammad's advance against Abu Sufián as far as Badr. The first story of the commentators given by Sale seems to be borne out by the statement, "They who hearkened unto God and his apostle *after a wound had befallen them.*" The following verse applies better to the second story. It is possible that two distinct revelations have been here blended together by the compilers of the Qurán.

(174) *Be ye afraid of them.* "The persons who thus endedeavoured

said, GOD is our support, and the most excellent patron. (175) Wherefore they returned with favour from GOD, and advantage: no evil befell them: and they followed what was well-pleasing unto GOD: for GOD is endowed with great liberality. (176) Verily that devil would cause you to fear his friends: but be ye not afraid of them: but fear me, if ye be true believers. (177) They shall not grieve thee who emulously hasten unto infidelity; for they shall never hurt GOD at all. GOD will not give them a part in the next life, and they shall suffer a great punishment. (178) Surely those who purchase infidelity with faith shall by no means hurt GOD at all, but they shall suffer a grievous punishment. (179) And let not the unbelievers think, because we grant them lives long and prosperous, that it is better for their souls: we grant them

---

to discourage the Muhammadans were, according to one tradition, some of the tribe of Abd Qais, who going to Madína, were bribed by Abu Sufián with a camel's load of dried raisins; and according to another tradition, it was Nuaim Ibn Masúd al Ashjai, who was also bribed with a she-camel ten months gone with young (a valuable present in Arabia). This Nuaim, they say, finding Muhammad and his men preparing for the expedition, told them that Abu Sufián, to spare them the pains of coming so far as Badr, would seek them in their own houses, and that none of them could possibly escape otherwise than by timely flight. Upon which Muhammad, seeing his followers a little dispirited, swore that he would go himself, though not one of them went with him. And accordingly he set out with seventy horsemen, every one of them crying out *Hashna Alláh*, *i.e.*, *God is our support.*"—*Sale, Baidháwi.*

Muir says Muhammad went forth with a force of 1500 men (*Life of Mahomet*, vol. iii. p. 221).

(175) *And advantage.* They had taken with them merchandise, and had held a fair at Badr for several days, disposing of their goods to great advantage. So *Baidháwi*, see *Sale*. From this fact Muir conjectures that Muhammad had knowledge of the change of purpose among the Quraish before he set out so boldly for Badr. See *Life of Mahomet*, vol. iii. p. 221, note.

(176) *That devil.* This probably refers to Abu Sufián. Some refer it to Nuaim, an emissary of the Quraish sent to Madína to excite fear among the Muslims. See note above on 174.

(177) *Who . . . hasten unto infidelity, i.e.*, the hypocrites of Madína, who professing themselves Muslims, talked like infidels (*Abdul Qádir*).

(179) See note on chap. ii. 211.

long and prosperous lives only that their iniquity may be increased; and they shall suffer an ignominious punishment. (180) GOD is not *disposed* to leave the faithful in the condition which ye are now in, until he sever the wicked from the good; nor is GOD *disposed* to make you acquainted with what is a hidden secret, but GOD chooseth such of his apostles as he pleaseth, *to reveal his mind unto:* believe therefore in GOD and his apostles; and if ye believe and fear *God,* ye shall receive a great reward. (181) And let not those who are covetous of what GOD of his bounty hath granted them imagine that *their avarice* is better for them: nay, rather it is worse for them. That which they have covetously reserved shall be bound as a collar about their neck on the day of the resurrection: unto GOD *belongeth* the inheritance of heaven and earth: and GOD is well acquainted with what ye do.

---

(180) *God is not disposed, &c.,* i.e., he will not suffer the good and sincere among you to continue indiscriminately mixed with the wicked and hypocritical.

A hidden secret. The author of the notes on the Roman Urdú Qurán thinks that Muhammad here disclaims all knowledge of the "hidden" things revealed to the *chosen apostles* of God. But the *Tafsír-i-Raufí* says the very reverse is the meaning of this passage. Muhammad here numbers himself among the *chosen* apostles, to whom God is pleased to make known the "hidden secrets" of his purpose. God does not, however, reveal secret things to hypocrites.

Believe . . . in God and his apostles. The use of the plural here shows that the revelations of God's *hidden* purposes made to apostles other than Muhammad were to be accepted by the Muslims. *There were then genuine and credible scriptures,* containing these revelations, in the hands of the contemporaries of Muhammad.

(181) *Those who are covetous.* The following tradition is given on the authority of *Abu Hurairah*:—" To whosoever God gives wealth, and he does not perform the charity due from it, his wealth will be made into the shape of a serpent on the day of resurrection, which shall not have any hair upon its head; and this is a sign of its poison and long life, and it has two black spots upon its eyes, and it will be twisted round his neck like a chain on the day of resurrection; then the serpent will seize the man's jawbone, and will say, 'I am thy wealth, the charity for which thou didst not give; and I am thy treasure, from which thou didst not separate any alms.'"—*Mishqát-al-Masábih,* book vi. chap. i. pt. 1.

R ¹⁹⁄₁₀.

‖ (182) GOD hath already heard the saying of those who said, Verily GOD is poor, and we are rich: we will surely write down what they have said, and the slaughter which they have made of the prophets without a cause; and we will say *unto them*, Taste ye the pain of burning. (183) This *shall they suffer* for the *evil* which their hands have sent before them, and because GOD is not unjust towards mankind; (184) who *also* say, Surely GOD hath commanded us, that we should not give credit to *any* apostle, until *one* should come unto us with a sacrifice, which should be consumed by fire. Say, Apostles have already come unto you

---

(182) *Verily God is poor.* "It is related that Muhammad, writing to the Jews of the tribe of Qainuqáa to invite them to Islám, and exhorting them, among other things, in the words of the Qurán, (chap. ii. 245), *to lend unto God on good usury.* Phineas Ibn Azúra, on hearing that expression, said, 'Surely God is poor, since they ask to borrow for him.' Whereupon Abu Baqr, who was the bearer of that letter, struck him on the face, and told him that if it had not been for the truce between them, he would have struck off his head; and on Phineas's complaining to Muhammad of Abu Baqr's ill usage, this passage was revealed."—*Sale, Baidháwi.*

The slaughter . . . of the prophets. See note on ver. 112.

(184) *A sacrifice . . . consumed by fire.* "The Jews, say the commentators, insisted that it was a peculiar proof of the mission of all the prophets sent to them that they could, by their prayers, bring down fire from heaven to consume the sacrifice, and therefore they expected Muhammad should do the like. And some Muhammadan doctors agree that God appointed this miracle as the test of all their prophets, except only Jesus and Muhammad (*Jaláluddín*): though others say any other miracle was a proof full as sufficient as the bringing down fire from heaven (*Baidháwi*).

"The Arabian Jews seem to have drawn a general consequence from some particular instances of this miracle in the Old Testament (Lev. ix. 24, &c.), and the Jews at this day say that first the fire which fell from heaven on the altar of the tabernacle (Lev. ix. 24), after the consecration of Aaron and his sons, and afterwards that which descended on the altar of Solomon's Temple at the dedication of that structure (2 Chron. vii. 1), was fed and constantly maintained there by the priests, both day and night, without being suffered once to go out, till it was extinguished, as some think, in the reign of Manasses (*Talmud Zebachim*, chap. vi.), but, according to the more received opinion, when the Temple was destroyed by the Chaldeans. Several Christians have given credit to this assertion of the Jews, with what reason I shall not here inquire: and the Jews, in consequence of this notion, might probably expect that a prophet who came to restore God's true religion should rekindle for them this

before me, with plain proofs, and with the *miracle* which ye mention: why therefore have ye slain them, if ye speak truth? (185) If they accuse thee of imposture, the apostles before thee have also been accounted impostors, who brought evident demonstrations, and the scriptures, and the book which enlighteneth *the understanding*. (186) Every soul shall taste of death, and ye shall have your reward on the

---

heavenly fire, which they have not been favoured with since the Babylonish captivity."—*Sale.*

There are a number of passages showing how Muhammad was challenged to work miracles in attestation of his prophetic claim, *e.g.,* chap. ii. 118, 119, vi. 34-36 and 109-111, x. 21, xvii. 92-95, xx. 134, &c. In every one of these passages the reply of Muhammad clearly indicates that he did not claim the power to work miracles. This matter is very clearly set forth in Prideaux's *Life of Mahomet,* 8th edition, p. 25, to which the reader is referred. I would also refer the reader to R. Bosworth Smith's *Muhammad and Muhammadanism,* 2d edition, pp. 185-191.

Why therefore have ye slain them, i.e., the former prophets wrought miracles and ye slew them; wherefore should I gratify your desire and cause fire to come down from heaven; would ye believe? Sale says, "Among these the commentators reckon Zacharias and John the Baptist!"

(185) *If they accuse thee of imposture.* This passage, following closely upon the apology of Muhammad for not giving the usual signs of apostleship demanded by the Jews and others, seems to give the ground of this accusation; *i.e.,* Muhammad's imposture was evident, *because* he refused to perform miracles which would prove that he had been sent from God. Muhammad's reply to this charge is not in accordance with facts—"The apostles before thee have been accounted impostors." It is not true that *all* apostles were regarded as impostors. Certainly, such as were so accused were enabled to work such miracles as proved even to their enemies that "there was a prophet of God in Israel," 1 Kings xviii. 36, &c. Such "evident demonstrations" were expected of Muhammad, but never given. Even his own followers have been driven to invent a multitude of stories detailing the miracles wrought by their prophet. These have been recorded in their traditions. The following are samples of the miracles thus invented:—"A camel weeps, and is calmed at the touch of Muhammad; the hair grows upon a boy's head when the prophet lays his hand upon it; a horse is cured from stumbling; the eye of a soldier is healed and made better than the other; he marked his sheep on the ear, and the species retain the mark to this day, &c."—*Arnold's Islám and Christianity,* p. 352. See *Mishqát-ul-Masábih,* Urdú edition, vol. iv. pp. 571-623.

(186) *Every soul shall taste of death.* Some Muslims understand this as applying to *all created* things. At the first sound of the last

day of resurrection; and he who shall be far removed from *hell* fire, and shall be admitted into paradise, shall be happy; but the present life is only a deceitful provision. (187) Ye shall surely be proved in your possessions, and *in* your persons; and ye shall bear from those unto whom the scripture was delivered before you, and from the idolaters, much hurt; but if ye be patient and fear *God*, this is a matter that is absolutely determined. (188) And when GOD accepted the covenant of those to whom the book *of the law* was given, *saying*, Ye shall surely publish it unto mankind, ye shall not hide it: yet they threw it behind their backs, and sold it for a small price: but woful *is the price* for which they have sold *it*. (189) Think not that they who rejoice at what they have done, and expect to

---

trump all angels will die, including Isráfíl, who will blow the trumpet. God will then raise Isráfíl, who will again sound the trump, and all the dead will rise to judgment.

Shall be admitted into paradise, i.e., at the resurrection. For the state of the dead between death and the resurrection, see Prelim. Disc., pp. 127–138.

(187) *Proved in your possessions, &c.* The *Tafsír-i-Raufi* refers this passage to the loss of property at the flight from Makkah, and the loss of life in the wars for the faith. It seems to me, however, the passage better applies to the temporary ascendancy of the Jews and hypocrites of Madína after the battle of Ohod.

(188) *Ye shall surely publish it, i.e.*, the prophecies concerning Muhammad contained in the Pentateuch. The claim set up here is virtually this, that the great burden of prophecy was the advent of Muhammad, just as Christians regard the spirit of prophecy to be the testimony of God to Jesus as the Christ. It would appear from this passage that Muhammad, consciously or unconsciously,—being deceived by designing converts from Judaism,—had conceived that the prophecies of the Old Testament concerning the *Coming One* related to him. Accordingly, those Jewish Rabbies who denied the existence of any prophecies relating to him are here stigmatised as having sold themselves to the work of perverting their Scriptures so as to oppose him.

Let it again be observed that the charge of corruption is not laid upon the volume of Scriptures extant in the days of Muhammad, but against the living *interpreters* of those Scriptures.

Woful is the price. "Whoever concealeth the knowledge which God has given him," says Muhammad, "God shall put on him a bridle of fire on the day of resurrection."—*Sale.*

(189) *They who rejoice, &c., i.e.*, who think they have done a com-

be praised for what they have not done; think not, *O prophet*, that they shall escape from punishment, for they shall suffer a painful punishment.

‖ (190) And unto GOD *belongeth* the kingdom of heaven and earth: GOD is almighty. (191) Now in the creation of heaven and earth, and the vicissitude of night and day, are signs unto those who are endued with understanding; (192) who remember GOD standing, and sitting, and *lying* on their sides; and meditate on the creation of heaven and earth, *saying*, O LORD, thou hast not created this in vain; far be it from thee: therefore deliver us from the torment of *hell* fire: (193) O LORD, surely whom thou shalt throw into the fire, thou wilt also cover with shame: nor shall the ungodly have any to help them. (194) O LORD, we have heard a preacher inviting *us* to the faith *and saying*, Believe in your LORD: and we believed. O LORD, forgive us therefore our sins, and expiate our evil

R $\frac{20}{11}$.

---

mendable deed in concealing and perverting the testimonies in the Pentateuch concerning Muhammad, and in disobeying God's commands to the contrary. "It is said that Muhammad once asking some Jews concerning a passage in their law, they gave him an answer very different from the truth, and were mightily pleased that they had, as they thought, deceived him. Others, however, think this passage relates to some pretended Muhammadans who rejoiced in their hypocrisy and expected to be commended for their wickedness."—*Sale, Baidháwi.*

(191) This verse belongs to the Makkan revelations. Comp. chap. ii. 165.

(192) *Who remember God standing, &c.*, viz., "at all times and in all postures. Al Baidháwi mentions a saying of Muhammad to one Imrán Ibn Husain, to this purpose: 'Pray standing, if thou art able; if not, sitting; and if thou canst not sit up, then as thou liest along.' Al Sháfa'i directs that the sick should pray lying on their right side."—*Sale.*

This passage describes the character of those mentioned in the previous verse.

(194) *A preacher.* This is the name which Muhammad constantly assumed at Makkah. See chap. vii. 2, chap. xiii. 29, 40, chap. xvi. 84, &c. Nought but the political power acquired at Madína changed the preacher into a soldier.

And expiate. The word used here is *kaffara*, which is the cognate of the Hebrew כָּפַר, *to cover, to expiate.* While, however, the *language* suggests atonement by sacrifice (and the idea was not

deeds from us, and make us to die with the righteous. (195) O LORD, give us also *the reward* which thou hast promised by thy apostles; and cover us not with shame

---

foreign to Muhammad's mind, for he offered sacrifices himself), yet in his teaching he everywhere as studiously denied the doctrine of salvation by atonement as he did the doctrine of the divinity of Christ. And yet he had the daring to appeal to the Jewish and Christian Scriptures as bearing witness to his prophetic pretensions, and to claim for his Qurán the excellency that it attested the doctrines of all the prophets.

It cannot be claimed for Muhammad that he was ignorant of Jewish belief and practice in respect to atoning sacrifices, for during his first year's residence at Madína "Mahomet kept the great day of atonement, with its sacrifices of victims, in conformity with the practice of the Jews; and had he continued on a friendly footing with them, he would probably have maintained this rite."—*Muir's Life of Mahomet*, vol. iii. p. 51. According to this author, Muhammad abandoned this Jewish rite in the second year of the Hijra, owing to his failure to win the Jews over to his cause. He then offered sacrifices himself. The following is the story of this transaction:—"After a service resembling that on the breaking of the fast, two fatted sucking kids with budding horns were placed before the prophet. Seizing a knife, he sacrificed one with his own hand, saying, 'O Lord! I sacrifice this for my whole people; all those that bear testimony to thy unity and to my mission.' Then he called for the other, and slaying it likewise, said, 'O Lord! this is for Mahomet, and for the family of Mahomet.' Of the latter kid both he and his family partook, and what was over he gave to the poor. The double sacrifice seems in its main features to have been founded on the practice of the Jewish priest at the Feast of the Atonement, when he sacrificed 'first for his own sins, and then for the people's' (Heb. vii. 27). This ceremony was repeated by Mahomet every year of his residence at Medina, and it was kept up there after his decease."—*Life of Mahomet*, vol. iii. pp. 52, 53.

In answer to the question why Muhammad should have ignored the doctrine of salvation by atonement, there is available no definite reply. It was, however, probably due to a variety of reasons. First, such a doctrine would contradict Muhammad's idea of a sovereign God. Such being the case, his conformity to Jewish and Arab practice was simply a matter of policy. Or again, we may well believe that the opposition by the Jews estranged him from everything distinctively Jewish. To accept the doctrine of the divinity of Christ would not only have seemed to militate against his idea of God's unity, but also would logically have led to a rejection of his prophetic claim. In like manner, the adoption of the doctrine of atoning sacrifices as necessary to salvation would not only have contradicted Muhammad's notion of God's sovereignty, but would logically have led to his adopting Judaism or Christianity as his

on the day of resurrection: for thou art not contrary to the promise.

‖ (196) Their LORD therefore answered them, *saying*, I will not suffer the work of him among you who worketh to be lost, whether he be male or female: the one of you is from the other. They therefore who have left their country, and have been turned out of their houses, and have suffered for my sake, and have been slain in battle; verily I will expiate their evil deeds from them, and I will surely bring them into gardens watered by rivers; a reward from GOD; and with GOD is the most excellent

---

religion, either of which conclusions would have rendered him unpopular with the Arabs, who, since the break with the Jews, had been constituted his chosen people. Either of these reasons would satisfactorily account for the fact that the doctrine of atonement as necessary to salvation is wanting in the teaching of Muhammad. When, however, he represents his own doctrine as that of all former prophets, and when, in all his allusions to the teaching of these prophets, he uniformly ignores the doctrine of salvation by atonement, we cannot but believe he did so deliberately. This is the rock upon which the cause of Islám falls, only to be dashed in pieces. The signal failure of the Qurán to attest this central doctrine of both the Old and New Testament Scriptures proves the Qurán, on its own testimony, to be a forgery, and Muhammad to be an impostor.

(196) *Male or female.* "These words were added, as some relate, on Omm Salma, one of the prophet's wives, telling him that she had observed God often made mention of the *men* who fled their country for the sake of their faith, but took no notice of the *women*."—Sale, Baidháwi.

The one of you, &c., *i.e.*, the one is born of the other. Rodwell translates "the one of you is the issue of the other." The teaching of the passage is that all, whether male or female, will be rewarded according to their works. Women are not by any means excluded from the blessings of Islám, and they have formed by no means the least devoted followers of Muhammad.

Verily I will expiate, &c. The word used here for *expiate* is the same as that used in ver. 194 (see note there). The idea attached to it here is that of *removal*.

Gardens watered by rivers. The imagery of paradise is coloured by Arab ideas of beauty and pleasure. Heaven is likened to a beautiful oasis carpeted in green, with its sparkling fountains, limpid streams, shady trees, and delicious fruits. On the question as to whether these earthly surroundings are to be understood in a literal or figurative sense, see note on ver. 15.

reward. (197) Let not the prosperous dealing of the unbelievers in the land deceive thee; *it is but* a slender provision; *and* then their receptacle shall be hell; an unhappy couch *shall it be.* (198) But they who fear the LORD shall have gardens through which rivers flow; they shall continue therein for ever: this is the gift of GOD; for what is with GOD shall be better for the righteous *than short-lived worldly prosperity.* (199) There are some of those who have received the scriptures who believe in GOD, and that which hath been sent down unto you, and that which hath been sent down to them, submitting themselves unto GOD; they sell not the signs of GOD for a small price: these shall have their reward with their

---

(197) *An unhappy couch.* This expression, used so frequently in the Qurán to describe the torment of hell, is probably used in contrast with the carnal and sensual delights of the Muslim heaven. There "they shall repose themselves on most delicate beds, adorned with gold and precious stones, under the shadow of the trees of paradise, which shall continually yield them all manner of delicious fruits; and there they shall enjoy most beautiful women, pure and clean, having black eyes, &c." But here, the couch shall be in the midst of fire, and be surrounded by smoke as with a coverlid, with nothing to eat "but the fruit of the tree Zaqún, which should be in their bellies like burning pitch," and nothing to drink "but boiling and stinking water," nor should they breathe ought but "exceeding hot winds," &c. (*Prideaux, Life of Mahomet,* p. 22).

(198) See notes on ver. 196.

For what is with God, &c. This passage, vers. 196–198, is said to have been revealed to comfort thé Muslims, who, being in poverty and want, were surrounded by prosperous enemies.

(199) *Some . . . who believe.* "The persons here meant some will have to be Abdullah Ibn Salám and his companions; others suppose they were forty Arabs of Najrán, or thirty-two Ethiopians, or else eight Greeks, who were converted from Christianity to Muhammadanism; and others say this passage was revealed in the ninth year of the Hijra, when Muhammad, on Gabriel's bringing him the news of the death of Ashámah, king of Ethiopia, who had embraced the Muhammadan religion some years before, prayed for the soul of the departed, at which some of his hypocritical followers were displeased, and wondered that he should pray for a Christian proselyte whom he had never seen."—*Sale, Jaláluddín, Baidháwi.*

See also verse 113, and note there.

LORD; for GOD is swift in taking an account. (200) O true believers, be patient and strive to excel in patience, and be constant-minded, and fear GOD, that ye may be happy.

God is swift, &c. See chap. ii. 201.

(200) *Be patient,* i.e., in fighting for religion. This is the conclusion of the exhortation to the disheartened followers of Muhammad, beginning with ver. 121.

CHAPTER IV.

ENTITLED SURAT UN NISA (WOMEN).

Revealed at Madína.

INTRODUCTION.

THIS chapter contains *revelations* suited to the circumstances of the Muslim community at Madína and the interests of the new religion after the defeat of Ohod. Questions relating to inheritance, the treatment of widows and orphans, forbidden degrees, &c., naturally arose. These questions find an answer here. Besides these, there are numerous passages containing exhortations to fight for the faith of Islám, together with denunciations against the Jews and the disaffected tribes of Madína and its vicinity. The various expeditions sent against these during the year following the battle at Ohod called for certain regulations, which are the subject of a portion of this chapter. And, finally, the Christians are referred to in the latter part of the chapter, where they are reproved, partly under cover of the Jews, for their faith in the crucifixion and death of Jesus, and their belief in the doctrine of the Trinity and the Sonship of Christ.

Probable Date of the Revelations.

Nearly all the stories told by the commentators to illustrate this chapter point to a period following the battle of Ohod, the expulsion of the Bani Nadhír, and the expedition against the tribes of the Bani Ghatafán at Dzát al Riqá. It follows, therefore, that the revelations of this chapter belong in general to a period extending from the beginning of A.H. 4 to the middle or latter part of A.H. 5. The following passages *may*, however, belong to a different period, viz., ver. 42, which probably belongs to A.H. 3, and vers. 104-114 and 134, which may belong to a date later than A.H. 5, but earlier than the subjugation of Makkah (see note on ver. 186).

Vers. 115-125 and 130-132 probably belong to the number of

the early Madína revelations. Nöeldeke inclines to place them among the later Makkan revelations, because the Jews are referred to in a friendly spirit. But this circumstance would rather point to Madína, where, during the first year of the Hijra, Muhammad courted the favour of the Jews. Still, the form of address, "O men" (ver. 132), points to Makkah. The question may therefore still be regarded as open, though we think the evidence, thus far, to be in favour of the early part of A.H. I.

Principal Subjects.

	VERSES
Man and his Creator	1
Orphans, the duty of guardians to such	2–5
The law of inheritance	6–13
The punishment of adulteresses	14, 15
Repentance enjoined	16, 17
Women's rights	18, 19
Forbidden and lawful degrees in marriage	20–27
Gaming, rapine, and suicide forbidden	28–30
Man's superiority over woman recognised	31–33
Reconcilement of man and wife	34
Parents, orphans, the poor, &c., to be kindly treated	35, 36
Hypocrisy in almsgiving condemned	37–41
Prayer forbidden to the drunken and polluted	42
Jewish mockers denounced	43–45
Idolatry the unpardonable sin	46–53
The rewards of faith and unbelief	54, 55
Trusts to be faithfully paid back	56
Disputes to be settled by God and his Apostle	57–68
Precautions, &c., in warring for the faith	69–74
The disobedient and cowardly reproved	75–84
Salutations to be returned	85
Treatment of hypocrites and apostates	86–90
Believers not to be slain or plundered	91–93
Believers in heathen countries to fly to Muslim lands	94–99
Special order for prayer in time of war	100–102
Exhortation to zeal for Islám	103
Fraud denounced	104–114, 133
Idolatry and Islám compared	115–125
Equity in dealing with women and orphans enjoined	126
Wives to be subject to the will of husbands	127–129
God to be feared	130–132
Muslims exhorted to steadfastness	134–138
Hypocrites to be shunned	139–143

	VERSES
The reward of hypocrisy and belief compared	144-151
Presumptuous and disobedient Jews destroyed.	152-154
The Jews calumniate Mary and Jesus	155-158
Certain kinds of food forbidden to Jews as punishment	159, 160
Muhammad's inspiration like that of other prophets	161-168
Christians reproved for their faith in Jesus as the Son of God and in the doctrine of the Trinity	169-174
The law of inheritance for distant relatives	175

IN THE NAME OF THE MOST MERCIFUL GOD.

‖ (1) O MEN, fear your LORD, who hath created you out of one man, and out of him created his wife, and from them two hath multiplied many men and women: and fear GOD by whom ye beseech one another; and *respect* women *who have borne you*, for GOD is watching over you. (2) And give the orphans *when they come to age* their substance; and render *them* not in exchange bad for good: and devour not their substance, *by adding it* to your own substance; for this is a great sin. (3) And if ye fear that ye shall not act with equity towards orphans

---

(1) *O men, &c.* This chapter is entitled WOMEN because it contains, for the most part, laws and precepts relating to them. The *men* are specially addressed, but the instruction is intended for both men and women. They are addressed in the original, "*O ye people.*"

From them two, &c. The unity of the human race is here distinctly declared. All men are of "one blood."

And respect women. The word translated *women* (in the Arabic, *wombs*) is the object of the verb *fear*. Palmer translates, "*Fear God, in whose name ye beg of one another, and the wombs.*" Sale, however, expresses the meaning by inserting the word *respect.*

(2) *Give the orphans, &c.* These orphans were the children of those who lost their lives in the wars for the cause of Islám. Not only the children but their property was intrusted to those who agreed to become guardians. These orphans were defrauded in various ways. Sometimes their property was appropriated by the guardians; others "exchanged bad for good," *e.g.,* by turning the good goats or camels of the orphan ward along with their own herds, and then selecting the bad ones as the orphan's share. This law was instituted by Muhammad to prevent this kind of abuse.

(3) *If ye fear that ye cannot act equitably, &c.* "The commentators understand this passage differently. The true meaning seems

of the female sex, take in marriage of such *other* women as please you, two, or three, or four, *and not more.* But

to be ·as it is here translated; Muhammad advising his followers that if they found they should wrong the female orphans under their care, either by marrying them against their inclinations, for the sake of their riches or beauty, or by not using or maintaining them so well as they ought, by reason of their having already several wives, they should rather choose to marry other women, to avoid all occasion of sin. Others say that when this passage was revealed, many of the Arabians, fearing trouble and temptation, refused to take upon them the charge of orphans, and yet multiplied wives to a great excess, and used them ill; or, as others write, gave themselves up to fornication; which occasioned the passage. And according to these, its meaning must be either that if they feared they could not act justly towards orphans, they had as great reason to apprehend they could not deal equitably with so many wives, and therefore are commanded to marry but a certain number; or else, that since fornication was a crime as well as wronging of orphans, they ought to avoid that also, by marrying according to their abilities."—*Sale, Baidháwi.*

The connection of this verse with the preceding is undoubted, and that connection is close. How the explanation of the commentators would remove the *fear* of *acting unjustly* with orphans of the female sex, I cannot see. Surely marrying two, or three, or four *other* women would hardly produce a moral change in a man who feared he could not act justly in the matter of a sacred trust. I therefore venture to suggest that Muhammad here advises his followers *to marry their orphan wards,* and so, by fixing upon them a lawful dowry and exalting them to the position of lawful wives, avoid the evil of committing a breach of .trust or an act of immorality. This view seems to me to be required by the preceding context. The word *other,* inserted by Sale and others before *women,* is not required. The Muslim may marry *of women* such as are pleasing to him, two, three, or four, whether his orphan wards or not.

Two, or three, or four. Literally, *two and two, three and three, and four and four.* The meaning is, that *each* might have two, or three, or four lawful wives. See Prelim. Disc., p. 206. Muhammad did not bind himself by this law. See chap. xxxiii. 49.

The statement of Mír Aulád Ali, professor of Oriental languages at Trinity College, Dublin, "that Muhammad had not *enjoined* polygamy," but only *permitted* it, quoted by Mr. R. Bosworth Smith (*Mohammed and Mohammedanism,* p. 144, note), is hardly borne out by this passage. Nor is such a statement borne out by the example of the Prophet. Nor is Mr. Smith's plea, that this permission may be placed in the same catagory as *slavery not forbidden in the Bible,* at all justified by the facts. Slavery is contrary to the whole spirit of the Bible, while polygamy is in accord with the whole spirit of the Qurán. Even the heaven of Islám is to witness the perpetuation of almost unlimited polygamy (see chaps. lv. and lvi.) The attempt to apologise for the polygamy of Islám, when made by

if ye fear that ye cannot act equitably towards so many, marry one only, or the slaves which ye shall have acquired.

Europeans, indicates either prejudice or a want of information on the part of the writer; when made by a few "enlightened Orientals," it indicates their desire to cover up what they, by an English education and by mingling in Christian society, have learned to be thoroughly ashamed of.

One only, or the slaves. Were the requirements of this rule strictly observed, there would be no polygamy in practice, for the simple reason that the impartial treatment of two or more wives is with man an impossibility. Muhammad did not fulfil this his own precept, as his marked preference, now for the Coptic Mary and again for the sprightly Ayesha, clearly shows.

But whilst *polygamy* would be impracticable, the floodgates of vice would be, *and now are,* opened wide by the permission to add to the one *wife* any number of slave girls. Those who quote this passage to show that Muhammad restricted polygamy and that monogamy is entirely in accord with Muhammadanism, fail to quote the words, "or the slaves which ye shall have acquired." The whole force of the *restriction* is evaporated by these words. There is absolutely no restriction in this direction. The number of concubines may be as great as any Osmánli could desire, and yet it receives the sanction of the Qurán.

Instead, therefore, of any "strong moral sentiment" being aroused by these laws, by which Muhammad "has succeeded, down to this very day, and to a greater extent than has ever been the case elsewhere, in freeing Muhammadan countries from those professional outcasts who live by their own misery,"* the very reverse is true. No countries under heaven present such a cesspool of seething corruption and sensuality as those ruled over by the Muslims. To be sure, the *form* under which it appears is different, but the fact, no man acquainted with the state of things in Muslim harems, can honestly deny. The distrust which Muslims show towards their own wives and daughters testifies to the low state of morality among them. "It is the Moslim theory that women can never, in any time, place, or circumstances, be trusted; they must be watched, veiled, suspected, secluded." "In these days, when so much has been written about the high ethical tone of Islám, we shall speak plainly on this subject, unpleasant though it is. We would reiterate the position already taken, that polygamy has *not* diminished licentiousness among the Mohammedans. The *sin of Sodom* is so common among them as to make them in many places objects of dread to their neighbours. The burning denunciations of the Apostle Paul in the first chapter of Romans, vers. 24 and 27, are applicable to tens of thousands in Mohammedan lands to-day." "In the city of Hamath, in Northern Syria, the Christian population, even to this day, are afraid to allow their boys from ten to fourteen years of age to appear

---

* R. B. Smith's *Mohammed and Mohammedanism,* p. 242.

This will be easier, that ye swerve not *from righteousness. And give women their dowry freely;* but if they voluntarily remit unto you any part if it, enjoy it with satisfaction and advantage. (4) And give not unto those who are weak of understanding the substance which GOD hath appointed you to preserve *for them;* but maintain them thereout, and clothe them, and speak kindly unto them. (5) And examine the orphans until they attain *the age of*

---

in the streets after sunset, lest they be carried off by the Moslems as victims of the horrible practice of Sodomy. Mohammadan pashas surround themselves with fair-faced boys, nominally scribes and pages, when in reality their object is of entirely another character." This, and much more, is told by Dr. Henry H. Jessup in his book entitled *The Mohammedan Missionary Problem*, pp. 46–48.

In India the case may not be as bad as it is in Turkey, but I think we can fairly agree with the Rev. J. Vaughan, who says:— "However the phenomenon may be accounted for, we, after mixing with Hindoos and Mussulmans for nineteen years back, have no hesitation in saying that the latter are, as a whole, some degrees lower in the social and moral scale than the former." Nor have we any hesitation in saying that the law here recorded, permitting as many as four lawful wives and any number of slave women besides, *with whom even the form of a marriage is in no way necessary to legalise cohabitation*, is responsible in large measure for this state of things. It is one of the darkest of the many spots which mar the pages of the Qurán.

Or the slaves. It is not even necessary that a Muslim have even one lawful wife. Should he feel it difficult to be impartial toward many wives, he may take his slave girls, whom he may treat as he please, and so avoid the responsibility of providing a dowry for even one wife!

Give women their dowry. The lawful and required amount of dowry is ten dirhams, but it may be fixed at any amount to which the contracting parties agree. See chap. ii. 229, note.

If they voluntarily remit, &c. A woman may legally insist upon the payment of the "lawful dowry," or that agreed upon by contract, in case she be divorced, unless she voluntarily remits it in part or altogether. In every case of dispute such remission must be proved by competent witnesses or by legal documents.

(4) *Those of weak understanding, i.e.,* idiots or persons of weak intellects, whose property is to be administered so as to provide for their necessities. Their treatment must also be kindly. Here is the Muslim lunatic asylum.

(5) *Examine the orphans.* If males, see to their intellect and capacity to care for themselves; if females, examine them as to their ability to perform household duties.

The age of marriage. "Or age of maturity, which is generally

marriage: but if ye perceive they are able to manage their affairs well, deliver their substance unto them; and waste it not extravagantly or hastily, because they grow up. Let him who is rich abstain *entirely from the orphans' estates;* and let him who is poor take *thereof* according to what shall be reasonable. And when ye deliver their substance unto them, call witnesses *thereof* in their presence: GOD taketh sufficient account *of your actions.* (6) Men ought to have a part of what *their* parents and kindred leave *behind them when they die:* and women *also* ought to have a part of what *their* parents and kindred leave, whether it be little, or whether it be much; a determinate part *is due to them.* (7) And when they who are of kin are present at the dividing *of what is left,* and also the orphans and the poor, distribute unto them *some part* thereof; and *if the estate be too small, at least*

---

reckoned to be fifteen; a decision supported by a tradition of their prophet; though Abu Hanífah thinks eighteen the proper age."—*Sale, Baidhāwi.*

Waste it not . . . hastily, i.e., when ye see them growing up rapidly to years of discretion, do not hasten to expend the orphan's inheritance, seeing it is soon to pass from your hands."—*Tafsír-i-Raufi.*

What shall be reasonable. "That is, no more than what shall make sufficient recompense for the trouble of their education."—*Sale, Baidhāwi.*

Call witnesses, to prevent future dispute and trouble.

(6) *Women also ought to have a part, &c.* "This law was given to abolish a custom of the pagan Arabs, who suffered not women or children to have any part of their husband's or father's inheritance, on pretence that they only should inherit who were able to go to war."—*Sale, Baidhāwi.*

Complaints were first made against this old Arab custom by Omm Kuha, in consequence of which this passage was revealed.—*Tafsír-i-Raufi.*

The importance of this reform cannot be overrated. Previous to this, women and helpless children might be disinherited by the adult male heirs, and thus be reduced to absolute penury, for no fault but that of being widows and orphans.

(7) *And speak comfortably.* The supposed ellipsis, filled in here by Sale, has not any real existence. See the same expression in ver. 4. The idea is that, in *any case,* some portion of the estate should be *cheerfully* given to the poor—they were to be treated kindly, notwithstanding that their presence would necessitate the

speak comfortably unto them. (8) And let those fear *to abuse orphans*, who if they leave behind them a weak offspring, are solicitous for them; let them therefore fear GOD, and speak that which is convenient. (9) Surely they who devour the possessions of orphans unjustly shall swallow down nothing but fire into their bellies, and shall broil in raging flames.

|| (10) GOD hath *thus* commanded you concerning your children. A male shall have as much as the share of two females; but if they be females *only, and* above two *in*

R $\frac{2}{13}$.

---

parting with some portion of the property about to be divided. This verse is abrogated by ver. 11 of this chapter. See *Preface, R. Urdû Qurán*, Lodiana edition, p. xx.

(8) *Let those fear.* There is in this verse a threat of retributive justice against those who would deal unjustly with the helpless orphan. Their own children might be dealt with in a similar manner.

No doubt Muhammad had learned the substance of this revelation by his own experience as an orphan. Certainly the anxiety he exhibited to alleviate the sad condition of such is most praiseworthy. His terrible curses against the oppressors of such (see next verse) evince the earnestness of his purpose to reform this abuse.

(10) *A male . . . two females.* "This is the general rule to be followed in the distribution of the estate of the deceased, as may be observed in the following cases."—*Sale.*

See also Prelim. Disc., p. 212.

Above two, or only two (*Tafsír-i-Raufi*). The two-third share of the property must be shared equally by the daughters being the sole heirs.

One, she shall have the half. "And the remaining third part, or the remaining moiety of the estate, which is not here expressly disposed of, if the deceased leaves behind him no son, nor a father, goes to the public treasury. It must be observed that Mr. Selden is certainly mistaken when, in explaining this passage of the Qurán, he says, that where there is a son and an only daughter, each of them will have a moiety: for the daughter can have a moiety but in one case only, that is, where there is no son; for if there be a son, she can have but a third, according to the above-mentioned rule."—*Sale.*

If he have a child = a son. It is implied that the parents would receive the same were the child a daughter. But of the remaining two-thirds, while the son would get the whole, a daughter would only get three-sixths or one-half of the whole estate. See note above.

His mother . . . the third, i.e., half as much as her husband (the father), a man being entitled to the share of two women.

number, they shall have two third parts of what *the deceased* shall leave; and if there be *but* one, she shall have the half. And the parents of *the deceased* shall have each of them a sixth part of what he shall leave, if he have a child; but if he have no child, and his parents be his heirs, then his mother shall have the third part. And if he have brethren, his mother shall have a sixth part, after the legacies which he shall bequeath and his debts *be paid*. Ye know not whether your parents or your children be of greater use unto you. *This is* an ordinance from GOD, and GOD is knowing and wise. (11) Moreover, ye may claim half of what your wives shall leave, if they have no issue; but if they have issue, then ye shall have the fourth part of what they shall leave, after the legacies which they shall bequeath and the debts *be paid*. They also shall have the fourth part of

---

In the case where there are brethren, the mother receives a sixth only. The remainder to be divided between his brethren and his father, if living. The father would receive a sixth of the whole, the remaining two-thirds of the estate being divided equally between the brothers. If he have sisters as well as brothers, we would infer from the following verse that they would share equally with the brothers.

The legacies. Those given for charitable purposes. According to Muhammadan law in India, a man cannot, by a will, devote more than one-third of his property in charity.

Your parents or your children. The meaning seems to be that parents and children are equally near related to the deceased. From this the inference is drawn that the brothers of the deceased can only be regarded as lawful heirs in case the father be deceased also. When living, the parents are the sole heirs, except where there be children. See *Tafsir-i-Raufi in loco.*

(11) *Fourth part . . . eighth part.* The principle that one man is equal to two women is preserved here. There being issue to deceased wives, they inherit the remainder of the property according to the law of ver. 10. So, too, in regard to what remains after a wife's eighth has been paid her.

Where there is no issue, the part remaining after the husband's or wife's share has been paid goes to more distant relatives or to the public treasury.

A distant relation. "For this may happen by contract, or on some other special occasion."—*Sale.*

The words in Arabic indicate *a man who has neither parents nor*

what ye shall leave, in case ye have no issue; but if ye have issue, then they shall have the eighth part of what ye shall leave, after the legacies which ye shall bequeath, and your debts *be paid*. And if a man or woman's *substance* be inherited by a distant relation, and he *or she* have a brother or sister; each of them two shall have a

---

children, and must therefore bequeath his property to more distant relatives.

Each of them. "Here, and in the next case, the brother and sister are made equal sharers, which is an exception to the general rule of giving a male twice as much as a female; and the reason is said to be, because of the smallness of the portions, which deserve not such exactness of distribution; for in other cases the rule holds between brother and sister, as well as other relations."—*Sale*.

The case of parents receiving each a sixth when there is a child is also an exception. See note, ver. 10.

Without prejudice to the heirs, *i.e.*, the distant relatives mentioned above. Abdul Qádir, commenting on this passage, says: "This relates to the inheritance of brothers and sisters, who have no claims so long as there be father or son alive. Should there be neither father nor son, then the brothers and sisters become heirs. There are three classes of these:—*First,* brothers and sisters by the same wife; *secondly,* by different wives; and *thirdly,* by different fathers. The inheritance belonging to these three classes is as follows:—If there be a single heir, he or she will receive a sixth part of the property; if more than one, then one-third of the property will be divided among them, no distinction being made between men and women. The first and second classes mentioned above rank as members of the deceased person's family *when there is left to him neither father nor son*. First the brothers by the same mother are heirs. If there be none such, then the brothers by a different mother. It is only in case there be no heirs of these classes that those of class third become heirs.

"This passage also declares that bequests for charitable purposes have the precedence, provided no injustice be done to the heirs. This may take place in two ways: either by deceased's having bequeathed in charity more than one-third of his property—he may not give in charity more than one-third of his property; or injustice may be done the heirs by willing to some one of the heirs more than his lawful share, through partiality. Such increased bequest, beyond a third of the property, or partial bestowal of property beyond the legal share, can only become legal by the consent of the heirs at the time of bequest.

"These five classes of heirs (children, parents, widower, widow, and brothers and sisters) all have fixed *portions* or fractional parts of the inheritance. Besides these, there are other heirs, called *Usbah* (distant relations), who have not *portions*. If there be no heirs having portions, then the *usbah* receive the whole property.

sixth part *of the estate*. But if there be more than this *number*, they shall be *equal* sharers in a third part, after *payment of* the legacies which shall be bequeathed and the debts, without prejudice *to the heirs. This is* an ordinance from GOD, and GOD is knowing and gracious. (12) These are the statutes of GOD. And whoso obeyeth GOD and his apostle, *God* shall lead him into gardens wherein rivers flow, they shall continue therein for ever; and this shall be great happiness. (13) But whoso disobeyeth GOD and his apostle, and transgresseth his statutes, *God* shall cast him into *hell* fire; he shall remain therein for ever, and he shall suffer a shameful punishment.

R ³⁄₁₄. ‖ (14) If any of your women be guilty of whoredom, produce four witnesses from among you against them,

---

But if there be both heirs with portions and *usbah*, then the latter receive what remains after the former have had their portions. An *usbah* must be a male, not a female, nor even a male connected on the mother's side only (*i.e.*, having no relationship by blood with the father's side). These are of four degrees: *First*, son and grandson; *second*, father and grandfather (on father's side); *third*, brothers and nephews (on father's side); *fourth*, uncle (father's elder brother), *his* son, and *his* grandson (these all rank alike). If there be several persons having claims, that one has the precedence who is nearest related to the deceased, *e.g.*, a son has the precedence of a grandson, a brother of a nephew, the brother of a step-brother, &c.

"Finally, among the children and brothers and sisters of the deceased, women have a portion, but among the *usbah* they have no claim. Should there be no heir of the kind already enumerated, then the *ziwilrihm* or relations by the 'female' (literally, *woman*) side, and who have no *portion*, become heirs, *e.g.*, a daughter's son, a maternal grandfather, a sister's son, a mother's brother, a maternal aunt, a father's sister, and their children, reckoned as in the case of the *usbah*."

(14) *Whoredom.* Either fornication or adultery.

Imprison in apartments, i.e., they were to be built into a wall, and be left there until they were dead.

Or God afford, &c. "Their punishment in the beginning of Muhammadanism was to be immured till they died, but afterwards this cruel doom was mitigated, and they might avoid it by undergoing the punishment ordained in its stead by the Sunnat, according to which the maidens are to be scourged with a hundred stripes, and to be banished for a full year, and the married women to be stoned."—*Sale, Jaláluddín.*

See also note, chap. iii. 23.

and if they bear witness *against them,* imprison them in *separate* apartments until death release them, or GOD affordeth them a way *to escape.* (15) And if two of you commit the like *wickedness,* punish them both: but if they repent and amend, let them both alone; for GOD is easy to be reconciled and merciful. (16) Verily repentance *will be accepted* with GOD from those who do evil ignorantly, and then repent speedily; unto them will GOD be turned: for GOD is knowing and wise. (17) But no repentance *shall be accepted* from those who do evil until *the time* when death presenteth itself unto one of them, *and he* saith, Verily I repent now; nor unto those

---

(15) *Two of you.* "The commentators are not agreed whether the text speaks of fornication or sodomy. Al Zamakhsharí, and from him, al Baidháwi, supposes the former is here meant; but Jaláluddín is of opinion that the crime intended in this passage must be committed between two men, and not between a man and a woman; not only because the pronouns are in the masculine gender, but because both are ordered to suffer the same slight punishment, and are both allowed the same repentance and indulgence; and especially for that a different and much severer punishment is appointed for the women in the preceding words. Abul Qásim Híbatullah takes simple fornication to be the crime intended, and that this passage is abrogated by that of the 24th chapter, where the man and the woman who shall be guilty of fornication are ordered to be scourged with a hundred stripes each."—*Sale.*

Punish them both. "The original is, *Do them some hurt or damage,* by which some understand that they are only to reproach them in public, or strike them on the head with their slippers (a great indignity in the East), though some imagine they may be scourged." —*Sale, Baidháwi, Jaláluddín.*

The *Tafsír-i-Raufi* declares the punishment is to be inflicted with the tongue, by reproaches and admonitions; at most, they are to be smitten with the hand. Surely the partiality shown in the award of punishment to the sexes sufficiently indicates the slavish position of Muslim women. This law of Islám falls far short of attesting the former Scriptures.

(16, 17) *Repentance.* The Muhammadans understand this verse to refer to the infidels, who may be forgiven on the ground of repentance, provided it be done before death, *i.e.,* as I understand it, if they repent sincerely. For Muslims there is always full and free pardon when they repent, or even say, "I seek forgiveness, O Lord."

This view of this passage is not borne out by the last clause, "*nor unto those who die in unbelief.*" The passage, therefore, probably refers to hypocritical professors of Islám.

who die unbelievers; for them have we prepared a grievous punishment. (18) O true believers, it is not lawful for you to be heirs of women against their will, nor to hinder them *from marrying others*, that ye may take away part of what ye have given them *in dowry;* unless they have been guilty of a manifest crime: but converse kindly with them. And if ye hate them, it may happen that ye may hate a thing wherein GOD hath placed much good. If ye be desirous to exchange a wife for *another* wife, and ye have already given one of them a talent, take not away anything therefrom: will ye take it by slandering *her*, and *doing her* manifest injustice? (19) And how can ye take it, since the one of you hath gone in unto the other, and they have received from you a firm covenant? (20) Marry not women whom your fathers have had to wife; (except what is already

---

(18) *Heirs of women.* "It was customary among the pagan Arabs, when a man died, for one of his relations to claim a right to his widow, which he asserted by throwing his garment over her; and then he either married her himself, if he thought fit, on assigning her the same dower that her former husband had done, or kept her dower and married her to another, or else refused to let her marry unless she redeemed herself by quitting what she might claim of her husband's goods. This unjust custom is abolished by this passage."—*Sale.*

This passage was occasioned, says the *Tafsír-i-Raufí*, by the wife of Abu Qáis, one of the companions, complaining to Muhammad against a son, who wished to treat her in accordance with the old custom.

Not hinder them. The allusion is to those who would hinder their father's widows from marrying others, in order to retain the property in the family. Some, however, think the allusion to be to those who maltreated their wives, in order to make them relinquish the dowry fixed upon them at marriage. The language will very well bear this interpretation. *Hindering* would then mean *imprisonment* in some part of the house.

Unless they have been guilty, i.e., of disobedience or shameless conduct. This passage carefully guards the right of a husband to punish his wife for whatever he may fancy a fault in her.

A wife for another wife. See notes on chap. ii. 229.

A talent. A large dowry.

Will ye take it by slandering her? *i.e.*, by giving out a false report of infidelity, in order to escape the necessity of forfeiting the dowry. See chap. ii. 229, note.

(20) *Women whom your fathers have had.* The pre-Islámite religion

past:) for this is uncleanness, and an abomination, and an evil way.

‖ (21) Ye are forbidden to *marry* your mothers, and B $\frac{4}{1}$. your daughters, and your sisters, and your aunts both on the father's and on the mother's side, and your brothers' daughters, and your sisters' daughters, and your mothers who have given you suck, and your foster-sisters, and your wives' mothers, and your daughters-in-law which are under your tuition, *born* of your wives unto whom ye have gone in, (but if ye have not gone in unto them, it shall be no sin in you *to marry them*,) and the wives of your sons who *proceed* out of your loins; and *ye are also forbidden* to take to wife two sisters, except what is already past: for GOD is gracious and merciful.

‖ (22) *Ye are* also *forbidden to take to wife* free women FIFTH SIPARA. *who are married*, except those *women* whom your right hands shall possess *as slaves*. *This is* ordained you from GOD. Whatever is beside this is allowed you; that ye may with your substance provide *wives* for yourselves, acting that which is right, and avoiding whoredom. (23)

---

of Arabia not only allowed such marriages, but made such women a lawful part of the son's inheritance. See Muir's *Life of Mahomet*, vol. ii. p. 52. The reform of Muhammad had respect to the future only. What was "already past" was allowed to remain unchanged.

(21) *Ye are forbidden to marry, &c.* It is quite certain that these prohibited degrees were *adapted* from the Jewish law. Compare Lev. xviii. 6-18. Muhammad did not consider himself bound by this law (see chap. xxxiii. 49, 50).

(22) *Free women, except, &c.* "According to this passage, it is not lawful to marry a free woman that is already married, be she a Muhammadan or not, unless she be legally parted from her husband by divorce; but it is lawful to marry those who are slaves or taken in war, after they shall have gone through the proper purifications, though their husbands be living. Yet, according to the decision of Abu Hanífah, it is not lawful to marry such whose husbands shall be taken or be in actual slavery with them."—*Sale, Baidháwi.*

Marriage, in the Muslim sense, is not required in the case of those who are held as slaves. Sale has used the word *marry* rather freely in his italicised phrases. It is not *marriage* that is here forbidden, but *certain women*, marriage being predicated only where, according to Muhammadan law, the ceremony is required.

And for the advantage which ye receive from them, give them their reward, according to what is ordained: but it shall be no crime in you to make any other agreement among yourselves, after the ordinance *shall be complied with;* for GOD is knowing and wise. (24) Whoso among you hath not means sufficient that he may marry free women, who are believers, *let him marry* with such of

---

(23) *Their reward, i.e.,* their dowry, which, is everywhere in the Qurán spoken of in this fashion. The allusion is very suggestive of the character of the marriage bond. The power of the bond of that pure and holy love which unites the Christian wife to her husband is unknown to Islám. If ever found in a Muslim household, it is there, not because of Islám, but in spite of it.

Any other arrangement. The amount of dowry may be increased or diminished at any time subsequent to marriage by the consent of the parties. A wife may remit the whole amount.

(24) *Whoso . . . hath not means, i.e.,* he who is too poor to support a wife, who is free, and therefore does not possess slave girls of his own, may marry slave women with the consent of their masters. In this case the dowry is fixed by the master.—*Tafsír-i-Raufi.*

Such . . . as are true believers. This is not the only passage antagonistic to Mr. R. Bosworth Smith's statements (*Muhammad and Muhammadanism,* p. 243) that Muhammad "laid down the principle that the captive who embraced Islám should be *ipso facto* free."

The Qurán provides not only for enslaving conquered infidels, thus justifying the cruellest war ever waged by Arab slave-traders in the heart of Africa, but it provides for their retention even when converted, and, although masters are forbidden to maltreat them, yet they are enjoined *to sell them in case they are displeased with them.* See Muir's *Life of Mahomet,* vol. iv. p. 239. "As regards female slaves," says the same author (vol. iii. p. 305) "under the thraldom of Mahometan masters, it is difficult to conceive more signal degradation of the human species; they are treated as an inferior class of beings. Equally restricted as if they had entered the marriage state, they are expressly excluded from any title to conjugal rights. They are purely at the disposal of their proprietors." Here the learned author is compelled to stop, being unable to say more without offence to morality, adding, that "the reader must believe at second-hand that the whole system is vile and revolting."

That system of slavery prevalent among the so-called Christian nations was utterly opposed to the clearest precepts of the Bible, and cannot be fairly compared with the system of slavery sanctioned by the Qurán, even granting the claim that the rigour of the latter is less than that of the former. The abolition of slavery by Christian nations was the natural result of obedience to the teaching of the Bible, applying in practice the doctrine of man's common brotherhood, and the duty of loving our neighbour as ourselves. The

your maid-servants whom your right hands possess, as are true believers; for GOD well knoweth your faith. Ye are the one from the other: therefore marry them with the consent of their masters; and give them their dower according to justice; *such as are* modest, not guilty of whoredom, nor entertaining lovers. And when they are married, if they be guilty of adultery, they shall suffer half the punishment which *is appointed* for the free women. This *is allowed* unto him among you who feareth to sin *by marrying free women;* but if ye abstain *from marrying slaves, it will be* better for you; GOD is gracious and merciful.

‖ (25) GOD is willing to declare *these things* unto R ⅖. you, and to direct you according to the ordinances of those who *have gone* before you, and to be merciful

---

abolition of slavery in Muslim states would be equivalent to the abrogation of a large part of the teaching of the Qurán. As a matter of fact, Muslim states never did anything voluntarily towards abolishing slavery, and we may safely predict that they never will. The social interest in slave women is too great, and too firmly rooted in the Qurán to permit it.

One from the other. "Being alike descended from Adam, and of the same faith."—*Sale, Baidháwi.*

Such as are modest, &c.—These crimes would cause them to forfeit their dowry.

Half the punishment.—" The reason of this is because they are not presumed to have had so good education. A slave, therefore, in such a case, is to have fifty stripes, and to be banished for half a year; but she shall not be stoned, because it is a punishment which cannot be inflicted by halves."—*Sale, Baidháwi.*

Who feareth to sin. Not merely *by marrying free women* when unable to support them or pay the dowry, but also *by remaining unmarried.—Tafsír-i-Raufí.*

If ye abstain, &c. "Because he could not marry a free woman and a slave" (*Abdul Qádir*), *i.e.*, no free woman would consent to be co-wife with a slave, but he could easily divorce the slave wife, and so avoid the difficulty.

The *Tafsír-i-Raufí* says the reason why abstaining from marrying slaves is here recommended is because of the "stain of slavery which would belong to the children."

(25) *The ordinances, &c.* The claim here made is that these laws concerning marriage are in accord with the teaching of the former prophets. I think we have here a declaration clearly indicating the source from which Muhammad drew his inspiration on this point. He does not, however, scruple to represent this new law as coming

unto you. GOD is knowing and wise. (26) GOD desireth to be gracious unto you; but they who follow *their* lusts, desire that ye should turn aside *from the truth* with great deviation. (27) GOD is minded to make *his religion* light unto you; for man was created weak. (28) O true believers, consume not your wealth among yourselves in vanity, unless there be merchandising among you by mutual consent: neither slay yourselves; for GOD is merciful towards you: (29) and whoever doth this maliciously and wickedly, he will surely cast him to be broiled in *hell* fire; and this is easy with GOD. (30) If ye turn aside from the grievous sins of those which ye

---

from God and place himself in the position of a disciple learning for the first time that this new revelation is in accord "with the ordinances of those who have gone before."

(26) *They who follow their lusts.* "Some commentators suppose that these words have a particular regard to the Magians, who formerly were frequently guilty of incestuous marriages, their prophet Zerdusht having allowed them to take their mothers and sisters to wife; and also to the Jews, who likewise might marry within some of the degrees here prohibited."—*Sale, Baidhāwi.*

According to the *Tafsīr-i-Raufi*, the allusion is to the Jews.

(27) *God is minded, &c.* The spirit of this verse, as well as the opinions of the commentators, clearly shows that the legislation in the preceding verses was intended to remove the temptation to fornication and adultery by facilitating marriage and concubinage.

God created man weak. This sentence indicates a low conception of morals, not to say of God's holiness. Man's immorality is excused on the ground that God made him liable to sins of incontinency. This doctrine plainly makes God the author of sin.

(28) *Consume not your wealth, &c., i.e.,* "employ it not in things prohibited by God, such as usury, extortion, rapine, gaming, and the like."—*Sale.*

Unless there be merchandising. The merchant's calling receives the imprimatur of the Qurán. The faithful are encouraged to *unite* together for purposes of trade.

Neither slay yourselves. This is understood to forbid suicide, which the heathen were in the habit of committing in honour of the idols (*Tafsīr-i-Raufi*); or it may be understood in a spiritual sense, as an exhortation to avoid all sin. The words may be translated *slay not your souls* (see *Sale*). Abdul Qádir understands the command to be *not to slay one another.*

(29) *And whosoever doeth this.* This statement best agrees with Abdul Qádir's interpretation, and therefore teaches that those who maliciously slay their brethren in the faith are doomed to hell fire.

(30) *If ye turn aside, &c.* Sins are divided by this and other pas-

are forbidden *to commit*, we will cleanse you from your *smaller* faults, and will introduce you *into paradise* with an honourable entry. (31) Covet not that which GOD hath bestowed on some of you preferably to others. Unto the men *shall be given* a portion of what they shall have gained, and unto the women *shall be given* a portion of what they shall have gained: therefore ask GOD of his bounty; for GOD is omniscient. (32) We have appointed unto every one kindred, *to inherit part* of what their parents and relations shall leave *at their deaths*. And unto those with whom your right hands have made an alliance, give their part *of the inheritance;* for GOD is witness of all things.

---

sages into two classes, *kabíra* and *saghíra*, or *great* and *small*. The commentators differ as to which are great. Some say they are seven: idolatry, murder, false charge of adultery against virtuous women, wasting the substance of orphans, usury, desertion in time of a religious war, and disobedience to parents (*Sale in loco*). Others enumerate seventeen (see Hughes's Notes, p. 139). Still others say there are as many as seven hundred great sins. The majority regard only those sins as *kabíra* which are *described* in the Qurán as meriting hell fire, the chief of all great sins being idolatry, or the associating of anything with God so as to express or imply a participation in the attributes of God.

Muhammad's teaching must lead his followers to carelessness in regard to all sins except those regarded as *kabíra*. As a matter of fact, this is true. Lying, deception, anger, lust, &c., are all numbered among the smaller and lighter offences. All such sins will be forgiven if men only keep clear of the great sins. Such passages exhibit to the Christian the sad fact that Muhammad had no true conception of the nature of sin. Great sins and small sins alike spring from an evil heart. But Muhammad seems not to have ascribed any moral character to simple states of the heart; the sins here described are the doing of what is *forbidden*. The Christian regards all such sin as rebellion against God, but Muhammad conceived of only a portion of these as great, which, if forgiven, would predicate the forgiveness of the smaller crimes also.

(31) *Covet not, &c.* "Such as honour, power, riches, and other worldly advantages. Some, however, understand this of the distribution of inheritances according to the preceding determinations, whereby some have a larger share than others."—*Sale*.

What they shall have gained, i.e., "What is gained *by men* in their warring for the faith in and in other good works; *by women,* in their chaste behaviour, and in submission to the will of their husbands."
—*Tafsír-i-Raufí in loco.*

(32) *Those with whom . . . an alliance.* "A precept conformable

R ⅜.   ‖ (33) **Men shall have the pre-eminence above women,** because of those *advantages* wherein GOD hath caused the one of them to excel the other, and for that which they expend of their substance *in maintaining their wives.* The honest women *are* obedient, careful in the absence *of their husbands,* for that GOD preserveth *them, by committing them to the care and protection of the men.* But those whose perverseness ye shall be apprehensive of, rebuke; and remove them into separate apartments, and chastise them. But if they shall be obedient unto you, seek not an occasion *of quarrel* against them: for GOD

to an old custom of the Arabs, that where persons mutually entered into a strict friendship or confederacy, the surviving friend should have a sixth part of the deceased's estate. But this was afterwards abrogated, according to Jaláluddín and al Zamakhsharí, at least as to infidels. The passage may likewise be understood of a private contract, whereby the survivor is to inherit a certain part of the substance of him that dies first."—*Sale, Baidháwi.*

Abdul Qádir says this law had relation to the circumstances which grew out of the "brotherhood" established by Muhammad soon after his arrival in Madína, whereby "each of the refugees selected one of the citizens as his brother. The bond was of the closest description, and involved not only a peculiar devotion to each other's interests in the persons thus associated, but in case of the death it superseded the claims of blood, the 'brother' becoming exclusive heir to all the property of the deceased."—*Muir's Life of Mahomet,* vol. iii. p. 17.

The custom was abolished after the lapse of eighteen months. It has, therefore, no present application to Muslims.

(33) *Men shall have the pre-eminence.* The ground of the pre-eminence of man over woman is here said to be man's natural superiority over woman. Women are an inferior class of human beings. "The advantages wherein God hath caused the one of them to excel the other" are said by the commentators to be "superior understanding and strength, and the other privileges of the male sex," *e.g.,* ruling in church and state, warring for the faith, and receiving double portions of the estates of deceased ancestors (see *Sale in loco).* Men are the *lords* of the women, and women become the virtual slaves of the men. The holy, happy estate of Eve in Eden can never be even approximately secured for her daughters under Islám.

Careful to preserve their husband's property and their own chastity. —*Sale, Baidháwi.*

Those whose perverseness, &c. Recreant wives are to be punished in three degrees: (1) They are to be rebuked, (2) if they remain rebellious, they are to be assigned separate apartments, and so be

is high and great. (34) And if ye fear a breach between the *husband and wife*, send a judge out of his family, and a judge out of her family: if they shall desire a reconciliation, GOD will cause them to agree; for GOD is knowing and wise. (35) Serve GOD, and associate no creature with him; and *show* kindness unto parents, and relations, and orphans, and the poor, and *your* neighbour who is of kin to you, and also *your* neighbour who is a stranger, and to *your* familiar companion, and the traveller, and *the captives* whom your right hands shall possess; for GOD loveth not the proud *or* vainglorious, (36) who are covetous, and recommend covetousness unto men, and conceal that which GOD of his bounty hath given them; (we have prepared a shameful punishment for the unbelievers;) (37) and who bestow their wealth *in charity* to be observed of men, and believe not in GOD, nor in the last day; and whoever hath Satan for a companion, an evil companion

---

banished from the bed; and (3) they are to be beaten, but not so as to cause any permanent injury.—*Abdul Qádir.*

Seek not an occasion. Muslims are here warned not to use the authority here granted to the men to beat their wives as a means of tyrannising over them and of abusing them, being reminded that "God is high and great" above them. The difference between the home-life of the Christian and that of the Muslim cannot be more clearly indicated than by a comparison of this verse with Gen. ii. 24, Eph. v. 28, and 1 Pet. iii. 7.

(34) *If ye fear a breach, &c.* This arrangement was intended to prevent divorce. The verse is closely connected with the one preceding. When beating should prove unsuccessful, arbitration might be resorted to, each party being represented by a friend.

(35) *Serve God . . . and show kindness, &c.* This passage gives the sum of the decalogue for a Muslim : God to be served—his unity to be preserved intact—relatives and neighbours, &c., to be kindly treated. It must be remembered that a Muslim's friend or neighbour is *a Muslim.* They are expressly forbidden to have friendships with Jews, Christians, or unbelievers. See chap. v. 56.

(36) *That which God . . . hath given them*, *i.e.*, "wealth, knowledge, or any other talent whereby they may help their neighbour." —*Sale.*

(37) *To be observed of men.* The duty of giving alms from a high motive is here enjoined. One is reminded of Matt. vi. 1–4. Abdul Qádir says : The miser who refuses to give in charity, and the man who gives to make a show of giving, are equally hateful in the sight of God.

hath he! (38) And what *harm would befall* them if they should believe in GOD and the last day, and give alms out of that which GOD hath bestowed on them? since GOD knoweth them *who do this.* (39) Verily GOD will not wrong *any one even* the weight of an ant: and if it be a good action, he will double it, and will recompense *it* in his sight with a great reward. (40) How *will it be with the unbelievers* when we shall bring a witness out of each nation *against itself,* and shall bring thee, *O Muhammad,* a witness against these *people?* (41) In that day they who have not believed, and have rebelled against the apostle *of God,* shall wish the earth was levelled with them; and they shall not *be able to* hide any matter from GOD.

R $\frac{7}{4}$.

|| (42) O true believers, come not to prayers when ye are drunk, until ye understand what ye say; nor when ye are polluted by emission of seed, unless ye be travelling

---

(38, 39) These verses teach the truth that no man is a loser by performing his duty toward God and man.

God will not wrong, &c., i.e., "either by diminishing the recompense due to his good actions, or too severely punishing his sins. On the contrary, he will reward the former in the next life far above their deserts. The Arabic word *dharra,* which is translated *an ant,* signifies a very small sort of that insect, and is used to denote a thing that is exceeding small, as a *mite."—Sale.*

(40) *A witness out of each nation.* This verse seems to clearly teach the doctrine that God sends a prophet to every distinct nation, and that Muhammad was sent to the Arabs. If so, this passage shows that Muhammad's idea of a universal Islám, though logically connected with the teaching of the Makkan Suras, yet only took a practical form at Madína, after military and political triumphs had cleared the way to foreign conquest. See also chap. ii. 143.

(42) *Come not to prayers when ye are drunk.* "It is related, that before the prohibition of wine, Abd'ur-Rahmán Ibn Auf made an entertainment, to which he invited several of the Apostle's companions; and after they had ate and drunk plentifully, the hour of evening prayer being come, one of the company rose up to pray, but being overcome with liquor, made a shameful blunder in reciting a passage of the Qurán; whereupon, to prevent the danger of any such indecency for the future, this passage was revealed."—*Sale, Baidháwi.*

See note on chap. ii. 218.

When polluted. Ordinarily ceremonial purity can only be had by performing ablutions in water. This verse provides for those

on the road, until ye wash yourselves. But if ye be sick, or on a journey, or any of you come from easing nature, or have touched women, and find no water; take fine clean sand and rub your faces and your hands *therewith;* for GOD is merciful and inclined to forgive. (43) Hast thou not observed those unto whom part of the Scripture was delivered? they sell error, and desire that ye may wander from the *right* way; but GOD well knoweth your enemies. GOD is a sufficient patron, and GOD is a sufficient helper. (44) Of the Jews there are some who pervert words from their places, and say, We have heard, and

---

who are so situated as to be unable to secure water. See Prelim. Disc., p. 167.

(43) *Those unto whom part, &c.* The Jews. They are said to *sell error* because they misrepresented the teachings of their sacred books from sordid motives.

(44) *Who pervert words from their places.* On the general subject of the corruption charged by Muslims against the Christians and Jews, much has already been said. I cannot, however, omit a somewhat lengthy quotation from *Muir's Life of Mahomet,* vol. iii. pp. 249 and 295, which affords a decided answer to this unfounded imputation of Muslims. The learned author says: "I pass over the passages in which the Jews are accused of 'hiding the signs of God,' or 'selling them for a small price.' For the meaning is evidently that the Jews merely refused to bring forward those texts which Mahomet believed to contain evidence in his favour. The renegade Jews applied the prophecies of the Messiah to Mahomet; the staunch Jews denied such application, and herein lay the whole dispute. There is no imputation or hint that any passages were *removed* from the sacred record. The Jews 'concealed the testimony of God' simply because they declined to bring it forward. The expression 'to sell a thing for a small price' is metaphorical, and signifies abandoning a duty for a worldly and sordid motive; it is used also of the disaffected citizens of Madína. [It might far more truly have been applied to the renegade Jews who purchased their safety and prosperity by pandering their evidence to Muhammad's ambition.]

"The passages in which 'dislocation' or 'perversion' is imputed are these: Sura ii. 75, v. 14, v. 47, iv. 43. The latter verse . . . well illustrates the meaning of *tahríf,* ordinarily but incorrectly translated *interpolation;* it signifies the *perversion* of a word or passage, by using it in a double or erroneous sense, or with a wrong contextual reference. The words *Raina,* &c., in the verse quoted (chap. ii. 103), are examples given by Mahomet himself. So with the passages of their Scriptures which the Jews wrested from their proper signification, as expressed in S. ii. 75, 'they perverted them *after they understood them.'*

have disobeyed; and do thou hear without understanding *our meaning*, and look upon us: perplexing with their tongues, and reviling the *true* religion. But if they had said, We have heard and do obey, and do thou hear and regard us; certainly it were better for them, and more right. But GOD hath cursed them by reason of their

---

"Next comes S. iii. 77. 'They twist their tongues in (reading) the Book, that ye may think it is out of the Book, though it is not out of the Book; and they say it is from God, and it is not from God.' *Twisting their tongues* is the same expression as in the verse above quoted, S. iv. 43. They read out passages which they *pretended* were from the Book, but were not (so Mahomet alleged); it was a deception of their tongues, not any corruption of their MSS.

"So also S. ii. 78. Here reference is evidently made to the ignorant Jews who copied out legends, traditions, or glosses from rabbinical books, and brought them forward as possessed of divine authority. Even if a more serious meaning were admitted, viz., that the same unscrupulous Jews copied out passages from the writings of their rabbins, &c., and brought them forward, pretending they were actual extracts from Scripture, the charge would indeed be one of fraud, but not by any means of corrupting the MSS. of the Old Testament.

"These are, I believe, the main passages alleged to contain evidence of corruption or interpolation, and even if they were capable of a more serious construction, which I believe them not to be, they must be construed in accordance with the general tenor of the Coran; and the very numerous passages, contemporary and subsequent, in which 'the Book,' as current in the neighbourhood and elsewhere, is spoken of as a genuine and authoritative record as containing the rule of faith and practice to be followed by Jews and Christians respectively, and as a divine record, belief in which is earnestly enjoined on the Moslems also. Assuredly such would not have been the language of Mahomet had he regarded either the Jewish or the Christian Scriptures as in any degree interpolated.

"The similitude of an ass laden with books, employed by Mahomet to describe the Jews in reference to their Scriptures (S. lxii. 5), exactly illustrates the point of his charge against them: they had indeed a precious charge in their possession, but they were ignorant of its value and use."

See notes on chap. ii. 75-78, and chap. iii. 77.

Look upon us. "The original word is *Râina*, which, being a term of reproach in Hebrew, Muhammad forbade their using to him."—*Sale.*

And regard us. "In Arabic *undhurna*, which, having no ill or equivocal meaning, he ordered them to use instead of the former."—*Sale.*

Sale understands the "*perverting* of words" charged upon the Jews in this verse to be illustrated here. See also note on chap. ii. 103.

infidelity; therefore a few *of them* only shall believe. (45) O *ye* to whom the scriptures have been given, believe in the *revelation* which ye have sent down, confirming that which is with you, before we deface *your* countenances, and render them as the back parts thereof, or curse them, as we cursed those who transgressed on the Sabbath-day, and the command of GOD was fulfilled. (46) Surely GOD will not pardon the giving him an equal, but will pardon any other *sin* except that, to whom he pleaseth; and whoso giveth a companion unto GOD hath devised a great wickedness. (47) Hast thou not observed those who justify themselves? But GOD justifieth whomsoever he pleaseth, nor shall *they* be wronged a hair. (48) Behold, how they imagine a lie against GOD; and therein is iniquity sufficiently manifest.

|| (49) Hast thou not considered those to whom part of the scripture hath been given? They believe in false gods and idols, and say of those who believe not, These are more rightly directed in the way *of truth* than they who believe *on Muhammad*. (50) Those are *the men*

---

(45) *Confirming that, &c.* This claim, so oft repeated, surely predicates the genuineness of the Scriptures in the hands of Jews and Christians at that time.

Those who transgressed. See note on chap. ii. 64.

(46) *God will not pardon, &c., i.e.,* idolatry, which includes the ascribing of divine attributes to a creature as well as idol-worship, is the unpardonable sin of Islám. It is unpardonable, however, only to those who, having received Islám or a knowledge of Islám, persist in this sin.

To whom he pleaseth, i.e., to those who repent before death and accept of Islám. These he forgives not on the ground of their good works, nor on account of any atonement, but because *he pleaseth.*

(47) *Those who justify,* "*i.e.,* the Christians and Jews, who called themselves *the children of God, and his beloved people.*"—Sale, Jaláluddín, Baidháwi.

A hair, literally *a fibre in the cleft of a date-stone.*

(48) *A lie against God.* The *lie* here seems to be their regarding themselves as the children of God. As applied to the Jews, compare John viii. 39-44.

(49) *They believe.* The commentators say this passage refers to certain Jews, who fraternised with the Makkan idolaters in their opposition to Muhammad. Modern Muslims, who join hands with

whom GOD hath cursed; and unto him whom GOD shall curse thou shalt surely find no helper. (51) Shall they have a part of the kingdom, since even then they would not bestow the smallest matter on men? (52) Do they envy *other* men that which GOD of his bounty hath given them? We formerly gave unto the family of Abraham a book *of revelations* and wisdom; and we gave them a great kingdom. (53) There is of them who believeth on him; and there is of them who turneth aside from him; but the raging fire of hell is *a* sufficient *punishment*. (54) Verily those who disbelieve our signs, we will surely cast to be broiled in *hell* fire; so often as their skins shall be well burned, we will give them other skins in exchange, that they may taste the *sharper* torment; for GOD is mighty and wise.

RUBA. ‖ (55) But those who believe and do that which is right, we will bring into gardens watered by rivers, therein shall they remain forever, *and* there shall they enjoy

---

idolaters in opposition to Christianity, receive no encouragement from passages like this.

False gods and idols. This is better translated *Jibt and Tághút*, reference being had to certain idols bearing these names See chap. ii. 256, note.

The story of the commentators, given by Sale, alleging that the Jews actually worshipped idols at Makkah, is most likely a fabrication.

(51) *Shall they have a part of the kingdom?* The reference is to Messiah's kingdom, in which the Jews would be restored to their former grandeur.

(52) *That which God hath given them,* viz., "the spiritual gifts of prophecy and divine revelations, and the temporal blessings of victory and success bestowed on Muhammad and his followers."—*Sale.*

The family of Abraham, i.e., the children of Israel. Reference is to the Jews before their apostasy in rejecting Jesus. Compare with preceding verse. See note in chap. iii. 33.

(53) *Who believe on him.* Sale refers the *him* to Muhammad, but manifestly *primary* allusion is to Abraham. The *inference* is that those who reject the religion of Muhammad also reject the religion of Abraham the Orthodox.

(54) *To be broiled, &c.* See note, chap. ii. 38.

(55) *Who believe and do, &c.* See notes, chap. ii. 25 and 223, and chap. iii. 15, 31, and 196.

wives free from all impurity; and we will lead them into perpetual shades. (56) Moreover GOD commandeth you to restore what ye are trusted with to the owners; and when ye judge between men, that ye judge according to equity: and surely an excellent *virtue it is* to which GOD exhorteth you; for GOD *both* heareth and seeth. (57) O true believers, obey GOD and obey the apostle, and those who are in authority among you; and if ye differ in anything, refer it unto GOD and the apostle, if ye believe in GOD and the last day: this is better, and a fairer *method of* determination.

|| (58) Hast thou not observed those who pretend they R ⅔.

---

(56) *God commandeth you, &c.* "This passage, it is said, was revealed on the day of the taking of Makkah, the primary design of it being to direct Muhammad to return the keys of the Kaabah to Othmán Ibn Talha Ibn Abdul Dár, who had then the honour to be keeper of that holy place, and not to deliver them to his uncle al Abbás, who having already the custody of the well Zamzam, would fain have had also that of the Kaabah. The Prophet obeying the divine order, Othmán was so affected with the justice of the action, notwithstanding he had at first refused him entrance, that he immediately embraced Muhammadanism; whereupon the guardianship of the Kaabah was confirmed to this Othmán and his heirs for ever."
—*Sale, Baidháwi.*

If this account of this *revelation* be correct, it is certainly out of place here, sandwiched in between passages of an earlier date. We think the reference is general, and that the passage is a sort of introduction to what follows. Note that the sentiment of this verse is expressive of high moral principle.

(57) *Those who are in authority.* This passage teaches the duty of submission to kings and judges, *so long as their decisions are in accord with the teaching of God and his Apostle (Abdul Qádir),* i.e., so long as they are in accord with the Qurán and the traditions.

The doctrine that Muhammad was "free from sin in what he ordered to be done, and in what he prohibited, in all his words and acts," for otherwise obedience to him would not be obedience to God, is based upon this verse among others (see *The Faith of Islám,* p. 12). But if so, the *Aulai al Amri,* or *those in authority,* must also be regarded as *sinless and infallible !*

The effort to establish the inspiration of the *Ahadís* or traditions of Islám on grounds like this requires not only inspired *Imáms* but also inspired *Ráwis.* But all admit that the latter were uninspired, wherefore the science of Muslim tradition is one of the most difficult as well as unsatisfactory departments of Muslim learning.

(58) *Those who pretend.* The hypocrites.

believe in what hath been revealed unto thee, and what hath been revealed before thee? They desire to go to judgment before Tághút, although they have been commanded not to believe in him; and Satan desireth to seduce them into a wide error. (59) And when it is said unto them, Come unto *the book* which GOD hath sent down, and to the apostle; thou seest the ungodly turn aside from thee with *great* aversion. (60) But how *will they behave* when a misfortune shall befall them, for that which their hands have sent before them? Then will they come unto thee, and swear by GOD, *saying,* If we intended any other than to do good, and to reconcile *the parties.* (61) GOD knoweth what is in the hearts of these *men;* therefore let them alone, and admonish them, and speak unto

---

Before Tághút. "That is, before the tribunals of infidels. This passage was occasioned by the following remarkable accident. A certain Jew having a dispute with a wicked Muhammadan, the latter appealed to the judgment of Qáb Ibn al Ashraf, the principal Jew, and the former to Muhammad. But at length they agreed to refer the matter to the Prophet singly, who giving it in favour of the Jew, the Muhammadan refused to acquiesce in his sentence, but would needs have it re-heard by Omar, afterwards Khalífah. When they came to him, the Jew told him that Muhammad had already decided the affair in his favour, but that the other would not submit to his determination; and the Muhammadan confessing this to be true, Omar bid them stay a little, and fetching his sword, struck off the obstinate Muslim's head, saying aloud, 'This is the reward of him who refuseth to submit to the judgment of God and his Apostle.' And from this action Omar had the surname of al Farúk, which alludes both to his *separating* that knave's head from his body, and to his *distinguishing* between truth and falsehood. The name of Tághút, therefore, in this place, seems to be given to Qáb Ibn al Ashraf."—*Sale, Baidháwi, Abdul Qádir.*

This story does not fit in well with the passage it is intended to illustrate, and is probably tagged on here by the commentators, who seem to feel that every allusion of the Qurán must be historically explained. The passage simply refers to the disaffected citizens of Madína, some of whom pretended to be favourable to Muhammad's cause when it was in their interest to do so (see ver. 60), and at other times showed too plainly their liking for the national idolatry, as is intimated in the next verse.

(60) *If we intended.* "For this was the excuse of the friends of the Muhammadan whom Omar slew, when they came to demand satisfaction for his blood."—*Sale, Baidháwi.*

them a word which may affect their souls. (62) We have not sent any apostle, but that he might be obeyed by the permission of GOD; but if they, after they have injured their own souls, come unto thee and ask pardon of GOD, and the apostle ask pardon for them, they shall surely find GOD easy to be reconciled and merciful. (63) And by thy LORD they will not *perfectly* believe until they make thee judge of their controversies; and shall not afterwards find in their own minds any hardship in what thou shalt determine, but shall acquiesce *therein* with *entire* submission. (64) And if we had commanded them, *saying*, Slay yourselves, or depart from your houses; they would not have done it except a few of them. (65) And if they had done what they were admonished, it would certainly have been better for them, and more efficacious for confirming *their faith;* and we should then have surely given them in our sight an *exceeding* great reward, (66) and we should have directed them in the right way. (67) Whoever obeyeth GOD and the apostle, they *shall be* with those

---

(62) *Obeyed by the permission of God.* The claim of Muhammad is that he should be implicitly obeyed. All controversies were to be decided by him, and all his decisions were to be "acquiesced in with entire submission." See next verse. There is a remarkable similarity between this claim of Muhammad and that of the Pope of Rome. He holds the keys of heaven and hell, and pardon is dependent upon his intercesion. He is their rightful judge, and his judgment is infallible. Muhammad seems to arrogate to himself a similar position in this passage.

(64) *If we had commanded, &c.* "Some understand these words of their venturing their lives in a religious expedition; and others, of their undergoing the same punishments which the Israelites did for their idolatry in worshipping the golden calf."—*Sale.*

See chap. ii. 53.

(67) *Whosoever obeyeth God and his Apostle.* Whilst it is true that rebellion against the messengers of God is rebellion against God, yet there is a vast difference between the teaching of the true messengers of God and that of Muhammad on this point. This habit of associating himself with God, and so making implicit obedience to him necessary to salvation, is not the least of the many blasphemies of Muhammad. Repudiating the divinity of our Lord, Muhammad here claims almost all our Lord claimed by virtue of his divine nature.

unto whom GOD hath been gracious, of the prophets, and the sincere, and the martyrs, and the righteous; and these are the most excellent company. (68) This is bounty from GOD; and GOD is sufficiently knowing.

‖ (69) O true believers, take your *necessary* precaution *against your enemies*, and *either* go forth *to war* in separate parties, or go forth all together, *in a body*. (70) There is of you who tarrieth behind; and if a misfortune befall you, he saith, Verily GOD hath been gracious unto me, that I was not present with them: (71) but if success attend you from GOD, he will say (as if there was no friendship between you and him), Would to GOD I had been with them, for I should have acquired great merit. (72) Let them therefore fight for the religion of GOD, who part with the present life in exchange for that which is to come; for whosoever fighteth for the religion of GOD, whether he be slain or be victorious, we will surely give him a great reward. (73) And what ails you, that ye fight not for GOD's true religion, and *in defence of* the weak among men, women, and children, who say, O LORD,

---

(69) *Necessary precaution.* This verse illustrates how that every dispatch from the orderly-room, so to speak, finds a place in the Qurán. This result is probably due to the faith of the Muslims that every word spoken by their Prophet was a revelation. Hence the inspired character of the traditions. These are, so far as they represent his teaching, fragmentary revelations.

The passage beginning here and ending with verse 83 has for its object the incitement of the Muslims to fight for Islám. By counsel, by reproaches, by taunts, by threats, by exhortation, and by promises the Muslims are urged to *fight for the religion of God.*

(70) *Who tarrieth.* The reference is to the hypocrites of Madína, particularly Ibn Ubái and his companions (*Tafsir-i-Raufi*).

(71) *As if . . . not friendship, i.e.,* "as one who attendeth not to the public but his own private interest. Or else these may be the words of the hypocritical Muhammadan himself, insinuating that he stayed not behind the rest of the army by his own fault, but was left by Muhammad, who chose to let the others share in his good fortune preferably to him."—*Sale, Baidháwi.*

(72) See notes on chap. ii. 190–195, and chap. iii. 157 and 170.

(73) *And what ails you, &c.*, viz., "those believers who stayed behind at Makkah, being detained there either forcibly by the idolaters or for want of means to fly for refuge to Madína. Al Baidháwi observes

bring us forth from this city, whose inhabitants are wicked; grant us from before thee a protector, and grant us from before thee a defender. (74) They who believe fight for the religion of GOD; but they who believe not fight for the religion of Tághút. Fight therefore against the friends of Satan, for the stratagem of Satan is weak.

|| (75) Hast thou not observed those unto whom it was said, Withhold your hands *from war*, and be constant at prayers, and pay the legal alms? But when war is commanded them, behold a part of them fear men as they should fear GOD, or with a great fear, and say, O LORD, wherefore hast thou commanded us to go to war, and hast not suffered us to wait *our* approaching end? (76) Say *unto them*, The provision of this life is *but* small; but the future *shall be* better for him who feareth *God;* and ye shall not be in the least injured *at the day of judgment.* (77) Wheresoever ye be, death will overtake you, although ye be in lofty towers. If good befall them, they say, This is from GOD; but if evil befall them, they say, This is from thee, *O Muhammad:* say, All is from GOD; and what aileth these people, that they are so far from understand-

R $\genfrac{}{}{0pt}{}{11}{8}$.

---

that *children* are mentioned here to show the inhumanity of the Quraish, who persecuted even that tender age."—*Sale.*

Bring us forth from this city. The *city* referred to here is Makkah. Muhammad pictures to his followers the forlorn condition of their brethren there as a motive to fight against the infidel Quraish. Weak helpless men, women, and children are crying to God for help and deliverance. Muhammad well knew how to fire the martial spirit of his countrymen.

"This petition, the commentators say, was heard. For God afforded several of them an opportunity and means of escaping, and delivered the rest at the taking of Makkah by Muhammad, who left Utáb Ibn Usaid governor of the city; and under his care and protection those who had suffered for their religion became the most considerable men in the place."—*Sale.*

(74) *The religion of Tághút.* See note, chap. ii. 256.

(75) *Those unto whom.* Those Muslims who were ready enough to observe the ordinary duties of Islám, but who disliked to fight. It is possible such were more averse to fighting against their relatives and neighbours than to the fear of death attributed to them here.

(77) *Wherever ye be, &c.* See notes on chap. iii. 155.

ing what is said *unto them?* (78) Whatever good befalleth thee, *O man*, it is from GOD; and whatever evil befalleth thee, it is from thyself. We have sent thee an apostle unto men, and GOD is a sufficient witness *thereof.* (79) Whoever obeyeth the apostle, obeyeth GOD; and whoever turneth back, we have not sent thee *to be* a keeper over them. (80) They say, Obedience: yet when they go forth from thee, part of them meditate by night *a matter* different from what thou speakest; but GOD shall write down what they meditate by night: therefore let them alone, and trust in GOD, for GOD is a sufficient protector. (81) Do they not attentively consider the Qurán? if it had been from any besides GOD, they would certainly have found therein many contradictions. (82) When any news cometh unto them, either of security or fear, they

---

(78) *Evil . . . is from thyself.* "These words are not to be understood as contradictory to the preceding, *that all proceeds from* God, since the evil which befalls mankind, though ordered by God, is yet the consequence of their own wicked actions."—*Sale.*

The passage is, however, contradictory of chap. vii. 179, 180; xv. 39–43; xvi. 95; xvii. 14–16, &c.

God . . . is witness. The allusion is probably to the verses (*ayát*) of the Qurán as being self-evidently miraculous. The ordinary testimony of God to his prophecy, viz., *prophecy* and *miracles*, was wanting. Of course this statement is only applicable to the Qurán. Tradition has provided an abundant supply of both.

(79) See note on ver. 67.

(81) *Do they not attentively consider the Qurán?* The belief that the Qurán was possessed in book form by many of the Muslims receives confirmation from this statement.

In this verse Muhammad sets up the claim that the Qurán is from God because it is free from contradictions. But notwithstanding his own convenient doctrine of abrogation (note in chap. ii. 105), he has left sufficient ground upon which to refute his prophetic pretensions on the basis of this his own claim. Compare chap. ii. 256 with chap. iv. 88; chap. v. 73 with ver. 76 of the same chapter; chap. ii. 61 with chap. iii. 84, &c. In addition to this, there is the more important as well as more palpable contradiction between the doctrine of the Qurán and that of the former Scriptures, though the former distinctly professes to confirm the latter. See notes on chap. ii. 90; chap. iii. 2, 31, 39, and 94, &c.

(82) *Any news.* This passage was occasioned thus: Muhammad sent a certain person to a neighbouring tribe to collect the legal alms. On the near approach of this messenger the people came forth

immediately divulge it; but if they told it to the apostle and to those who are in authority among them, such of them would understand *the truth of* the matter, as inform themselves thereof *from the apostle and his chiefs.* And if the favour of GOD and his mercy *had* not *been* upon you, ye had followed the devil, except a few *of you.* (83) Fight therefore for the religion of GOD, and oblige not any to what is difficult, except thyself; however, excite the faithful *to war,* perhaps GOD will restrain the courage of the unbelievers; for GOD is stronger *than they,* and more able to punish. (84) He who intercedeth *between men* with a good intercession shall have a portion thereof; and he who intercedeth with an evil intercession shall have a portion thereof; for GOD overlooketh all things. (85) When ye are saluted with a salutation, salute *the person* with a better salutation, or *at least* return the same; for GOD taketh an account of all things.

---

to receive him, but he, supposing them to have come out to kill him, fled into Madína and spread the report of the disaffection of the tribe.—*Tafsír-i-Raufí.*

Ye had followed the devil. "That is, if God had not sent his Apostle with the Qurán to instruct you in your duty, ye had continued in idolatry and been doomed to destruction, except only those who, by God's favour and their superior understanding, should have true notions of the divinity; such, for example, as Zaid Ibn Amru Ibn Nufail and Waraqa Ibn Naufal, who left idols and acknowledged but one God before the mission of Muhammad."—*Sale, Baidháwi.*

(83) *Oblige not, &c.* "It is said this passage was revealed when the Muhammadans refused to follow their Prophet to the lesser expedition of Badr, so that he was obliged to set out with no more than seventy (chap. iii. ver. 174). Some copies vary in this place, and instead of *lá tukallifu,* in the second person singular, read *lá nukallifu,* in the first person plural, 'We do not oblige,' &c. The meaning being, that the Prophet only was under an indispensable necessity of obeying God's commands, however difficult, but others might choose, though at their peril."—*Sale.*

Perhaps God will restrain. This is said to have been fulfilled in the return of Abu Sufián, who had started on the second expedition to Badr. The character of this prophecy, if such were intended, is made sufficiently clear by reference to note on chap. iii. 175.

(84) *God overlooketh all things, i.e.,* God sees all things, even the secret motives which inspire your efforts at reconciliation, whether they be good or bad, and will therefore certainly reward accordingly.

(85) *A better salutation.* "By adding something further. As

NISF.

R $\frac{12}{9}$.

|| (86) GOD! there is no GOD but he; he will surely gather you together on the day of resurrection; there is no doubt of it: and who is more true than God in what he saith?

|| (87) Why are ye *divided* concerning the ungodly into two parties; since GOD hath overturned them for what they have committed? Will ye direct him whom GOD hath led astray; since for him whom GOD shall lead astray, thou shalt find no *true* path? (88) They desire that ye should become infidels, as they are infidels, and that ye should be equally *wicked with themselves.* Therefore take not friends from among them, until they fly *their country* for the religion of GOD; and if they turn back *from the faith,* take them, and kill them wherever

---

when one salutes another by this form, 'Peace be unto thee,' he ought not only to return the salutation, but to add, 'and the mercy of God and his blessing.' "—*Sale.*

The salutation in Arabic is *As salámo álaikum,* and the reply should be *wa álaikomussalám o rahmat ulláh,* or if the address be *As salám álaikum o rahmat ulláh,* the reply should add *wa barakátoh.* This salutation is used only in addressing a Muslim. If addressed to a Muslim, he may only reply as above directed when he recognises in the speaker a Muslim. The use of it is, therefore, equivalent to a profession of Islám. It is the watchword of the Muslim.

(87) *Two parties.* "This passage was revealed, according to some, when certain of Muhammad's followers, pretending not to like Madína, desired leave to go elsewhere, and having obtained it, went farther and farther, till they joined the idolaters; or, as others say, on occasion of some deserters at the battle of Ohod, concerning whom the Muslims were divided in opinion whether they should be slain as infidels or not."—*Sale.*

Whom God hath led astray, i.e., by eternally decreeing his course of evil, or by a righteous reprobation.

(88) *They desire, &c.* "The people here meant, say some, were the tribe of Khuzáah, or, according to others, the Aslamians, whose chief, named Hilál Ibn Uwaimar, agreed with Muhammad, when he set out against Makkah, to stand neuter; or, as others rather think, Banu Baqr Ibn Zaid."—*Sale, Baidháwi, Jaláluddín.*

No covenant of friendship was to be entered into with these, except in the case of those who became refugees, and of whose sincerity there could be no doubt. Should they afterwards apostatise, they were to be slain. This law was inexorably executed in all Muslim countries for over twelve hundred years. Death is still the penalty that may be legally inflicted on every convert from Islám to Christianity in every country not yet under Christian domination.

ye find them; and take no friend from among them, nor any helper, (89) except those who go unto a people who are in alliance with you, or those who come unto you, their hearts forbidding them either to fight against you, or to fight against their own people. And if GOD pleased he would have permitted them to have prevailed against you, and they would have fought against you. But if they depart from you, and fight not against you, and offer you peace, GOD doth not allow you *to take or kill* them. (90) Ye shall find others who are desirous to enter into confidence with you, and *at the same time* to preserve a confidence with their own people; so often as they return to sedition, they shall be subverted therein; and if they depart not from you, and offer you peace, and restrain their hands *from warring against you*, take them and kill them wheresoever ye find them; over these have we granted you a manifest power.

|| (91) It is not *lawful* for a believer to kill a believer, unless *it happen* by mistake; and whoso killeth a believer by mistake, *the penalty shall be* the freeing of a believer

R $\frac{13}{10}$.

---

(89) *Except those, &c., i.e.*, "the Bani Mudlaj, who had agreed to remain neutral between Muhammad and the Quraish."—*Tafsír-i-Raufi*. The importance of this treaty is indicated in the latter part of this verse.

(90) *Ye shall find others.* "The persons hinted at here were the tribes of Asad and Ghatfán, or, as some say, Banu Abdaldár, who came to Madína and pretended to embrace Muhammadanism, that they might be trusted by the Muslims, but when they returned, fell back to their old idolatry."—*Sale, Baidháwi.*

The history of Muslim wars with the Bani Quraidha and the Jews of Khaibar illustrate how faithfully the fierce injunction of this verse was carried out.

(91) *Unless by mistake.* "That is, by accident and without design. This passage was revealed to decide the case of Ayásh Ibn Abi Rábia, the brother by the mother's side of Abu Jahl, who, meeting Haráth Ibn Zaid on the road, and not knowing that he had embraced Muhammadanism, slew him."—*Sale, Baidháwi.*

A believer from slavery, i.e., a slave who has professed Islám. The hope of freedom must have been a strong inducement to unbelieving slaves to profess the religion of their masters.

A fine, "which is to be distributed according to the law of inheritance given in the beginning of this chapter."—*Sale, Baidháwi.*

VOL. II. G

from slavery, and a fine to be paid to the family of *the deceased,* unless they remit *it* as alms: and if *the slain person* be of a people at enmity with you, and be a true believer, *the penalty shall be* the freeing of a believer; but if he be of a people in confederacy with you, a fine to be paid to his family, and the freeing of a believer. And he who findeth not *wherewith to do this* shall fast two months consecutively *as* a penance *enjoined* from GOD; and GOD is knowing and wise. (92) But whoso killeth a believer designedly, his reward shall be hell; he shall remain therein *forever;* and GOD shall be angry with him, and shall curse him, and shall prepare for him a great punishment. (93) O true believers, when ye are on a march in defence of the true religion, justly discern *such as ye shall happen to meet,* and say not unto him who saluteth you, thou art not a true believer; seeking the accidental goods of the present life; for with GOD is much spoil. Such have ye formerly been; but GOD hath been gracious unto

---

When, however, the deceased believer's people are unbelievers, no *fine* is to be paid. The legal fine as the price of blood is one hundred camels, as follows:—Twenty males one year old, twenty females of one year, twenty of two years, twenty of three years, and twenty of four years old. If the slain person be a woman, the fine is half this sum. In the case of a slave, the price must be paid to the master. If the fine be paid in coin, then the blood price is one thousand dinars gold, or ten thousand dirhams in silver. Half this sum to be paid for a woman.

But if he be of a people in confederacy, &c. The same rule as to fine was applied to the case of a person slain, who, though not a Muslim, yet belonged to a tribe or nation with whom a treaty of peace had been formed.

(92) This verse was intended to abolish the blood feuds so prevalent among the Arabs, and no doubt it ministered to the welding together of the various factions under the banner of Islám. How many millions of Muslims have been consigned to hell by this law since the death of Muhammad the annals of Islám abundantly declare. The punishment is, say the commentators, *purgatorial*, and the Muslim will eventually be restored to paradise, for, according to the Qurán, no true Muslim can be for ever lost. This view of the matter is, however, contradicted by this very passage, which says the murderer "shall remain therein for ever,"—the same language used in speaking of the fate of infidels.

(93) *Say not . . . thou art not a true believer.* The desire for

you; therefore make a just discernment, for GOD is well acquainted with that which ye do.

|| (94) Those believers who sit still *at home*, not having any hurt, and those who employ their fortunes and their persons for the religion of GOD, shall not be held equal. GOD hath prepared those who employ their fortunes and their persons *in that cause* to a degree *of honour* above those who sit at home; GOD hath indeed promised every one paradise, but GOD hath preferred those who fight *for the faith* before those who sit still, *by adding unto them* a great reward, (95) by degrees *of honour conferred on them* from him, and *by granting them* forgiveness and mercy; for GOD is indulgent *and* merciful. (96) Moreover unto those whom the angels put to death, having injured their own

R $\frac{14}{11}$.

---

plunder, which Muhammad had stirred up, had become so insatiable, that even Muslims were slain on the pretence that they were infidels, in order that they might be lawfully plundered. See *Muir's Life of Mahomet*, vol. iii. p. 307.

With God is much spoil. The motive here was certainly suited to Arab minds: Don't rob and murder Muslims for the sake of spoil, for God will give you the opportunity of spoiling many infidels. Muhammad did not scruple to pander to the worst passions of human nature in order to advance his political ends. Let it be remembered, however, this language does not purport to be Muhammad's, but that of the only true God! See our note in Prelim. Disc., p. 118.

(94) *Not having any hurt, i.e.,* "not being disabled from going to war by sickness or other just impediment. It is said that when this passage was first revealed there was no such exception therein, which occasioned Ibn Umm Maqtúm, on his hearing it repeated, to object, 'And what though I be blind?' Whereupon Muhammad, falling into a kind of trance, which was succeeded by strong agitations, pretended he had received the divine direction to add these words to the text."—*Sale, Baidháwi.*

The Makkan preacher declared that force was not to be used in religion, but the Madína politician promises the highest honours to those who spend life and property in warring for the faith. The prophet has now become a soldier and a general of armies. Like Jeroboam, Muhammad, having built his altars in Bethel and Dan, no longer hesitates to make any use of the holy name and religion of Jehovah which would seem to advance his political aspirations.

(96) *Whom the angels put to death.* "These were certain inhabitants of Makkah, who held with the hare and ran with the hounds, for though they embraced Muhammadanism, yet they would not

souls, *the angels* said, Of what *religion* were ye? they answered, We were weak in the earth. *The angels* replied, Was not GOD's earth wide *enough*, that ye might fly therein *to a place of refuge?* Therefore their habitation shall be hell; and an evil journey *shall it be thither:* (97) except the weak among men, and women, and children, who were not able to find means, and were not directed in the way; (98) these peradventure GOD will pardon, for GOD is ready to forgive, *and* gracious. (99) Whosoever flieth *from his country* for the sake of GOD's true religion, shall find in the earth many forced *to do the same*, and plenty *of provisions*. And whoever departeth from his house, and flieth unto GOD and his apostle, if death overtake him *in the way*, GOD will be obliged to reward him, for GOD is gracious *and* merciful.

R $\frac{15}{12}$ ‖ (100) When ye march *to war* in the earth, it shall be

---

leave that city to join the Prophet, as the rest of the Muslims did, but, on the contrary, went out with the idolaters, and were therefore slain with them at the battle of Badr."—*Sale, Jalāluddīn.*

The *angels* who slew these Muslims were of the three thousand who assisted the faithful (chap. iii. 13, note), but the angels who examined them were Munkir and Nakír, "two fierce-looking black angels with blue eyes, who visit every man in his grave and examine him with regard to his faith in God and Muhammad."—*Sell's Faith of Islám*, p. 145.

(97) *Except the weak, &c.* None were excused from the duty of *flight (Hijrat)* excepting those who were unable to perform it. Muslims still recognise the duty of flight from the Dár al Harb to the Dár al Islám. This duty is so imperative that even a doubt is thrown upon the case of the "weak," &c. in the next verse.

The purpose of this law is evident from the circumstances of the Prophet at the time of its enunciation. He needed the help of the faithful. All must therefore fly to Madína for refuge. When there, all must fight "in the way of God."

(99) *If death overtake him*. "This passage was revealed, says al Baidháwi, on account of Jundub Ibn Dhamra. This person being sick, was, in his flight, carried by his sons on a couch, and before he arrived at Madína, perceiving his end approached, he clapped his right hand on his left, and solemnly plighting his faith to God and his Apostle, died."—*Sale.*

God will be obliged. Rodwell's translation is better, "His reward from God is sure."

(100 *and* 101) The service here sanctioned was called "The Service of Danger." It was introduced during the return of Muhammad

no crime in you if ye shorten your prayers, in case ye fear the infidels may attack you; for the infidels are your open enemy. (101) But when thou, *O Prophet*, shalt be among them, and shalt pray with them, let a party of them arise to prayer with thee, and let them take their arms; and when they shall have worshipped, let them stand behind you, and let another party come that hath not prayed, and let them pray with thee, and let them be cautious and take their arms. The unbelievers would that ye should neglect your arms and your baggage *while ye pray,* that they might turn upon you at once. It shall be no crime in you, if ye be incommoded by rain or be sick, that ye lay down your arms; but take your *necessary* precaution: GOD hath prepared for the unbelievers an ignominious punishment. (102) And when ye shall have ended *your* prayer, remember GOD, standing, and sitting, and *lying* on your sides. But when ye are secure *from danger*, complete *your* prayers: for prayer is commanded the faithful, *and* appointed *to be said* at the stated times. (103) Be not negligent in seeking out the *unbelieving* people, though

---

and his army from Dzát al Rica, where they had captured many women. The following passage from Muir's *Life of Muhomet*, vol. iii. p. 224, relating to this *service*, well expresses the character of the revelations of this period (A.H. 5). He says: "I quote the revelation which sanctioned this practice, less for its own interest, than to illustrate the tendency of the Coran now to become the vehicle of military commands. In the Coran, victories are announced, success promised, actions recounted, failure is explained, bravery applauded, cowardice or disobedience chided, military or political movements are directed; and all this as an immediate communication from the Deity. The following verses resemble in part what one might expect to find in the 'General Orders' of some Puritan leader or commander of a crusade in the Holy Land." Here he quotes the verses under comment.

We should like to know how the apologists for Muhammad would reconcile this practical use of inspiration to political ends with their dictum that he can no longer be regarded as an impostor.

(102) *Standing, sitting, &c.* See note on chap. iii. 192.

(103) Sale, on the authority of Baidháwi, says, "This verse was revealed on the occasion of the unwillingness of Muhammad's men to accompany him in the lesser expedition of Badr." The *Tafsīr-i-Raufi* refers it to the pursuit of Abu Sufián after the battle of Ohod. The "seeking out the unbelieving people" was not *to save*, but to destroy them.

ye suffer *some inconvenience;* for they *also* shall suffer as ye suffer, and ye hope for *a reward* from GOD which they cannot hope for; and GOD is knowing *and* wise.

R $\frac{16}{13}$.

‖ (104) We have sent down unto thee the book *of the Qurán* with truth, that thou mayest judge between men through that *wisdom* which GOD showeth thee *therein;* and be not an advocate for the fraudulent; (105) but ask pardon of GOD *for thy wrong intention,* since GOD is indulgent *and* merciful. (106) Dispute not for those who deceive one another, for GOD loveth not him who is a deceiver *or* unjust. (107) *Such* conceal themselves from men, but they conceal not themselves from GOD; for he is

---

(104) *Be not an advocate for the fraudulent.* "Tíma Abu Ubairak, of the sons of Dhafar, one of Muhammad's companions, stole a coat of mail from his neighbour, Kitáda Ibn al Numán, in a bag of meal, and hid it at a Jew's, named Zaid Ibn al Samín. Tíma being suspected, the coat of mail was demanded of him, but he denying he knew anything of it, they followed the track of the meal, which had run through a hole in the bag, to the Jew's house, and there seized it, accusing him of the theft; but he producing witnesses of his own religion that he had it of Tíma, the sons of Dhafar came to Muhammad, and desired him to defend his companion's reputation and condemn the Jew; which he having some thoughts of doing, this passage was revealed, reprehending him for his rash intention, and commanding him to judge, not according to his own prejudice and opinion, but according to the merit of the case."—*Sale, Baidháwi, Jaláluddín, Yahya.*

(105) *Ask pardon, i.e.,* for the purpose, entertained for a while, of acquitting the Muslim and of unjustly condemning the Jew. This passage affords an unanswerable argument against those modern Muslims who claim that Muhammad was sinless.

(106) *Who deceive one another.* The friends of Tíma, who were importunate in their demands for favour to the Muslims.

A deceiver or unjust. "Al Baidháwi, as an instance of the divine justice, adds, that Tíma, after the fact above mentioned, fled to Makkah and returned to idolatry; and there, undermining the wall of a house in order to commit a robbery, the wall fell in upon him and crushed him to death."—*Sale.*

Many other stories of a like nature have been related by the commentators. See *Tafsír-i-Raufi* under ver. 14.

(107) *A saying which pleaseth him not, i.e.,* "When they secretly contrive means, by false evidence or otherwise, to lay their crime on innocent persons."—*Sale.*

This verse and 108–114 refer to the case of Tíma and his associates. The whole passage shows how much superior the morality of

with them when they imagine by night a saying which pleaseth *him* not, and GOD comprehendeth what they do. (108) Behold, ye are they who have disputed for them in this present life; but who shall dispute with GOD for them on the day of resurrection, or who will become their patron? (109) Yet he who doth evil or injureth his own soul, and afterwards asketh pardon of God, shall find God gracious *and* merciful. (110) Whoso committeth wickedness, committeth it against his own soul: GOD is knowing *and* wise. (111) And whoso committeth a sin or iniquity, and afterwards layeth it on the innocent, he shall surely bear *the guilt of* calumny and manifest injustice.

|| (112) If the indulgence and mercy of GOD had not R $\frac{17}{14}$. been upon thee, surely a part of them had studied to seduce thee; but they shall seduce themselves only, and shall not hurt thee at all. GOD hath sent down unto thee the book *of the Qurán* and wisdom, and hath taught thee that which thou knewest not; for the favour of GOD hath been great towards thee.

|| (113) There is no good in the multitude of their SULS. private discourses, unless *in the discourse* of him who recommendeth alms, or that which is right, or agreement amongst men: whoever doth this out of a desire to please GOD, we will surely give him a great reward. (114) But whoso separateth himself from the apostle, after *true* direction hath been manifested unto him, and followeth any other way than that of the true believers, we will cause him to obtain that to which he is inclined, and will cast him to be burned in hell; and an unhappy journey shall it be *thither*.

Muhammad was to that of his *Arab* followers. Did he learn it from his Jewish converts?
(109) *Who . . . asketh pardon*. See note on chap. ii. 199.
(112) *A part of them*. The friends of Tíma alluded to above.
(114) *We will cause him to obtain, &c.* This refers to all deceivers and dishonest persons represented by Tíma (ver. 106). This passage has probably suggested the numerous stories of the commentators related to illustrate it.

R 18/15.   ‖ (115) Verily GOD will not pardon the giving him a companion, but he will pardon *any crime* besides that, unto whom he pleaseth : and he who giveth a companion unto GOD is surely led aside into a wide mistake; (116) the *infidels* invoke beside him only female *deities*, and

---

(115) *God will not pardon, &c.* See note on ver. 46.
(116) *Only female deities.* "Namely, Al Lát, al Uzza and Minát, the idols of the Makkans; or the angels whom they called the *daughters of God.*"—*Sale.* See Prelim. Disc., pp. 39-43. The *Tafsír-i-Raufi* and the *Tafsír-i-Hussaini* tell us that the idols at Makkah were made in the form of women, and that the goddesses thus represented were called the *daughters of* God.

And only invoke rebellious Satan, i.e., when they pray to the idols. Muhammad everywhere recognises the personality of Satan as a being possessed of mighty power for evil, and he seems to have had a strong conviction of his own exposure to his influences. See chap. vi. 67, 112, xvi. 100, xix. 86, xx. 53, 54, cxiv. 1-6, &c.

Muir accounts for Muhammad's apostasy and his belief in his inspiration, in part at least, by reference to direct Satanic influence (see his *Life of Mahomet,* vol. ii. chap. iii.) This theory, while scouted by Muslims and apologists for Islám, is decidedly the most satisfactory of any yet enunciated, and to a believer in the Word of God there should be no difficulty in accepting it. It accounts for the sincere efforts at reform inaugurated at Makkah when Muhammad seemed to be really a preacher of righteousness. It accounts for his fall, and for all the deception and iniquity practised by him in later years under the garb of religion, and by what he presumed to be divine right. It accounts for his deliberate imposture, while fancying himself directed by God, for it is not impossible for Satan to have, so to speak, reflected back upon the mind of Muhammad the devices of his own heart, and so by a *revelation* not only confirm his own views, but also *lead him to fancy his every thought to be born of inspiration,* so that he came practically to identify himself with God, though really identified with Satan ! I think that something like this is absolutely necessary to account for Muhammad's having, even in giving military orders, &c. (see vers. 100, 101), *invariably* spoken in the person as well as in the name of God.

I am aware of the reply of Mr. R. Bosworth Smith (in his *Mohammed and Mohammedanism,* p. 116, note), that "if the Spirit of Evil did suggest the idea to Mohammed, he never so completely outwitted himself, since friend and foe must alike admit that it was Mohammed's firm belief in supernatural guidance that lay at the root of all he achieved." But this is exactly what the Lying Spirit of false prophecy desires. Did Ahab's prophet think that he spoke by the dictum of a lying spirit when he withstood the prophet of God before the kings of Israel and Judah ?

Again, as to Muhammad's achievements, we think Satan has no reason to believe he overstepped the matter in the accomplishment

only invoke rebellious Satan. (117) GOD cursed him; and he said, Verily I will take of thy servants a part cut off *from the rest*, (118) and I will seduce them, and will insinuate *vain* desires into them, and I will command them, and they shall cut off the ears of cattle; and I will command them, and they shall change GOD's creature. But whoever taketh Satan for his patron, besides GOD, shall surely perish with a manifest destruction. (119) He maketh them promises, and insinuateth into them vain desires: yet Satan maketh them only deceitful promises. (120) The receptacle of these shall be hell; they shall find no refuge from it. (121) But they who believe and do good works we will surely lead them into gardens, through which rivers flow; they shall continue therein for ever, *according to* the true promise of GOD; and who is more true than GOD in what he saith? (122) It shall not be according to your desires, nor *according to* the desires of those who have received the scriptures. Whoso doth evil shall be rewarded for it; and shall not find any

---

of these. What better achievement could he devise than the establishment of a religion which would destroy the souls of men by denying the atoning blood which alone can destroy his power? Idolatry is certainly his strong tower, but when monotheism can be made to serve the same end, his fortress is rendered doubly strong.

(117) *God cursed him*, or *God curse him*. The usual idiom would require *we* cursed him. The word *say* introduced, however, makes all consistent. See chap. i., note on ver. 2.

A part cut off, " or a part *destined* or *predetermined* to be seduced by me."—*Sale.*

(118) *Cut off the ears.* This was an ancient Arab custom, whereby they marked the animals devoted to their idols.

They shall change God's creature, i.e., they shall devote their property to the service of Satan by offering it to idols (*Abdul Qádir*). Baidháwi thinks the allusion is to the mutilation and disfigurement of the human body, *e.g.*, marking their bodies with figures, by pricking and dying them with wood or indigo, sharpening their teeth by filing, by unnatural amours, &c. See Sale's note.

(122) *Nor according to the desires, &c.* "That is, the promises of God are not to be gained by acting after your own fancies, nor yet after the fancies of the Jews or Christians, but by obeying the commands of God. This passage, they say, was revealed on a dispute which arose between those of the three religions, each preferring his own and

patron or helper beside GOD; (123) but whoso doth good works, whether he be male or female, and is a true believer, they shall be admitted into paradise, and shall not in the least be unjustly dealt with. (124) Who is better in point of religion than he who resigneth himself unto GOD, and is a worker of righteousness, and followeth the law of Abraham the orthodox? since GOD took Abraham for his friend; (125) and to GOD *belongeth* whatsoever is in heaven and on earth; GOD comprehendeth all things.

---

condemning the others. Some, however, suppose the persons here spoken to in the second person were not the Muhammadans, but the idolaters."—*Sale, Baidhâwi, &c.*

"Those who have received the Scriptures" must refer to false professors of the religion revealed in their Scriptures, else the passage contradicts the claim of the Qurán that Islám is the religion of the former Scriptures.

(123) *Male or female.* This passage clearly disproves the opinion of those who imagine that women are excluded from the paradise of Islám. See also notes on chap. iii. 196, chap. ix. 73, and chap. xlviii. 5. The ground of salvation given here is *good works*, which works are, however, *such as Islám requires.*

(124) *He who resigneth himself, i.e.,* a Muslim, one who submits himself to the divine will. Such are said to be the followers of "the law of Abraham the Orthodox."

God took Abraham for his friend. Compare 2 Kings xx. 7, Isa. xli. 8, and James ii. 23. "Muhammadans usually call that patriarch, as the Scripture also does, Khalíl Ullah, the *friend of God,* and simply al Khalíl; and they tell the following story:—That Abraham in a time of dearth sent to a friend of his in Egypt for a supply of corn; but the friend denied him, saying in his excuse, that though there was a famine in their country also, yet had it been for Abraham's own family, he would have sent what he desired, but he knew he wanted it only to entertain his guests and give away to the poor, according to his usual hospitality. The servants whom Abraham had sent on this message, being ashamed to return empty, to conceal the matter from their neighbours, filled their sacks with the fine white sand, which in the East pretty much resembles meal. Abraham being informed by his servants, on their return, of their ill success, the concern he was under threw him into a sleep; and in the meantime Sarah, knowing nothing of what had happened, opening one of the sacks, found good flour in it, and immediately set about making of bread. Abraham awaking and smelling the new bread, asked her whence she had the flour. 'Why,' says she, 'from your friend in Egypt.' 'Nay,' replied the patriarch, 'it must have come from no other than my friend God Almighty.'"—*Sale, Baidháwi, Jaláluddín, Yahya.*

‖ (126) They will consult thee concerning women; R ⅔. Answer, GOD instructeth you concerning them, and that which is read unto you in the book *of the Qurán* concerning female orphans, to whom ye give not that which is ordained them, neither will ye marry them, and concerning weak infants, and that ye observe justice towards orphans: whatever good ye do, GOD knoweth it. (127) If a woman fear ill usage, or aversion from her husband, it shall be no crime in them if they agree the matter amicably between themselves; for a reconciliation is better *than a separation.* Men's souls are naturally inclined to covetousness: but if ye be kind *towards women,* and fear *to wrong them,* GOD is well acquainted with what

---

(126) *They will consult thee concerning women, i.e.,* "as to the share they are to have in the distribution of the inheritances of their deceased relations; for it seems that the Arabs were not satisfied with Muhammad's decision on this point against the old customs." —*Sale.*

God instructeth you, i.e., as in the earlier portion of the chapter.

Neither will ye marry them. "Or the words may be rendered in the affirmative, *and whom ye desire to marry.* For the pagan Arabs used to wrong their female orphans in both instances; obliging them to marry against their inclinations, if they were beautiful or rich; or else not suffering them to marry at all, that they might keep what belonged to them."—*Sale, Baidháwi.*

Rodwell translates, "And whom ye refuse to marry." See also note on ver. 3.

Weak infants. See notes on vers. 6 and 8.

(127) *If a woman fear, &c.* The *Tafsír-i-Raufi* says this verse was occasioned by a man's having sought an excuse for divorcing his wife. His wife, however, having a number of children, besought him not to do so, saying he might take to himself as many wives as he chose.

This verse, then, encourages wives to be reconciled to their husbands, by remitting some portion of their dower, or by granting them other wives, and thereby assuming the unenviable place of co-wife. On the other hand, it encourages the husbands to practise this kind of domestic oppression: "It shall be no crime in them if they agree" in this manner.

Souls are naturally inclined to covetousness. This is said to refer to Sauda, one of Muhammad's wives, who besought him to marry her, that she might be amongst his wives at the resurrection! It would seem, however, rather to be intended to justify the covetousness of husbands referred to above.

ye do. (128) Ye can by no means carry yourselves equally between women *in all respects*, although ye study *to do it;* therefore turn not *from a* wife with all *manner of* aversion, nor leave her like one in suspense: if ye agree, and fear *to abuse your wives*, GOD is gracious *and* merciful; (129) but if they separate, GOD will satisfy *them* both of his abundance; for GOD is extensive *and* wise, (130) and unto GOD *belongeth* whatsoever is in heaven and on earth. We have already commanded those unto whom the scriptures were given before you, and *we command* you also, *saying*, Fear GOD; but if ye disbelieve, unto GOD *belongeth* whatsoever is in heaven and on earth; and GOD is self-sufficient, *and* to be praised; (131) for unto GOD *belongeth* whatsoever is in heaven and on earth, and GOD is a sufficient protector. (132) If he pleaseth he will take you away, O men, and will produce others *in your stead;* for GOD is able to do this. Whoso desireth the reward of this world, verily with GOD is the reward of this world, and *also* of that which is to come; GOD *both* heareth *and* seeth.

|| (133) O true believers, observe justice when ye bear witness before GOD, although *it be* against yourselves, or *your* parents, or relations; whether *the party* be rich, or *whether he be* poor; for GOD is more worthy than them both; therefore follow not *your own* lust *in bearing testimony* so that ye swerve *from justice*. And whether ye wrest *your evidence* or decline *giving it*, GOD is well

---

(128) *Carry yourselves equally.* See note on ver. 3.
Like one in suspense, "or like one that neither has a husband, nor is divorced, and at liberty to marry elsewhere."—*Sale.*
(129) *God will satisfy them.* They will have peace, or God will bless them with a better match.
(130) *We have already commanded, &c.* This seems to indicate that these laws, thus instituted, are in accord with the laws of the Bible. If so, the Qurán again comes far short of confirming the former Scriptures.
God is self-sufficient, i.e., needing the service of no creature.
(132) Illustrative of God's sovereign power and *self-sufficiency.*

acquainted with that which ye do. (134) O true believers, believe in GOD and his apostle, and the book which he hath caused to descend unto his apostle, and the book which he hath formerly sent down. And whosoever believeth not in GOD, and his angels, and his scriptures, and his apostles, and the last day, he surely erreth in a wide mistake. (136) Moreover they who believed, and afterwards became infidels, and then believed *again*, and after that disbelieved, and increased in infidelity, GOD will by no means forgive them, nor direct them into the *right* way. (137) Declare unto the ungodly that they shall suffer a painful punishment. (138) They who take the unbelievers for their protectors, besides the faithful, do they seek for power with them? since all power belongeth unto GOD. (139) And he hath already revealed unto you, in the book *of the Qurán, the*

---

(134) *Observe justice when ye bear witness.* The duty of truthfulness in witness-bearing is clearly inculcated here.

(135) *The book which he hath formerly sent down.* "It is said that Abdullah Ibn Salám and his companions told Muhammad that they believed in him, and in his Qurán, and in Moses, and the Pentateuch, and in Ezra, but no farther; whereupon this passage was revealed, declaring that a partial faith is little better than none at all, and that a true believer must believe in all God's prophets and revelations without exception."—*Sale, Baidháwi.*

The duty of believing the Scriptures of the Old and New Testaments is here again inculcated. But so certainly impossible is the fulfilment, that Muslims reject the Gospels, and holding to the Qurán, deny the teaching of all former prophets. See notes on chap. ii. 105.

(136) *Who . . . increased in infidelity.* "These were the Jews, who first believed in Moses, and afterwards fell into idolatry by worshipping the golden calf; and though they repented of that, yet in after ages rejected the prophets who were sent to them, and particularly Jesus the son of Mary, and now filled up the measure of their unbelief by rejecting of Muhammad."—*Sale, Baidháwi.*

Abdul Qádir applies the passage to hypocritical professors of Islám. All such will die and suffer the penalty of infidelity.

The passage also teaches the reprobation of such hypocrites. They shall be given over to destruction, for they shall neither be pardoned nor directed.

(139) *He hath already revealed.* This passage expresses the *substance* of what is contained in chap. vi. If any particular verse is indicated, it is probably chap. vi. 10.

following passage—WHEN YE SHALL HEAR THE SIGNS OF GOD, THEY SHALL NOT BE BELIEVED, BUT THEY SHALL BE LAUGHED TO SCORN. Therefore sit not with them *who believe not*, until they engage in different discourse ; for *if ye do*, ye will certainly *become* like unto them. GOD will surely gather the ungodly and the unbelievers together in hell. (140) They who wait *to observe what befalleth* you, if victory be *granted* you from GOD, say, Were we not with you ? But if any advantage happen to the infidels, they say *unto them*, Were we not superior to you, and have we not defended you against the believers ? GOD shall judge between you on the day of resurrection : and GOD will not grant the unbelievers means *to prevail* over the faithful.

R $\frac{21}{1}$. ‖ (141) The hypocrites act deceitfully with GOD, but he will deceive them ; and when they stand up to pray, they stand carelessly, affecting to be seen of men, and remember not GOD, unless a little, (142) wavering between *faith and infidelity, and adhering* neither unto these nor unto those : and for him whom GOD shall lead astray thou shalt find no true path. (143) O true believers, take not the unbelievers for *your* protectors besides the faithful. Will ye furnish GOD with an evident argument *of impiety* against you ? (144) Moreover the hypocrites shall be in the lowest bottom of *hell* fire,

---

Sit not with them. Muslims are not allowed even to *listen* to the adverse criticisms of unbelievers, lest they should become like them. These scoffers were no doubt Jews, whose arguments were to the Muslims unanswerable. Anything like a fair investigation would have been disastrous to the cause of Islám. Ignorant bigotry has ever been its strongest defence.

(140) *They who wait.* The hypocrites who played fast and loose with the Muslims and their enemies. When the former were victorious, as at Badr, these desired to share the booty, on pretence of having been in sympathy with the victors. When, however, the latter gained the day, as at Ohod, the hypocrites could show how the victory was due to their withdrawing from the Muslims !

(141) *He will deceive them.* This is a good illustration of the play upon words frequently met with in the Qurán. See chap. iii. 53.

(144) *The lowest bottom of hell fire.* See Prelim. Disc., p. 148.

and thou shalt not find any to help them *thence*. (145) But they who repent and amend, and adhere firmly unto GOD, and approve the sincerity of their religion to GOD, they shall be *numbered* with the faithful; and GOD will surely give the faithful a great reward. (146) And how should GOD go about to punish you, if ye be thankful and believe? for GOD is grateful and wise.

|| (147) GOD loveth not the speaking ill *of any one* in public, unless he who is injured *call for assistance;* and GOD heareth and knoweth: (148) whether ye publish a good *action*, or conceal it, or forgive evil, verily GOD is gracious *and* powerful. (149) They who believe not in GOD and his apostles, and would make a distinction between GOD and his apostles, and say, We believe in some *of the prophets* and reject others of *them*, and seek to take a *middle* way in this *matter;* (150) these are really unbelievers: and we have prepared for the unbelievers an ignominious punishment. (151) But they who believe in GOD and his apostles, and make no distinction between any of them, unto those will ye surely give their reward; and GOD is gracious *and* merciful.

|| (152) They who have received the scriptures will demand of thee, that thou cause a book to descend unto

---

(146) *God is grateful.* The idea that God is placed under some sort of obligation to true Muslims is certainly suggested by the language of this verse, but the *meaning* is that he acts towards believers as if he were grateful. The passage may be quoted to illustrate the use of the word *repent* in Gen. vi. 6.

(147) *Unless he who is injured.* The words *call for assistance* are incorrectly supplied. The phrase gives an exception to the rule that evil-speaking is displeasing to God. The oppressed may speak evil of their oppressors. See *Tafsír-i-Raufí in loco.*

(149) *They who believe not, &c.* See chap. ii. 285.

(150) *These are really unbelievers.* The reference is to the Jews, who said, "We believe in Moses and Ezra, but we reject Jesus and Muhammad" (*Tafsír-i-Raufí*).

(152) *That thou cause a book to descend, i.e.,* "the Jews, who demanded of Muhammad, as a proof of his mission, that they might see a book of revelations descend to him from heaven, or that he would produce one written in a celestial character, like the two tables of Moses."—*Sale.*

them from heaven: they formerly asked of Moses a greater *thing* than this; for they said, Show us GOD visibly. Wherefore a storm of fire from heaven destroyed them, because of their iniquity. Then they took the calf *for their God*, after that evident proofs *of the divine unity* had come unto them: but we forgave *them* that, and gave Moses a manifest power *to punish them.* (153) And we lifted the mountain of *Sinai* over them *when we exacted from them* their covenant; and said unto them, Enter the gate *of the city* worshipping. We also said unto them, Transgress not on the Sabbath-day. And we received from them a firm covenant, *that they would observe these things.* (154) Therefore for that they have made void their covenant, and have not believed in the signs of GOD, and have slain the prophets unjustly, and have said, Our hearts are circumcised; (but GOD hath sealed them up, because of their unbelief; therefore they shall not believe, except a few *of them:*) (155) and for that they have not believed *in Jesus,* and have spoken against Mary a grievous calumny; (156) and have said, Verily we have slain Christ Jesus the son of Mary, the apostle of GOD; yet

---

Show us God visibly. See notes on chap. ii. 54 and 62; comp. Exod. xxiv. 9, 10, and 11.

A storm of fire, &c. There is no truth in this statement, which is here given as so much inspired history. See note, chap. iii. 39.

They took the calf. Note on chap. ii. 50.

(153) *We lifted the mountain, &c.* See note on chap. ii. 62 and 64.

(154) *For that.* "There being nothing in the following words of this sentence to answer to the casual *for that,* Jaláluddín supposes something to be understood to complete the sense, as, *therefore we have cursed them,* or the like."—*Sale.*

(156) *A grievous calumny.* "By accusing her of fornication."—*Sale.*

They slew him not. See notes on chap. iii. 53 and 54.

Who disagreed. "For some maintained that he was justly and really crucified; some insisted that it was not Jesus who suffered, but another who resembled him in the face, pretending the other parts of his body, by their unlikeness, plainly discovered the imposition; some said he was taken up into heaven; and others, that his manhood only suffered, and that his godhead ascended into heaven."—*Sale, Baidháwi.*

they slew him not, neither crucified him, but he was represented *by one* in his likeness; and verily they who disagreed concerning him were in a doubt as to this *matter*, and had no *sure* knowledge thereof, but followed only an *uncertain* opinion. They did not really kill him; (157) but GOD took him up unto himself: and GOD is mighty *and* wise. (158) And *there shall not be one* of those who have received the scriptures who shall not believe in him before his death; and on the day of resur-

They did not really kill him. But the former Scriptures teach the contrary. The death of Christ was foretold to take place at the *first advent* (Dan. ix. 24). Jesus himself, according to the gospel, often foretold his death, and afterwards refers to it as past; the same Scriptures testify to his death as an accomplished fact, and all gospel preaching for eighteen centuries has been based upon it. The historians, Jewish, Heathen, and Christian, attest the fact. In short, there is no fact of either history or revelation so certainly established as that which is here contradicted. This one passage is sufficient to refute Muhammad's claim to be a prophet of God. And the Qurán, instead of attesting the former Scriptures, is found to attest a fiction of Christian heresy.

(158) *And there shall not be one of those, &c.* "This passage is expounded two ways:—

"Some, referring the relative *his* to the first antecedent, take the meaning to be that no Jew or Christian shall die before he believes in Jesus: for they say, that when one of either of those religions is ready to breathe his last, and sees the angel of death before him, he shall then believe in that prophet as he ought, though his faith will not then be of any avail. According to a tradition of Hijáj, when a Jew is expiring, the angels will strike him on the back and face, and say to him, 'O thou enemy of God! Jesus was sent as a prophet unto thee, and thou didst not believe on him;' to which he will answer, 'I now believe him to be the servant of God;' and to a dying Christian they will say, 'Jesus was sent as a prophet unto thee, and thou hast imagined him to be God, or the son of God;' whereupon he will believe him to be the servant of God only, and his apostle.

"Others, taking the above-mentioned relative to refer to Jesus, suppose the intent of the passage to be, that all Jews and Christians in general shall have a right faith in that prophet before his death, that is, when he descends from heaven and returns into the world, where he is to kill Antichrist, and to establish the Muhammadan religion, and a most perfect tranquillity and security on earth."— *Sale, Baidháwi, Jaláluddín, Yahya, Zamakhsharí.*

The latter view seems to be the most reasonable. See note on chap. iii. 54.

He shall be a witness against them. His witness, says Sale, on

CHAP. IV.] (114) [SIPARA VI.

rection he shall be a witness against them. (159) Because of the iniquity of those who Judaise, we have forbidden them good things, which had been *formerly* allowed them; and because they shut out many from the way of GOD, (160) and have taken usury, which was forbidden them *by the law*, and devoured men's substance vainly: we have prepared for such of them as are unbelievers a painful punishment. (161) But those among them who are well grounded in knowledge, and the faithful, who believe in that which hath been sent down unto thee, and that which hath been sent down *unto the prophets* before thee, and who observe the stated times of prayer, and give alms, and believe in GOD and the last day, unto these will we give a great reward.

R $\frac{23}{3}$.
|| (162) Verily we have revealed *our will* unto thee, as we have revealed *it* unto Noah and the prophets who succeeded him; and *as* we revealed *it* unto Abraham, and Ismáíl, and Isaac, and Jacob, and the tribes, and unto

the authority of Baidháwi, shall be "against the Jews for rejecting him, and against the Christians for calling him God and the Son of God." See note on chap. v. 116-119.

(159) *We have forbidden them good things.* See notes on chap. iii. 93.

(161) *Those . . . who are well grounded.* Such as Abdullah Ibn Salám (*Tafsír-i-Raufí*). It seems that those were well grounded in the faith who accepted Islám. Infidelity and incorrigible stupidity went hand in hand in rejecting the claims of Muhammad.

(162) *We have revealed our will unto thee, &c.* This jumble of names, presented without any respect to chronology, is probably due to Muhammad's receiving his information second-hand and piecemeal through Jewish informants. Yet Muhammad claims to have been inspired, as were all the prophets. He also asserts that his inspiration was of precisely the same character as that of all the persons here enumerated, *i.e.*, they received the message directly from Gabriel, by direct communication and audible voice, the tinkling sound of bells in his ears, &c., which Muslims call *Wahi* and *Ilhám* (see Sell's *Faith of Islám,* p. 37, and Hughes's *Notes on Muhammadanism,* p. 47).

The Bible shows clearly that some of those mentioned here were not prophets at all, and that few of them knew aught of the inspiration claimed by Muhammad. Here again the Qurán denies historical fact and contradicts the book it professes to attest.

We have given the Qurán. This clause should have been omitted. The text is clear without it.

Jesus, and Job, and Jonas, and Aaron, and Solomon; and *we have given thee the Qurán as* we gave the psalms unto David : (163) *some* apostles *have we sent,* whom we have formerly mentioned unto thee; and *other* apostles *have we sent,* whom we have not mentioned unto thee; and GOD spake unto Moses, discoursing *with him;* (164) apostles declaring good tidings and denouncing threats, lest men should have an argument *of excuse* against GOD, after the apostles *had been sent unto them:* GOD is mighty *and* wise. (165) GOD is witness of that *revelation* which he hath sent down unto thee; he sent it down with his *special* knowledge; the angels also are witnesses *thereof;* but GOD is a sufficient witness. (166) They who believe not, and turn aside *others* from the way of GOD, have erred in a wide mistake. (167) Verily those who believe not and act unjustly, GOD will by no means forgive, neither will he direct them into *any other* way than the way of hell; they shall remain therein forever; and this is easy with GOD. (168) O men, now is the apostle come unto you, with truth from your LORD; believe, therefore; *it will be* better for you. But if ye disbelieve, verily unto GOD *belongeth* whatsoever *is* in heaven and on earth ; and GOD is knowing *and* wise. (169) O ye who have received the scriptures, exceed not the just bounds in your religion,

---

(163) *God spake unto Moses.* This Muslims understand to be the highest form of *wahi (revelation),* or inspiration, as the word is incorrectly translated. In this respect, say they, Moses resembled Muhammad. *Tafsír-i-Raufi in loco.*

(165) *God is witness.* The occasion of this revelation was the infidelity of certain Jews, who being asked to testify to his prophecy before certain Quraish chiefs, declared that they did not recognise him as a prophet (*Tafsír-i-Raufi*). The witness of God is in the incomparable language and style of the Qurán ; the witness of angels has reference to the testimony of Gabriel. See the plural form used for the singular, chap. iii. 39, note.

(166) *Turned aside others, i.e.,* the chiefs of the Quraish, who were turned aside by the answer of the Jews referred to in the note on the preceding verse.

(168) *With truth from your Lord.* A new assertion of his prophetic claim. See notes on vers. 116, 156, and 162.

(169) *Exceed not the just bounds, i.e.,* "either by rejecting or con-

neither say of GOD *any other* than the truth. Verily Christ Jesus the son of Mary *is* the apostle of GOD, and his Word, which he conveyed into Mary, and a spirit *proceeding* from him. Believe therefore in GOD and his apostles, and say not, *There are* three *Gods;* forbear *this;* it will be better for you. GOD is but one GOD. Far be it from him that he should have a son; unto him *belongeth* whatever *is* in heaven and on earth; and GOD is a sufficient protector.

R $\frac{24}{4}$.
 || (170) Christ doth not proudly disdain to be a servant unto GOD; neither the angels who approach near *to his presence:* and whoso disdaineth his service and is puffed up with pride, *God* will gather them all to himself *on the last day.* (171) Unto those who believe and do that which is right he shall give their rewards, and shall *superabundantly* add unto them of his liberality: but those who are disdainful and proud, he will punish with a grievous punishment; (172) and they shall not find any

---

temning Jesus, as the Jews do; or raising him to an equality with God, as do the Christians."—*Sale, Baidháwi.*

His word, . . . a spirit proceeding from him. See notes on chap. ii. 86, and chap. iii. 39.

Say not . . . three, "Namely, God, Jesus, Mary. For the Eastern writers mention a sect of Christians which held the Trinity to be composed of those three; but it is allowed that this heresy has been long since extinct (*Elmacin,* p. 227). The passage, however, is equally levelled against the Holy Trinity, according to the doctrine of the orthodox Christians, who, as Al Baidháwi acknowledges, believe the divine nature to consist of three persons, the Father, the Son, and the Holy Ghost; by the Father, understanding God's essence; by the Son, his knowledge; and by the Holy Ghost, his life."—*Sale.*

See also *Prelim. Disc.,* p. 64.

The commentators Baidháwi, Jaláluddín, and Yahya agree in interpreting the *three* to mean "God, Jesus, and Mary," in the relation of Father, Mother, and Son. This misrepresentation of the Scripture doctrine again stamps the Qurán as a fabrication, and furnishes the evidence of its being such on the ground of its own claims. The history of the Church, as well as the Bible, proves the statement of the text, as interpreted by authoritative commentators, to be false; for even granting that some obscure Christian sect did hold such a doctrine of the Trinity (of which statement we have yet to learn the truth), yet the spirit of Muhammad's inspiration represents it as the faith of the Christians *generally.* In almost every case

to protect or to help them, besides GOD. (173) O men, now is an evident proof come unto you from your LORD, and we have sent down unto you manifest light. (174) They who believe in GOD and firmly adhere to him, he will lead them into mercy from him, and abundance; and he will direct them in the right way to himself. (175) They will consult thee *for thy decision in certain cases;* say *unto them,* GOD giveth you *these* determinations concerning the more remote degrees of kindred. If a man die without issue, and have a sister, she shall have the half of what he shall leave: and he shall be heir to her, in case she have no issue. But if there be two *sisters,* they shall have *between them* two third parts of what he shall leave; and if there be *several, both* brothers and sisters, a male shall have as much as the portion of two females. GOD declareth unto you *these precepts,* lest ye err: and GOD knoweth all things.

---

where the Qurán refers to the Christian faith, it is to inveigh against the idea that God has a son. See chap. ix. 31, xix. 31, xliii. 59.

(173) *Manifest light, i.e.,* the teaching of the Qurán.

(175) See notes on vers. 10 and 11.

And he shall be heir to her, i.e., where there is a brother and a sister, the sister inherits half the brother's property in case he die first without issue. On the other hand, in case the sister die first without issue, the brother inherits all her property.

CHAPTER V.

ENTITLED SURAT UL MÁIDA (THE TABLE).

Revealed at Madína.

INTRODUCTION.

ALTHOUGH, as is usual with all the long chapters of the Qurán, this chapter refers to a variety of matters of a general and miscellaneous character, *e.g.*, rules respecting purification, laws concerning lawful and unlawful food, yet there are four points which attract the special notice of the reader. These are (1) the extended reference to the rites of the pilgrimage to Makkah; (2) the fierce hatred of the Prophet towards the Jews and his denunciations against them; (3) the laboured effort to refute the Christian doctrine of the Trinity and the Sonship of Christ; and (4) the repeated warning given to Muslims not to make friends of either Jews or Christians. Wherefore both the historic references of this chapter as well as the *animus* of the revelation point to a period late in the life of Muhammad as that to which it belongs—a period when successful warfare had made the Prophet indifferent alike to Jewish hatred and Christian friendship.

The statement of ver. 4, "This day have I perfected your religion for you," &c., has led some writers to regard this chapter as the last of the chapters of the Qurán, taken in their chronological order. Muslim authorities agree that this verse and a few others at the beginning of this chapter fairly claim the last place on the list of *revelations*. However, excepting this short section, there is nothing in this chapter to lead us to believe it to be chronologically the last in the Qurán. Nöeldeke and Muir both agree in placing chap. ix. at the end of the chronological list of Suras, the former, however, admitting that there are some verses in this chapter which fairly claim posteriority to all others in the Qurán. He refers especially to ver. 4, which he thinks was revealed when Muhammad, with perhaps a presentiment of death being near, could say that all his enemies had lost their courage and that his religion was completed. It is for this reason he places it last in his historico-critical observations.

The revelations of this chapter are therefore of Madína origin.

Probable Date of the Revelations.

Following Nöeldeke for the most part, the dates within which the revelations of this chapter were made are as follows:—

Vers. 1-11 belong to A.H. 10. The date of ver. 12 cannot be ascertained with certainty. Vers. 13 and 14 may be placed almost anywhere between A.H. 2 and 7, the probability being that they belong nearer to the latter than to the former date. Vers. 45-55, though referred by most Muslim writers to a period prior to the massacre of the Baní Quraidha, should nevertheless be placed later, *i.e.*, prior to the expedition against the Jews of Khaibar in A.H. 7.

Vers. 56-63, according to Muslim authorities, belong to the latter part of A.H. 3 or the early part of A.H. 4.

Of vers. 64-88, the most that can be said is that they belong to a period between A.H. 4 and 8, after many wars with the Jews, and before the final outbreak with the Christians. Vers. 89-104 belong to A.H. 4-6. The date of the remaining verses is uncertain, but may be fixed approximately at A.H. 5-8.

Principal Subjects.

	VERSES
Covenants are to be fulfilled	1
Lawful meats	2
Heathen pilgrims not to be molested	3
Islám completed—last revelation of the Qurán	4
Certain kinds of food, gaming, and lots forbidden	4, 5
Muslims permitted to eat the food of Jews and Christians, and to marry their women	6
The law of purifications	7
Believers reminded of the covenant of Aqabah	8
Muslims should forget old quarrels with brethren	9-11
God's favour to Muslims	12
Disobedience of Jews and Christians exposed	13-15
Jews and Christians are exhorted to accept Islám	16-18
The divinity of Christ denied	19, 20
Jews and Christians not the children of God	21
Muhammad sent as a warner	22
Israel's rebellion at Kadesh Barnea	23-29
The story of Cain and Abel	30-34

	VERSES
The sin of homicide	35, 36
The punishment of theft accompanied by apostasy	37, 38
The faithful exhorted to fight for religion	39
The punishment of infidels	40, 41
The penalty of theft	42–44
Muhammad to judge the Jews and Christians by the law, gospel, and the Qurán	45–55
Muslims forbidden to fraternise with Jews and Christians	56
Hypocrites threatened	57, 58
Believers warned and instructed	59–61
Muslims not to associate with infidels	62, 63
The Jews exhorted and warned	64, 65
The hypocrisy and unbelief of the Jews rebuked	66–69
Promises to believing Jews and Christians	70
Muhammad required to preach	71
He attests Jewish and Christian Scriptures	72
Believing Jews, Sabeans, and Christians to be saved	73
The Jews rejected and killed the prophets of God	74, 75
The doctrines of the Trinity and Christ's Sonship rejected	76–81
Disobedient Jews cursed by their prophets	82–84
Jewish hatred and Christian friendship compared	85–88
Muslims to use lawful food, &c.	89, 90
Expiation for perjury	91
Wine and lots forbidden	92–94
Law concerning hunting and gaming during pilgrimage	95–97
Pilgrimage and its rites enjoined	98–100
The Prophet not to be pestered with questions	101, 102
Heathen Arab customs denounced	102–104
Wills to be attested by witnesses	105–107
The prophets ignorant of the characters of their followers	108
Jesus—his miracles—God's favour to him	109, 110
The apostles of Jesus were Muslims	111
A table provided by Jesus for the apostles	112–114
Jesus did not teach his followers to worship him and his mother	115–118
The reward of the true believer	119
God is sovereign	120

IN THE NAME OF THE MOST MERCIFUL GOD. SECOND MANZIL.

|| (1) O TRUE believers, perform your contracts. (2) Ye R $\frac{1}{5}$. are allowed *to eat* the brute cattle, other than what ye are commanded *to abstain from*; except the game which ye are allowed *at other times, but not* while ye are on pilgrimage *to Makkah;* GOD ordaineth that which he pleaseth. (3) O true believers, violate not the holy rites of GOD, nor the sacred month, nor the offering, nor the ornaments hung *thereon*, nor those who are travelling to the holy house, seeking favour from their LORD, and to please *him*. But when ye shall have finished *your pilgrimage*, then hunt. And let not the malice of some, in that they hindered you *from entering* the sacred temple, provoke you to transgress, *by taking revenge on them in the sacred months*. Assist one another according to justice and piety, but assist not one another in injustice and malice: therefore fear GOD; for GOD is severe in punish-

---

(1) *Perform your contracts.* The command is general, and is introductory to the matters following.

(2) *Ye are allowed, &c.* See below, on vers. 4-6; also chap. ii. 174. The only flesh forbidden in the Qurán, if properly slain, is that of the swine; but tradition and custom decide many animals unfit for food. Wild animals, otherwise lawful, are forbidden during the pilgrimage.

(3) *Holy rites, i.e.,* the rites connected with pilgrimage to Makkah. This passage relates to the *heathen* pilgrims and their offerings, tolerated for a short time after the capture of Makkah.

Sacred month. See Prelim. Disc., sect. vii.

The offering. An animal devoted to sacrifice might not be captured even from an infidel. A garland on the neck of an animal indicated its sacred character. It is related in the *Tafsír-i-Raufi* that a camel was stolen from Muhammad at Madína. Some time afterwards, when on a pilgrimage, he recognised his stolen camel in a caravan on its way to Makkah; but seeing the garland on its neck, he forbade his followers taking it. This story may be apocryphal, but it illustrates the force of this law.

The malice of some, i.e., in the pilgrimage A.H. 6, when the Muslims were stopped at Hudaibaya. See Prelim. Disc., p. 89.

Assist one another, &c., in the pilgrimage. The sense is closely connected with what precedes.

ing. (4) Ye are forbidden *to eat* that which dieth of itself, and blood, and swine's flesh, and that on which the name of any besides GOD hath been invocated; and that which hath been strangled, or killed by a blow, or by a fall, or by the horns *of another beast*, and that which hath been eaten by a wild beast, except what ye shall kill *yourselves;* and that which hath been sacrificed unto idols. *It is likewise unlawful for you* to make division by casting lots with arrows. This is an impiety. On this day woe be unto those who have apostatised from their religion; therefore fear not them, but fear me. This day have I perfected your religion for you, and have completed my mercy upon you; and I have chosen for you Islám, *to be your* religion. But whosoever shall be driven

---

(4) *Ye are forbidden, &c.* See notes on chap. ii. 174.

Eaten by a wild beast, i.e., the flesh of an animal killed by a wild beast is forbidden unless it be found before life is extinct. In this case the flesh may be eaten, provided the hunter cuts its throat in the usual manner.

Sacrificed to idols. "The word also signifies certain stones which the pagan Arabs used to set up near their houses, and on which they superstitiously slew animals in honour of their gods."—*Sale, Baidháwi.*

These stones of the Ishmaelites were probably such as are referred to in Gen. xxviii. 18–22. They were the altars upon which sacrifices were offered to the idols Lát and Uzza, but which pointed to the blood which speaketh better things than the blood of Abel. It is probable that every animal slain for food was offered as a sacrifice.

Lots with arrows. See note on chap. ii. 218, and Prelim. Disc., p. 196. Three arrows were ordinarily used. On one was written *My God commands me,* on another was written *My God forbids me,* and the third was blank. If the first were drawn, the way was clear; if the second were drawn, the matter was left in abeyance for one year, when arrows were again drawn; if the blank were drawn, it was returned to the bag and another trial was made, and so on until either first or second should be drawn (*Tafsír-i-Raufi*).

On this day. "This passage, it is said, was revealed on Friday evening, being the day of the pilgrims visiting Mount Arafát the last time Muhammad visited the temple of Makkah, therefore called the pilgrimage of valediction."—*Sale.*

This day have I perfected your religion. "And therefore the commentators say that after this time no positive or negative precept was given."—*Sale.*

by necessity through hunger *to eat of what we have forbidden*, not designing to sin, surely GOD *will be* indulgent and merciful *unto him.* (5) They will ask thee what is allowed them as *lawful to eat.* Answer, Such things as are good are allowed you; and what ye shall teach animals of prey *to catch,* training them up for hunting after the manner of dogs, *and* teaching them according to the *skill* which GOD hath taught you. Eat therefore of that which they shall catch for you; and commemorate the name of GOD thereon; and fear GOD, for GOD is swift in taking an account. (6) This day are ye allowed to eat such things as are good, and the food of those to whom the scriptures were given is *also* allowed as lawful unto you; and your food is allowed as lawful unto them. And *ye are also allowed to marry* free women that are believers, and also free women of those who have received the scriptures before you, when ye shall have assigned them their dower, living chastely *with them,* neither committing fornication, nor taking *them for* concubines. Whoever shall renounce the faith, his work shall be vain, and in the next life he shall be of those who perish.

---

(5) *Commemorate the name of God thereon.* Sale says, "Either when ye let go the hound, hawk, or other animal after the game, or when ye kill it." The rule is to say *Bismillah alláho Akbar,* or simply *Bismillah,* when the dog or hawk is let go.

The requirements of these verses look as if they were either delivered on two different occasions, or they represent the same command as repeated by two different persons to those who compiled the Qurán in its present form.

(6) *The food of those to whom the Scriptures, &c.* This one passage is sufficient to refute the position of those Muslims in India who regard Christians as infidels, and forbid their co-religionists to eat and drink with them.

Free women of those who, &c. Muslims are allowed to have Christian and Jewish wives, but Muslim women may not have Christian or Jewish husbands. Such Christian women, however, may not be taken as concubines.

Muhammad did not feel himself bound by this law in the case of the Jewess Riháua, whom he took for his concubine immediately after the cruel slaughter of the Bani Quraidha; nor in the case of the Coptic Mary. This law may, however, have been delivered after these women had been taken into the Prophet's harem.

‖ (7) O true believers, when ye prepare yourselves to pray, wash your faces, and your hands unto the elbows; and rub your heads, and your feet unto the ankles; and if ye be polluted by having lain with a woman, wash yourselves *all over*. But if ye be sick, or on a journey, or any of you cometh from the privy, or *if* ye have touched women, and ye find no water, take fine clean sand, and rub your faces and your hands therewith: GOD would not put a difficulty upon you; but he desireth to purify you, and to complete his favour upon you, that ye may give thanks. (8) Remember the favour of GOD towards you, and his covenant which he hath made with you, when ye said, We have heard, and will obey. Therefore fear GOD, for GOD knoweth the innermost parts of the breasts *of men*. (9) O true believers, observe justice when ye appear as witnesses before GOD, and let not hatred towards any induce you to do wrong: *but* act justly; this will approach nearer unto piety; and fear GOD, for GOD is fully acquainted with what ye do. (10) GOD hath promised unto those who believe and do that which is right that they shall receive pardon and a great reward. (11) But they who believe not and accuse our signs of falsehood, they

---

(7) *He desireth to purify you.* This verse, as well as the chapter on purifications in the *Mishqát ul Masábih*, abundantly show that this external purity is all Islám knows of holiness. The word *holy* conveys no other idea to a Muslim's mind.

(8) *We have heard.* Sale says, "These words are the form used at the inauguration of a prince; and Muhammad here intends the oath of fidelity which his followers had taken to him at Al Aqabah." (See *Prelim Disc.*, p. 81.)

(9) *Let not hatred, &c.* According to the *Tafsír-i-Raufí* this passage has reference to those who, having once persecuted the Muslims, afterwards embraced Islám. Muslims are here exhorted to forgive all such injuries.

(11) *They . . . who accuse our signs, &c.* This is another passage showing (1) that the charge of imposture was made in Muhammad's lifetime; (2) that the language and style of the Qurán was not so striking as to convince Muhammad's contemporaries that they were inimitable; and (3) that Muhammad's only argument in reply was his usual threat.

shall be the companions of hell. (12) O true believers, remember GOD's favour towards you, when certain men designed to stretch forth their hands against you, but he restrained their hands from *hurting* you; therefore fear GOD and in GOD let the faithful trust.

 ‖ (13) GOD formerly accepted the covenant of the chil- R ⅜.

---

(12) *He restrained their hands.* "The commentators tell several stories as the occasion of this passage. One says that Muhammad and some of his followers being at Usfán (a place not far from Makkah, in the way to Madína), and performing their noon devotions, a company of idolaters who were in view repented they had not taken that opportunity of attacking them, and therefore waited till the hour of evening prayer, intending to fall upon them then; but God defeated their design by revealing *the verse of Fear.* Another relates that the Prophet going to the tribe of Quraidha (who were Jews) to levy a fine for the blood of two Muslims who had been killed by mistake by Amru Ibn Ummaya al Dhimri, they desired him to sit down and eat with them, and they would pay the fine: Muhammad complying with their request, while he was sitting they laid a design against his life, one Amru Ibn Jásh undertaking to throw a millstone upon him; but God withheld his hand, and Gabriel immediately descended to acquaint the Prophet with their treachery, upon which he rose up and went his way. A third story is, that Muhammad having hung up his arms on a tree under which he was resting himself, and his companions being dispersed some distance from him, an Arab of the desert came up to him and drew his sword, saying, 'Who hindereth me from killing thee?' to which Muhammad answered, 'God;' and Gabriel beating the sword out of the Arab's hand, Muhammad took it up, and asked him the same question, 'Who hinders me from killing thee?' the Arab replied, 'Nobody,' and immediately professed Muhammadanism. Abulfida tells the same story, with some variation of circumstances."—*Sale, Baidháwi.*

We have little reason to regard any of these stories, excepting the first, as true. They possess the marks of the improbable and the apocryphal. Nevertheless they are reproduced by all commentators and expositors of the Qurán, and are believed by all good Muslims. The passage apparently points to the *lesser pilgrimage* and events connected therewith.

(13) *Twelve leaders.* The following is the Muslim account of these twelve leaders as given by Sale on the authority of Baidháwi:—

"After the Israelites had escaped from Pharaoh, God ordered them to go against Jericho, which was then inhabited by giants,* of

---

* These giants, say the Muslims, were from 800 to 3300 yards in height; their grapes were so large it required five persons to lift a cluster, and the pomegranates were so large that five persons could get into the shell at once.

dren of Israel, and we appointed out of them twelve leaders; and GOD said, Verily I am with you: if ye observe prayer, and give alms, and believe in my apostles, and assist them, and lend unto GOD on good usury, I will surely expiate your evil *deeds* from you, and I will lead you into gardens wherein rivers flow: but he among you who disbelieveth after this, erreth from the straight path. (14) Wherefore because they have broken their covenant, we have cursed them, and hardened their hearts; they dislocate the words *of the Pentateuch* from their places, and have forgotten part of what they were admonished; and thou wilt not cease to discover deceitful practices among them, except a few of them. But forgive them, and pardon them, for GOD loveth the beneficent. (15) And from those who say, We are Christians, we have received their covenant; but they have forgotten part of what they were admonished; wherefore we have raised up enmity and hatred among them, till the day of resurrection; and GOD will *then* surely declare unto them what they have been doing. (16) O ye who have received the

---

the race of the Canaanites, promising to give it into their hands; and Moses, by the divine direction, appointed a prince or captain over each tribe to lead them in that expedition (Num. i. 4, 5); and when they came to the borders of the land of Canaan, sent the captains as spies to get information of the state of the country, enjoining them secrecy; but they, being terrified at the prodigious size and strength of the inhabitants, disheartened the people by publicly telling what they had seen, except only Caleb the son of Yafunna (Jephunneh), and Joshua the son of Nun" (Num. xiii. xiv.)

As usual, the message to the Israelites is represented as the same as that given to the Arabs by Muhammad.

Good usury. The reward of those who spent their money in the wars for the faith.

I will surely expiate. See note on chap. iii. 194. It is altogether probable that the word *expiate* was used in conformity with Jewish idiom, but certainly not in a Jewish sense.

(14) *They dislocate the words.* See note on chap. iv. 44.

But forgive them. "That is, if they repent and believe, or submit to pay tribute. Some, however, think these words are abrogated by the verse of the *Sword.*"—*Sale, Baidháwi.*

(15) *Forgotten part, i.e.,* the prophecies of the gospel concerning Muhammad as the Paraclete (*Tafsír-i-Raufí*).

Enmity and hatred. The reference is to the sectarian quarrels among Christians.

scriptures, now is our apostle come unto you, to make manifest unto you many *things* which ye concealed in the scriptures, and to pass over many *things*. (17) Now is light and a perspicuous book *of revelations* come unto you from GOD. (18) Thereby will GOD direct him who shall follow his good pleasure into the paths of peace; and shall lead them out of darkness into light by his will, and shall direct them in the right way. (19) They are infidels who say, Verily GOD is Christ the son of Mary. Say unto them, And who could obtain anything from GOD *to the contrary*, if he pleased to destroy Christ the son of Mary, and his mother, and all those who are on the earth?

---

(16) *Which ye concealed, e.g.,* "the verse of stoning adulterers (chap. iii. 23), the description of Muhammad, and Christ's prophecy of him by the name of AHMED" (chap. lxi. 6).—*Sale, Baidháwi.*

And to pass over other things. The things thus passed over were all that made Christianity a religion at all. The *additions,* made under pretence of restoring lost revelations, were distinctly Muslim in their character. How such a proceeding can be reconciled with a character for honest sincerity is beyond my ken.

(17) *Now is light . . . come unto you, i.e.,* the light of prophecy, which resided in Muhammad and all the predecessors of Muhammad up to Adam. This light was the first creation of God, and through this light all the works of God were made manifest (*Tafsir-i-Raufi*). Muhammadan mystics have little difficulty in persuading themselves in this way that Muhammad and the Qurán are divine in the sense that they are the light of God, manifesting him as the light of the sun reveals to us the orb of day with all its retinue of worlds.

The orthodox, however, take more sober views of the passage, and understand the truth of Islám as recorded in the Qurán to be all that is intended.

(19) *The infidels.* Christians are here called by the same name as that which is applied to idolaters, because their clear confession of the divine nature and attributes of Christ declares them to be guilty of this unpardonable sin of Islám. In almost all the earlier chapters of the Qurán, Christians are spoken of as "the people of the book," and the status assigned to them is far above that of either Jews or idolaters. In the latter revelations the *Nazarines* are, as here, plainly called idolaters. This inconsistency may be explained either by supposing Muhammad to have been ignorant of Christianity until a late period of his life, or by presuming that he chose to ignore them when he could, and to patronise where he could not ignore, until his pretensions as a prophet and his power as a politician had been established. We think the last to be most in accord with probability,

(20) For unto GOD *belongeth* the kingdom of heaven and earth, and whatsoever *is contained* between them; he createth what he pleaseth, and GOD is almighty. (21) The Jews and the Christians say, We are the children of GOD and his beloved. Answer, Why therefore doth he punish you for your sins? Nay, but ye are men, of those whom he hath created. He forgiveth whom he pleaseth, and punisheth whom he pleaseth; and unto GOD *belongeth* the kingdom of heaven and earth, and of what *is contained* between them both; and unto him shall *all things* return. (22) O ye who have received the scriptures, now is our apostle come unto you, declaring unto you *the true religion*, during the cessation of apostles, lest ye should say, There came unto us no bearer of good tidings, nor any warner: but now is a bearer of good tidings and a warner come unto you; for GOD is almighty.

---

and as being most easily reconciled with traditions which accredit Muhammad with a knowledge of Christianity even before he claimed to be a prophet, and which even declare his wife Khadijah to have been a Christian.

If he pleased to destroy Christ. This passage decidedly proves that whatever purpose Muhammad had in using the terms "*Word of God*," "*Spirit from God*," &c. (see chaps. ii. 86 and iii. 39), he certainly never intended to sanction the doctrine of Christ's divinity in any way.

(21) *Why . . . doth he punish you?* Compare with Heb. xii. 5–8. This verse shows that Muhammad, while using the phraseology of Christians, did not understand its import. *A son of God* seemed to him to certainly express the idea of a divine nature, hence he says, "Nay, but ye are men," &c.

(22) *The cessation of the apostles.* "The Arabic word *al fatra* signifies the intermediate space of time between two prophets, during which no new revelation or dispensation was given; as the interval between Moses and Jesus, and between Jesus and Muhammad, at the expiration of which last Muhammad pretended to be sent."—*Sale.*

The *Tafsír-i-Raufi* says there were one thousand prophets intervening successively between Moses and Jesus, but none between Jesus and Muhammad. During the whole period of 2300 years, according to Arab reckoning, between Moses and Muhammad, no prophet appeared among the children of Ishmáíl. Surely the promise was to Isaac, even on Muslim showing.

|| (23) *Call to mind* when Moses said unto his people, R $\frac{4}{8}$. O my people, remember the favour of GOD towards you, since he hath appointed prophets among you, and constituted you kings, and bestowed on you what he hath given to no *other* nation in the world. (24) O my people, enter the holy land, which GOD hath decreed you, and turn not your backs, lest ye be subverted and perish. (25) They answered, O Moses, verily there are a gigantic people in the *land;* and we will by no means enter it, until they depart thence; but if they depart thence, then will we enter *therein.* (26) And two men of those who feared GOD, unto whom GOD had been gracious, said, Enter ye upon them *suddenly by* the gate *of the city;* and when ye shall have entered the same, ye shall surely be victorious: therefore trust in GOD, if ye are true believers. (27) They replied, O Moses, we will never enter *the land* while they remain therein: go therefore thou and thy LORD

---

(23) *Kings.* There is almost certainly an anachronism here; but Muslims regard the words as a prophecy of Moses concerning kings to come, or they understand by the expression that God had "made them *kings* or *masters* of themselves by delivering them from Egyptian bondage" (*Sale*).

What he hath given, &c. Baidháwi says, "Having divided the Red Sea for you, and guided you by a cloud, and fed you with quails and manna, &c." The allusion is with more probability assigned to the *peculiar blessings* of Israel as the chosen people of God.

(24) *Holy land.* This expression, like the language of the previous verse, was received from the vocabulary of contemporary Jews or Christians. But it is here put in the mouth of Moses.

(25) *Gigantic people.* See note on ver. 13.

(26) *Two men.* Caleb and Joshua.

Enter . . . by the gate. This illustrates Muhammad's idea of the mission of the Israelites to Canaan, and of Joshua's resources in his efforts to conquer Jericho. He is confident of success through stratagem. Yet this whole caricature of the history of the rebellion of the children of Israel at Kadesh Barnea is put in the mouth of God and related as authentic story. What can account for such a phenomenon but satanic possession or wilful imposture? Certainly nothing from a Christian standpoint. The only other possible supposition is the faith of the Muslim that this is inspired history, and that everything contradictory to it is false.

and fight; for we will sit here. (28) Moses said, O LORD, surely I am not master of any except myself and my brother; therefore make a distinction between us and the ungodly people. (29) GOD answered, Verily, the *land shall be forbidden them forty years; during which time they shall wander like men astonished* on the earth; therefore be not thou solicitous for the ungodly people.

R $\frac{5}{9}$.

|| (30) Relate unto them also the history of the two sons of Adam, with truth. When they offered *their* offering, and it was accepted from one of them, and was not accepted from the other, Cain said *to his brother*, I will

---

(28) *Except myself and my brother.* Moses would seem to have forgotten Caleb and Joshua. The author of the *Tafsir-i-Raufi* conjectures that it is Aaron who is called *Lord* in ver. 27 ; but this theory is contrary to the dignity bestowed on Moses everywhere in the Qurán.

Therefore make a distinction, &c. Compare Numb. xiv. 11-20.

(29) *They shall wander.* "The commentators pretend that the Israelites, while they thus wandered in the desert, were kept within the compass of about eighteen (or, as some say, twenty-seven) miles ; and that though they travelled from morning to night, yet they constantly found themselves the next day at the place from whence they set out."—*Sale.*

(30) *Relate with . . . truth.* See note on chap. ii. 145.

The two sons of Adam, Cain and Abel ; called by Muhammadans Kábíl and Hábíl.

When they offered, &c. "The occasion of their making this offering is thus related, according to the common tradition in the East. Each of them being born with a twin sister, when they were grown up, Adam, by God's direction, ordered Cain to marry Abel's twin sister, and that Abel should marry Cain's (for it being the common opinion that marriages ought not to be had in the nearest degrees of consanguinity, since they must necessarily marry their sisters, it seemed reasonable to suppose they ought to take those of the remoter degree ; but this Cain refusing to agree to, because his own sister was the handsomest, Adam ordered them to make their offerings to God, thereby referring the dispute to his determination. The commentators say Cain's offering was a sheaf of the very worst of his corn, but Abel's a fat lamb, of the best of his flock."—*Sale, Baidháwi, Jaláluddín.*

"The offering of Abel was accepted by fire descending from heaven and consuming it, while that of Cain was untouched."—*Tafsir-i-Raufi, Tafsir-i-Husaini.*

Abel answered, &c. "This conversation between the two brothers," says Sale, "is related somewhat to the same purpose in the Jerusalem Targum and that of Jonathan ben Uzziel."

certainly kill thee. Abel answered, GOD only accepteth *the offering* of the pious;

|| (31) If thou stretchest forth thy hand against me, to NISF. slay me, I will not stretch forth my hand against thee, to slay thee; for I fear GOD, the LORD of all creatures. (32) I choose that thou shouldest bear my iniquity and thine own iniquity; and that thou become a companion of *hell* fire; for that is the reward of the unjust. (33) But his soul suffered him to slay his brother, and he slew him; wherefore he became *of the number* of those who perish. (34) And GOD sent a raven, which scratched the earth, to show him how he should hide the shame of his brother, *and* he said, Woe is me! am I unable to be like this raven,

---

(31) *I will not stretch forth my hand, &c.* Baidháwi says Abel was much stronger than Cain, and that he could easily have prevailed against him if he had chosen to fight.

(32) *A companion of hell fire.* This fierce revengeful spirit comports well with the character of the Arabian Prophet, but comes far short of the truth when applied to the brother of Cain.

(33) *He slew him.* The commentators say he did not know how to kill his brother until the devil, appearing in human form, killed in his sight a bird by laying its head on one stone and smiting it with another. Cain then went at night-time to his brother, who was sleeping with his head pillowed on a stone, and striking him on the head with a stone, slew him (*Tafsir-i-Raufi*).

(34) *A raven . . . to show him, &c.* The Jewish tradition, which makes Adam to be indebted to a raven for his knowledge as to how to dispose of the body of his murdered son, is here so distorted as actually to make God to sympathise with the murderer in his anxiety to conceal the corpse of his victim.

"Cain, having committed this fratricide, became exceedingly troubled in his mind, and carried the dead body about on his shoulders for a considerable time, not knowing where to conceal it, till it stank horridly; and then God taught him to bury it by the example of a raven, who having killed another raven in his presence, dug a pit with his claws and beak, and buried him therein."—*Sale, Baidháwi.*

The commentators say that, previous to the burial, Cain carried the body of his brother about for forty days (others say a year), ever struggling to keep off birds of prey and ravenous beasts; that his skin became black, and a voice ever shouted in his ears, "Be thou for ever in terror," and that at last he was murdered by his own son. The punishment of Cain is said to be equal to half the punishment of all the rest of mankind. His repentance was therefore in vain. See the *Tafsir-i-Raufi in loco.*

that I may hide my brother's shame? and he became *one* of those who repent. (35) Wherefore we commanded the children of Israel, that he who slayeth a soul, without having slain a soul, or committed wickedness in the earth, *shall be* as if he had slain all mankind: but he who saveth *a soul* alive, *shall be* as if he had saved the lives of all mankind. (36) Our apostles formerly came unto them, with evident *miracles;* then were many of them after this transgressors on the earth. (37) But the recompense of those who fight against GOD and his apostle, and study to act corruptly in the earth, *shall be*, that they shall be slain, or crucified, or have their hands and their feet cut off on the opposite *sides*, or be banished the land. This shall be their disgrace in this world, and in the next

---

(35) *Without having slain a soul.* From this the inference is drawn that a murderer may be slain without crime (*Abdul Qádir*).

Wickedness in the earth, "Such as idolatry or robbing on the highway."—*Sale, Baidháwi.*

All mankind. See Rodwell's note here, showing the Jewish origin of this sentiment.

(37) *The recompense, &c.* A party of eight Bedouin Arabs, having professed Islám at Madína, was appointed to guard the camels of Muhammad sent to graze at Ayr, near Madína. The Bedouins drove off the camels and wounded some herdsmen who had gone in pursuit, killing one in a barbarous manner. Muhammad, having been informed of this transaction, sent twenty horsemen in pursuit, who captured the robbers, recovering all the camels but one. In punishment Muhammad ordered the arms and legs of the eight men to be cut off, their eyes to be put out, and their trunks to be impaled until life was extinct. This horrible barbarity seems to have appeared excessive, and accordingly this verse was revealed. (See Muir's *Life of Mahomet*, vol. iv. pp. 19 and 20.) The barbarities herein sanctioned are still practised in every Muhammadan country. As to the infliction of these punishments, Sale, on the authority of Baidháwi and others, says, "The lawyers are not agreed. But the commentators suppose that they who commit murder only are to be put to death in the ordinary way; those who murder and rob too, to be crucified; those who rob without committing murder, to have their right hand and their left foot cut off; and they who assault persons and put them in fear, to be banished. It is also a doubt whether they who are crucified shall be crucified alive, or be first put to death, or whether they shall hang on the cross till they die."

world they shall suffer a grievous punishment; (38) except those who shall repent before ye prevail against them; for know that GOD *is* inclined to forgive, *and* merciful.

|| (39) O true believers, fear GOD, and earnestly desire R $\frac{6}{10}$. a near conjunction with him, and fight for his religion, that ye may be happy. (40) Moreover they who believe not, although they had whatever *is* in the earth, and as much more withal, that they might therewith redeem themselves from punishment on the day of resurrection; it shall not be accepted from them, but they shall suffer a painful punishment. (41) They shall desire to go forth from the fire, but they shall not go forth from it, and their punishment shall be permanent. (42) If a man or a woman steal, cut off their hands, in retribution for that which they have committed; *this is* an exemplary punishment *appointed* by GOD; and GOD is mighty *and* wise. (43) But whoever shall repent after his iniquity and amend,

---

(38) *Except those who shall repent.* If the offenders be unbelievers, and previous to their being forcibly seized they profess Islám, they are to be forgiven; even stolen property may not be taken from them. If they be Muslims, they are to be pardoned; stolen property being returned and the price of blood being paid in case murder have been committed. See the *Tafsír-i-Raufi in loco.*

(39) *A near conjunction.* The original word means *a helper* or *a means of accomplishing anything.* The meaning here is that believers should seek the means of near approach to God, which means, say the commentators, is obedience to his commandments.

(42) *Cut off their hands.* "But this punishment, according to the Sunnat, is not to be inflicted unless the value of the thing stolen amount to four dinars, or about forty shillings. For the first offence the criminal is to lose his right hand, which is to be cut off at the wrist; for the second offence, his left foot, at the ankle; for the third, his left hand; for the fourth, his right foot; and if he continue to offend, he shall be scourged at the discretion of the judge." *Sale, Jaláluddín.*

Savary says this law is not observed by the Turks, who use the *bastonnado* in ordinary cases, often beheading robbers of notoriety. But if so, the Turk is inconsistent with his religion, for "this is an exemplary punishment appointed of God."

(43) *But whoever shall repent.* "That is, God will not punish him for it hereafter; but his repentance does not supersede the execution of the law here, nor excuse him from making restitution. Yet,

verily GOD will be turned unto him, for GOD *is* inclined to forgive, *and* merciful. (44) Dost thou not know that the kingdom of heaven and earth is GOD's? He punisheth whom he pleaseth, and he pardoneth whom he pleaseth; for GOD is almighty. (45) O apostle, let not them grieve thee who hasten to infidelity, *either* of those who say, We believe, with their mouths, but whose hearts believe not; or of the Jews, who hearken to a lie, *and* hearken to other people; *who* come unto thee: they pervert the words *of the law* from their *true* places, *and* say, If this be brought unto you, receive it; but if it be not brought unto you, beware *of receiving aught else;* and in behalf of him whom GOD shall resolve to seduce, thou shalt not prevail with GOD at all. They whose hearts GOD shall not please to

---

according to al Sháfa'í, he shall not be punished if the party wronged forgive him before he be carried before a magistrate."—*Sale, Baidháwi.*

See above on vers. 37 and 38.

(45) See notes on chap. iv. 43-50. The passage is directed against apostates, hypocrites, and Jews.

And hearken to other people. "These words are capable of two senses, and may either mean that they attended to the lies and forgeries of their Rabbins, neglecting the remonstrances of Muhammad, or else that they came to hear Muhammad as spies only, that they might report what he said to their companions, and represent him as a liar."—*Sale, Baidháwi.*

If this be brought unto you, &c. "That is, if what Muhammad tells you agrees with Scripture, as corrupted and dislocated by us, then you may accept it as the Word of God; but if not, reject it. These words, it is said, relate to the sentence pronounced by that prophet on an adulterer and adulteress, both persons of some figure among the Jews. For they, it seems, though they referred the matter to Muhammad, yet directed the persons who carried the criminals before him, that if he ordered them to be scourged and to have their faces blackened (by way of ignominy), they should acquiesce in his determination; but in case he condemned them to be stoned, they should not. And Muhammad pronouncing the latter sentence against them, they refused to execute it, till Ibn Súriya (a Jew), who was called upon to decide the matter, acknowledged the law to be so. Whereupon they were stoned at the door of the mosque."—*Sale, Baidháwi.*

That which is forbidden, i.e., usury, which in Oriental languages is said to be *eaten.* Forbidden *meats* could only be intended providing the persons addressed here included Christians as well as Jews.

cleanse shall suffer shame in this world, and a grievous punishment in the next: who hearken to a lie, *and* eat that which is forbidden. (46) But if they come unto thee *for judgment*, either judge between them, or leave them; and if thou leave them, they shall not hurt thee at all. But if thou *undertake* to judge, judge between them with equity; for GOD loveth those who observe justice. (47) And how will they submit to thy decision, since they have the law, containing the judgment of GOD? Then will they turn their backs, after this; but those are not true believers.

|| (48) We have surely sent down the law, containing direction and light: thereby did the prophets, who professed the true religion, judge those who judaised; and

R $\frac{7}{11}$.

---

(46) *Or leave them*, *i.e.*, "take thy choice whether thou wilt determine their differences or not. Hence al Sháfa'í was of opinion that a judge was not obliged to decide causes between Jews or Christians; though if one or both of them be tributaries, or under the protection of the Muhammadans, they are obliged, this verse not regarding them. Abu Hanífa, however, thought that the magistrates were obliged to judge all cases which were submitted to them."—*Sale, Baidháwi.*

(47) *They have the law.* See note on chap. iv. 44. Sale says that "in the following passage Muhammad endeavours to answer the objections of the Jews and Christians, who insisted that they ought to be judged, the former by the law of Moses, and the latter by the gospel. He allows that the law was the proper rule of judging till the coming of Jesus Christ, after which the gospel was the rule; but pretends that both are set aside by the revelation of the Qurán, which is so far from being contradictory to either of the former, that it is more full and explicit; declaring several points which had been stifled or corrupted therein, and requiring a vigorous execution of the precepts in both, which had been too remissly observed, or rather neglected, by the latter professors of those religions."

On the doctrine of abrogation alluded to by Sale, see note on chap. ii. 105. The statements of this passage alike contradict the idea that Muhammad regarded the Christian or Jewish Scriptures as *corrupted* in any way whatever, and that of the *abrogation* of those Scriptures; for, if corrupted, how could he say *the Jews of Madína* "*have the law, containing the judgment of God*"? And, if abrogated, how could he say in ver. 49, "We have therein (in the *law* (Tauret), see ver. 48) commanded them," &c., quoting almost literally a portion of the law of Exod. xxi. 23–27, and adding, "Whoso judgeth not according to *what God hath revealed*, they are unjust and infidels"?

(48) *The true religion*, *i.e.*, Islám, the one true religion of all ages of the world. See note on chap. ii. 136.

the doctors and priests *also judged* by the book of GOD, which had been committed to their custody; and they were witnesses thereof. Therefore fear not men, but fear me; neither sell my signs for a small price. And whoso judgeth not according to what GOD hath revealed, they are infidels. (49) We have therein commanded them, that they *should give* life for life, and eye for eye, and nose for nose, and ear for ear, and tooth for tooth; and *that* wounds *should also be punished by* retaliation: but whoever should remit it as alms, it *should be accepted as* an atonement for him. And whoso judgeth not according to what GOD hath revealed, they are unjust. (50) We also caused Jesus the son of Mary to follow the footsteps of *the prophets*, confirming the law which *was sent down* before him;

Committed to their custody; and ... witnesses. The only fair interpretation of this passage is that the Scriptures of the Jews were *preserved from all corruption* by the jealous watchfulness of those "doctors and priests" who had been appointed as the custodians of the precious treasure. These keepers of the LAW are the witnesses to the character of that which has been committed to their charge. ("They are vigilant to prevent any corruption therein."—*Sale.*) Wherefore he exhorts the *Jews whom he is here addressing*, "Therefore, O Jews, fear not men, but fear me (*i.e.*, God); neither sell my signs for a small price," *i.e.*, by perverting the meaning of your Scriptures, as in ver. 45.

(49) Compare with Exod. xxi. 23-27. Muhammad could not have had the Scriptures before him, else he would have quoted more fully.

An atonement. This expression conveys here the Mosaic idea of *satisfaction,* but does not seem to have been used by Muhammad in the Bible sense, the meaning being that when the injured person forgave the transgressor, no punishment should be inflicted by others on this account. The popular belief among Muslims agrees with this, viz., that God cannot forgive an offence against a man or beast unless the offender first be pardoned by those whom he has injured. See also note on chap. iii. 194.

This passage, as well as chap. xv. 35, is said to be abrogated by chap. ii. 178. That passage certainly professes to relax the law of retaliation prescribed by Moses. If so, there appears to be a contradiction between these two passages which cannot fairly be reconciled by the convenient doctrine of abrogation, for in this case the passage abrogated was revealed several years after the passage which abrogates it.

(50) *Confirming also the law.* The testimony to the law is the gospel of Jesus, and the testimony confirming both is the Qurán.

and we gave him the gospel, containing direction and light; confirming also the light which *was given* before it, and a direction and admonition unto those who fear God: (51) that they who have received the gospel might judge according to what GOD hath revealed therein: and whoso judgeth not according to what GOD hath revealed, they are transgressors. (52) We have also sent down unto thee the book *of the Qurán* with truth, confirming that scripture which *was revealed* before it; and preserving the same safe *from corruption.* Judge therefore between them according to that which GOD hath revealed; and follow not their desires *by swerving* from the truth which hath come unto thee. Unto every one of you have we given a law and an open path; (53) and if GOD had pleased, he had surely made you one people; but *he hath thought fit to give you different laws*, that he might try you in that which he hath given you *respectively.* Therefore strive to excel each other in good works: unto GOD shall ye all return, and *then* will he declare unto you that concerning

---

See v. 52. Portions may be abrogated, and so cease to be of binding force to whom they are so abrogated, but all remains *true*. The eternal truths of God as to his own nature and attributes, his moral law, historical fact, &c., cannot be abrogated (see chap. ii. 105 note), and therefore the Qurán again points the way to its own refutation.

(52) See notes on chaps. ii. 75-78; iii. 77; iv. 44.

(53) *One people, i.e.*, "He had given you the same laws, which should have continued in force through all ages, without being abolished or changed by new dispensations; or he could have forced you all to embrace the Muhammadan religion."—*Sale, Baidháwi.*

This passage seems to have been intended to reconcile all parties to Islám, notwithstanding its differences when compared with Judaism and Christianity. These were intended as a trial of faith. But, in accordance with the teaching of the preceding verses, the claim should have been that *God had made them one people*, possessing the same religion and acknowledging the same divine messengers, and that that wherein they differed was due to *their own sin and unbelief*, and not to God's will. The fact of irreconcilable differences between the "people of the book" and himself seems to have forced itself into the consciousness of the oracle of Islám, and made consistency in the statement of prophetic claims and the facts of experience an impossibility. See also Arnold's *Islám and Christianity*, pp. 172 and 174.

which ye have disagreed. (54) Wherefore *do thou, O prophet,* judge between them according to that which GOD hath revealed, and follow not their desires; but beware of them, lest they cause thee to err from part of those *precepts* which GOD hath sent down unto thee; and if they turn back, know that GOD is pleased to punish them for some of their crimes; for a great number of men are transgressors. (55) Do they therefore desire the judgment of *the time of* ignorance? but who is better than GOD, to judge between people who reason aright?

‖ (56) O true believers, take not the Jews or Christians for *your* friends; they are friends the one to the other; but whoso among you taketh them for *his* friends, he *is* surely *one* of them: verily GOD directeth not unjust people. (57) Thou shalt see those in whose hearts there is an infirmity, to hasten unto them, saying, We fear lest

---

(54) *Beware of these.* "It is related that certain of the Jewish priests came to Muhammad with a design to entrap him; and having first represented to him that if they acknowledged him for a prophet, the rest of the Jews would certainly follow their example, made this proposal—that if he would give judgment for them in a controversy of moment which they pretended to have with their own people, and which was agreed to be referred to his decision, they would believe him; but this Muhammad absolutely refused to comply with."—*Sale, Baidháwi.*

This story of the commentators looks very like the one given in note on ver. 45. That the passage is a reply to some effort on the part of the Jews to tempt Muhammad is clear enough. The following verse points to some law abolishing the practices of the heathen Arabs as the point of attack. The story of Baidháwi in the note in ver. 45, if true, would sufficiently explain the character of the Jewish proposal.

(56) *Take not Jews and Christians for your friends.* See note on chap. iii. 118. The statement that Jews and Christians "*are friends one of another*" is another slip of the pen that recorded the history of the Qurán. The spirit of hatred and contempt inculcated here is entirely inconsistent with the teaching of ver. 53. Yet this is the spirit of Islám as it now is. Religious toleration in Muhammadan countries is the toleration of contempt.

(57) *We fear, &c.* "These were the words of Ibn Ubbai, who, when Obádah Ibn al Sámat publicly renounced the friendship of the infidels, and professed that he took God and his Apostle for his

some adversity befall us; but it is easy for GOD to give victory, or a command from him, that they may repent of that which they concealed in their minds. (58) And they who believe will say, Are these *the men* who have sworn by GOD, with a most firm oath, that they surely *held* with you? their works are become vain, and they are of those who perish. (59) O true believers, whoever of you apostatiseth from his religion, GOD will certainly bring *other* people *to supply his place*, whom he will love,

---

patrons, said that he was a man apprehensive of the fickleness of fortune, and therefore would not throw off his old friends, who might be of service to him hereafter."—*Sale, Baidháwi.*

A command "to extirpate and banish the Jews, or to detect and punish the hypocrites."—*Sale.*

This verse and the one following refer to the Jews of the tribes of Nadhír and Quraidha.

(59) *Whoever of you apostatiseth, &c.* "This is one of those accidents which it is pretended were foretold by the Qurán long before they came to pass. For in the latter days of Muhammad, and after his death, considerable numbers of the Arabs quitted his religion and returned to Paganism, Judaism, or Christianity. Al Baidháwi reckons them up in the following order:—1. Three companies of Banu Mudlaj, seduced by Dhu'lhamár al Aswad al Ansí, who set up for a prophet in Yaman, and grew very powerful there. 2. Banu Hunaifah, who followed the famous false prophet Musailama. 3. Banu Assad, who acknowledged Tulaiha Ibn Khuwailad, another pretender to divine revelation, for their prophet. All these fell off in Muhammad's lifetime. The following, except only the last, apostatised in the reign of Abu Baqr. 4. Certain of the tribe of Fizárah, headed by Uyaima Ibn Husáin. 5. Some of the tribe of Ghatfán, whose leader was Qurrah Ibn Salmah. 6. Banu Sulaim, who followed al Fahjáah Ibn Abd Yalíl. 7. Banu Yarbú, whose captain was Málik Ibn Nuwairah Ibn Qais. 8. Part of the tribe of Tamín, the proselytes of Sajáj the daughter of al Mundhár, who gave herself out for a prophetess. 9. The tribe of Kindah, led by al Asháth Ibn Qais. 10. Banu Baqr Ibn al Wayil in the province of Bahrain, headed by al Hutam Ibn Zaid. And 11. Some of the tribes of Ghassán, who, with their prince Jabálah Ibn al Ayshám, renounced Muhammadanism in the time of Omar, and returned to their former profession of Christianity.

"But as to the persons who fulfilled the other part of this prophecy, by supplying the loss of so many renegades, the commentators are not agreed. Some will have them to be the inhabitants of Yaman, and others the Persians; the authority of Muhammad himself being vouched for both opinions. Others, however, suppose them to be two thousand of the tribe of al Nakhá (who dwelt in Yaman), five

CHAP. V.]   (140)   [SIPARA VI.

and who will love him; *who shall be* humble towards the believers, *but* severe to the unbelievers; they shall fight for the religion of GOD, and shall not fear the obloquy of the detractor. This *is* the bounty of GOD; he bestoweth it on whom he pleaseth: GOD *is* extensive *and* wise. (60) Verily your protector is GOD, and his apostle, and those who believe, who observe the stated times of prayer, and give alms, and who bow down *to worship.* (61) And whoso taketh GOD, and his apostle, and the believers for his friends, *they are* the party of GOD, *and* they *shall be* victorious.

R $\frac{9}{13}$

‖ (62) O true believers, take not such of those to whom the scriptures were delivered before you, or of the infidels, for your friends, who make a laughing-stock and a jest of your religion; but fear GOD, if ye be true believers; (63) *nor those who,* when ye call to prayer, make a laughing-stock and a jest of it; this *they do* because they are people who do not understand. (64) Say, O ye who have received the scriptures, do ye reject us *for any other reason* than because we believe in GOD, and that *revelation* which

---

thousand of those of Kindah and Bajílah, and three thousand of unknown descent, who were present at the famous battle of Kadisia, fought in the Khalífat of Omar, and which put an end to the Persian empire."—*Sale.*

For an account of the pretenders who rose up against Muhammad towards the end of his lifetime, see Muir's *Life of Mahomet,* vol. iv. chap. xxxii.

(60) *Stated times of prayer, &c.* See note, chap. ii. 42.

(62) *Who makes . . . a jest of your religion, i.e.,* certain Jews who mocked the Muslims when at prayer (*Tafsír-i-Raufi*). Baidhawi gives the following story as translated by Sale :—" These words were added on occasion of a certain Christian who, hearing the *Muadhdhin,* or crier, in calling to prayers, repeat this part of the usual form, ' I profess that Muhammad is the apostle of God,' said aloud, 'May God burn the liar;' but a few nights after his own house was accidentally set on fire by a servant, and himself and his family perished in the flames."

(64) The Jews and Christians are here again told that a profession of Islám is consistent with their own Scriptures. The passage belongs to a period before Muhammad had broken with Jews and Christians.

hath been sent down unto us, and that which was formerly sent down, and for that the greater part of you are transgressors? (65) Say, Shall I denounce unto you a worse *thing* than this, *as to* the reward *which ye are to expect* with GOD? He whom GOD hath cursed, and with whom he hath been angry, having changed *some* of them into apes and swine, and *who* worship Taghut, they *are* in the worse condition, and err more *widely* from the straightness of the path. (66) When they came unto you, they said, We believe: yet they entered *into your company* with infidelity, and went forth *from you* with the same; but GOD well knew what they concealed. (67) Thou shalt see many of them hastening unto iniquity and malice, and to eat things forbidden; and woe *unto them for* what they have done. (68) Unless *their* doctors and priests forbid them uttering wickedness and eating things forbidden, woe *unto them for* what they shall have committed. (69) The Jews say, The hand of GOD is tied up. Their hands shall be tied up, and they shall be cursed for that which they have said. Nay, his hands are both stretched forth; he bestoweth as he pleaseth: that which hath been sent down unto thee from thy LORD shall increase the transgression and infidelity of many of them; and we have put enmity and hatred between them, until the day of resurrection. So often as they shall kindle a fire for war GOD shall extinguish it; and they shall set their minds to act corruptly in the earth, but GOD loveth

---

(65) *Having changed ... them into apes.* See note on chap. ii. 64.

(67) *Things forbidden.* See notes on ver. 4.

(69) *The hand of God is tied up.* "That is, he is become niggardly and close-fisted. These were the words of Phineas, Ibn Azúra (another indecent expression of whom, almost to the same purpose, is mentioned elsewhere), when the Jews were much impoverished by a dearth which the commentators will have to be a judgment on them for their rejecting of Muhammad; and the other Jews who heard him, instead of reproving him, expressed their approbation of what he had said."—*Sale, Baidháwi.*

Their hands shall be tied up, i.e., they shall appear in the judg-

not the corrupt doers. (70) Moreover, if they who have received the scriptures believe and fear *God*, we will surely expiate their sins from them, and we will lead them into gardens of pleasure; and if they observe the law, and the gospel, and *the other scriptures* which have been sent down unto them from their LORD, they shall

---

ment with their hands tied up to their necks. See Prelim. Disc., p. 144.

That which hath been sent down, &c. This statement is put in the form of a prophecy, though the fulfilment had taken place years before the oracle spake. There is, however, underlying this statement, the prophetic claim of Muhammad still firmly maintained at this late period of his life. This claim has not changed its form. He still places himself in the catalogue of true prophets, and his religion is still presented as the one only true religion, the rejection of which by the Jews adds to their transgression, as did their rejection of Jesus.

God shall extinguish it, "Either by raising feuds and quarrels among themselves, or by granting the victory to the Muslims. Al Baidháwi adds, that on the Jews neglecting the true observance of their law, corrupting their religion, God had successively delivered them into the hands, first of Bakht Nasr or Nebuchadnezzar, then of Titus the Roman, and afterwards of the Persians, and has now at last subjected them to the Muhammadans."—*Sale.*

(70) *We will surely expiate their sins.* The word translated *expiate* is the same as that used above (ver. 49) and in chap. iii. 194 (see notes). The meaning attached to it here is simply that of *removal* or *taking away.*

And . . . which hath been sent down, &c. Sale fills in the ellipsis by supplying the words, "the other scriptures." But this is hardly correct. The expression here is certainly the same in import as that of the preceding verse, where the Qurán is undoubtedly meant. The meaning, then, is that those Jews and Christians, who, while holding on to their own Scriptures, believe *also in the Qurán*, shall be blessed in both heaven and earth, "from above them and from under their feet." The inference would therefore seem to follow that *every true Muslim must accept the Old and New Testament Scriptures, along with the Qurán, as the Word of God.* The doctrine of abrogation can have no force here, for this Sura was the last revealed, and therefore its requirements, while they may abrogate passages in the earlier chapters, can by no means be abrogated. Of course, practically no Muslim does truly accept the former Scriptures along with the Qurán, nor indeed can he be blamed for failing to do the impossible, but it is of great importance that he should know what he is here required to do. There is no more manifest display of Muhammad's ignorance of the true teaching of the former Scriptures than this; no more violent contradiction of the plainest instincts of common sense.

surely eat *of good things* both from above them and from under their feet. Among them there are people who act uprightly; but how evil is that which many of them do work!

‖ (71) O apostle, publish *the whole of* that which hath been sent down unto thee from thy LORD; for if thou do not, thou dost not *in effect* publish any part thereof: and GOD will defend thee against *wicked* men; for GOD directeth not the unbelieving people. (72) Say, O ye who have received the scriptures, ye are not *grounded* on anything, until ye observe the law and the gospel and that which hath been sent down unto you from your LORD. That

R $\frac{19}{14}$.

---

(71) *Publish the whole, &c.* "That is, if they do not complete the publication of all thy revelations without exception, thou dost not answer the end for which they were revealed; because the concealing of any part renders the system of religion which God has thought fit to publish to mankind by thy ministry lame and imperfect."— *Sale, Baidháwi.*

This is another mark indicating that this chapter was the last of the revelations of the Qurán.

God will defend thee. "Until this verse was revealed, Muhammad entertained a guard of armed men for his security; but on receiving this assurance of God's protection, he immediately dismissed them." —*Sale, Baidháwi.*

(72) This verse, by implication, condemns the practices of every Muslim. See notes on vers. 69 and 70. The purpose of the revelation was, however, to persuade the *Jews and Christians* to embrace Islám. To quote this passage in proof of Muhammad's sincerity is therefore really a begging of the question. Can his apologists show us a single passage *requiring* Arab or Gentile Muslims to believe the Scriptures of the Old and New Testament in addition to the Qurán, as necessary to salvation? So far as I know, *such requirement is purely*, but, as we admit, justly, *inferential*, nevertheless there is no reason to believe Muhammad intended any such inference to be drawn. His great object was to maintain his prophetic claim, and if possible to win over to his side the Jews, Christians, and Sabians. In his anxiety to accomplish this, he made statements, like that of the passage under consideration, which implied more than he intended to teach. Certainly the universal faith of Muslims for thirteen centuries shows what Muhammad's real teaching was. None such have ever felt bound to believe the doctrines of the Jewish and Christian Scriptures, except in the sense that all such are conserved by the Qurán and to be found in it. The statement, twice repeated, that "that which hath been sent down unto thee from thy Lord will surely increase the transgression and infidelity of many of them,"

which hath been sent down unto thee from thy LORD will surely increase the transgression and infidelity of many of them: but be not thou solicitous for the unbelieving people. (73) Verily, they who believe, and those who Judaise, and the Sabians, and the Christians, whoever *of them* believeth in GOD and the last day, and doth that which is right, *there shall come* no fear on them, neither shall they be grieved. (74) We formerly accepted the covenant of the children of Israel, and sent apostles unto them. So often as an apostle came unto them with that which their souls desired not, they accused some of them of imposture, and some of them they killed: (75) And they imagined that there should be no punishment *for those crimes*, and they became blind, and deaf. Then was GOD turned unto them; afterwards many of them *again* became blind and deaf; but GOD saw what they did. (76) They are surely infidels who say, Verily GOD is Christ the Son of Mary; since Christ said, O children of Israel, serve GOD, my LORD and your LORD. Whoever shall give a companion unto GOD, GOD shall exclude him from paradise, and his habitation shall be *hell* fire; and the ungodly shall have none to help them. (77) They are certainly infidels who say, GOD is the third of three; for there is no GOD besides one GOD; and if they refrain not from what they say, a painful torment shall surely be inflicted on such of them as are unbelievers. (78) Will

---

creates in the mind of the thoughtful reader a conviction that Muhammad *knew* something at least of the irreconcilable differences between the doctrines of the Qurán and those of the Bible, and that therefore the Jews and Christians would not believe in him or his Qurán.

(73) See note on chap. ii. 61.
(74) *They accused . . . of imposture.* Chap. iii. 185, note.
(75) *Because blind and deaf.* "Shutting their eyes and ears against conviction and the remonstrances of the law, as when they worshipped the calf."—*Sale.*
(76) See notes on ver. 19 above. The teaching of Jesus, according to this verse, was identical with that of Muhammad.
(77) *God . . . the third of three.* See notes on chap. iv. 169. The *Tafsir-i-Raufi* says the Marcusians believed in the Trinity of God, Mary, and Jesus, but in this the communicator is mistaken.

they not therefore be turned unto GOD and ask pardon of him, since GOD is gracious *and* merciful? (79) Christ the son of Mary is no more than an apostle; *other* apostles have preceded him; and his mother was a woman of veracity: they *both* ate food. Behold, how we declare unto them the signs *of God's unity;* and then behold how they turn aside *from the truth.* (80) Say *unto them,* Will ye worship, besides GOD, that which can cause you neither harm nor profit? GOD *is* he who heareth *and* seeth. (81) Say, O ye who have received the scriptures, exceed not *the just bounds* in your religion *by speaking* beside the truth; neither follow the desires of people who have heretofore erred, and who have seduced many, and have gone astray from the straight path.

|| (82) Those among the children of Israel who believed R $\frac{11}{1}$. not were cursed by the tongue of David, and of Jesus the son of Mary. This *befell them* because they were rebellious and transgressed: they forbade not one another the wickedness which they committed; and woe *unto them for* what they committed. (83) Thou shalt see many of them take for their friends those who believe not. Woe *unto them* for what their souls have sent before them, for that GOD is incensed against them, and they shall remain in torment *for ever.* (84) But if they had believed in God

---

(79) Compare chap. iii. 39.
A woman of veracity, i.e., "never pretending to partake of the divine nature, or to be the mother of God." — *Sale, Julâluddín.* Compare note on chap. iv. 169.
(81) *Exceed not, &c.* See chap. iv. note 169.
Who have ... erred. "Their prelates and predecessors, who erred in ascribing divinity to Christ before the mission of Muhammad." — *Sale, Baidhâwi.*
(82) *Cursed ... by Jesus.* See note, chap. ii. 64. The curse said to have been pronounced by Jesus against the Jews probably has reference to his prophetic denunciations and warnings in general, especially his prophecy concerning the destruction of Jerusalem and the fall of the Jewish nationality. The *woes* of this passage may have been suggested by the woes of our Lord against the Scribes, Pharisees, and hypocrites.
(83) *What their souls have sent before them.* See chap. ii. 94.

and the prophet, and that which hath been revealed unto him, they had not taken them for *their* friends; but many of them are evil-doers. (85) Thou shalt surely find the most violent of *all* men in enmity against the true believers *to be* the Jews and the idolaters; and thou shalt surely find those among them *to be* the most inclinable to *entertain* friendship for the true believers who say, We are Christians. This *cometh to pass* because there are priests and monks among them, and because they are not elated with pride.

SEVENTH SIPARA.

|| (86) And when they hear that which hath been sent down to the apostle *read unto them*, thou shalt see their

---

(85) This revelation must be relegated to a period earlier than is usually assigned to the verses of this chapter. The bitter enmity attributed to the Jews points to a period succeeding A.H. 3, while the friendly feeling shown towards Christians points to a time preceding A.H. 8, for in A.H. 9 Muhammad contemptuously cast aside both Jews and Christians. The mention of "the Jews and the idolaters" together may refer to a period near to the end of A.H. 4 or the beginning of A.H. 5, when the Jews, owing to the expulsion of the Bani Nadhír, began to show their readiness to help the Quraish against the common enemy.

The kindliness attributed to the Christians, who are here said to call themselves *Nazarenes*, was due (1) to the friendly treatment Muhammad had received at their hands during his journeys to Syria in the early years of his life, and (2) to the kindness shown by the African Najáshi towards the Muslim exiles from Makkah.

Priests and monks. The original words are *qissísina wa ruhbánan.* They are translated by Abdul Qádir *well-read and worshippers;* in the Persian translation, *wise and sitters-in-a-corner* (Dervishes). All English translators follow Geiger, who derives both words from Syriac terms, and ascribes to them the meaning of the text.

The principles of forbearance and love, inculcated by the Lord Jesus, and still manifested in some degree by the corrupt Churches of Muhammad's time, had impressed his mind favourably. It is probable that his admiration was due especially to the fact that they offered little or no opposition to his prophetic claims. Some of them seem to have become Muslims (see next verse). On the story of Muhammad's intercourse with the monk Sergius or Bahaira, see chap. x. 17, note.

(86) *When they hear, &c.* The following stories, invented by the Muslims to illustrate this passage, are related by Sale on the authority of Baidháwi and Abulfida :—"The persons directly intended in this passage were either Asháma, king of Ethiopia, and several bishops and priests, who, being assembled for that purpose, heard Jaafar Ibn Abi

eyes overflow with tears because of the truth which they perceive *therein,* saying, O LORD, we believe; write us down therefore with those who bear witness *to the truth.* (87) And what *should hinder* us from believing in GOD and the truth which hath come unto us, and from earnestly desiring that our LORD would introduce us *into paradise* with the righteous people? (88) Therefore hath GOD rewarded them, for what they have said, with gardens through which rivers flow; they shall continue therein *forever;* and this is the reward of the righteous. But they who believe not, and accuse our signs of falsehood, they *shall be* the companions of hell.

|| (89) O true believers, forbid not the good things which R $\frac{12}{2}$.

Tálib, who fled to that country in the first flight, read the 29th and 30th, and afterwards the 18th and 19th chapters of the Qurán; on hearing of which the king and the rest of the company burst into tears and confessed what was delivered therein to be conformable to truth; that prince himself, in particular, becoming a proselyte to Muhammadanism: or else thirty, or as others say seventy, persons sent ambassadors to Muhammad by the same king of Ethiopia, to whom the prophet himself read the 36th chapter, entitled Y.S. Whereupon they began to weep, saying, 'How like is this to that which was revealed unto Jesus!' and immediately professed themselves Muslims."

The point of this revelation is that Christians hearing the Qurán at once recognised it as the word of God, and that its teachings were *in perfect accord* with those of Jesus, and that they were thereby persuaded to accept Islám. The tears shed were those of joy.

This passage therefore implies that these converts had the Christian Scriptures in their possession, that they were acquainted with their teaching, and that they, by comparing them with the Qurán, at once recognised Muhammad as the prophet of God The copies of their Scriptures were genuine, and if, as Muslims assert, the true gospel be no longer in existence, we may fairly ask why Muslims allowed them to become corrupt, seeing they had equal responsibility in the preserving of them? and further, we may challenge them to prove that the copies in possession of the early converts of Islám and their Christian contemporaries ever were corrupted.

(89) *Forbid not the good things.* "These words were revealed when certain of Muhammad's companions agreed to oblige themselves to continual fasting and watching, and to abstain from women, eating flesh, sleeping on beds, and other lawful enjoyments of life, in imitation of some self-denying Christians; but this the Prophet disapproved, declaring that he would have no *monks* in his religion."
—*Sale, Jaláluddín.*

GOD hath allowed you; but transgress not, for GOD loveth not the transgressors. (90) And eat of what GOD hath given you for food, *that which is* lawful *and* good: and fear GOD, in whom ye believe. (91) GOD will not punish you for an inconsiderate word in your oaths; but he will punish you for what ye solemnly swear *with deliberation.* And the expiation of such *an oath shall be* the feeding of ten poor men with such moderate *food* as ye feed your own families withal; or to clothe them; or to free the neck *of a true believer from captivity:* but he who shall not find *wherewith to perform one of these three things* shall fast three days. This is the expiation of your oaths, when ye swear *inadvertently.* Therefore keep your oaths. Thus GOD declareth unto you his signs, that ye may give thanks. (92) O true believers, surely wine, and lots, and images, and divining arrows *are* an abomination of the work of Satan; therefore avoid them that ye may prosper. (93) Satan seeketh to sow dissension and hatred among you by means of wine and lots, and to divert you from

---

However, in ver. 85, these *priests and monks* are the special objects of Muhammad's praise. The passage, according to Abdul Qádir and the *Tafsir-i-Raufi*, has a general reference, and teaches that there is no merit in works of supererogation.

(91) *An inconsiderate word.* See note on chap. ii. 225. Perjury, according to the Imáms Azim and Sháfa'i, is swearing deliberately to that which is *at the time* thought to be false by the person swearing. They therefore classify all thoughtless oaths used in conversation or *mistakes* made under oath under the head of "inconsiderate words." The passage so understood contradicts the doctrine of Jesus.

Inadvertently. This word should not have been introduced by the translator. The inadvertent oaths require no expiation. On the word *expiation* see chap. iii. 194.

(92) See notes on chap. ii. 218 and chap. iv. 42.

(93) *Satan seeketh to sow dissension, &c.* We here learn the real reason for prohibiting the practices of gambling and drinking—a reason, utilitarian though it be, yet sufficient. This law of Islám, considered by itself, reflects great glory on Muhammad and his religion; yet, regarded as a part of the whole system of Islám, it appears to great disadvantage. It is seen to be a purely political measure, based on no solid groundwork of moral principle, and inconsistent with much that is permitted by Islám. The same principle of utility would have led to the *distinct prohibition* of all intoxicating drugs and of polygamy.

remembering GOD and from prayer: will ye not therefore abstain *from them?* Obey GOD and obey the apostle, and take heed *to yourselves:* but if ye turn back, know that the duty of our apostle is only to preach publicly. (94) In those who believe and do good works, it is no sin that they have tasted *wine or gaming before they were forbidden;* if they fear *God,* and believe, and do good works, and *shall for the future* fear *God,* and believe, and *shall persevere to* fear *him* and *to* do good; for GOD loveth those who do good.

|| (95) O true believers, GOD will surely prove you in R $\frac{13}{3}$. *offering you plenty of* game, which ye may take with your hands or your lances, that GOD may know who feareth him in secret; but whoever transgresseth after this shall suffer a grievous punishment. (96) O true believers, kill no game while ye are on pilgrimage; whosoever among

---

The duty of our apostle, &c. See Prelim. Disc., p. 83. This passage looks very like a fragment of a Makkan chapter.

(94) *If they fear, &c.* "The commentators endeavour to excuse the tautology of this passage by supposing the threefold repetition of *fearing* and *believing* refers either to the three parts of time, past, present, and future, or to the threefold duty of man, towards God, himself, and his neighbour, &c."—*Sale, Baidháwi.*

(95) *God will prove you.* "This temptation or trial was at al Hudaibiya, where Muhammad's men, who had attended him thither with an intent to perform a pilgrimage to the Kaabah, and had initiated themselves with the usual rights, were surrounded by so great a number of birds and beasts, that they impeded their march; from which unusual accident some of them concluded that God had allowed them to be taken; but this passage was to convince them of the contrary."—*Sale, Baidháwi, Jaláluddín.*

(96) *On pilgrimage, i.e.,* while ye are *muhrims. Muhrims* are those Muslims who have put on the *ihrám* or peculiar dress donned on entering the sacred precincts of Makkah to indicate that they are now on the way to the sacred Kaabah. The law forbidding hunting was established in accordance with the peaceful character of the sacred places within the boundaries called *Haram.* Certain hurtful animals might be killed, but this was also in accord with the law which permitted Muslims to fight infidels within the sacred months, provided they did so in self-defence. See chap. ii. 210.

Domestic animals. "That is, he shall bring an offering to the temple of Makkah, to be slain there and distributed among the poor, of some domestic or tame animal, equal in value to what he shall have killed; as a sheep, for example, in lieu of an antelope; a

you shall kill any designedly shall restore the like of what he shall have killed in domestic animals, according to the determination of two just persons among you, to be brought as an offering to the Kaabah; or in atonement thereof shall feed the poor; or instead thereof shall fast, that he may taste the heinousness of his deed. GOD hath forgiven what is past, but whoever returneth *to transgress,* GOD will take vengeance on him; for GOD is mighty *and* able to avenge. (97) It is lawful for you to fish in the sea, and to eat *what ye shall catch,* as a provision for you and for those who travel; but it is unlawful for you to hunt by land while ye are performing the rights of pilgrimage; therefore fear GOD, before whom ye shall be assembled *at the last day.* (98) GOD hath appointed the Kaabah, the holy house, an establishment for mankind;

---

pigeon for a partridge, &c. And of this value two prudent persons were to be judges. If the offender was not able to do this, he was to give a certain quantity of food to one or more poor men; or if he could not afford that, to fast a proportionable number of days."— *Sale, Jalâluddín, Abdul Qâdir.*

That ye may taste, &c. We see here again the idea attached to *atonement* in the Qurán. It is not to free from condemnation by vicarious suffering, but is in its nature a *punishment,* and intended as a warning to transgressors.

(97) *Lawful . . . to fish.* This law has reference to pilgrimage, though of general application. The commentators understand fish found in all bodies of water, whether fountains, rivulets, rivers, or ponds, and lakes, as well as the sea. They differ in applying the law to amphibious creatures.

Unlawful . . . to hunt, i.e., during pilgrimage, after the *ihrám* has once been put on. See notes on 95.

(98) *The Kaabah.* See notes on chap. ii. 125 and 189.

An establishment, i.e., "the place where the practice of their religious ceremonies is chiefly established; where those who are under any apprehension of danger may find a sure *asylum,* and the merchant certain gain, &c."—*Sale, Jalâluddín.*

Sacred month. "Baidhâwi understands this to be the month of Dhu'l Hajja, wherein the ceremonies of the pilgrimage are performed; but Jalâluddín supposes all the four sacred months are here intended. See Prelim. Disc., sect. vii."—*Sale.*

Ornaments. See note on ver. 3.

That ye might know, &c. How the observance of the rites of pilgrimage can convince any one of God's omniscience is enough to puzzle the clearest-headed Muslim.

and *hath ordained* the sacred month, and the offering, and the ornaments hung *thereon*. This *hath he done* that ye might know that GOD knoweth whatsoever *is* in heaven and on earth, and that GOD is omniscient. Know that GOD is severe in punishing, and that GOD *is also* ready to forgive, *and* merciful. (99) The duty of our apostle is to preach only; and GOD knoweth that which ye discover, and that which ye conceal. (100) Say, Evil and good shall not be equally esteemed of, though the abundance of evil pleaseth thee; therefore fear GOD, O ye of understanding, that ye may be happy.

|| (101) O true believers, inquire not concerning things R $\frac{14}{4}$. which, if they be declared unto you, may give you pain; but if ye ask concerning them when the Qurán is sent down, they will be declared unto you: GOD pardoneth *you as to* these matters; for GOD is ready to forgive, *and* gracious. (102) People who have been before you formerly inquired concerning them; and afterwards disbelieved therein. GOD hath not ordained *anything* concerning Bahaira, nor Sáïba, nor Wasíla, nor Hámi; but the

---

(99) *The duty of our apostle.* See note on ver. 93.

(101) *Inquire not, &c.* "The Arabs continually teasing their Prophet with questions, which probably he was not always prepared to answer, they are here ordered to wait till God should think fit to declare his pleasure by some farther revelation: and to abate their curiosity, they are told, at the same time, that very likely the answers would not be agreeable to their inclinations. Al Baidháwi says, that when the pilgrimage was first commanded, Suráka Ibn Málik asked Muhammad whether they were obliged to perform it every year. To this question the Prophet at first turned a deaf ear; but being asked it a second and a third time, he at last said, 'No; but if I had said yes, it would have become a duty, and if it were a duty, ye would not be able to perform it; therefore give me no trouble as to things wherein I give you none:' whereupon this passage was revealed."—*Sale.*

(102) *Bahaira . . . Hámi.* "These were the names given by the pagan Arabs to certain camels or sheep which were turned loose to feed, and exempted from common services in some particular cases, having their ears slit, or some other mark that they might be known; and this they did in honour of their gods (Prelim. Disc., p. 199). Which superstitions are here declared to be no ordinances of God, but the inventions of foolish men."—*Sale.*

CHAP. V.]   (152)   [SIPARA VII.

unbelievers have invented a lie against GOD: and the greater part of them do not understand. (103) And when it was said unto them, Come unto that which GOD hath revealed, and to the apostle; they answered, That *religion* which we found our fathers *to follow* is sufficient for us. What, though their fathers knew nothing and were not *rightly* directed? (104) O true believers, take care of your souls! He who erreth shall not hurt you while ye are *rightly* directed: unto GOD shall ye all return, and he will tell you that which ye have done. (105) O true believers, let witnesses be taken between you, when death approaches any of you, at the time of *making* the

---

A camel devoted to an idol had its ears slit, and was called *Bahaira*. Any animal devoted to an idol and let run loose to roam whither it pleased was called *Sáiba*. It was unlawful to kill or eat any animal thus consecrated. If a man should devote the offspring of his animals yet unborn, saying, "If a male is born I will sacrifice it to an idol, and if a female I will keep it," and the result should be the birth of twins, one a male and the other a female, he would in that case keep the male alive as sacred to the idol; such an animal was called *wasíla*. A camel that had been the mother of ten camels fit to carry a rider or a burden was allowed to roam at liberty in any pasture, and was called *Hámi* (*Tafsír-i-Raufi* and *Abdul Qádir*). This account differs somewhat from Rodwell's. See his note *in loco*.

(103) *That religion, &c.* This is a very common reply on the part of idolaters even in these days. But for the sword of Islám the Arabs would no doubt have remained in the religion of their fathers for many years after the death of the Makkan preacher.

(104) See note on chap. iii. 118.

(105) *Let witnesses be taken, &c.* Sale gives the following story, on the authority of Baidháwi, as the occasion of the revelations in this and the following verse:—" The occasion of the preceding passage is said to have been this. Tamím al Dári and Addi Ibn Yazíd, both Christians, took a journey into Syria to trade, in company with Budhail, the freedman of Amru Ibn al Aas, who was a Muslim. When they came to Damascus, Budhail fell sick and died, having first wrote down a list of his effects on a piece of paper, which he hid in his baggage, without acquainting his companions with it, and desired them only to deliver what he had to his friends of the tribe of Sahm. The survivors, however, searching among his goods, found a vessel of silver of considerable weight and inlaid with gold, which they concealed, and on their return delivered the rest to the deceased's relations, who, finding the list of Budhail's writing, demanded the vessel of silver of them, but they denied it; and the affair being brought before Muhammad, these words, viz., *O true believers, take witnesses*, &c., were revealed, and he ordered them to be sworn at the

testament; *let there be* two *witnesses,* just men, from among you; or two others of *a* different *tribe or faith* from yourselves, if ye be journeying in the earth, and the accident of death befall you. Ye shall shut them both up after the *afternoon* prayer, and they shall swear by GOD, if ye doubt *them, and they shall say,* We will not sell *our evidence* for a bribe, although *the person concerned* be one who is related *to us,* neither will we conceal the testimony of GOD, for then should we certainly be *of the number* of the wicked. (106) But if it appear that both have been guilty of iniquity, two others shall stand up in their place,

---

pulpit in the mosque, just as afternoon prayer was over, and on their making oath that they knew nothing of the plate demanded, dismissed them. But afterwards, the vessel being found in their hands, the Sahmites, suspecting it was Budhail's, charged them with it, and they confessed it was his, but insisted that they had bought it of him, and that they had not produced it because they had no proof of the bargain. Upon this they went again before Muhammad, to whom these words, *And if it appear,* &c., were revealed ; and thereupon Amru Ibn al Aas and al Mutallib Ibn Abi Rafáa, both of the tribe of Sahm, stood up, and were sworn against them ; and judgment was given accordingly."

Two others. Two different parties may be referred to here, and hence the difference of interpretation, indicated by italics in the text. Those who hold that the witnesses must be Muslims understand the *two others* to mean two Muslims of different family or tribe. Others, holding that the witnesses intended here may belong to any religion, still practically agree with the principle that only Muslims should be witnesses, inasmuch as they regard this portion of the verse as being abrogated. The former view is certainly the correct one.

The stories of the commentators show that Muhammad actually decided the two Christians to be guilty of a breach of trust on the adverse testimony of two Muslims. While this is entirely in accord with the spirit of Islám, it does not commend the justice of the Lawgiver. It may, however, be seriously doubted whether the story of the commentators is anything more than a fabrication. Their being brought out during the afternoon prayer, the oath prescribed, and the purport of ver. 107, all indicate that the law has nothing to do with Christians whatever.

The afternoon prayer, i.e., Asar, "because," says Sale, on the authority of Baidháwi, "that was the time of people's assembling in public, or, say some, because the guardian angels then relieve each other, so that there would be four angels to witness against them if they gave false evidence. But others suppose they might be examined after the hour of any other prayer, when there was a sufficient assembly."

CHAP. V.]　　　　　　(154)　　　　　　[SIPARA VII.

of those who have convicted them *of falsehood*, the two nearest *in blood*, and they shall swear by GOD, *saying*, Verily our testimony is more true than the testimony of these two, neither have we prevaricated ; for *then* should we become *of the number* of the unjust. (107) This will be easier, that *men* may give testimony according to the plain intention thereof, or fear lest a *different* oath be given, after their oath. Therefore fear GOD and hearken; for GOD directeth not the unjust people.

R $\frac{15}{5}$.　|| (108) On a *certain* day shall GOD assemble the apostles, and shall say unto them, What answer was returned you *when ye preached unto the people to whom ye were sent?* They shall answer, We have no knowledge, but thou art the knower of secrets. (109) When GOD shall say, O Jesus son of Mary, remember my favour towards thee, and towards thy mother; when I strengthened thee with the holy spirit, that thou shouldst speak unto men in the cradle, and when thou wast grown up; (110) and when I taught thee the scripture, and wisdom, and the law, and the gospel: and when thou didst create

---

(107) This verse shows the purpose for which the law of witnesses was given, viz., to deter from corrupt practices by the knowledge that a solemn oath might be called for, and that even perjured persons might be confronted by the oaths of the witnesses and thereby be condemned. *Two* witnesses were necessary. Compare with Deut. xix. 15.

(108) *On a certain day, i.e.,* on the judgment-day.

Thou art the knower. That is, we are ignorant whether our proselytes were sincere, or whether they apostatised after our deaths ; but thou well knowest, not only what answer they gave us, but the secrets of their hearts, and whether they have since continued firm in their religion or not.—*Sale.*

This passage contradicts the idea that the prophets will intercede for their followers on the judgment-day.

(109) *The Holy Spirit.* See note on chap. ii. 86.

Speak . . . in the cradle. See notes on chap. iii. 46.

(110) *The gospel.* Muslims believe the New Testament Scriptures (*Injīl*) were sent down to Jesus just as the Qurán was given to Muhammad. Christ is here represented as having been taught of God *as Muhammad was.* Muhammad is the type of all apostles.

The figure of a bird. See note on chap. iii. 48.

Blind . . . leper . . . dead from their graves. Three classes of mir-

of clay as it were the figure of a bird by my permission, and didst breathe thereon, and it became a bird, by my permission, and thou didst heal one blind from his birth, and the leper, by my permission; and when thou didst bring forth the dead *from their graves* by my permission; and when I withheld the children of Israel from *killing* thee, when thou hadst come unto them with evident *miracles*, and such of them as believed not said, This is nothing but manifest sorcery. (111) And when I commanded the apostles of *Jesus*, saying, Believe in me and in my messenger; they answered, We do believe; and do thou bear witness that we are resigned *unto thee*. (112) *Remember* when the apostles said, O Jesus son of Mary, is thy LORD able to cause a table to descend unto us from heaven? He answered, Fear GOD, if ye be true believers.

---

acles referred to here, all of which testified to the divinity Muhammad is here *so careful to deny*. The constant use of the phrase "*By my permission*" seems to indicate clearly one of two things: either a deliberate effort to combat the Christian doctrine of the divinity of Christ, or to apologise for the absence of similar miracles in his own case. Of the two, the first is most probable, for *at this late day* there was no occasion to vindicate his own apostleship from charges of this kind. The *signs* of the Qurán and the successes of Islám were now considered sufficient proof of his apostleship.

From killing thee. See notes on chap. iii. 53, 55, and iv. 156.

Sorcery. See Sale's note on chap. iii. 48, and Rodwell *in loco*.

(111) *Apostles.* In Arabic *Al hawáriín*, a word descriptive of the chosen followers of Jesus. It does not convey any idea of apostleship in the ordinary sense of the word. If derived from the Ethiopic *hawyra* (Rodwell), the *etymological* meaning would indicate *one sent;* but if derived from *hur*, it would mean *friends or helpers*, and so correspond with the idea of the *Ansár*, or helpers of Muhammad.

We are resigned, i.e., we are Muslims. Such expressions show that Muhammad regarded his followers as identified with the true followers of all other prophets.

(112) *A table.* This word supplies the title of this chapter. It is thought to allude to the Table of the Lord or Christ's Last Supper. It might as well allude to the miracles of loaves and fishes given in Matt. xiv. and xv. A similar inquiry is attributed to the children of Israel, Ps. lxxviii. 19. The passage is far from being confirmatory of the former Scriptures, if the following opinions of the commentators indicate anything of what Muhammad believed on this subject:—"This miracle is thus related by the commentators. Jesus having, at the request of his followers, asked it of God, a red table

(113) They said, We desire to eat thereof, and that our hearts may rest at ease, and that we may know that thou hast told us the truth, and that we may be witnesses thereof. (114) Jesus the son of Mary said, O GOD our LORD, cause a table to descend unto us from heaven, that *the day of its descent* may become a festival day unto us, unto the first of us, and unto the last of us, and a sign from thee; and do thou provide food for us, for thou art

---

immediately descended in their sight between two clouds, and was set before them : whereupon he rose up, and having made the ablution, prayed, and then took off the cloth which covered the table, saying, "In the name of God, the best provider of food." What the provisions were with which this table was furnished is a matter wherein the expositors are not agreed. One will have them to be nine cakes of bread and nine fishes ; another, bread and flesh ; another, all sorts of food except flesh ; another, all sorts of food except bread and flesh ; another, all except bread and fish ; another, one fish, which had the taste of all manner of food ; and another, fruits of Paradise ; but the most received tradition is, that when the table was uncovered, there appeared a fish ready dressed, without scales or prickly fins, dropping with fat, having salt placed at its head, and vinegar at its tail, and round it all sorts of herbs except leeks, and five loaves of bread, on one of which there were olives, on the second honey, on the third butter, on the fourth cheese, and on the fifth dried flesh. They add, that Jesus, at the request of the apostles, showed them another miracle, by restoring the fish to life, and causing its scales and fins to return to it ; at which the standers-by being affrighted, he caused it to become as it was before : that one thousand three hundred men and women, all afflicted with bodily infirmities or poverty, ate of these provisions, and were satisfied, the fish remaining whole as it was at first ; that then the table flew up to heaven in the sight of all ; and that all who had partaken of this food were delivered from their infirmities and misfortunes ; and that it continued to descend for forty days together at dinner-time, and stood on the ground till the sun declined, and was then taken up into the clouds. Some of the Muhammadan writers are of opinion that this table did not really descend, but that it was only a parable ; but most think the words of the Qurán are plain to the contrary. A further tradition is, that several men were changed into swine for disbelieving this miracle and attributing it to magic art ; or, as others pretend, for stealing some of the victuals from off it. Several other fabulous circumstances are also told, which are scarce worth transcribing."—*Sale, Baidháwi, Thalábi.*

(114) *A festival day.* This expression seems to point to the Eucharist as the subject of this passage. It may, however, rather refer to the love-feasts of the early Christians, which were observed every Sunday.

the best provider. (115) GOD said, Verily I will cause it to descend unto you; but whoever among you shall disbelieve hereafter, I will surely punish him with a punishment wherewith I will not punish any other creature.

‖ (116) And when GOD shall say *unto Jesus at the last* RUBA. *day*, O Jesus son of Mary, hast thou said unto men, Take me and my mother for two gods beside GOD? he shall answer, Praise be unto thee! it is not for me to say that which I ought not; if I had said so, thou wouldst surely have known it: thou knowest what is in me, but I know not what is in thee; for thou art the knower of secrets. (117) I have not spoken to them *any other* than what thou didst command me, *namely*, Worship GOD, my LORD and your LORD: and I was a witness *of their actions* while I stayed among them; but since thou hast taken me to thyself, thou hast been the watcher over them; for thou art witness of all things. (118) If thou punish them, they are surely thy servants; and if thou forgive them, thou art mighty *and* wise. (119) GOD will say, This day shall their veracity be of advantage unto those who speak truth; they shall have gardens wherein rivers flow, they shall remain therein forever: God hath been well pleased

R $\frac{16}{6}$.

---

(116) *Two gods beside God.* See notes on chap. iv. 169, and v. 77. Muir says, "So far as I can judge from the Coran, Mahomet's knowledge of Christianity was derived from the Orthodox party, who styled Mary 'Mother of God.' He may have heard of the Nestorian heresy, and it is possibly referred to among the 'sects' into which Jews and Christians are said in the Coran to be divided; but, had he ever obtained a closer acquaintance with the Nestorian doctrine, at least in the earlier part of his career, it would (according to the analogy of his practice with respect to other subjects) have been more definitely mentioned in his revelation. The truth, however, is, that Mahomet's acquaintance with Christianity was at the best singularly dim and meagre."—*Life of Mahomet*, vol. ii. p. 19, note.

I know not what is in thee. This passage expressly contradicts the teaching of Jesus in John x. 15.

(117) *My Lord and your Lord.* The strained effort of Muhammad to refute the doctrine of Christ's divinity is here manifest. See note on ver. 110.

Since thou hast taken me, &c., "or *since thou hast caused me to*

in them, and they have been well pleased in him. This *shall be* great felicity. (120) Unto GOD *belongeth* the kingdom of heaven and of earth, and of whatever therein is; and he is almighty.

---

die; but as it is a dispute among the Muhammadans whether Christ actually died or not before his assumption, and the original may be translated either way, I have chosen the former expression, which leaves the matter undecided."—*Sale.*

See notes on chap. iii. 54, and chap. iv. 156.

(120) Thus the Qurán ends as it begins, with a declaration of the sovereignty of God—the cardinal doctrine of Islám.

CHAPTER VI.

ENTITLED SURAT AL ANÁM (CATTLE).

Revealed at Makkah.

INTRODUCTION.

THIS chapter owes its title to the frequent mention of certain cattle in connection with the idolatrous rites of the people of Makkah. It relates to the controversy of Muhammad with the inhabitants of his native city during the period immediately preceding his flight to Madína. This is evident from the tone of the revelations. Everywhere the Quraish are spoken of as hopelessly infidel, as given over to unbelief, abandoned of God, and doomed to perdition. Having rejected the *signs* of the Qurán, they will not hear though an angel were to speak audibly to them, though a written book were to descend to them from heaven, or though the Prophet were to ascend into the heavens or delve into the earth to bring them a sign to their own liking.

Other passages contain commands addressed to the Prophet to withdraw from the idolaters and to have no fellowship with them. From all this it is clear that Muhammad had matured his plan of leaving Makkah and of retiring to Madína.

Probable Date of the Revelations.

From what has been said above, and relying especially upon the command of ver. 106, *to retire from the idolaters*, which all authorities agree in referring to the Hijra, we may fairly conclude that most of the revelations of this chapter were rehearsed in public for the first time during the year immediately preceding that event. There are, however, a few verses which belong to the number of Madína revelations. These are vers. 92–94 and 151–153. Noëldeke thinks the latter three are referred to Madína without good reason. The requirements of ver. 152 certainly fit in best with the circumstances of Islám after the Hijra. Their date may be considered as doubtful. This is, in our opinion, true also of vers. 118-121, 145, 146, and 159-165. The command to abstain from certain kinds of meat is said, on the authority of tradition, to have been delivered after the Night Journey, and might therefore have been delivered before the Hijra. But the requirements of the law of permitted and forbidden meats are so certainly an imitation of the Jewish law on the same subject, as to lead us to think that all passages referring to this law of Islám belong to Madína though found in chapters belonging to Makkah. As Muir has already pointed out, the habit was formed soon after the Hijra "of throwing into a former Sura newly-revealed passages connected with its subject." * Wherefore many passages like these, relating to rites borrowed from the Jews, may belong to Madína, though *recited* in a Makkan chapter.

Principal Subjects.

	VERSES
Praise to the Almighty and Omniscient Creator	1-3
The wilful unbelief of the Makkah infidels	4, 5
They are threatened with the divine judgment	6
The people of Makkah hopelessly unbelieving	7
Why angels were not sent to the infidels	8, 9
Those who rejected the former prophets were punished	10, 11
Why the true God should be served	12-18
God the witness between Muhammad and the infidels	19
The Jews recognise Muhammad as a prophet	20
Idolaters on the judgment-day—their condition	21-23
Scoffing idolaters rebuked and threatened	24-29
The condition of believers and unbelievers after death	30, 31
Unbelievers make God a liar	32, 33
God's word and purposes unchangeable	33
Miracles of no avail to convince infidels	34
God will raise the dead to life	35
Why God did not grant the signs asked by unbelievers	36
Animals and birds to be brought into judgment	37
Infidels are deaf and dumb	38
Idolaters will call upon God in their distress	39, 40
Adversity and prosperity alike unmeaning to infidels	41-44
God is the only helper in trouble	45
Unbelievers, if impenitent, sure to perish	46-48
Muhammad unacquainted with the secrets of God	49
There shall be no intercessor on the judgment-day	50

---

* Life of Mahomet, vol. ii. p. 268, note.

	VERSES
The motives of professing Muslims not to be judged	51–54
Muhammad declines the proposals of idolaters	55–57
God the Omniscient and Sovereign Ruler	58–61
God the Almighty Deliverer	62–64
Muhammad charged with imposture	65
Unbelievers will certainly be punished	66
Mockers to be avoided by Muslims	67–69
The punishment of idolaters certain and dreadful	70, 71
Muslims commanded to obey God only	71–74
Abraham's testimony against idolatry	75–84
The prophets who succeeded Abraham	85–91
The unbelieving Jews (of Madína) rebuked	92
The Qurán confirms the former Scriptures	93
The fate of those who forge Scriptures	94
Idolaters deserted by their gods on the judgment-day	95
The God of nature the true God	96–100
God has no offspring	101–103
God's favour in sending the Qurán	104, 105
The command to retire from Makkah	106–108
Muhammad not permitted to work miracles	109
The people of Makkah given over to unbelief	110–113
Muhammad the prophet of God	114
The direction of Muslims and idolaters contrasted	114–117
Law of permitted and forbidden meats	118–121
The righteous and unbelievers compared	122
Wicked leaders of the people—conduct and punishment	122–125
The blessedness of the faithful	126, 127
God's threatenings against unbelieving men and genii	128–130
God always warns men before punishing idolatry	131
Rewards and punishments shall be according to works	132, 133
The punishment of unbelievers certain	134
The idolaters of Makkah rebuked	135, 136
Evil customs of the Quraish exposed	137–139
The idolaters of Makkah threatened	140
The fruit of trees to be eaten	141
Controversy between the Quraish and Muhammad concerning forbidden meats referred to	142–144
The law concerning forbidden meats rehearsed	145
The Jewish law of forbidden meats	146
God will punish those who accuse the prophets of imposture	147
The idolaters of Makkah are reprobate	148, 149
Their testimony unworthy of credit	150

	VERSES
Forbidden things rehearsed	151-153
The Qurán attests the teaching of Moses and Jesus	154-157
The fate of the wicked on the judgment-day	158
Sectaries reproved	159
The reward of the righteous and wicked compared	160
Islám the true religion	161, 162
Muhammad's self-consecration to God	163
The idolaters exhorted to believe in God	164, 165

IN THE NAME OF THE MOST MERCIFUL GOD.

R ⁷⁄

‖ (1) PRAISE be unto GOD, who hath created the heavens and the earth, and hath ordained the darkness and the light: nevertheless they who believe not in the LORD equalise *other gods with him*. (2) It is he who hath created you of clay, and then decreed the term *of your lives;* and the prefixed term is with him: yet do ye doubt *thereof.* (3) He is GOD in heaven and in earth; he knoweth what ye keep secret and what ye publish, and knoweth what ye deserve. (4) There came not unto them any sign of the signs of their LORD, but they retired from the same; (5) and they have gainsaid the truth after that it hath come unto them; but a message shall come unto them concern-

---

(1) *Darkness and the light.* Literally, *darknesses and the light*, from which form some commentators infer that by *darknesses* is intended the *many* false religions, and by *light* the *one* true faith of Islám. These make God to be the author of evil as well as good. See the *Tafsír-i-Raufi in loco*.

Abdul Qádir thinks the passage is directed against the eternal duality of the Magian religion. This also makes God the author of both good and evil.

Equalise, i.e., they regard their idols as equal with God.

(2) *The term, &c.* "By the last *term* some understand the time of the resurrection. Others think that by the first term is intended the space between creation and death, and by the latter that between death and the resurrection."—*Sale.*

(3) *He knoweth, &c.* The omniscience of God is here very forcibly expressed. The speaker is, according to Muslim faith, God, and the passage should be introduced by *Say* (see note on chap. i.) These words are addressed to the unbelievers mentioned in ver. 1.

(5) *A message shall come.* Coming destruction, either in this

ing that which they have mocked at. (6) Do they not consider how many generations we have destroyed before them? We had established them in the earth in a manner wherein we have not established you; we sent the heaven to rain abundantly upon them, and we gave *them* rivers which flowed under *their feet:* yet we destroyed them in their sins, and raised up other generations after them. (7) Although we had caused to descend unto thee a book *written* on paper, and they had handled it with their hands, the unbelievers had surely said, This *is* no other than manifest sorcery. (8) They said, Unless an angel be sent down unto him, *we will not believe.* But if we had sent down an angel, verily the matter had been decreed, and they should not have been borne with, *by having time granted them to repent.* (9) And if we had appointed an

---

world or the world to come, is here suggested. Some refer it to the final success of Islám, which is here predicted.

(6) *Many generations.* Sale thinks the ancient tribes of Ád and Thámúd are here referred to. See Prelim. Disc., pp. 20–22.

(7) *A book written on paper.* The Qurán being *repeated* piecemeal to the people, according to the circumstances or necessities of the Prophet, it was very natural they should regard the whole as the composition of Muhammad himself. The *Tafsír-i-Raufi* relates that three chiefs of the Quraish came to Muhammad saying they would not believe him to be a prophet, or his Qurán to be from God, unless four angels were to descend from heaven with a written book and testify to his apostleship. It was then that this passage was revealed. This story, however, does not fit on to the passage well, and must be regarded as an invention of the commentators, the chief incidents being suggested by the passage itself. It is, however, sufficiently clear that the Quraish did not see anything sufficiently miraculous in the style of the Qurán to convince them of its heavenly origin.

(8) *Unless an angel.* Muhammad claimed to have received the Qurán from Gabriel. This is probably the angel referred to here, the Quraish having claimed the right to see the angel-visitor of their townsman before believing in his prophetic pretensions.

Verily the matter had been decreed. "That is to say, as they would not have believed even if an angel had descended to them from heaven, God has shown his mercy in not complying with their demands; for if he had, they would have suffered immediate condemnation, and would have been allowed no time for repentance."—*Sale.*

angel *for our messenger*, we should have sent him *in the form of* a man, and have clothed *him* before them, as they are clothed. (10) *Other* apostles have been laughed to scorn before thee, but *the judgment* which they made a jest of encompassed those who laughed them to scorn.

R ⅖.

|| (11) Say, Go through the earth, and behold what hath been the end of those who accused *our prophets* of imposture. (12) Say, Unto whom *belongeth* whatsoever is in heaven and earth? Say, Unto GOD; he hath prescribed unto himself mercy. He will surely gather you together on the day of resurrection; there is no doubt of it. They who destroy their own souls *are those who* will not believe. (13) Unto him *is owing* whatsoever happeneth by night or by day; *it is* he who heareth and knoweth. (14) Say, Shall I take any other protector than GOD, the creator of heaven and earth, who feedeth *all* and is not fed *by any?* Say, Verily I am commanded to be the first

---

(9) *The form of a man.* Had the angels appeared to the Quraish, they would have appeared as men, therefore there would have been nothing more convincing in the appearance of the heavenly messengers than in that of a human being who was a prophet. Sale observes that Gabriel always appeared to Muhammad in human form, because even a prophet could not bear the sight of an angel in his proper form.

(10) *Other apostles . . . laughed to scorn.* This illustrates the kind of argument used by Muhammad at Makkah. He was a prophet of God because he said so, the inimitable Qurán being witness. The very fact that unbelievers scoffed at him and his message was an additional argument, for so were all prophets treated. Not a word is said of miracles, for there were none. Nor is there any allusion to the testimony of former prophets as applying to him, all such passages belonging to the Madína chapters. How very different all this from the conduct of the true prophets!

(11) *Go through the earth, &c.* See note on chap. iii. 137.

(12) *He hath prescribed unto himself mercy.* Literally, *he hath written upon his being mercy.* He delights in mercy, and when unbelievers are condemned and punished, it is owing to *their having destroyed themselves.* It is plain that with passages like this before them, Muhammadans may fairly claim that they do not deny the freedom of the human will while holding to the absolute sovereignty of God. But see note on chap. iii. 155.

(14) *The first.* "That is, the first of my nation."—*Sale.* Muhammad had not yet conceived of himself as a prophet for all

who professeth Islám, and *it was said unto me*, Thou shalt by no means be *one* of the idolaters. (15) Say, Verily I fear, if I should rebel against my LORD, the punishment of the great day: (16) from whomsoever it shall be averted on that day, *God* will have been merciful unto him; this *will be* manifest salvation. (17) If GOD afflict thee with any hurt, there is none who can take it off *from thee* except himself; but if he cause good to befall thee, he is almighty; (18) he is the supreme *Lord* over his servants, and he *is* wise *and* knowing. (19) Say, What thing is the strongest in bearing testimony? Say, GOD; *he is* witness between me and you. And this Qurán was revealed unto me that I should admonish you thereby, and *also* those unto whom it shall reach. Do ye really profess that there are other gods together with GOD? Say, I do not profess *this.* Say, Verily he is one GOD; and I am guiltless of

---

the world. Brinckman remarks, that "if Muhammed was the first of the Arabians to become a Moslem, all the Arabians before him must have been infidels and estranged from God, and yet he chooses one of them to be the seal of the prophets and to convert the world." But this is the point upon which Muhammad depended to show his own likeness to Abraham, who was chosen from among idolaters. Chap. ii. 131, 132.

(19) *What is . . . strongest . . . in testimony.* "This passage was revealed when the Quraish told Muhammad that they had asked the Jews and Christians concerning him, who assured them they found no mention or description of him in their books of Scripture. "Therefore," said they, "who bear witness to thee that thou art the apostle of God?"—*Sale, Baidháwi, Jaláluddín.*

Muhammad's reply is, "God, he is witness between me and you," allusion being made to the miraculous character of the verses (signs) of the Qurán.

This Qurán was revealed unto me. The Qurán is here, as everywhere else, referred to as a *complete volume,* and a distinct claim for its plenary inspiration is set up. Every word and letter is copied from the divine original. Vain then is the hope of the apologists for Muhammad that Muslims "will soon see that there may be an appeal to the Mohammed of Mecca from the Mohammed of Medina," and "that with the growth of knowledge of the real character of our faith, Mohammedans must recognise that the Christ of the gospel was something ineffably above the Christ of those Christians from whom alone Mohammed drew his notions of him," &c. (R. Bosworth Smith's *Mohammed and Muhammedanism,* p. 337). Such a hope is based upon the idea that Muslims will come to believe that the

what ye associate *with him*. (20) They unto whom we have given the scripture know *our apostle*, even as they know their own children ; *but* they who destroy their own souls will not believe.

R ⅜.

‖ (21) Who is more unjust than he who inventeth a lie against GOD, or chargeth his signs with imposture? Surely the unjust shall not prosper. (22) And on the day *of resurrection* we will assemble them all; then will we say unto those who associated *others with God*, Where are your companions, whom ye imagined *to be those of God?* But they shall have no other excuse than that they shall say, By GOD our LORD, we have not been idolaters. (23) Behold, how they lie against themselves, and what they have *blasphemously* imagined *to be the companion of God*

Qurán is the composition of Muhammad, and that he was mistaken in his estimate of Christ and Christianity. When they come to believe this, they will not be long in casting the whole thing aside, and so either become Christians, or, as is often the case, they will disbelieve all religions, and so sink into infidelity. The rationalising teachings of the few *enlightened Muslims,* which have inspired the *hope* alluded to above, are to all orthodox Muhammadans as gall and wormwood. They clearly recognise that the result of their teaching would not be to reconcile Christianity and Islám, but to destroy the foundation principles of both. The writer has been asked by at least one learned Muslim author for assistance to refute the rationalistic writings of Sayad Ahmad Khán, C.S.I. In presenting this request I was reminded that in combating this doctrine Muslims and Christians stood on common ground, inasmuch as we had here a common enemy which each was alike interested in defeating. Was he mistaken in his estimate of the danger which threatened Islám from this source? We think not. Islám is based upon the Qurán, and anything which will undermine the faith of Muslims in the Qurán as the very Word of God, anything which will serve to transfer the authorship from God to Muhammad, must result in the rejection of Islám altogether.

(20) *They unto whom we have given the Scriptures, &c., i.e.,* the Jews at Makkah. Muir thinks the Jews were at this time inclined to respect the prophetic claims of Muhammad (*Life of Mahomet,* vol. ii. p. 184). See also note on chap. ii. 147.

(21) *A lie against God.* "Saying the angels are the daughters of God, and intercessors for us with him," &c.—*Sale, Baidháwi.*

(22) *Your companions, i.e.,* "your idols and false gods."—*Sale.*

(23) *Flieth from them.* "Their imaginary deities prove to be nothing, and disappear like vain phantoms and chimeras."—*Sale.*

flieth from them. (24) There is of them who hearkeneth unto thee *when thou readest the Qurán;* but we have cast veils over their hearts, that they should not understand it, and a deafness in their ears: and though they should see all *kinds of* signs, they will not believe therein; *and their infidelity will arrive to that height* that they will even come unto thee to dispute with thee. The unbelievers will say, This is nothing but silly fables of ancient *times*. (25) And they will forbid *others* from *believing therein*, and will retire afar off from it; but they will destroy their own souls only, and they are not sensible *thereof.* (26) If thou didst see when they shall be set over the fire of *hell!* and they shall say, Would to GOD we might be sent back *into the world;* we would not charge the signs of our LORD with imposture, and we would become true believers: (27) nay, but that is become manifest unto them, which they formerly concealed; and though they should be sent back *into the world,* they would surely return to that which was forbidden them; and they are surely liars. (28) And they said, There is no *other life* than our present life; neither

---

(24) *Silly fables.* This no doubt referred to the numerous stories, learned from Jewish, Arab, and Magian tradition, with which the Qurán abounds. Such statements serve to show that there was nothing in the style or matter of the Qurán to impress the people with its miraculous character. Sale says, on the authority of Baidháwi, that the persons referred to in this verse were Abu Sufián, Walíd, Nudhár, Utbá, Abu Jahl, and their comrades. These having listened to Muhammad repeating the Qurán, Nudhár was asked what he said. He replied with an oath that he knew not, only that he moved his tongue and told a parcel of foolish stories, as he had done to them.

(25) *They will forbid, &c.* They will neither accept of Islám themselves, nor permit others to do so. Some refer the passage to Abu Tálib, Muhammad's uncle and protector, who, though forbidding the enemies of his nephew from injuring him, yet declined to accept Islám. See *Tafsír-i-Raufi.*

(27) *Become manifest, i.e,* " their hypocrisy and vile actions; nor does their promise proceed from any sincere intention of amendment, but from the anguish and misery of their condition."—*Sale, Baidháwi.*

(28) *No other life, &c.* The ideas of the future life attributed to the Quraish here were such as are still prevalent among idolaters.

[CHAP. VI.] (168) [SIPARA VII.

R $\tfrac{4}{10}$.

shall we be raised again. But if thou couldest see when they shall be set before their LORD! (29) He shall say *unto them*, Is not this in truth *come to pass?* They shall answer, Yea, by our LORD. God shall say, Taste therefore the punishment *due unto you*, for that ye have disbelieved. ‖ (30) They are lost who reject as a falsehood the meeting of GOD *in the next life*, until the hour cometh suddenly upon them. *Then will* they say, Alas! for that we have behaved ourselves negligently in *our lifetime;* and they shall carry their burdens on their backs; will it not be evil which they shall be loaden with? (31) This present life is no other than a play and a vain amusement; but surely the future mansion *shall be* better for those who fear *God:* will they not therefore understand? (32) Now we know that what they speak grieveth thee: yet they do not accuse thee of falsehood; but the ungodly contra-

---

As Paul's doctrine of the resurrection and judgment was foolishness to the Greeks, so was the same doctrine regarded by the idolaters of Makkah. The astonishment of these unbelievers at the resurrection day is very graphically set forth in what follows.

(30) *The hour.* "The last day is here called *the hour*, as it is in Scripture (1 John v. 25, &c.); and the preceding expression of *meeting* God on that day is also agreeable to the same (1 Thess. iv. 17)."—*Sale.*

The same is true of the expression *suddenly.* This is, however, due to Muhammad's having learned all he knew on this subject from Jewish and Christian sources. Compare note on ver. 28.

Burdens on their backs. "When an infidel comes forth from his grave, says Jaláluddín, his works shall be represented to him under the ugliest form that ever he beheld, having a most deformed countenance, a filthy smell, and a disagreeable voice; so that he shall cry out, 'God defend me from thee! what art thou? I never saw anything more detestable!' To which the figure will answer, 'Why dost thou wonder at my ugliness? I am thy evil works. Thou didst ride upon me while thou wast in the world; but now will I ride upon thee, and thou shalt carry me.' And immediately it shall get upon him; and whatever he shall meet shall terrify him, and say, 'Hail, thou enemy of God! Thou art he who was meant by (these words of the Qurán), *and they shall carry their burdens*,' &c."—*Sale, Jaláluddín, Tafsír-i-Raufí.*

(31) *The future mansion shall be better*, because there remain for the faithful other delights which shall never fail.—*Tafsír-i-Raufí.* Compare chap. ii. 25.

(32) *Not . . . thee . . . but . . . God.* "That is, it is not thou but

dict the signs of GOD. (33) And apostles before thee have been accounted liars: but they patiently bore their being accounted liars, and their being vexed, until our help came unto them: for there is none who can change the words of GOD: and thou hast received some information concerning those who have been *formerly* sent *from him.*

|| (34) If their aversion *to thy admonitions* be grievous NISF. unto thee, if thou canst seek out a den *whereby thou mayest penetrate* into *the inward parts of* the earth, or a ladder *by which thou mayest ascend* into heaven, that thou mayest show them a sign, *do so, but thy search will be fruitless;* for if GOD pleased he would bring them all to the *true* direction: be not therefore *one* of the ignorant. (35) He will give a favourable answer unto those only who shall

---

God whom they injure by their impious gainsaying of what has been revealed to thee. It is said that Abu Jahl once told Muhammad that they did not accuse him of falsehood, because he was known to be a man of veracity, but only they did not believe the revelations which he brought them; which occasioned this passage."—*Sale, Baidháwi.*

(33) *Apostles before thee, &c.* See note on chap. iii. 185.

Patiently bore. The attitude of the preacher of Makkah, as here indicated, is in wide contrast with that of the warrior-prophet of Madína. Yet the latter could liken himself to the prophets of old as readily as could the former. Compare note on chap. iii. 146.

Some information. This information *purports* to have been received by inspiration, and is detailed in a number of the chapters revealed at Makkah, where the persecutions of former prophets are described, together with the punishments incurred by the persecutors, *e.g.*, chaps. xxxvii., l., &c. Most of it was learned, as we know, from Jewish Scripture and tradition, of which it is here said, *There is none who can change the words of God.* But a comparison of the Qurán with the Bible will show that Muhammad did effectually change the words of God whenever he attempted to relate the histories of the prophets.

(34) *A den ... or a ladder.* The Quraish had demanded a sign, and Muhammad, according to the commentators, was anxious to gratify their wish, in the hope they would believe. But he is here reproved by the declaration that these unbelievers would not believe even were they to witness the very miracles they demanded of him, and by the assurance that they were infidels only because God had not been pleased to bring them into the true way. The passage is one among many proof texts to show that Muhammad did not work miracles.

(35) *Those only who shall hearken.* The *Tafsír-i-Raufi* says the

hearken *with attention :* and GOD will raise the dead; then unto him shall they return. (36) The *infidels* say, Unless some sign be sent down unto him from his LORD, *we will not believe :* answer, Verily GOD is able to send down a sign : but the greater part of them know *it* not. (37) There is no *kind of* beast on earth, nor fowl which flieth with its wings, but *the same is* a people like unto you : we have not omitted anything in the book *of our decrees :* then unto their LORD shall they return. (38) They who accuse our signs of falsehood *are* deaf and dumb, *walking* in darkness : GOD will lead into error whom he pleaseth, and whom he pleaseth he will put in the right way ? (39) Say, What think ye ? if the punishment of GOD come upon you, or the hour *of the resurrection* come upon you, will ye call upon any other than GOD, if ye speak truth ? (40) Yea, him shall ye call upon, and he shall free *you* from that which ye shall ask him *to deliver you from*, if he pleaseth; and ye shall forget that which ye associated *with him.*

---

infidels are as the dead : they cannot hear. Hence God will not hear them. And yet, though dead, God will raise them to life, and they shall hear, but then it will be too late to avail them for good.

(36) *But . . . know not* that such a sign would probably result in their destruction ; for it is the command of God that if any one, having demanded a sign, refuse to believe, he shall be utterly destroyed.—*Tafsír-i-Raufí.*

This verse also shows that Muhammad wrought no miracles.

(37) *A people like unto you.* "Being created and preserved by the same omnipotence and providence as ye are."—*Sale.* They will also be brought into judgment. See *Tafsír-i-Raufí in loco* and Prelim. Disc., p. 146.

We have not omitted anything in the book. "That is, in the *Preserved Table*, wherein God's decrees are written, and all things which came to pass in the world, as well the most minute as the more momentous, are exactly recorded."—*Sale.* See Prelim. Disc., p. 164.

This verse, with ver. 58 below, and chap. xvi. 91, is "held to prove that all law was provided for by anticipation in the Qurán" *(The Faith of Islám,* pp. 19, 20).

(38) See note on chap. iii. 185.

(39, 40) See notes above on vers. 22–27.

|| (41) We have already sent *messengers* unto *sundry* R $\frac{5}{11}$. nations before thee, and we afflicted them with trouble and adversity that they might humble themselves: (42) yet when the affliction *which we sent* came upon them, they did not humble themselves; but their hearts became hardened, and Satan prepared for them that which they committed. (43) And when they had forgotten that concerning which they had been admonished, we opened unto them the gates of all things; until, while they were rejoicing for that which had been given them, we suddenly laid hold on them, and behold, they *were* seized with despair; (44) and the utmost part of the people which had acted wickedly was cut off: praise be unto GOD, the LORD of all creatures! (45) Say, What think ye? if GOD should take away your hearing and your sight, and should seal up your hearts; what god besides GOD will restore them unto you? (46) See how variously we show forth the signs *of God's unity;* yet do they turn aside *from them.* Say *unto them,* What think ye? if the punishment of GOD come upon you suddenly or in open view, will *any* perish except the ungodly people? (47) We send not *our* messengers otherwise than bearing good tidings and

---

(41-44) *We afflicted them.* The effect of which was to harden them, implying that the prosperity of the Quraish indicated God's mercy. And yet, when God, willing to show kindness to other nations, *opened unto them the gates of all things* by prospering them in worldly things, as he now was prospering the people of Makkah, and they continued unmindful of both judgments and mercies, sudden destruction came upon them. The allusion here is to the dealing of God with the children of Israel. The reading of the passage suggests Prov. i. 24-33; Isa. lxvi. 3, 4, &c.

Praise be unto God, &c. As the destruction of infidels is the deliverance of the faithful from their tyranny, it becomes us to praise the Destroyer.—*Tafsír-i-Raufí.*

(46) *See how variously, &c.* "Laying them before you in different views, and making use of arguments and motives drawn from various considerations."—*Sale.*

Suddenly or in open view, i.e., at night or in daytime.—*Tafsír-i-Raufí.*

Sale says, on the authority of Baidháwi, "either without previous notice, or after some warning given."

denouncing threats. Whoso therefore shall believe and amend, on them shall no fear come, neither shall they be grieved: (48) but whoso shall accuse our signs of falsehood, a punishment shall fall on them, because they have done wickedly. (49) Say, I say not unto you, The treasures of GOD are in my power: neither *do I say*, I know the secrets *of God:* neither do I say unto you, Verily I am an angel: I follow only that which is revealed unto me. Say, Shall the blind and the seeing be held equal? do ye not therefore consider?

R $\frac{6}{12}$.

‖ (50) Preach it unto those who fear that they shall be assembled before their LORD: they shall have no patron nor intercessor except him; that peradventure they may take heed to themselves. (51) Drive not away those who call upon their LORD morning and evening, desiring *to see* his face: it belongeth not unto thee to pass any judgment on them, nor doth it belong unto them to pass any judg-

---

(48) *Whoso shall accuse our signs, &c.* This phrase has occurred no less than five times before in this chapter, vers. 11, 21, 26, 32, and 38. This illustrates Muhammad's anxiety to remove this stigma from himself. Strange to say, this persistency of Muhammad in asserting his claim to be a true prophet is regarded by some writers as conclusive proof that he was not an impostor. But surely, granting the false assumption to have been once made, there could be no other course open to him, excepting retraction and disgrace. Besides, impostors have never been noted for anything more than for their audacity and impudent self-assertion, *e.g.*, Joseph Smith, the Mormon prophet. The false prophet of Islám and rival of Muhammad, Musailama, persisted in his claim to the very last—yea, died in defence of his claim.

(49) *I say not unto you, &c.* In ver. 34 Muhammad was denied the power of working miracles. Here he declares himself unacquainted with the "secrets of God," literally *hidden* things, by which he confesses that he does not possess the gift of prophecy. How different the claim of Jesus! John viii. 38, 42; x. 15, 30, 37, &c.

(50) *No patron nor intercessor.* This passage is directly contradictory to the doctrine of Muslims, that Muhammad will intercede for his followers on the judgment-day. See notes on chap. ii. 47, 123, and 254.

(51) *Drive not away, &c.* "These words were occasioned when the Quraish desired Muhammad not to admit the poor or more inferior people, such as Ammár, Suhaib, Khubbáb, and Salmán,

ment on thee: therefore *if* thou drive them away, thou wilt become *one* of the unjust. (52) Thus have we proved some part of them by other part, that they may say, Are these *the people* among us unto whom GOD hath been gracious? Doth not GOD most truly know *those who are* thankful? (53) And when they who believe in our signs shall come unto thee, say, Peace *be* upon you. Your LORD hath prescribed unto himself mercy; so whoever among you worketh evil through ignorance, and afterwards repenteth and amendeth, *unto him will* he surely *be* gracious *and* merciful. (54) Thus have we distinctly propounded *our* signs, that the path of the wicked might be made known.

|| (55) Say, Verily I am forbidden to worship *the false* R $\frac{7}{13}$. *deities* which ye invoke besides GOD. Say, I will not follow your desires; for then should I err, neither should I be *one* of *those who are rightly* directed. (56) Say, I *behave* according to the plain declaration, *which I have*

---

into his company, pretending that then they would come and discourse with him; but he refusing to turn away any believers, they insisted at least that he should order them to rise up and withdraw when they came, which he agreed to do. Others say that the chief men of Makkah expelled all the poor out of their city, bidding them go to Muhammad, which they did, and offered to embrace his religion; but he made some difficulty to receive them, suspecting their motive to be necessity, and not real conviction, whereupon this passage was revealed."—*Sale, Baidháwi, Jaláluddín.*

It belongeth not to thee, &c., i.e., "rashly to decide whether their intentions be sincere or not, since thou canst not know their heart, and their faith may possibly be more firm than that of those who would persuade thee to discard them."—*Sale.*

(52) *Proved some part . . . by other part.* "That is to say, the noble by those of mean extraction, and the rich by the poor, in that God chose to call the latter to the faith by the former."—*Sale, Baidháwi, &c.*

(53) *Say, Peace be upon you.* See chap. iv. 85, note.
Prescribed . . . mercy. See on ver. 12, above.

(55) This verse suggests the thought that Muhammad may have been tempted to make a compromise with the idolatry of the Kaabah. May he not have been urged to do so by some of his friends? Or the passage may belong to a period subsequent to the temporary lapse of the prophet, referred to in chap. xxii. 53 and 54.

received from my LORD; but ye have forged lies concerning him. That which ye desire should be hastened is not in my power; judgment *belongeth* only unto GOD; he will determine the truth; and he is the best discerner. (57) Say, If what ye desire should be hastened were in my power, the matter had been determined between me and you: but GOD well knoweth the unjust. (58) With him are the keys of the secret *things;* none knoweth them besides himself: he knoweth that which is on the dry land and in the sea: there falleth no leaf but he knoweth it; neither *is there* a single grain in the dark parts of the earth, neither a green thing, nor a dry thing, but it is *written* in the perspicuous book. (59) It is he who causeth you to sleep by night, and knoweth what ye merit by day; he also awaketh you therein, that the prefixed term *of your lives* may be fulfilled; then unto him shall ye return, and he shall declare unto you that which ye have wrought.

R $\frac{8}{14}$.

|| (60) He is supreme over his servants, and sendeth the guardian *angels to watch* over you, until, when death overtaketh one of you, our messengers cause him to die: and

---

(56) *That which ye desire, &c.* "This passage is an answer to the audacious defiances of the infidels, who bade Muhammad, if he were a true prophet, to call for a shower of stones from heaven, or some other sudden and miraculous punishment, to destroy them."—*Sale, Baidháwi.*

(57) *The matter had been determined* by the judgment of God upon your impiety, and the bestowal of the punishment which ye have challenged.—*Tafsír-i-Raufi.* The fierce reply intended, according to Baidháwi's interpretation, is premature. That spirit was not yet manifested.

(58) *The perspicuous book.* The Preserved Table, or *Luh-i-Mahfúz.* See note on ver. 37. This verse, with the three following it, very graphically sets forth the omniscience and omnipresence of the Sovereign Ruler of the Universe. Compare with Job xxxviii. 1-14; Ps. l. 10-12, and Ps. cxxxix. 1-16.

(59) *Causeth you to sleep.* Literally *taketh up your souls,* sleep being regarded as the sister of Death.

(60) *Guardian angels.* See Prelim. Disc., pp. 118-120.

Our messengers. "That is, the Angel of Death and his assistants." See Prelim. Disc., p. 119.

they will not neglect *our commands*. (61) Afterwards shall they return unto GOD, their true LORD: doth not judgment *belong* unto him? He is the most quick in taking an account. (62) Say, Who delivereth you from the darkness of the land and of the sea, *when* ye call upon him humbly and in private, *saying*, Verily if thou deliver us from these *dangers*, we will surely be thankful? (63) Say, GOD delivereth you from them, and from every grief of mind; *yet* afterwards ye give *him* companions. (64) Say, He is able to send on you a punishment from above you, or from under your feet, or to engage you in dissension, and to make some of you taste the violence of others. Observe how variously we show forth *our* signs, that peradventure they may understand. (65) This people hath accused the *revelation which thou hast brought* of falsehood, although it be the truth. Say, I am not a guardian over you: (66) every prophecy hath its fixed time *of accomplishment*; and he will hereafter know *it*. (67) When thou seest those who are engaged in *cavilling at or ridiculing* our signs, depart from them until they be engaged in

---

(61) *He is quick.* See Prelim. Disc., p. 137.
(62) *The darkness.* The word is in the plural number, and means *dangers* or *distresses*. See also note on ver. 1.
If thou deliver us. Sale says, "The Kufic copies read it in the third person, *if he deliver us,*" &c.
(63) *Afterwards ye gave him companions.* In distress they called on God, and so recognised him as the only Preserver; but in prosperity they turned away from him to their idols.
(64) *A punishment from above.* "That is, by storms from heaven, as he destroyed the unbelieving people of Noah and of Lot, and the army of Abráhá, the lord of the elephant."—*Sale, Baidháwi.*
Or from under your feet, as he destroyed Pharaoh and his host in the Red Sea, or Korah and his company.
Dissension, by warfare and civil strife.
(66) *Every prophecy hath its fixed time.* The word translated *prophecy* means *news, thing, word,* and the passage means that everything has a fixed time for its accomplishment; that is, there is a time for those who oppose the messengers of God and who blaspheme to receive their just punishment.
(67) *Depart from them.* The infidels having begun to mock the Muslims whenever they found them repeating the Qurán in their company, the order was given to withdraw from them whenever they should begin to laugh or jest.—*Tafsir-i-Raufi.*

some other discourse: and if Satan cause thee to forget *this precept*, do not sit with the ungodly people after recollection. (68) They who fear God are not at all accountable for them, but *their duty is* to remember, that they may take heed to themselves. (69) Abandon those who make their religion a sport and a jest, and whom the present life hath deceived; and admonish *them* by *the Qurán*, that a soul becometh liable to destruction for that which it committeth; it shall have no patron nor intercessor besides GOD: (70) and if it could pay the utmost price of redemption, it would not be accepted from it.

R $\frac{9}{15}$.

‖ (71) They who are delivered over to perdition for that which they have committed shall have boiling water to drink, and shall suffer a grievous punishment, because they have disbelieved. Say, shall we call upon that, besides GOD, which can neither profit us nor hurt us? and shall we turn back on our heels, after that GOD hath directed us, like him whom the devils hath infatuated, wandering amazedly in the earth, *and yet* having companions who call him into the *true* direction, *saying*, Come unto us? Say, The direction of GOD is the *true* direction: we are commanded to resign ourselves unto

---

(68) *Not at all accountable.* "And therefore need not be troubled at the indecent and impious talk of the infidels, provided they take care not to be infected by them. When the preceding passage was revealed, the Muslims told their prophet that if they were obliged to rise up whenever the idolaters spoke irreverently of the Qurán, they could never sit quietly in the temple nor perform their devotions there; whereupon these words were added."—*Sale, Baidháwi, Jaláluddín.*

(69) *A sport and a jest*, i.e., by worshipping idols, consecrating sacred animals, as Bahaira, Sáhiba, &c.—*Tafsír-i-Raufi.* See a similar passage in chap. v. 62.

No patron nor intercessor. See note on ver. 50. The expression is here applied to unbelievers who have died in their sins.

(71) *Boiling water.* See chap. ii. 38, note.

Like him whom the devils, &c. He whom God has rejected as a reprobate is like a man snatched away from a caravan and cast down in a lone wilderness; his companions call to him to come to them, but he is dragged away by evil spirits and ghouls.—*Tafsír-i-Raufi.*

the LORD of all creatures; (72) and *it is also commanded us, saying,* Observe the stated times of prayer, and fear him; for it is he before whom ye shall be assembled. (73) It is he who hath created the heavens and the earth in truth; and whenever he saith *unto a thing,* Be, it is. (74) His word is the truth; and his will be the kingdom on the day whereon the trumpet shall be sounded: he knoweth whatever is secret, and whatever is public; he is the wise, the knowing.

|| (75) *Call to mind* when Abraham said unto his father, Suls. Ázar, Dost thou take images for gods? Verily I perceive

---

(72) *The stated times of prayer.* See note on chap. ii. 38.
(74) *The trumpet, &c.* See Prelim. Disc., p. 135.
(75) *Ázar.* "This is the name which the Muhammadans give to Abraham's father, named in Scripture Terah. However, some of their writers pretend that Ázar was the son of Terah, and D'Herbelot says that the Arabs always distinguish them in their genealogies as different persons; but that because Abraham was the son of Terah according to Moses, it is therefore supposed (by European writers) that Terah is the same with the Ázar of the Arabs. How true this observation may be in relation to some authors, I cannot say, but I am sure it cannot be true of all; for several Arab and Turkish writers (Baidháwi, Yahya, &c.) expressly make Ázar and Terah the same person. Ázar, in ancient times, was the name of the planet Mars, and the month of March was so called by the most ancient Persians; for the word originally signifying *fire* (as it still does), it was therefore given by them and the Chaldeans to that planet, which partaking, as was supposed, of a fiery nature, was acknowledged by the Chaldeans and Assyrians as a god or planetary deity, whom in old times they worshipped under the form of a pillar: whence Ázar became a name among the nobility, who esteemed it honourable to be denominated from their gods, and is found in the composition of several Babylonish names. For these reasons a learned author supposes Ázar to have been the heathen name of Terah, and that the other was given him on his conversion (Hyde de Rel. Vet. Persar.) Al Baidháwi confirms this conjecture, saying that Ázar was the name of the idol which he worshipped. It may be observed that Abraham's father is also called Zarah in the Talmud, and Athar by Eusebius."—*Sale.*

Dost thou take images for gods? "That Ázar, or Terah, was an idolater is allowed on all hands; nor can it be denied, since he is expressly said in Scripture to have served strange gods (Josh. xxiv. 2, 14). The Eastern authors unanimously agree that he was a statuary, or carver of idols; and he is represented as the first who made images of clay, pictures only having been in use before, and taught that they were to be adored as gods. However, we are told his em-

that thou and thy people *are* in a manifest error. (76) And thus did we show unto Abraham the kingdom of heaven and earth, that he might become *one* of those who firmly believe. (77) And when the night overshadowed him, he saw a star, *and* he said, This is my LORD; but when it set, he said, I like not *gods* which set. (78) And when he saw the moon rising, he said, This is my LORD; but when he saw it set, he said, Verily if my LORD direct me not, I shall become *one* of the people who go astray. (79) And when he saw the sun rising, he said, This is my LORD, this is the greatest; but when it set, he said, O my people, verily I am clear of that which ye associate *with God:* (80) I direct my face unto him who hath created

---

ployment was a very honourable one, and that he was a great lord, and in high favour with Nimrod, whose son-in-law he was, because he made his idols for him, and was excellent in his art. Some of the Rabbins say Terah was a priest, and chief of the order."—*Sale.*

(76) *Abraham.* The story of Abraham as told in the writings of the Muslims is embellished by much that is of a miraculous character. The king, Nimrod, having had a dream of a wonderful child being born who should destroy his idols, commanded all the male children to be slain. The mother of Abraham, without exhibiting the usual signs of pregnancy, brought forth her son in a cave outside of Babylon, and hiding him there, informed her husband that she had had a child, but that he was dead and buried. The next day she repaired to the cave and found her son sucking his thumbs, and to her surprise she discovered that milk flowed from one thumb and honey from the other. In fifteen months Abraham had grown from childhood to the size and maturity of a boy of fifteen years. His mother then informed her husband of her deception, and took him to the cave to see his son. Azar was delighted, and immediately determined to present him to the king, which he could do with safety, seeing he would appear to have been born many years before the cruel edict went forth. The child, however, soon began to show his reverence for the true God and his contempt for idolatry. One day he asked his mother, " Who is your protector ?" She replied, " Your father." Said he, " Who is my father's protector?" to which his mother replied, " Nimrod." "And who is Nimrod's protector?" said Abraham. His mother, being affrighted, said, " Stop now; you must not ask such questions; it is dangerous to do so." And so the story goes. See *Tafsír-i-Raufi in loco.*

(77-84) *This is my Lord, &c.* "Since Abraham's parents were idolaters, it seems to be a necessary consequence that himself was one also in his younger years; the Scripture not obscurely intimates

the heavens and the earth; *I am* orthodox, and am not *one* of the idolaters. (81) And his people disputed with him: *and* he said, Will ye dispute with me concerning GOD? since he hath now directed me, and I fear not that which ye associate *with him*, unless that my LORD willeth a thing; *for* my LORD comprehendeth all things by *his* knowledge: will ye not therefore consider? (82) And how should I fear that which ye associate *with God*, since ye fear not to have associated with GOD that concerning which he hath sent down unto you no authority? which therefore of the two parties is the more safe, if ye understand *aright?* (83) They who believe, and clothe not their faith with injustice, they shall enjoy security, and they *are rightly* directed.

|| (84) And this is our argument wherewith we furnished R $\frac{10}{16}$. Abraham *that he might make use of it* against his people: we exalt unto degrees *of wisdom and knowledge* whom we

---

as much (Josh. xxiv. 2, 14); and the Jews themselves acknowledge it (Joseph. Ant., lib. i. c. 7). At what age he came to the knowledge of the true God and left idolatry, opinions are various. Some Jewish writers tell us he was then but three years old, and the Muhammadans likewise suppose him very young, and that he asked his father and mother several shrewd questions when a child. Others, however, allow him to have been a middle-aged man at that time. Maimonides, in particular, and R. Abraham Zacuth think him to have been forty years old, which age is also mentioned in the Qurán. But the general opinion of the Muhammadans is, that he was about fifteen or sixteen. As the religion wherein Abraham was educated was the Sabian, which consisted chiefly in the worship of the heavenly bodies (Prelim. Disc., sect. i.), he is introduced examining their nature and properties, to see whether they had a right to the worship which was paid them or not; and the first which he observed was the planet Venus, or, as others (Baidháwi) will have it, Jupiter. This method of Abraham's attaining to the knowledge of the Supreme Creator of all things is conformable to what Josephus writes, viz., that he drew his notions from the changes which he had observed in the earth and the sea, and in the sun and the moon, and the rest of the celestial bodies; concluding that they were subject to the command of a superior power, to whom alone all honour and thanks are due. The story itself is certainly taken from the Talmud. Some of the commentators, however, suppose this reasoning of Abraham with himself was not the first means of his conversion, but that he used it only by way of argument to convince the idolaters among whom he then lived."—*Sale.*

please; for thy LORD is wise *and* knowing. (85) And we gave unto them Isaac and Jacob; we directed *them* both: and Noah had we before directed, and of his posterity David and Solomon; and Job, and Joseph, and Moses, and Aaron: thus do we reward the righteous; (86) and Zacharias, and John, and Jesus, and Elias; all *of them were* upright men: (87) and Ismael, and Elisha, and

Of this account of Abraham's conversion it may be fairly said (1), That it is taken for the most part from Jewish tradition, as already shown by Sale; (2) that something of Muhammad's own experience is here predicated of Abraham; and (3) that, in Muhammad's conception, Abraham was a prophet in all respects like himself. And yet, according to his own claim, this garbled tale was received entirely by revelation from the Angel Gabriel—Muhammad merely repeating the words given to him. Was there nothing of imposition in all this?

(85) The order in which Muhammad has here recited the names of the "prophets" indicates his ignorance of history, and clearly shows that he did not have access to the written Scriptures of the Old and New Testament. Of twenty-five *prophets* mentioned in the Qurán, eighteen are named here.

His posterity. "Some refer the relative *his* to Abraham, the person chiefly spoken of in this passage; some to Noah, the next antecedent, because Jonas and Lot were not (say they) of Abraham's seed; and others suppose the persons named in this and the next verse are to be understood as the descendants of Abraham, and those in the following verse as those of Noah."—*Sale, Baidháwi.*

The conjunctions make it necessary to refer the *his* to Noah. The attempt to refer it to Abraham was due to the declaration that David and Solomon were descended from Noah prior to Abraham, which the commentators desired to remove.

Job. The commentators say he was of the race of Esau, but he is everywhere mentioned in the Qurán *after* Solomon, so that a suspicion at least is admissible that in Muhammad's mind he was descended from David and Solomon, or that he lived after them. See chap. xxi. 83, and xxxviii. 40.

(86) *Zacharias,* like Aaron in the preceding verse and Ismaíl in the one following, is numbered among the prophets, contrary to the teaching of the Bible. It is rather remarkable that Ismaíl is placed at the end of the catalogue of the successors of Abraham. This is probably due to the change of attitude towards the Jews, which took place after the Hijra, from which time it became the policy of Muhammad to exalt Ismaíl, in order to please the Arabs. Zachariah, the father of John the Baptist, is probably confounded with the prophet of the same name.

And Elias. See notes on chap. xxxvii. 123–131.

(87) *Elisha, i.e.,* the son of Shaphat, whom the commentators say was the son of Akhtúb.—*Tafsír-i-Raufi.*

Jonas, and Lot; all *these* have we favoured above *the rest of* the world; (88) and *also divers* of their fathers, and their issue, and their brethren; and we chose them, and directed them into the right way. (89) This is the direction of GOD; he directeth thereby such of his servants as he pleaseth; but if they had been guilty of idolatry, that which they wrought would have become utterly fruitless unto them. (90) Those *were the persons* unto whom we gave the scripture, and wisdom, and prophecy; but if these believe not therein, we will commit the care of them to a people who shall not disbelieve the same. (91) Those *were the persons* whom GOD hath directed, therefore follow their direction. Say *unto the inhabitants of Makkah*, I ask of you no recompense for *preaching the Qurán;* it is no other than an admonition unto *all* creatures.

|| (92) They make not a due estimation of GOD, when R $\frac{11}{17}$. they say, GOD hath not sent down unto man anything at

---

Jonas. See chap. x. 98, chap. xxi. 87, and chap. xxxvii. 139, and notes there.

Lot. See chap. vii. 81.

(88) *Their fathers, &c.* This verse strengthens the statement under ver. 85. Muhammad had forgotten the names of other prophets of whom he had heard, and accordingly the spirit of his inspiration makes this very general statement. See also note on chap. iii. 34.

(89) *Guilty of idolatry.* See note on chap. iv. 46.

(90) *If these believe not.* Baidháwi makes these words to refer to the Quraish. They, however, agree with the teaching of the Bible in regard to the Jews, to whom they may very well refer. See Rodwell's translation. This passage may be quoted to show that the Scriptures of the former prophets were extant in Muhammad's day, and that they were not only genuine, but that Jewish unbelief was incapable of corrupting them. They would be committed to the care of another people.

(91) *An admonition unto all creatures, i.e.,* the *direction* given to all the prophets, and now declared by Muhammad to be the teaching of God for all men. We see here the theory of a universal Islám already present in Muhammad's mind. See chap. ii. 193.

(92) *They make not a due estimation of God.* "That is, they know him not truly, nor have just notions of his goodness and mercy towards man. The persons here meant, according to some commentators, are the Jews, and according to others the idolaters (Baidháwi).

all: Say, who sent down the book which Moses brought, a light and a direction unto men; which ye transcribe on papers, whereof ye publish *some part,* and great part *whereof* ye conceal? and ye have been taught *by Muhammad* what ye knew not, neither your fathers. Say, GOD *sent it down:* then leave them to amuse themselves with their vain discourse. (93) This book which we have sent down *is* blessed; confirming that which was *revealed* before it; and *is delivered unto thee* that thou mayest preach *it* unto the metropolis *of Makkah* and to those who are round about it. And they who believe in the next life will believe therein, and they will diligently observe their *times of* prayer. (94) Who is more wicked than he who forgeth a lie concerning GOD? or saith, *This* was revealed unto me; when nothing had been revealed unto him? and who saith, I will produce a revelation like unto that which GOD hath sent down? If thou didst see when

---

"This verse and the two next, as Jaláluddín thinks, were revealed at Madína."—*Sale.*

If the passage be referred to the Jews, the meaning of the phrase *God hath not sent down unto man anything at all* is that God never *sent down* a book to man, as Muhammad taught, but gave the word by the inspiration of holy men. See Prelim. Disc., pp. 111–114.

Which ye transcribe, &c. These words also show that Muhammad's charge of corrupting the Scriptures had no reference to the original text but to the practice of the Jews, whom he believed to have *suppressed or concealed* those portions referring to himself as a prophet. See note on chap. iv. 44.

Their vain discourse. This clause points to Madína as the place to which this and the following verse belong. Muhammad did not use this tone at Makkah.

(93) *This book . . . confirming, &c.* See note on chap. ii. 50.

Metropolis of Makkah. This should have been *of Madína,* seeing the passage belongs there. The term *metropolis* would suit Madína much better than the then heathen Makkah. The clause following, *and to those who are round about it,* also points to Madína, for Muhammad did not preach to those *round about* Makkah until his unsuccessful visit to Tayif shortly before the Hijra.

(94) *This was revealed unto me, &c.* "Falsely pretending to have received revelations from him, as did Musailama, al Aswad, al Ansi, and others, or doing as did Abdullah Ibn Saad Ibn Abi Sarah, who for some time was the Prophet's amanuensis, and when these words were dictated to him as revealed, viz., 'We created man of a purer

the ungodly *are* in the pangs of death, and the angels reach out their hands, *saying*, Cast forth your souls; this day shall ye receive an ignominious punishment for that which ye have falsely spoken concerning GOD; and because ye have proudly rejected his signs. (95) And now are ye come unto us alone, as we created you at first, and ye have left that which we had bestowed on you behind your backs; neither do we see with you your intercessors, whom ye thought to have been partners *with God* among you: now is *the relation* between you cut off, and what ye imagined hath deceived you.

|| (96) GOD causeth the grain and the date-stone to put forth: he bringeth forth the living from the dead, and he

R $\frac{12}{18}$.

---

kind of clay,' &c. (chap. xxiii. 12–14), cried out, by way of admiration, 'Blessed be God the best Creator!' and being ordered by Muhammad to write these words down also as part of the inspired passage, began to think himself as great a prophet as his master. Whereupon he took upon himself to corrupt and alter the Qurán according to his own fancy, and at length apostatising, was one of the ten who were proscribed at the taking of Makkah (Prelim. Disc., p. 93), and narrowly escaped with life on his recantation, by the interposition of Othmán Ibn Affán, whose foster-brother he was."—*Sale, Baidháwi.*

I will produce a revelation like, &c. Muhammad's claim was that the Qurán was the word of God because it was inimitable, and over and over the challenge was given to *Bring a chapter like unto it.* See chap. ii. 23, x. 39, and chap. xvii. 90. Here, by *assuming* the Qurán to be the word of God, he declares the very attempt to meet his challenge the most wicked of acts, whereas his opponents only claimed to be able to write a revelation equal to that of the writing of Muhammad in literary merit, thus meeting the challenge. This passage clearly indicates that Muhammad's contemporaries did not regard the Qurán as inimitable.

This passage also belongs to the list of verses quoted to prove Muhammad's sincerity in believing in his own inspiration; but see note on ver. 48.

The angels. See notes on ver. 60.

(95) *Alone, i.e.,* "without your wealth, your children, or your friends, which ye so much depended on in your lifetime."—*Sale.*

Your intercessors. Idols and false gods.

(96–102) This passage sets forth God as the all-wise, powerful, and merciful Creator, everywhere manifesting himself in nature, and therefore worthy of the worship and honour which was bestowed by the idolaters upon the mere creature. It is one of the most elevated and beautiful passages in this chapter. We learn from it the

bringeth forth the dead from the living. This *is* GOD. Why therefore are ye turned away *from him?* (97) He causeth the morning to appear; and hath ordained the night for rest, and the sun and the moon for computing *of time*. This is the disposition of the mighty, the wise *God.* (98) It is he who hath ordained the stars for you, that ye may be directed thereby in the darkness of the land and of the sea. We have clearly shown forth *our* signs unto people who understand. (99) It is he who hath produced you from one soul; and *hath provided for you* a sure receptacle and a repository. We have clearly shown forth *our* signs unto people who are wise. (100) It is he who sendeth down water from heaven, and we have thereby produced the springing buds of all things, and have thereout produced the green thing, from which we produce the grain growing in rows, and palm-trees from whose branches proceed clusters of dates *hanging* close together; and gardens of grapes, and olives, and pomegranates, *both* like and unlike to one another. Look on their fruits when they bear fruit, and their growing to maturity. Verily herein are signs unto people who believe. (101) *Yet* they have set up the genii as partners with GOD, although he created them: and they have falsely attributed unto him sons and daughters, without knowledge. Praise be unto him, and

---

power which the preacher of Makkah exerted in opposition to the idolatry of his countrymen—the power of truth against falsehood.

(96) *The living from the dead, &c.* Compare with chap. iii. 27. He bringeth forth life from the seed or the egg.

(98) *The land.* Literally, of the wilderness or desert, in traversing which the stars serve the Arab in the same way as they do the mariner. They worshipped the stars, but forgot the God who made them.

(99) *One soul.* Adam. The unity of the human race is here recognised.

Receptacle and repository. "Namely, in the loins of your fathers and the wombs of your mothers."—*Sale, Baidháwi.*

(101) *The genii.* "This signifies properly the *genus* of rational *invisible* beings, whether angels, devils, or that intermediate species usually called *genii*. Some of the commentators, therefore, in this place, understand the angels whom the pagan Arabs worshipped ;

far be that from him which they attribute *unto him!* *He is* the maker of heaven and earth: how should he have issue since he hath no consort? he hath created all things, and he is omniscient. (102) This is GOD your LORD; there is no GOD but he, the creator of all things; therefore serve him: for he taketh care of all things. (103) The sight comprehendeth him not, but he comprehendeth the sight; he *is* the gracious, the wise. (104) Now have evident demonstrations come unto you from your LORD; whoso seeth *them the advantage thereof will redound* to his own soul: and whoso is *wilfully* blind, *the consequence will be* to himself. I am not a keeper over you. (105) Thus do we variously explain *our* signs, that they may say, Thou hast studied diligently, and that we may declare them unto people of understanding. (106) Follow that which hath been revealed unto thee from thy LORD; there

R $\frac{13}{19}$.

---

and others the devils, either because they became their servants by adoring idols at their instigation, or else because, according to the Magian system, they looked on the devil as a sort of creator, making him the author and principle of all evil, and God the author of good only."—*Sale, Baidháwi.*

The genii of Islám are a distinct class of beings—some good, but generally evil. Some of them were converted to Islám. See notes on chap. xlvi. 28, and chap. lxxii.

Sons and daughters. See Prelim. Disc., pp. 38 and 70.

(102) *How should he have issue, &c.* This passage was directed against the Makkah idolaters, but is commonly quoted against the doctrine of the sonship of Christ. See note, chap. ii. 116.

(103) *The sight comprehendeth him not, &c.* Literally, the eyes cannot find him, and he findeth the eyes. So the Urdu and Persian translations.

(104) *Evident demonstrations.* Not only the testimony to God in his own works, alluded to above, but also the *signs* of the Qurán.

(105) *Thou hast studied diligently.* "That is, thou hast been instructed by the Jews and Christians in these matters, and only retailest to us what thou hast learned of them. For this the infidels objected to Muhammad, thinking it impossible for him to discourse on subjects of so high a nature, and in so clear and pertinent a manner, without being well versed in the doctrines and sacred writings of those people."—*Sale.*

The passage seems to us rather to predicate the superiority of the teaching of the Qurán over the thoughts and popular beliefs of the Arabs. Certainly the next verse, which must be read in connection with this, points to the idolaters alone.

is no GOD but he: retire therefore from the idolaters. (107) If GOD had *so* pleased, they had not been guilty of idolatry. We have not appointed thee a keeper over them; neither art thou a guardian over them. (108) Revile not the *idols* which they invoke besides GOD, lest they maliciously revile GOD, without knowledge. Thus have we prepared for every nation their works: hereafter unto GOD shall they return, and he shall declare unto them that which they have done. (109) They have sworn by GOD, by the most solemn oath, that if a sign came unto them, they would certainly believe therein: Say, Verily signs are in the power of GOD alone; and he permitteth

---

(107) *A keeper . . . a guardian.* A similar expression occurs in ver. 104. The purport of the saying is that God has chosen some and rejected others, and that he had not sent the Prophet to be a *keeper* or *guardian* to any of those who had been given over to reprobation. These would not believe, having been blinded and hardened. See vers. 110-113 below.

(108) *Revile not the idols.* The Quraish had declared that unless the Muslims should cease reviling their idols they would revile the name of God.—*Tafsir-i-Raufi.* The passage belongs to the period when Muhammad finally broke with the Quraish, having come to look upon them as rejected of God. He requires his followers to separate from them (ver. 106), and here they are commanded to abstain from aggressive action, seeing nothing would come of it but that the name of God would be reviled. The attitude of the Muslims towards them was to be one of passive defiance and conscious superiority. This passage is regarded as now abrogated. Certainly it never has been acted upon by the Muhammadans since the rise of Muslim power in the world.

(109) *Signs are in the power of God alone.* "In this passage Muhammad endeavours to excuse his inability of working a miracle, as had been demanded of him; declaring that God did not think fit to comply with their desires; and that if he had so thought fit, yet it had been in vain, because if they were not convinced by the Qurán, they would not be convinced by the greatest miracle."—*Sale.*

Sale compares this statement of Muhammad with that of Jesus in Luke xvi. 31. But surely there is no comparison. Jesus did not simply rely upon the testimony of Moses, though *in his case* that might have been sufficient. But Muhammad, instead of resting his claim upon the testimony of inspired writings already received by the Quraish, bases it upon his own Qurán. The Quraish, and probably also the Jews, demanded a miracle—*a single miracle*—and swear most solemnly they will believe his claim if only he will give them one sign of his apostleship; but Muhammad, confessing him-

you not to understand, that when they come, they will not believe. (110) And we will turn aside their hearts and their sight *from the truth*, as they believed not therein the first time; and we will leave them to wander in their error.

‖ (111) And though we had sent down angels unto them, and the dead had spoken unto them, and we had gathered together before them all things in one view; they would not have believed, unless GOD had so pleased: but the greater part of them know *it* not. (112) Thus have we appointed unto every prophet an enemy; the devils of men, and of genii: who privately suggest the one to the other specious discourses to deceive; but if thy LORD pleased, they would not have done it. Therefore leave them, and that which they have falsely imagined;

EIGHTH SIPARA.

R $\frac{14}{1}$.

---

self unable to work even this one miracle, falls back upon the inimitable Qurán and the doctrine of reprobation. What could be clearer than the fact that Muhammad, at least up to this date, wrought no miracle? It would seem that Muhammad was brought under pressure by the demand of his own disciples that he should show the unbelievers a sign. But his only reply is that God "permitted you not to understand, that when they come they will not believe." He leads his followers *to expect signs* in the future, but such signs will not avail for the salvation of the infidels. See the next two verses. Rodwell's translation is here in error. The allusion is not to past unbelief, but to the future. The verbs are all in the Aorist tense.

(111) *Though we had sent down angels, &c.* "For the Makkans required that Muhammad should either show them an angel descending from heaven in their sight, or raise their dead fathers, that they might discourse with them, or prevail on God and his angels to appear to them in a body."—*Sale.*

So the commentators; but the interpretation is probably inferred from the text. The *Tafsír-i-Raufí* relates that the infidels had demanded that the mountain Safa should be changed into gold. Muhammad prayed for power to work this miracle, but was dissuaded from the undertaking by Gabriel, who warned him that were such a miracle wrought and any remain in unbelief, they would be instantly destroyed. Such are the devices of Muslims to explain away passages of the Qurán at variance with their teaching, and the teaching of the traditions, on the subject of Muhammad's power to work miracles.

(112) *An enemy; the devils, &c.* The enemy of the prophets referred to here is not Satan, but a demon (the original is *Shayátín, devils*). These are *the devils of men and the genii.* Some think that

(113) and let the hearts of those be inclined thereto who believe not in the life to come: and let them please themselves therein, and let them gain that which they are gaining. (114) Shall I seek after any *other* judge besides GOD *to judge between us?* It is he who hath sent down unto you the book *of the Qurán* distinguishing *between good and evil;* and they to whom we gave the scripture know that it is sent down from thy LORD, with truth. Be not therefore *one* of those who doubt *thereof.* (115) The words of thy LORD are perfect, in truth and justice; there is none who can change his words: he *both* heareth *and* knoweth. (116) But if thou obey the greater part of them who are in the earth, they will lead thee aside from the path of GOD: they follow an *uncertain* opinion only, and speak nothing but lies; (117) verily thy LORD well knoweth those who go astray from his path, and well

---

the infidels are referred to under this appellation. But it seems far more reasonable to suppose the allusion to be to evil spirits. The meaning, then, is that every prophet is beset by an evil spirit, whose evil suggestions must be distinguished from those of the Angel Gabriel. The word translated *privately suggest* is the same which is translated *revelation* (wahí). We know that Muhammad did on one occasion confess to having been deceived by a *revelation* of the devil. See notes on chap. liii. 19, 20.

Genii. See note on ver. 101. They are here associated with men as subject to demoniacal influences.

(113) *Let the hearts . . . be inclined thereto, i.e.,* their idolatry and obstinate unbelief are due to the influence of devils, wherefore withdraw from them and permit them to be subject to these influences, and so allow them to obtain the reward of their evil-doing.

(114) *The book distinguishing.* See notes on chap. iii. 3. This is all the miracle required by those who believe.

They to whom we gave the Scripture know. See note on ver. 20.

(115) *None who can change his words.* "Some interpret this of the immutability of God's decree, and the certainty of his threats and promises; others, of his particular promise to preserve the Qurán from any such alterations or corruptions as they imagine to have happened to the Pentateuch and the Gospel (Prelim. Disc., sect. iv.), and others, of the unalterable duration of the Muhammadan law, which they hold is to last till the end of the world, there being no other prophet, law, or dispensation to be expected after it."

See also note on ver. 33.

(116) *An opinion only,* "imagining that the true religion was that which their idolatrous ancestors professed."—*Sale.*

knoweth those who are *rightly* directed. (118) Eat of that whereon the name of GOD hath been commemorated, if ye believe in his signs; (119) and why do ye not eat of that whereon the name of GOD hath been commemorated? since he hath plainly declared unto you what he hath forbidden you; except that which ye be compelled to eat of by necessity; many lead *others* into error, because of their appetites, being void of knowledge; but thy LORD well knoweth *who are* the transgressors. (120) Leave both the outside of iniquity and the inside thereof: for they who commit iniquity shall receive the reward of that which they shall have gained. (121) Eat not therefore of that whereon the name of GOD hath not been commemorated; for this is certainly wickedness: but the devils will suggest unto their friends, that they dispute with you *concerning this precept;* but if ye obey them, ye *are* surely idolaters.

|| (122) Shall he who hath been dead, and whom we have restored unto life and unto whom we have ordained a light, whereby he may walk among men, *be* as he whose similitude is in darkness, from whence he shall not come R $\frac{15}{2}$.

(118-121) See notes on chap. ii. 174, and chap. v. 4-6. The *Tafsír-i-Raufi* gives the opinion of some commentators that the flesh of animals which have died without being slaughtered is here specially referred to. The heathen Arabs had endeavoured to persuade some of the Muslims to eat of such flesh, on the ground that if what was slaughtered by man was allowable for food, much more that which was killed by God! The reply of the Prophet is that nothing but necessity would make such flesh lawful for food. Rodwell thinks these verses should follow ver. 153; but such misplacement of passages is very common.

The outside of iniquity and the inside, i.e., "both open and secret sins."—*Sale.* The lengthy discussions of the Muslim commentators on this clause illustrate their general ignorance of heart purity. See chap. v. 7, note.

(121) *Devils will suggest.* See note on ver. 112.

(122) Sale says the persons alluded to in this verse "were Hamza, Muhammad's uncle, and Abu Jahl; others, instead of Hamza, name Omar or Ammár." But there is no need of giving the passage any more special reference than that there is infinite difference between a believer and an infidel.

forth? Thus was that which the infidels are doing prepared for them. (123). And thus have we placed in every city chief leaders of the wicked *men* thereof, that they may act deceitfully therein; but they shall act deceitfully against their own souls only; and they know *it* not. (124) And when a sign cometh unto them, they say, We will by no means believe until *a revelation* be brought unto us, like unto that which hath been delivered unto the messengers of GOD. GOD best knoweth whom he will appoint for his messenger. Vileness in the sight of GOD shall fall upon those who deal wickedly, and a grievous punishment, for that they have dealt deceitfully. (125) And whomsoever GOD shall please to direct, he will open his breast to *receive the faith of* Islám: but whomsoever he shall please to lead into error, he will render his breast straight *and* narrow, as though he were climbing up to heaven. Thus doth GOD inflict a terrible punishment on those who believe not. (126) This is the right way of thy LORD. Now have we plainly declared *our* signs unto those people who will consider. (127) They shall have a dwelling of peace with their LORD, and he shall be their patron, because of that which they have wrought. (128)

---

(123) *Leaders of the wicked*, as Pharaoh, Nimrod, and others (*Abdul Qádir*). Others refer the passage to the influential leaders of the opposition to Muhammad in tribes other than the Quraish.

(124) *A sign*, *i.e.*, a verse of the Qurán.

We will not believe, &c. "These were the words of the Quraish, who thought there were persons among themselves more worthy of the honour of being God's messenger than Muhammad."—*Sale*.

Whom he will appoint, &c. "Literally, *Where he will place his commission.* God, says al Baidháwi, bestows not the gift of prophecy on any one on account of his nobility or riches, but for their spiritual qualifications; making choice of such of his servants as he pleases, and who he knows will execute their commissions faithfully."—*Sale*.

(125) *Whomsoever God shall please to direct.* This verse makes a man's salvation to depend solely on the will of God. Muslims are such because God has opened their hearts to Islám, and the infidels are lost because God has rendered them as incapable of believing as they are of ascending up to heaven. He *leads them into error* in order to inflict upon them *a terrible punishment*.

Think on the day whereon God shall gather them all together, *and shall say,* O company of genii, ye have been much concerned with mankind; and their friends from among mankind *shall* say, O LORD, the one of us hath received advantage from the other, and we are arrived at our limited term which thou hast appointed us. *God* will say, *Hell* fire *shall be* your habitation, therein shall ye remain *forever;* unless as GOD shall please *to mitigate your pains,* for thy LORD *is* wise *and* knowing. (129) Thus do we set some of the unjust over others of them, because of that which they have deserved.

‖ (130) O company of genii and men, did not messengers from among yourselves come unto you, rehearsing my signs unto you, and forewarning you of the meeting of this your day ? They shall answer, We bear witness against ourselves: the present life deceived them: and they shall bear witness against themselves that they were

R $\frac{16}{3}$.

---

(128) *A company of genii.* See vers. 101 and 112, with notes.
Much concerned with mankind "in tempting and seducing them to sin."—*Sale.*
Advantage. "The advantage which men received from the evil spirits was their raising and satisfying their lusts and appetites ; and that which the latter received in return was the obedience paid them by the former," &c.—*Sale, Baidháwi, Jaláluddín.*
Term. See note on ver. 2.
Unless as God shall please, &c. "The commentators tell us that this alleviation of the pains of the damned will be when they shall be taken out of the fire to drink the boiling water, or to suffer the extreme cold called al Zamharir, which is to be one part of their punishment; but others think the respite which God will grant to some before they are thrown into hell is here intended. According to the exposition of Ibn Abbás, these words may be rendered, *Unless him whom God shall please* to deliver thence."—*Sale, Baidháwi, Jaláluddín.*
See also Prelim. Disc., sect. ix. p. 149.
(130) *Messengers from among yourselves.* "It is the Muhammadan belief that apostles were sent by God for the conversion both of *genii* and of men; being generally of human race (as Muhammad, in particular, who pretended to have a commission to preach to both kinds); according to this passage, it seems there must have been prophets of the race of *genii* also, though their mission be a secret to us."—*Sale.*
Some regard the seven *genii* who came to Muhammad (see chap. lxxii.) as God's messengers to their own kind.

unbelievers. (131) This *hath been the method of God's dealings with his creatures*, because thy LORD would not destroy the cities in *their* iniquity, while their inhabitants were careless. (132) Every one shall *have* degrees *of recompense* of that which they shall do; (133) for thy LORD is not regardless of that which they do, and thy LORD is self-sufficient *and* endued with mercy. If he pleaseth he can destroy you, and cause such as he pleaseth to succeed you, in like manner as he produced you from the posterity of other people. (134) Verily that which is threatened you, shall surely come to pass; neither shall ye cause *it* to fail. (135) Say *unto those of Makkah*, O my people, act according to your power; verily I will act *according to my duty:* and hereafter shall ye know whose will be the reward of paradise. The ungodly shall not prosper. (136) *Those of Makkah* set apart unto GOD a portion of that which he hath produced of the fruits of the earth, and of cattle; and say, This *belongeth* unto GOD (according to their imagination), and this unto our companions. And that which is *destined* for their companions cometh not unto GOD; yet that which *is set apart* unto

(131) *Would not destroy, &c.* These *cities* are evidently the same mentioned in ver. 123. The doctrine taught here is that God sends a messenger to every people to warn and instruct them in his way, which, according to the Qurán, is Islám. He could not justly punish them, says the *Tafsír-i-Raufi*, unless he should first send them a prophet.

(132) *Degrees of recompense.* The rewards of the wicked, as well as of the righteous, shall be in proportion to their light and privilege. This principle of justice seems to be clearly enunciated here.

(133) *Self-sufficient*, literally one *rich* or wealthy, needing not the help of others.

If he pleaseth he can destroy you, &c. The allusion is to the tribes of Ád and Thámúd, &c., reported to have been destroyed on account of their wickedness. See Prelim. Disc., pp. 21, 22.

(135) *Verily I will act.* "That is, ye may proceed in your rebellion against God and your malice towards me, and be confirmed in your infidelity; but I will persevere to bear your insults with patience, and to publish those revelations which God has commanded me."—*Sale, Baidháwi.*

(136) *This belongeth unto God, &c.* The commentators say the idolaters divided the produce of their fields and flocks into two parts,

GOD cometh unto their companions. How ill do they judge! (137) In like manner have their companions induced many of the idolaters to slay their children, that they might bring them to perdition, and that they might render their religion obscure and confused unto them. But if GOD had pleased, they had not done this: therefore leave them and that which they falsely imagine. (138) They also say, These cattle and fruits of the earth are sacred; none shall eat thereof but who we please (according to their imagination); and *there are* cattle whose backs are forbidden *to be rode on, or laden with burdens;* and *there are* cattle on which they commemorate not the name of GOD *when they slay them;* devising a lie against him. *God* shall reward them for that which they falsely devise.

---

one for God and one for the idols, or rather *inferior deities*, called here and throughout this passage *companions*. Should the portion of God prove greater at the time of harvest, they changed the portions, giving the largest portion to the gods, saying that the Almighty God was not in need of so much as the poorer gods.

Sale, on the authority of Baidháwi and Jaláluddín, says, "The share set apart for God was employed chiefly in relieving the poor and strangers, and the share of the idols for paying their priests and providing sacrifices for them;" which statement quite accounts for their confidence in God's ability to take care of his own interests.

See also Prelim. Disc., pp. 36 and 37.

(137) *To slay their children.* "Either by that inhuman custom, which prevailed among those of Kindah and some other tribes, of burying their daughters alive so soon as they were born, if they apprehended they could not maintain them; or else by offering them to their idols, at the instigation of those who had the custody of their temples."—*Sale, Baidháwi.*

See notes on chaps. xvi. 60, 61, and lxxxi. 8, 9.

That they might bring them to perdition, &c. The deities of the idolaters are here declared to be evil spirits, whose object is the destruction of men by obscuring the way of salvation taught by the prophet Ismail.

If God had pleased, &c. See note on ver. 125.

(138) *Who we please.* "That is, those who serve our idols, and are of the male sex; for the women were not allowed to eat of them."—*Sale, Baidháwi.*

Whose backs are forbidden. See Prelim. Disc., pp. 199-202, and note on chap. v. 102.

Cattle on which, &c. See notes on chap. ii. 174, and chap. v. 2, 4-6.

(139) And they say, That which is in the bellies of these cattle *is* allowed to our males *to eat*, and *is* forbidden to our wives: but if it prove abortive, then they are *both* partakers thereof. *God* shall give them the reward of their attributing *these things to him:* he *is* knowing *and* wise. (140) They are utterly lost who have slain their children foolishly,. without knowledge; and have forbidden that which GOD hath given them for food, devising a lie against GOD. They have erred, and were not *rightly* directed.

RUBA.

R $\frac{17}{4}$.

‖ (141) He it is who produceth gardens of *vines, both those which are* supported on trails *of wood,* and *those which are* not supported, and palm-trees, and the corn affording various food, and olives, and pomegranates, alike and unlike unto one another. Eat of their fruit when they bear fruit, and pay the due thereof on the day whereon ye shall gather it; but be not profuse, for *God* loveth not those who are too profuse. (142) And *God hath given you* some cattle fit for bearing of burdens, and *some* fit for slaughter only. Eat of what GOD hath given you for food; and follow not the steps of Satan, for he is your declared enemy. (143) Four pair *of cattle hath God given you;* of sheep one pair,

---

(139) *That which, &c.* "That is, the fœtus or embryos of the Bahaira and the Sáiba (chap. v. 102) which shall be brought forth alive."—*Sale.*

Of this the men alone might eat, but "if it prove abortive," the women were allowed to partake.

(140) See note on ver. 137.

(141) *Supported . . . and not supported,* or cultivated fruit-trees and vines, and those which grow wild.

Pay the due. "That is, give alms thereof to the poor. And these alms, as al Baidháwi observes, were what they used to give before the *zakát,* or legal alms, was instituted; which was done after Muhammad had retired from Makkah, where this verse was revealed. Yet some are of another opinion, and for this very reason will have the verse to have been revealed at Madína."—*Sale.*

Be not profuse, i.e., "charity begins at home."—*Sale.*

(142) *Follow not the steps of Satan, i.e.,* by observing the idolatrous customs referred to above.

(143, 144) *Four pair.* Alluding to the *four* classes of sacred animals. See chap. v. 102, and note.

Hath God forbidden, &c. The *Tafsír-i-Raufi* says this passage was revealed in order to silence Auf-Ibn-Málik, who complained against

and of goats one pair. Say *unto them*, Hath *God* forbidden the two males, *of sheep and of goats*, or the two females; or that which the wombs of the two females contain? Tell me with certainty, if ye speak truth. (144) And of camels *hath God given you* one pair, and of oxen one pair. Say, hath he forbidden the two males *of these*, or the two females; or that which the wombs of the two females contain? Were ye present when GOD commanded you this? And who is more unjust than he who deviseth a lie against GOD, that he may seduce men without understanding? Verily GOD directed not unjust people.

|| (145) Say, I find not in that which hath been revealed R 18/5. unto me anything forbidden unto the eater, that he eat it not, except it be that which dieth of itself, or blood poured forth, or swine's flesh; for this is an abomination: or *that which is* profane, having been slain in the name of some other than of GOD. But whoso shall be compelled by necessity *to eat of these things*, not lusting, nor *wilfully transgressing*, verily thy LORD *will be* gracious *unto him* and merciful. (146) Unto the Jews did we forbid every

---

Muhammad for having allowed his followers the food of sacred animals, which was forbidden by their fathers. If the prohibition was on the ground of their being *males*, then *all* males would be forbidden; if their being *females* were the ground, then *all* females would be prohibited; and if the unborn fœtus were forbidden, then all animals would be forbidden, seeing such were either male or female!

Sale, on the authority of Baidháwi, says :—"In this passage Muhammad endeavours to convince the Arabs of their superstitious folly in making it unlawful, one while, to eat the males of these four kinds of cattle; another while, the females; and at another time, their young."

Who is more unjust than he, &c. "The person particularly intended here, some say, was Amru Ibn Luhai, king of Hajáz, a great introducer of idolatry and superstition among the Arabs." See Prelim. Disc., sect. i. p. 42.—*Sale.*

(145) See note on ver. 118. There is no contradiction of chap. v. 2-6, as Brinckman and others suppose. This includes all kinds of flesh specified there.

Whoso shall be compelled. This exception is added to every passage of the Qurán repeating the law of permitted and forbidden meats. See chap. ii. 174, chap. v. 4, and chap. xvi. 116.

beast having an *undivided* hoof; and of bullocks and sheep, we forbade them the fat of both; except that which should be on their backs, or their inwards, or which should be intermixed with the bone. This have we rewarded them with, because of their iniquity; and we are surely speakers of truth. (147) If they accuse thee of imposture, say, Your LORD is endued with extensive mercy; but his severity shall not be averted from wicked people. (148) The idolaters will say, If GOD had pleased, we had not been guilty of idolatry, neither our fathers; and *pretend that* we have not forbidden *them* anything. Thus did they who were before them accuse *the prophets* of imposture, until they tasted our severe punishment. Say, Is there with you any *certain* knowledge *of what ye allege*, that ye may produce it unto us? Ye follow only a *false* imagination; and ye utter only lies. (149) Say, therefore, Unto GOD *belongeth* the most evident demonstration; for if he had pleased, he had directed you all. (150) Say, Produce your witnesses, who can bear testimony that GOD hath forbidden this. But if they bear testimony *of this*, do not thou bear testimony with them, nor do thou follow the desires of those who accuse our signs of falsehood, and who believe not in the life to come, and equalise *idols* with their LORD.

---

(146) *Except that . . . on their backs.* This passage contradicts the teaching of the Mosaic law. Compare Levit. iii. 9–11 and 17, with vii. 23–25.

(148) *The idolaters will say, &c.* Yet this is just what the Qurán teaches in the next verse! The same doctrine is taught in vers. 125 and 137 of this chapter. See notes there. The idolaters *justified their idolatry* on this ground.

Accuse . . . of imposture. See note on chap. iii. 189.

A false imagination. See note on ver. 116.

(150) *If they bear testimony, &c.* In the beginning of this verse the Quraish are challenged to bring testimony to prove that God had forbidden the flesh of the sacred animals, Bahaira, Sáiba, &c. Here Muhammad is told not to believe the testimony even if produced in answer to the challenge! One would think a challenge under such circumstances was scarcely worth putting forth.

Equalise. See note on ver. 1.

|| (151) Say, Come; I will rehearse that which your LORD hath forbidden you; *that is to say*, that ye be not guilty of idolatry, and *that ye show* kindness to *your* parents, and that ye murder not your children *for fear* lest ye be reduced to poverty; we will provide for you and them; and draw not near unto heinous crimes, neither openly nor in secret; and slay not the soul which GOD hath forbidden *you to slay*, unless for a just cause. This hath he enjoined you that ye may understand. (152) And meddle not with the substance of the orphan, otherwise than for the improving *thereof*, until he attain his age of strength: and use a full measure, and a just balance. We will not impose *a task* on *any* soul beyond its ability. And when ye pronounce *judgment* observe justice, although it be *for or against* one who is near of kin, and fulfil the covenant of GOD. This hath *God* commanded you, that ye may be admonished; (153) and *that ye may know* that this is my right way: therefore follow it, and follow not the path *of others*, lest ye be scattered from the path *of God*. This hath he commanded you, that ye may take heed. (154) We gave also unto Moses the book *of the law;* a perfect rule unto him who should do right, and a determination concerning all things *needful,*

---

(151) See notes on ver. 137. Sale says, " This and the two following verses Jaláluddín supposes to have been revealed at Madína." The requirements certainly belong to a date later than the Hijra.

Unless for a just cause. " As for murder, apostasy, or adultery."—*Sale.*

(152) *The substance of the orphan.* See notes on chap. iv. 2-5.

A full measure. Compare Deut. xxv. 13-16.

A task . . . beyond ability. " But the pilgrimage, the Ramadhán fast, the killing of unbelievers, and several other things, are very often beyond the power of many Moslems."—*Brinckman.* But no Muslim is *required* to perform what is " beyond his power." This is the very lesson taught in this verse. See chap. iv. 27.

(154) Rodwell thinks the *abruptness* with which this passage is introduced predicates a lost passage preceding this. It, however, simply illustrates the crudeness of the work wrought by the compilers of the Qurán.

The book of the law, a perfect rule, &c. This testimony to the Pentateuch and the way of salvation indicated therein is entirely against

and a direction and mercy; that *the children of Israel* might believe the meeting of their LORD.

R 20/7.

‖ (155) And this book which we have *now* sent down is blessed; therefore follow it, and fear *God* that ye may obtain mercy: (156) lest ye should say, The scriptures were only sent down unto two people before us; and we neglected to peruse them with attention: (157) or lest ye should say, If a book *of divine revelations* had been sent down unto us, we should surely have been better directed than they. And now hath a manifest declaration come unto you from your LORD, and a direction and mercy: and who is more unjust than he who deviseth lies against the signs of GOD, and turneth aside from them? We will reward those who turn aside from our signs with a grievous punishment, because they have turned aside. (158) Do they wait for *any other* than that the angels should come unto them, *to part their souls from their bodies,* or that thy LORD should come *to punish them;*

the Qurán, which denies the cardinal doctrine of salvation by sacrifice and atoning blood. Yet in the following verses the assertion is made that the teaching of the Qurán and of "the Scriptures . . . sent down unto the people before"—that is, to the Jews and Christians—is the same.

(156) *And we neglected to peruse them.* Abdul Qádir translates, "and we did not know to read and to teach them;" or, as Muir translates, "but we are unable to read in their language" (*Life of Mahomet,* vol. ii. p. 68, note). Muir conjectures that Muhammad was led to make the prophetic claim by thoughts suggested by the *objections* of his townsmen in language like the following:—"It is well for Jews and Christians to follow the purer faith thou speakest of. *They,* we know, have had prophets bringing them a message of the will of God. Let *us* be content with the light our Maker hath given unto us, and remain as we are. *If a prophet had been sent unto us, we should no doubt have followed his directions, and been equally devout and spiritual in our worship as the Jews and Christians."* See whole discussion given at reference already quoted.

(157) *Better directed than they.* "Because of the acuteness of our wit, the clearness of our understanding, and our facility of learning sciences, as appears from our excelling in history, poetry, and oratory, notwithstanding we are illiterate people."—*Sale, Baidháwi.* A nice bit of Arab conceit.

Now hath a manifest declaration, &c. The prophetic claim is here again set up. See notes on vers. 19 and 48.

or that some of the signs of thy LORD should come to pass, *showing the day of judgment to be at hand?* On the day whereon some of thy LORD's signs shall come to pass, its faith shall not profit a soul which believed not before, or wrought not good in its faith. Say, Wait ye *for this day;* we surely do wait *for it.* (159) They who make a division in their religion and become sectaries, have thou nothing to do with them; their affair *belongeth* only unto GOD. Hereafter shall he declare unto them that which they have done. (160) He who shall appear with good works shall receive a tenfold recompense for the same; but he who shall appear with evil works shall receive only an equal *punishment* for the same; and they shall not be treated unjustly. (161) Say, Verily my LORD hath directed me into a right way, (162) a true religion, the sect of Abraham the orthodox; and he was no idolater. (163) Say, Verily my prayers, and my worship, and my life, and my death *are dedicated* unto GOD, the LORD of all crea-

---

(158) *Signs of thy Lord.* "Al Baidháwi, from a tradition of Muhammad, says that ten signs will precede the last day, viz., the smoke, the beast of the earth, an eclipse in the east, another in the west, and a third in the peninsula of Arabia, the appearance of Antichrist, the sun's rising in the west, the eruption of Gog and Magog, the descent of Jesus on earth, and fire shall break forth from Aden."—*Sale.* See also Prelim. Disc., sect. iv. p. 62.

Its faith shall not profit, &c. "For faith in the next life will be of no advantage to those who have not believed in this; nor yet faith in this life without good works."—*Sale.*

(159) *Sectaries.* "That is, who believe in part of it and disbelieve other parts of it, or who form schisms therein. Muhammad is reported to have declared that the Jews were divided into seventy-one sects, and the Christians into seventy-two; and that his own followers would be split into seventy-three sects; and that all of them would be damned except only one of each."—*Sale, Baidháwi.*

As there were no sectaries among the Muslims at this time, it is quite certain that the purport of this passage is that Muhammad should avoid the Jews and Christians; and if so, this verse must be referred to Madína rather than to Makkah. Commentators, who interpret the passage thus, say it has been abrogated by the command to fight against infidels. See *Tafsír-i-Raufi in loco.*

(162) *The sect of Abraham the orthodox.* See note on chap. iii. 95, and chap. iv. 124.

(163) *Verily my prayers, &c.* This entire consecration of self to

tures: he hath no companion. This have I been commanded: I am the first Muslim. (164) Say, Shall I desire any other LORD besides GOD? since he is the LORD of all things; and no soul shall acquire *any merits or demerits* but for itself; and no burdened *soul* shall bear the burden of another. Moreover, unto your LORD shall ye return; and he shall declare unto you that concerning which ye *now* dispute. (165) It is he who hath appointed you to succeed *your predecessors* in the earth, and hath raised some of you above others by *various* degrees *of worldly advantages*, that he might prove you by that which he hath bestowed on you. Thy LORD is swift in punishing; and he *is also* gracious *and* merciful.

---

the true God is what Muhammad here declares to be the religion of Islám.

I am the first Muslim. See note on ver. 14.

(164) *No burdened soul, &c.* "This was revealed in answer to the preceding instances of the idolaters, who offered to take the crime upon themselves if Muhammad would conform to their worship."—*Sale, Baidháwi.*

That no sinner shall bear the sin of another is true; but Muhammad went further, denying that the burden of the sinner could be borne by any one. See note on chap. iii. 194.

(165) *Appointed you to succeed.* The original word is *khalífah*, which is applied to the successors of Muhammad.

The meaning, according to the *Tafsír-i-Raufí*, is either that the Quraish were appointed the successors of various peoples in Arabia, or that the Muslims are appointed the successors of the Arab idolaters. The latter seems to be the true meaning. If so, this portion of the chapter may belong to the Madína revelations.

CHAPTER VII.

ENTITLED SURAT AL ARÁF (THE PARTITION WALL).

Revealed at Makkah.

INTRODUCTION.

THIS chapter owes its title to the reference to *the partition wall* between heaven and hell in ver. 4, which is called *al Aráf*. It may be said to contain Muhammad's vindication of his prophetic claims. Accordingly, it abounds with stories of the experiences of former prophets, and of the judgments that overtook those who refused to accept their doctrine and the signs of their prophetic authority. Even the most careless reader can hardly fail to see that all these prophets are facsimiles of Muhammad himself. Their character and authority, their message and accompanying claims to inspiration, the incredulity and hardness of heart shown by the tribes to whom they were sent, the consequent rejection of the prophets, and the threatenings of the sudden and dreadful judgments of God upon unbelievers, all these correspond to the experience of Muhammad; and the inference suggested by each story is that the rejection of the Prophet of Makkah would bring with it judgments on the Quraish similar to and dreadful as those which befell those tribes who rejected the former prophets.

Probable Date of the Revelations.

The allusion to a famine in ver. 95 (compare chap. x. 22, 23, and xxiii. 77–79), and a subsequent period of prosperity in ver. 96, together with the tone of the whole chapter, point to a period immediately preceding the Hijra as the date to which it should be assigned.

The only passages to be excepted are vers. 158–160, and 164–171. The former of these passages evidently belongs to Madína, as appears: (1) From the title, *Illiterate Prophet*, or Gentile Prophet, as contrasted with the prophets of Judaism and Christianity. This contrast points to Madína rather than to Makkah. (2.) From the expression *the law and the gospel*, which, as Nöeldeke points out, never occurs in other than Madína revelations. (3.) From the words *and assist him*, which certainly refer to the Ansárs or helpers of Madína; and (4.) From the fact that this passage breaks the thread of discourse at ver. 157, which is taken up again at ver. 161. This passage was probably added by Muhammad himself at Madína.

Most commentators agree, also, in referring vers. 164-171 to Madína. Nöeldeke, however, differs from them, and regards it as belonging to Makkah. When, however, it is remembered that Muhammad's custom in the Qurán is to give the *most detailed* accounts of Jewish history and tradition in the *earliest* chapters containing such narratives, afterward alluding to the same stories with more or less brevity, it must be granted that this passage belongs to Madína, inasmuch as the substance of it is given at length in the early Madína chapters.

Principal Subjects.

	VERSES
Muhammad not to doubt the Qurán	1, 2
The people exhorted to believe in it	3
Many cities destroyed for their unbelief	4, 5
Prophets and their hearers on the judgment-day	6-9
The ingratitude of infidels	10
The creation of Adam	11
Satan refuses to worship Adam	11, 12
He is driven from Paradise	13
He is respited until the resurrection	14, 15
He avows his purpose to beguile man	16, 17
God threatens Satan and his victims	18, 19
The fall of Adam and Eve	20-24
They are expelled from Paradise	25, 26
Indecent customs condemned	27-29
God to be sought in prayer	30, 31
True worshippers to be decently clad	32-34
Every nation has a fixed term of life	35
The doom of those who reject the apostles of God	36-42
The blessed reward of true believers	43-45
God's curse on the infidels	45-46
The veil of Aráf and its inhabitants	47-50
The rejecters of God's apostles to be forgotten	51, 52
A warning against rejecting Muhammad	53, 54
The Creator and Lord of the worlds to be served	55-59

	VERSES
Noah rejected by his people—their fate	60–65
Húd rejected by the Ádites—their fate	66–73
Sálih rejected by the Thamúdites—their destruction	74–80
Lot rejected and the Sodomites destroyed	81–85
Shuaib rejected by the Madianites, and their doom	86–94
Unbelievers at Makkah unaffected either by adversity or prosperity	95, 96
The dreadful fate of those cities who rejected the apostles of God and charged them with imposture	97–101
They are reprobated	102, 103
Moses is sent to Pharaoh and his princes	104, 105
The miracles of the serpent and leprous hand	106–108
The magicians of Egypt called	109–115
Contest by miracles between Moses and the magicians	116–120
Several magicians converted to Moses	121–123
Pharaoh's anger kindled against them	124–127
Pharaoh and his princes persecute Moses and his people	128
Moses exhorts his people to patient trust in God	129, 130
Adversity and prosperity alike unavailing to bring Pharaoh to repentance	131, 132
The Egyptian unbelievers plagued	133, 134
The hypocrisy of the Egyptians	135
They are destroyed in the Red Sea	136
The people of Moses triumph, and possess the eastern and western land	137
The children of Israel become idolatrous	138, 141
Moses makes Aaron his deputy, and fasts forty days	142
He desires to see the glory of God, but repents his rashness	143
God gives Moses the law on two tables	144, 145
Infidels threatened for calling their prophets impostors	146, 147
The people of Moses worship the golden calf	148
They repent their sin	149
Moses in indignation assaults Aaron	150
He prays for forgiveness for himself and Aaron	151
He calls for vengeance on the idolaters	152
God merciful to believers	153
Moses's anger is appeased	154
He chooses seventy elders	155
Moses prays for deliverance from destruction by lightning	155, 156
The *Illiterate Prophet* foretold by Moses	156, 159

	VERSES
Some Jews rightly directed	160
The Israelites divided into twelve tribes	161
The rock smitten, and manna and quails given	161
The command to enter the city saying *Hittatun*, and the fate of the disobedient	162, 163
The Sabbath-breakers changed into apes	164–167
Dispersion of the Jews among the nations	168, 169
Some of their successors faithful to the law of Moses	170, 171
God shakes Mount Sinai over the Israelites	172
God's covenant with the children of Adam	173–175
The curse of Balaam a warning to infidels	176–179
Many genii and men created for hell	180
The names of God not to be travestied	181, 182
God's method of leading infidels to destruction	183, 184
Muhammad not possessed of a devil	185
No hope for the reprobate	186
The coming of the "last hour" sudden	187
Muhammad no seer, only a preacher	188
Adam and Eve were guilty of idolatry	189, 190
The folly of idolatry	191–198
Muhammad commanded to use moderation	199
He is to repel Satan by using the name of God	200, 201
The people of Makkah incorrigible	202
They charge Muhammad with imposture	203
The Qurán to be listened to in silence and holy meditation	204–206

IN THE NAME OF THE MOST MERCIFUL GOD.

|| (1) A. L. M. S. (2) A book hath been sent down unto thee: and therefore let there be no doubt in thy breast concerning it; that thou mayest preach the same, and *that it may be* an admonition unto the faithful. (3) Follow that which hath been sent down unto you from your LORD: and follow no guides besides him: how little will

---

(1) See note on chap. ii. 1. Some conjecture that these letters represent the sentence *Amara li Muhammad sándiq*, "thus spake to me Muhammad the truthful." See Rodwell's note *in loco*.

(2) *Let there be no doubt.* See note on chap. ii. 2. Arnold's remark on this passage is worthy of careful consideration:—"The

ye be warned! (4) How many cities have we destroyed; which our vengeance overtook by night, or while they were reposing themselves at noon-day! (5) And their supplication, when our punishment came upon them, was no other than that they said, Verily we have been unjust. (6) We will surely call those to an account unto whom *a prophet* hath been sent; and we will *also* call those to account who have been sent *unto them*. (7) And we will declare *their actions* unto them with knowledge; for we are not absent *from them*. (8) The weighing *of men's actions* on that day shall be just; and they whose balances *laden with their good works* shall be heavy, are those who *shall be* happy; (9) but they whose balances shall be light, are those who have lost their souls, because they injured our signs. (10) And now have we placed you on the earth, and have provided you food therein; *but* how little are ye thankful!

|| (11) We created you, and afterwards formed you; R $\frac{"}{\tau}$.

---

author of the Korán betrays precisely the disquietude and suspicion which invariably indicate *fraud*, and never exist in guileless, honest, and truthful minds."—*Islám and Christianity*, p. 316. And yet this constant and persistent assertion of honesty and truthfulness is regarded by many as certain evidence of his sincerity.

(4) *Cities destroyed . . . by night*, as in the case " of Sodom and Gomorrah, to whom Lot was sent." *Or . . . noon-day*, "as happened to the Midianites, to whom Shuaib preached."—*Sale, Tafsír-i-Raufi.*

(5) *Verily we have been unjust.* They will make this confession, thinking thereby to secure deliverance, not knowing that the time of repentance and confession has gone by.—*Tafsír-i-Raufi.*

(6) The prophets will testify for or against the people to whom they have been sent, and the people will witness to the faithfulness of the prophets.—*Tafsír-i-Raufi.*

(8) *The weighing, &c.* See Prelim. Disc., p. 144.

The balances. One of these shall be called *Light* and the other *Darkness.* The good actions shall be placed in *Light* and the evil ones in *Darkness.* The length of the beam of these scales, according to Ibn Abbás, will be equal to a journey of 50,000 years.—*Tafsír-i-Raufi.*

(9) *Because they injured our signs.* The one great object of Muhammad in picturing the terrors of the judgment-day was to frighten his townsmen into accepting his prophetic claims. The one great reason for a soul's being lost will be that it rejected the prophetic claims of Muhammad.

and then said unto the angels, Worship Adam; and they *all* worshipped *him,* except Iblís, *who* was not one of those who worshipped. (12) *God* said *unto him,* What hindered thee from worshipping *Adam,* since I had commanded thee? He answered, I am more excellent than he: thou hast created me of fire, and hast created him of clay. (13) *God* said, Get thee down therefore from *paradise;* for it is not *fit* that thou behave thyself proudly therein: get thee *hence;* thou shalt *be* one of the contemptible. (14) He answered, Give me respite until the day of resurrection. (15) *God* said, Verily thou shalt be *one* of those *who are* respited. (16) The *devil* said, Because thou hast depraved me, I will lay wait for *men* in thy strait way; (17) then will I come upon them from before, and from behind, and from their right hands, and from their left; and thou shalt not find the greater part of them thankful. (18)

---

(11) *Created and . . . formed you.* The creation probably has reference to the *souls* of mankind, all of which were created before Adam was formed, the forming having special reference to the preparation of bodies for the souls. But see also chap. vi. 99 and notes there.

Worship Adam, &c. See notes on the parallel passage in chap. ii. 34.

(12) *Thou hast created me of fire.* The idea that angels are created of fire may have been obtained from Jewish sources. See Arnold's learned note in *Islám and Christianity,* p. 101.

Heb. i. 7 gives no ground for such an opinion, for there the angels are said to be *spirits.* The *ministers* called a flame of fire may refer to 2 Kings ii. 11, vi. 7, &c.

The *Tafsír-i-Raufi* has a long note here, showing how mistaken Satan was in supposing creatures made of fire to be superior to those made of clay.

(15) *One of the respited.* "As the time till which the devil is reprieved is not particularly expressed, the commentators suppose his request was not wholly granted; but agree that he shall die, as well as other creatures, at the second sound of the trumpet."—*Sale, Baidháwi.*

(17) *Then will I come upon them, &c., i.e.,* "I will attack them on every side that I shall be able. The other two ways, viz., from above and from under their feet, are omitted, say the commentators, to show that the devil's power is limited."—*Sale, Baidháwi.*

The Qurán clearly teaches that Satan has no power to destroy true believers. See chap. xvi. 101.

God said *unto him*, Get thee hence, despised, and driven *far away :* (19) verily whoever of them shall follow thee, I will surely fill hell with you all.

|| (20) But *as for thee*, O Adam, dwell thou and thy wife NISF. in paradise; and eat *of the fruit thereof* wherever ye will; but approach not this tree, lest ye become *of the number of the unjust.* (21) And Satan suggested to them both, that he would discover unto them their nakedness, which was hidden from them; and he said, Your LORD hath not forbidden you this tree *for any other reason* but lest ye should become angels, or lest ye become immortal. (22) And he sware unto them, *saying*, Verily, I am *one* of those who counsel you aright. (23) And he caused them to fall through deceit. And when they had tasted of the tree, their nakedness appeared unto them; and they began to join together the leaves of paradise, to cover themselves. And their LORD called to them, *saying*, Did I not forbid you this tree : and *did I not* say unto you, Verily Satan is your declared enemy? (24) They answered, O LORD, we have dealt unjustly with our own souls; and if thou forgive us not, and be not merciful unto us, we shall *surely* be of those who perish. (25) *God* said, Get ye down, the one of you an enemy unto the other; and ye shall have a dwelling-place upon the earth, and a provision for a season.

(18) *Despised and driven away.* See note, chap. iv. 117. Rodwell translates it, *a scorned and banished one.*

(20) See notes on chap. ii. 35.

(21) *Lest ye become immortal.* Muhammad did not distinguish between the Tree of Life and the Tree of the Knowledge of Good and Evil. According to this passage, Adam and Eve should have been rendered immortal by eating the forbidden fruit. Compare chap. xx. 118 and 119.

(22) *He sware.* The *Tafsir-i-Raufi* comments thus :—Adam, may the peace of God be on him! thought no one could perjure himself, and thus was deceived by Satan.

(23) *The tree.* See chap. ii. 35, note.

Their nakedness. They were hitherto clothed in light or garments of Paradise, or enrobed by their long hair.

Leaves. Either of the grape-vine or the fig-tree.—*Tafsir-i-Raufi.*

(24) *They answered, &c.* Compare Gen. iii. 10-13 to see how the former Scriptures are attested here.

(25) See notes on chap. ii. 37. Compare Gen. iii. 15.

(26) He said, Therein shall ye live, and therein shall ye die, and from thence shall ye be taken forth *at the resurrection.*

|| (27) O children of Adam, we have sent down unto you apparel, to conceal your nakedness, and fair garments; but the clothing of piety is better. This *is one* of the signs of God; that peradventure ye may consider. (28) O children of Adam, let not Satan seduce you, as he expelled your parents out of paradise, by stripping them of their clothing, that he might show them their nakedness: verily he seeth you, *both* he and his companions, whereas ye see not them.—We have appointed the devils *to be* patrons of those who believe not: (29) and when they commit a filthy action, they say, We found our fathers *practising* the same; and GOD hath commanded us *to do* it. Say, Verily GOD commandeth not filthy actions. Do ye speak concerning GOD that which ye know not? (30) Say, My LORD hath commanded me *to observe* justice;

---

(27) *Apparel.* "Not only proper materials, but also ingenuity of mind and dexterity of hand to make use of them."—*Sale.*

(28-34) *Let not Satan seduce you, &c.* "This passage was revealed to reprove an immodest custom of the pagan Arabs, who used to encompass the Kaabah naked, because clothes, they said, were the signs of their disobedience to God. The Sunnat orders that when a man goes to prayers he should put on his better apparel, out of respect to the divine majesty before whom he is to appear. But as the Muhammadans think it indecent, on the one hand, to come into God's presence in a slovenly manner; so they imagine, on the other, that they ought not to appear before him in habits too rich or sumptuous, and particularly in clothes adorned with gold or silver, lest they should seem proud."—*Sale, Jaláluddín, Baidháwi.*

The Quraish seem to have defended their indecent practice on the ground of custom.

(29) Muhammad declares them to be under the beguiling influence of Satan, who had by deception exposed the shame of Adam and Eve. Seeing, then, that their progenitor himself had been deceived by Satan, the authority of their forefathers could not be relied on for the establishment of filthy customs contrary to the nature of a pure God: "God commandest not filthy actions."

Ye see them not. "Because of the subtlety of their bodies and their being void of all colour."—*Sale.*

(30) *My Lord hath commanded me to observe justice,* should be translated, *My Lord hath commanded aright, i.e.,* in the Qurán.

therefore set your faces *to pray* at every place of worship, and call upon him, approving unto him the sincerity of *your* religion. As he produced you at first, *so unto him* shall ye return. (31) A part *of mankind* hath he directed; and a part hath been justly led into error, because they have taken the devils for *their* patrons besides GOD, and imagine they are *rightly* directed. (32) O children of Adam, take your decent apparel at every place of worship, and eat and drink, but be not guilty of excess; for he loveth not those who are guilty of excess.

‖ (33) Say, Who hath forbidden the decent apparel of GOD, which he hath produced for his servants, and the good things *which he hath provided* for food? Say, these things *are* for those who believe, in this present life, *but* peculiarly on the day of resurrection. Thus do we distinctly explain *our* signs unto people who understand. (34) Say, Verily my LORD hath forbidden filthy actions, both that which is discovered thereof, and that which is concealed, and also iniquity and unjust violence; and *hath forbidden you* to associate with GOD that concerning which

---

Place of worship. Literally *every masjid.* Rodwell is surely mistaken in saying that the word "is usually applied only to that of Makkah, and that the term commonly used for the larger mosques is *ájami.*" The term *masjid* is certainly used everywhere in India for the ordinary mosque; and, though larger places are called *jama* (or *djami*), this term is added on to the other, *e.g., jama masjid.*

The word, as used here, probably has no reference to any particular building, but to the places where the Muslims offer prayer, *i.e.,* wherever they may be at the hour of prayer. If we understand the reference to be to the qibla of each masjid (so Rodwell), then we must count this passage among the Madína revelations.

(32) *Decent apparel.* See general note by Sale on ver. 28.

And eat and drink. "The sons of Amar, it is said, when they performed the pilgrimage to Makkah, used to eat no more than was absolutely necessary, and that not of the more delicious sort of food neither; which abstinence they looked upon as a piece of merit; but they are here told the contrary."—*Sale, Jaláluddín.*

(33) *But peculiarly, &c.* "Because then the wicked, who also partook of the blessings of this life, will have no share in the enjoyments of the next."—*Sale.*

(34) *Filthy actions, &c.* See notes above.

To associate with God, i.e., to worship idols or inferior deities.

he hath sent you down no authority, or to speak of GOD that which ye know not. (35) Unto every nation *there is a prefixed term*; therefore when their term is expired, they shall not have respite for an hour, neither shall they be anticipated. (36) O children of Adam, verily apostles from among you shall come unto you, who shall expound my signs unto you: whosoever therefore shall fear *God* and amend, there shall come no fear on them, neither shall they be grieved. (37) But they who shall accuse our signs of falsehood, and shall proudly reject them, they shall be the companions of *hell*-fire; they shall remain therein for ever. (38) And who is more unjust than he who deviseth a lie concerning GOD, or accuseth his signs of imposture? Unto these shall be given their portion *of worldly happiness*, according to *what is written in* the book *of God's decrees*, until our messengers come unto them, *and* shall cause them to die; saying, Where *are the idols* which ye called upon besides God? They shall answer, They have disappeared from us. And they shall bear witness against themselves that they were unbelievers. (39) *God* shall say *unto them at the resurrection*, Enter ye with the nations which have preceded you, of genii and of men, into *hell*-fire; so often as one nation shall enter, it shall curse its sister, until they shall all have successively entered therein. The latter of them shall say of the former of them: O LORD, these have seduced us, therefore inflict on them a double punishment of the fire *of hell*. *God*

---

(35) *Every nation.* Literally *every following*, whether of a true or false prophet.

(36–38) See notes on chap. vi. 48, 60, and iii. 185.

(38) *Where are the idols.* See note on chap. vi. 23.

(39) *Genii and men.* See below on ver. 180.

Its sister. "That is, the nation whose example betrayed them into their idolatry and other wickedness."—*Sale.*

Doubled unto all. "Unto those who set the example, because they not only transgressed themselves, but were also the occasion of the others' transgression; and unto those who followed them, because of their own infidelity and their imitating an ill example."—*Sale, Baidháwi, Jaláluddín.*

shall answer, *It shall be* doubled unto all: but ye know it not: (40) and the former of them shall say unto the latter of them, Ye have not therefore any favour above us; taste the punishment for that which ye have gained.

|| (41) Verily they who shall charge our signs with R 5/12 falsehood, and shall proudly reject them, the gates of heaven shall not be opened unto them, neither shall they enter into paradise, until a camel pass through the eye of a needle, and thus will we reward the wicked doers. (42) Their couch shall be in hell, and over them shall be coverings *of fire;* and thus will we reward the unjust. (43) But they who believe, and do that which is right (we will not load any soul but according to its ability), they shall be the companions of Paradise; they shall remain therein for ever. (44) And we will remove all grudges from their minds; rivers shall run at their feet, and they shall say, Praised be GOD, who hath directed us into this

---

(41) *They who shall charge, &c.* See notes on iii. 185, and vi. 48.
The gates shall not be opened, &c. " That is, when their souls shall, after death, ascend to heaven, they shall not be admitted, but shall be thrown down into the dungeon under the seventh earth."—*Sale, Jaláluddín.* See also Prelim. Disc., p. 129.
The eye of a needle. Compare Matt. xix. 24. See Rodwell's note on this passage.
(42) See note on chap. iii. 197.
(43) *We will not load any soul, &c.* See chap. iv. 27, and notes there.
(44) *Will remove all grudges, &c.* " So that, whatever differences or animosities there had been between them in their lifetime, they shall now be forgotten, and give place to sincere love and amity. This Ali is said to have hoped would prove true to himself and his inveterate enemies, Othmán, Talha, and Al Zubair."—*Sale, Baidháwi.* See also note on iii. 15.
For that which ye have wrought. Here salvation is said to be given in virtue of the good works wrought by Muslims. Brinckman says, " This is one of the numerous places in the Koran which deceives a man, makes him proud, self-righteous, and denies the whole Atonement. It would be a trying question for any Muslim to answer, Tell me of your good works, what they have been, and the good works you have neglected to do."—*Notes on Islám,* p. 99. But the *good works* of a Muslim are his professing the Muslim faith and per-

felicity! For we should not have been *rightly* directed if GOD had not directed us; now *are we convinced by demonstration that* the apostles of our LORD came *unto us* with truth. And it shall be proclaimed unto them, This is Paradise, whereof ye are made heirs *as a reward* for that which ye have wrought. (45) And the inhabitants of Paradise shall call out to the inhabitants of *hell*-fire, *saying*, Now have we found that which our LORD promised us *to be* true: have ye *also* found that which your LORD promised you *to be* true? They shall answer, Yea. And a crier shall proclaim between them, The curse of GOD *shall be* on the wicked; (46) who turn *men* aside from the way of GOD, and seek *to render* it crooked, and who deny the life to come. (47) And between the *blessed and the damned* there shall be a veil; and men *shall stand* on Al Aráf who shall know every one *of them* by their marks; and shall call unto the inhabitants of paradise, *saying,*

---

forming the five stated duties belonging to his religion. See notes on chap. ii. 3-5, 37, 38; iii. 194; iv. 55, 121-123.

A crier. "This crier, some say, will be the angel Israfíl."—*Sale.*

(47) *A veil*, or a wall, which is designated *Al Aráf.* See Prelim. Disc., p. 152.

And men. The commentators differ as to who these are to be. The most common understanding is that those whose good and bad deeds are equal, and who are therefore neither fit for heaven nor worthy of hell, will be placed upon this wall. Others suppose these to be martyrs and notable believers, who receive this knowledge of the reward they are to receive, and also of the pains from which they have escaped. Still others think they are angels in the form of men. See Prelim. Disc., p. 152, and *Tafsir-i-Raufi in loco.*

Their marks. The blessed are distinguished by the whiteness and the damned by the blackness of their faces.—*Tafsir-i-Raufi.*

They shall not enter therein, &c. "From this circumstance it seems that their opinion is the most probable who make this intermediate partition a sort of purgatory for those who, though they deserve not to be sent to hell, yet have not merits sufficient to gain them immediate admittance into Paradise, and will be tantalised here for a certain time with a bare view of the felicity of that place."—*Sale.*

They will, however, eventually be received into heaven, for when the command to worship will be given to the universe just before the final judgment, these will prostrate themselves, and thus the balance on the side of virtue will become heavier, and they will be admitted into heaven.—*Tafsir-i-Raufi.*

Peace be upon you: *yet they shall not enter therein, although they earnestly desire it.* (48) And when they shall turn their eyes towards the companions of *hell*-fire, they say, O LORD, place us not with the ungodly people!

|| (49) And those who stand on Al Aráf shall call unto certain men, whom they shall know by their marks, *and shall say,* What hath your gathering *of riches* availed you, and that you were puffed up with pride? (50) Are these the men on whom you swear that GOD would not bestow mercy? Enter ye into Paradise; *there shall come* no fear on you, neither shall ye be grieved. (51) And the inhabitants of *hell*-fire shall call unto the inhabitants of Paradise, *saying,* Pour upon us some water, or of those *refreshments* which GOD hath bestowed on you. They shall answer, Verily GOD hath forbidden them unto the unbelievers, (52) who made a laughing-stock and a sport of their religion, and whom the life of the world hath deceived: therefore this day will we forget them, as they did forget the meeting of this day, and for that they denied our signs *to be from God.* (53) And now have we brought unto those *of Makkah* a book *of divine revelations:* we have explained it

---

(49) *Certain men.* "The chiefs and ringleaders of the infidels" (*Sale, Baidháwi*), *e.g.,* Walíd Bin Mughaira, Abu Jahl, and Áas Bin Wail.—*Tafsír-i-Raufi.*

(50) *Are these the men, &c.* The poorer believers, *e.g.,* Bilál and Amár, &c., some of whom had been slaves.

Enter ye. "These words are directed, by an apostrophe, to the poor and despised believers above mentioned. Some commentators, however, imagine these and the next preceding words are to be understood of those who will be confined in Al Aráf; and that the damned will, in return for their reproachful speech, swear that they shall never enter Paradise themselves; whereupon God of his mercy shall order them to be admitted by these words."—*Sale, Baidháwi.*

(51-54) Compare this passage with the story of the rich man and Lazarus (Luke xvi. 19-26).

(52) See notes on chap. vi. 69.

(53) *A book, i.e.,* the Qurán, spoken of here as a complete volume. Assuming the pre-existence of the Qurán, as Muslims do, there could be no ground for the charge of imposture referred to in the Prelim. Disc., p. 96. But regarding Muhammad as its author, as his European apologists, in common with ourselves, do, we think there is in this language very good reason for believing that author to have

with knowledge; a direction and mercy unto people who shall believe. (54) Do they wait *for any other* than the interpretation thereof? On the day whereon the interpretation thereof shall come, they who had forgotten the same before shall say, Now *are we convinced by demonstration that* the messengers of our LORD came *unto us* with truth: shall we therefore have any intercessors, who will intercede for us? or shall we be sent back *into the world*, that we may do other *works* than what we did *in our lifetime? But* now have they lost their souls; and that which they impiously imagined hath fled from them.

R $\frac{7}{14}$.

‖ (55) Verily, your LORD is GOD, who created the heavens and the earth in six days; and then ascended *his* throne: he causeth the night to cover the day; it succeedeth the same swiftly: *he* also *created* the sun, and the moon, and the stars, *which are* absolutely subject unto his command. Is not the whole creation and the empire *thereof* his? Blessed be GOD, the LORD of all creatures!

---

been an impostor. There can be no reasonable doubt that the meaning which Muhammad intended to attach to this expression is that *a book* was sent down to him from heaven through the medium of the Angel Gabriel, as the Taurát or Pentateuch had been sent down to Moses, which, though revealed to his disciples piecemeal, *was nevertheless a complete volume*. Indeed, it may fairly be doubted whether this expression ever is used in the Qurán to designate *a portion* of the Qurán, except in the sense that it is a part of a whole already existing.

(54) *The interpretation*, i.e., the fulfilment of its promises and threats.

Intercessors. Allusion is to the gods whom they worshipped, and whom they regarded as intercessors.

Sent back. The expression looks like an allusion to the doctrine of metempsychosis.

That which they imagined; their false gods. See chap. vi. 23, note.

(55) *Six days*. Compare Gen. i. 14–19, and Exod. xx. 11. Some understand the creation days to be each one thousand solar years in length.—*Tafsír-i-Raufi*.

Then ascended. The commentators place this sentence among the *Mutashábihát* or difficult passages of the Qurán, which none but God and his prophet understand. The *Tafsír-i-Raufi* says, God only knows the truth of this matter; as the *how* about God himself is a mystery, so is the *how* about his ascent upon the throne of the heavens a mystery.

(56) Call unto your LORD humbly and in secret; for he loveth not those who transgress. (57) And act not corruptly in the earth after its reformation; and call upon him with fear and desire: for the mercy of GOD is near unto the righteous. (58) It is he who sendeth the winds, spread abroad before his mercy, until they bring a cloud heavy *with rain*, which we drive into a dead country; and we cause water to descend thereon, by which we cause all *sorts of* fruits to spring forth. Thus will we bring forth the dead *from their graves;* that peradventure ye may consider. (59) From a good country shall its fruit spring forth *abundantly*, by the permission of its LORD; but from the *land* which is bad it shall not spring forth otherwise than scarcely. Thus do we explain the signs *of divine providence* unto people who are thankful.

|| (60) We formerly sent Noah unto his people: and he said, O my people, worship GOD: ye have no other GOD than him. Verily I fear for you the punishment of the

R $\frac{8}{15}$.

Empire his. Because he sits in the throne of heaven.

(56) *Humbly and in secret, i.e.,* "not behaving themselves arrogantly while they pray, or praying with an obstreperous voice, or a multitude of words and vain repetitions."—*Sale, Baidháwi.*

Muslim prayers now come far short of fulfilling either the letter or spirit of this injunction. Compare Matt. vi. 5-7.

(57) *Act not corruptly,* by strife, and blasphemy, and idolatry, *after its reformation, i.e.,* "after God hath sent his prophets and revealed his laws for the reformation and amendment of mankind." —*Sale.*

(58) *A dead country.* This refers probably to those parts of the desert which depend upon the rain alone for productive power.

Thus will he bring forth the dead. Compare 1 Cor. xv. 35-38. This doctrine of the resurrection was undoubtedly one of the most attractive of those borrowed from Judaism, and well calculated to commend him to the Arabs as a prophet. The term *nushran*, translated by Sale *spread abroad*, is *bushran* in all the copies current in India, and is rendered *heralds*, as in Rodwell's translation.

(60) *Noah.* "Noah the son of Lamech, according to the Muhammadan writers, was one of the six principal prophets, though he had no written revelations delivered to him, and the first who appeared after his great-grandfather Idris or Enoch. They also say he was by trade a carpenter, which they infer from his building the ark, and that the year of his mission was the fiftieth, or, as others say, the fortieth of his age."—*Sale.*

great day. (61) The chiefs of his people answered *him*, We surely perceive thee *to be* in a manifest error. (62) He replied, O my people, there is no error in me; but I am a messenger from the LORD of all creatures. (63) I bring unto you the messages of my LORD; and I counsel you aright; for I know from GOD, that which ye know not. (64) Do ye wonder that an admonition hath come unto you from your LORD by a man from among you, to warn you, that ye may take heed to yourselves, and that peradventure ye may obtain mercy? (65) And they accused him of imposture: but we delivered him and those who *were* with him in the ark, and we drowned those who charged our signs with falsehood; for they were a blind people.

‖ (66) And unto *the tribe of* Ád *we sent* their brother Húd. He said, O my people, worship GOD: ye have no

---

Noah's experience, as pictured here, is the experience of Muhammad himself. His nation was a nation of idolaters, who persistently refused to accept his preaching concerning the true God, who rejected his prophetic claims, and accused him of imposture, and who perished on account of their infidelity.

The great day. "Either the day of the resurrection, or that whereon the flood was to begin."—*Sale.*

(64) *By a man.* "For said they, If God had pleased, he would have sent an angel, and not a man; since we never heard of such an instance in the times of our fathers."—*Sale, Baidháwi.*

In this interpretation of this expression the commentators have followed the example of their Prophet, and made the objections of the antediluvians to Noah's prophetic claim to be the same as those made by the Quraish to Muhammad's pretensions. See chap. vi. 111, and notes thereon.

(65) *Those . . . in the ark.* "That is, those who believed on him, and entered into that vessel with him. Though there be a tradition among the Muhammadans, said to have been received from the Prophet himself, and conformable to the Scripture, that eight persons, and no more, were saved in the ark, yet some of them report the number variously. One says they were but six, another ten, another twelve, another seventy-eight, and another fourscore, half men and half women, and that one of them was the elder Jorham, the preserver, as some pretend, of the Arabian language."—*Sale, Zamakhshari, Jaláluddin.*

(66) *Ád.* "Ád was an ancient and potent tribe of Arabs, and zealous idolaters. They chiefly worshipped four deities, Sákia, Háfidha, Rázika, and Sálima; the first, as they imagined, supplying them with rain, the second preserving them from all dangers abroad,

other GOD than him; will ye not fear *him?* (67) The chiefs of those among his people who believed not answered, Verily we perceive that thou *art guided* by folly; and we certainly esteem thee *to be one* of the liars. (68) He replied, O my people, *I am* not *guided by* folly; but I am a messenger unto you from the LORD of all creatures. (69) I bring unto you the messages of my LORD; and I am a faithful counsellor unto you. (70) Do ye wonder that an admonition hath come unto you from your LORD by a man from among you, that he may warn you? Call to mind how he hath appointed you successors unto the people of Noah, and hath added unto you in stature largely. Remember the benefits of GOD, that ye may prosper. (71) They said, Art thou come unto us, that we should worship GOD alone, and leave *the deities* which our fathers worshipped? Now bring down that *judgment* upon us with which thou threatenest us, if thou speakest truth. *Húd answered,* Now shall there suddenly fall upon you from your LORD vengeance and indignation. (72) Will ye dispute with me concerning the names which ye have named and your fathers, as to

---

the third providing food for their sustenance, and the fourth restoring them to health when afflicted with sickness, according to the signification of the several names."—*Sale.* See also the Prelim. Disc., p. 20.

Húd. See Prelim. Disc., p. 21, and my note there. Húd, like Noah, had experiences like unto those of Muhammad. The language ascribed to him and "his people" is mostly verbatim, the same as that ascribed to Noah and the antediluvians.

Chiefs . . . who believed not. Some of the chiefs did believe on Húd. Baidháwi says one of them was Murthad Ibn Saad.

(70) *Successors unto the people of Noah.* "Dwelling in the habitations of the antediluvians, who preceded them not many centuries, or having the chief sway in the earth after them; for the kingdom of Shidád, the son of Ád, is said to have extended from the sands of Alaj to the trees of Omán."—*Sale, Baidháwi.*

And . . . stature. See Prelim. Disc., p. 22.

(71) *Bring down that judgment.* This was just what the infidel Quraish said to Muhammad. See chap. vi. 56.

(72) *The names.* The idols, whose *names* are given in note on ver. 66.

which GOD hath not revealed unto you any authority? (73) Do ye wait therefore, and I will be *one* of those who wait with you. And we delivered him, and them who *believed* with him, by our mercy; and we cut off the uttermost part of those who charged our signs with falsehood, and were not believers.

R 10/17. ‖ (74) And unto *the tribe of* Thamúd *we sent* their brother Sálih. He said, O my people, worship GOD: ye have no GOD besides him. Now hath a manifest proof come unto you from your LORD. This she-camel of GOD *is* a sign unto you: therefore dismiss her freely, that she may feed in GOD'S earth; and do her no hurt, lest a

---

(73) *We cut off, &c.* The following note by Sale contains a specimen of the kind of history to be met with on the pages of any Muslim commentary on the Qurán:—

"The dreadful destruction of the Ádites we have mentioned in another place (Prelim. Disc., p. 21), and shall only add here some further circumstances of that calamity, and which differ a little from what is there said; for the Arab writers acknowledge many inconsistencies in the histories of these ancient tribes. The tribe of Ád, having been for their incredulity previously chastised with a three years' drought, sent Kail Ibn Ithar and Murthad Ibn Saad, with seventy other principal men, to the temple of Makkah to obtain rain. Makkah was then in the hands of the tribe of Amalek, whose prince was Muáwiyah Ibn Baqr; and he, being without the city when the ambassadors arrived, entertained them there for a month in so hospitable a manner, that they had forgotten the business they came about, had not the king reminded them of it, not as from himself, lest they should think he wanted to be rid of them, but by some verses which he put into the mouth of a singing-woman. At which, being roused from their lethargy, Murthad told them the only way they had to obtain what they wanted would be to repent and obey their prophet: but this displeasing the rest, they desired Muáwiyah to imprison him, lest he should go with him; which being done, Kail with the rest entering Makkah, begged of God that he would send rain to the people of Ád. Whereupon three clouds appeared, a white one, a red one, and a black one; and a voice from heaven ordered Kail to choose which he would. Kail failed not to make choice of the last, thinking it to be laden with the most rain; but when this cloud passed over them, it proved to be fraught with the divine vengeance, and a tempest broke forth from it which destroyed them all."

(74) *Thamúd.* An ancient tribe of Arabs. See Prelim. Disc., p. 22.

Sálih. "Baidháwi deduces his genealogy thus: Sálih the son of

painful punishment seize you. (75) And call to mind how he hath appointed you successors unto *the tribe of Ád*, and hath given you a habitation on earth; ye build *yourselves* castles on the plains thereof, and cut out the mountains into houses. Remember therefore the benefits of GOD, and commit not violence in the earth, acting corruptly. (76) The chiefs among his people who were puffed up with pride, said unto those who were esteemed weak, *namely*, unto those who believed among them, Do ye know that Sálih hath been sent from his LORD? They answered, We do surely believe in that wherewith he hath been sent. (77) Those who were elated with pride replied, Verily we believe not in that wherein ye

---

Obaid, the son of Asaf, the son of Masikh, the son of Obaid, the son of Hadhír. the son of Thámúd."—*Sale*. But these genealogies are quite worthless, being almost without exception an adaptation of Jewish genealogies to Arab tradition. See notes on Prelim. Disc., pp. 24, 25. As usual, Sálih is *a brother* of the people to whom he is sent, as Muhammad was a brother of the people to whom he pretended to have been sent.

The remarks made on the prophetic experiences of Noah and Húd, vers. 60 and 66, will apply also to those of Sálih. This Sálih seems to be a prophet of Muhammad's own invention. See note in Prelim. Disc., p. 21.

This she-camel . . . a sign. "The Thamúdites insisting on a miracle, proposed to Sálih that he should go with them to their festival, and that they should call on their gods, and he on his, promising to follow that deity which should answer. But after they had called on their idols a long time to no purpose, Junda Ibn Amru, their prince, pointed to a rock standing by itself, and bade Sálih cause a she-camel big with young to come forth from it, solemnly engaging that if he did, he would believe; and his people promised the same. Whereupon Sálih asked it of God, and presently the rock, after several throes, as if in labour, was delivered of a she-camel answering the description of Junda, which immediately brought forth a young one ready weaned, and, as some say, as big as herself. Junda, seeing this miracle, believed on the Prophet, and some few with him; but the greater part of the Thamúdites remained, notwithstanding, incredulous."—*Sale*.

(75) *Cut out . . . houses.* See Prelim. Disc., p. 23.

(76) *Who were esteemed weak.* This passage undoubtedly expresses the social position of the Muslims when this passage was revealed. As yet they were few in number, mostly poor, and held in contempt by their townsmen.

believe. (78) And they cut off the feet of the camel, and insolently transgressed the command of their LORD, and said, O Sálih, cause that to come upon us which thou hast threatened us, if thou art *one* of those who have been sent *by God.* (79) Whereupon a terrible noise from heaven assailed them; and in the morning they were found in

(78) *They cut off the feet of the camel, &c.* "This extraordinary camel frighting the other cattle from their pasture, a certain rich woman named Onaiza Omm Ganím, having four daughters, dressed them out, and offered one Kidár his choice of them if he would kill the camel. Whereupon he chose one, and with the assistance of eight other men hamstrung and killed the dam, and pursuing the young one, which fled to the mountain, killed that also and divided his flesh among them. Others tell the story somewhat differently, adding Sadaqa Bint al Mukhtár as a joint conspiratress with Onaiza, and pretending that the young one was not killed; for they say that having fled to a certain mountain named Kára, he there cried three times, and Sálih bade them catch him if they could, for then there might be hopes of their avoiding the divine vengeance; but this they were not able to do, the rock opening after he had cried, and receiving him within it."—*Sale, Baidháwi.*

Rodwell thinks it possible that the camel-killing which resulted in a war between the Banu Taghlib and the Bani Baqr, A.D. 490, afforded to Muhammad the groundwork of this story of the persecution of Sálih. It seems clear that some such story was current among the heathen Arabs, which Muhammad found convenient to his use, and which he adapted to further his prophetic claims.

Cause that to come, &c. They said this "because they trusted in their strong dwellings, hewn in the rocks, saying the tribe of Ád perished only because their houses were not built with sufficient strength."—*Sale.*

(79) *A terrible noise.* "Like violent and repeated claps of thunder, which some say was no other than the voice of the Angel Gabriel, and which rent their hearts. It is said that after they had killed the camel, Sálih told them that on the morrow their faces should become yellow, the next day red, and the third day black, and that on the fourth God's vengeance should light on them; and that the first three signs happening accordingly, they sought to put him to death, but God delivered him by sending him into Palestine."—*Sale, Baidháwi.*

The following episode in the history of Muhammad is here related by Sale as follows, on the authority of Abulfida:—"Muhammad, in the expedition of Tabúk, which he undertook against the Greeks in the ninth year of the Hijra, passing by Hijr, where the ancient tribe had dwelt, forbade his army, though much distressed with heat and thirst, to draw any water there, but ordered them, if they had drunk of that water, to bring it up again, or if they had kneaded any meal with it, to give it to their camels; and wrapping up his face in his garment, he set spurs to his mule, crying out, 'Enter not

their dwellings prostrate on their breasts *and dead.* (80) And Sâlih departed from them, and said, O my people, now have I delivered unto you the message of my LORD, and I advised you well, but ye love not those who advise *you* well. (81) And *remember* Lot, when he said unto his people, Do ye commit a wickedness wherein no creature hath sent you an example? (82) Do ye approach lustfully unto men, leaving the women? Certainly ye are people who transgress *all modesty.* (83) But the answer of his people was no other than that they said *the one to the other,* Expel them your city; for they are men who preserve themselves pure *from the crimes which ye commit.* (84) Therefore we delivered him and his family, except his wife; she was *one* of those who stayed *behind:* and

---

the houses of those wicked men, but rather weep, lest that happen unto you which befell them;' and having so said, he continued galloping full speed with his face muffled up, till he had passed the valley."

(80) *The message.* This message was probably delivered at the parting of Sálih from the people, though some think it was delivered after the calamity.

(81) *Lot.* "The commentators say, conformably to the Scripture, that Lot was the son of Haran, the son of Azar or Terah, and consequently Abraham's nephew, who brought him with him from Chaldea into Palestine, where they say he was sent by God to reclaim the inhabitants of Sodom and the other neighbouring cities which were overthrown with it from the unnatural vice to which they were addicted."—*Sale.*

Lot certainly was not sent to Sodom as a prophet. What Peter says of him in his 2nd Epistle, ii. 8, in no way implies that he was a *preacher* of righteousness, as Sale fancies. His only claim to be even a *righteous* person is based on his having, in the midst of many vices, held on to "the faith of Abraham." We think the Qurán is here fairly chargeable with again contradicting the Scriptures it professes to attest.

No creature. The original has it, *Min il 'alamína,* none *from among the learned.*

(83) *Expel them,* viz., "Lot and those who believe on him."—*Sale.* The *Tafsír-i-Raufi* says, *Expel Lot and his sons and those who believe on him.* The statement of the Qurán clearly implies that some of the Sodomites, besides Lot and his daughters, mentioned in chap. xi. 77, 78, escaped from the destruction which fell on the remainder.

(84) *She . . . stayed.* Commentators are not agreed whether she remained in the city or went forth some distance with Lot. See Sale's note, given in chap. xi. 80. The language of both these pas-

we rained a shower *of stones* upon them. (85) Behold therefore what was the end of the wicked.

(86) And unto Madian *we sent* their brother Shuaib. He said *unto them*, O my people, worship GOD; ye have no GOD

---

sages certainly favours the view of those who believe she remained in the city.

(85) *A shower.* In chap. xi. 81 it is distinctly said this shower was of "stones of baked clay." This whole passage, as well as the parallel passages in chaps. xi. 76-82; xv. 58-77; xxvi. 160-174; xxvii. 55-59, &c., contradicts the statements of Gen. xix. in many particulars. Surely the taunts of those referred to in ver. 203 of this chapter were well directed. Granting the ignorance of Muhammad in respect to the sacred stories he attempts to narrate here,— of which ignorance we have abundant illustration in this chapter,— still the fact remains that Muhammad, receiving his information from parties themselves ill-informed, recorded the result in the Qurán, declaring that he received it directly from heaven through the Angel Gabriel.

(86) *Madian.* "Or Midian, was a city of Híjáz, and the habitation of a tribe of the same name, the descendants of Midian, the son of Abraham by Keturah (Gen. xxv. 2), who afterwards coalesced with the Ishmaelites, as it seems; Moses naming the same merchants who sold Joseph to Potiphar in one place Ishmaelites, and in another Midianites. (Comp. Gen. xxxix. 1, and xxxvii. 36.) This city was situated on the Red Sea, south-east of Mount Sinai, and is doubtless the same with the Modiana of Ptolemy; what was remaining of it in Muhammad's time was soon after demolished in the succeeding wars, and it remains desolate to this day. The people of the country pretend to show the well whence Moses watered Jethro's flocks."—*Sale.*

Shuaib. Muslim writers generally identify Shuaib with Jethro, the father-in-law of Moses. Baidháwi says he was the son of Mikaíl, the son of Yashjar, the son of Midian, and the *Tafsír-i-Raufi* relates that he was descended from Lot, Midian having married the daughter of Lot.

"In the commentary of the Syrian Ephream, Jethro is called Shuaib."—*Notes on the Roman Urdú Qurán.*

An evident demonstration. No miracles wrought by Shuaib are described either in the Qurán or the Traditions, yet Muslim writers tell us that when he desired to ascend a mountain, it invariably stooped down to receive him, and then rose up to its ordinary place! See *Tafsír-i-Raufi in loco.*

Sale gives the following on the authority of Baidháwi and D'Herbelot:—"This demonstration the commentators suppose to have been a power of working miracles, though the Qurán mentions none in particular. However they say (after the Jews) that he gave his son-in-law that wonder-working rod with which he performed all those miracles in Egypt and the desert, and also excellent advice and instructions (Exod. xviii. 13), whence he had the surname of Khatib al anbiyáh, or the *preacher to the prophets.*"

besides him. Now hath an evident demonstration come unto you from your LORD. Therefore give full measure and just weight, and diminish not unto men *aught of* their matters: neither act corruptly in the earth after its reformation. This will be better for you, if ye believe. (87) And beset not every way, threatening *the passenger*, and turning aside from the path of GOD him who believeth in him, and seeking to make it crooked. And remember, when ye were few and *God* multiplied you: and behold what hath been the end of those who acted corruptly. (88) And if part of you believe in that wherewith I am sent, and part believe not, wait patiently until GOD judge between us; for he is the best judge.

‖ (89) The chiefs of his people, who were elated with pride, answered, We will surely cast thee, O Shuaib, and those who believe with thee, out of our city: or else thou shalt certainly return unto our religion. He said, What! though we be averse *thereto?* (90) We shall surely imagine a lie against GOD if we return unto your religion, after that GOD hath delivered us from the same: and we have no *reason* to return unto it, unless GOD our LORD shall please *to abandon us.* Our LORD comprehendeth everything by *his* knowledge. In GOD do we put our trust. O LORD, do thou judge between us and our nation with

NINTH SIPARA

Give full measure. One of the great crimes of the Midianites was keeping two different kinds of weights and measures, buying by one and selling by the other. *Baidhâwi, Tafsîr-i-Raufi.*

After reformation. See on ver. 57.

(87) *Beset not every way, &c.* "Robbing on the highway, it seems, was another crying sin, frequent among these people. But some of the commentators interpret this passage figuratively of their besetting the way of truth, and threatening those who gave ear to the remonstrances of Shuaib."—*Sale, Baidhâwi.*

(88) *Wait patiently, &c.* This is no doubt what Muhammad himself taught his hearers at Makkah. It would appear that, unable to work miracles, he either hoped for the power to do so (see notes on chap. vi. 109–111), or he trusted that something would turn up to favour his cause in the future.

(89) *We will surely cast thee . . . out of our city.* Rodwell relates a Jewish tradition of similar import regarding Jethro. See *Korân,*

truth; for thou art the best judge. (91) And the chiefs of his people who believed not said, If ye follow Shuaib, ye shall surely perish. (92) Therefore a storm from heaven assailed them, and in the morning they were found in their dwellings *dead and* prostrate. (93) They who accused Shuaib of imposture *became* as though they had never dwelt therein; they who accused Shuaib of imposture perished themselves. (94) And he departed from them, and said, O my people, now have I performed unto you the messages of my LORD; and I advised you aright: but why should I be grieved for an unbelieving people?

R 1/2. || (95) We have never sent any prophet unto a city but we afflicted the inhabitants thereof with calamity and adversity, that they might humble themselves. (96) Then we gave *them* in exchange good in lieu of evil, until they abounded, and said, Adversity and prosperity formerly happened unto our fathers *as unto us.* Therefore we took vengeance on them suddenly, and they perceived it not *beforehand.* (97) But if the inhabitants of *those* cities had believed and feared *God*, we would surely have opened to them blessings both from heaven and earth. But they charged *our apostles* with falsehood, wherefore we took

---

p. 117 *note.* This passage seems to point to the time when the Quraísh proscribed Muhammad and his followers and sympathisers, and compelled them to retire to "the Sheb of Abu Tálib," about five or six years before the Hijra.

(91) *A storm* "like that which destroyed the Thamúdites."—*Sale.* Some translate the word *earthquake.* See *Tafsir-i-Raufi.*

(93) The fate of the Quraísh is here prefigured. See notes on chap. iii. 185, and notes above on vers. 2, 60, 66, and 74.

(94) *Why should I be grieved, &c.* Comp. Matt. xxiii. 37, and Luke xix. 41, 42; xxiii. 34.

(95) See note on chap. vi. 131. There is here, in all probability, allusion to some calamity which had befallen the city of Makkah. Some say it was a famine.

(97–100) *Those cities, i.e.,* those described above as inhabited by the people of Noah, Húd, Sálih, Lot, and Shuaib, whose dreadful fate is set forth as a warning to those who refuse to believe on Muhammad. *The great crime of these people was that they charged their prophets with being impostors.* Was not Muhammad conscious of his own imposture? See note on ver. 2.

vengeance on them for that which they had been guilty of. (98) Were the inhabitants therefore of *those* cities secure that our punishment should not fall on them by night while they slept? (99) Or were the inhabitants of *those* cities secure that our punishment should not fall on them by day while they sported? (100) Were they therefore secure from the stratagem of GOD? But none will think himself secure from the stratagem of GOD except the people who perish.

|| (101) And hath it not manifestly appeared unto those R 13/3. who have inherited the earth after the *former* inhabitants thereof, that if we please we can afflict them for their sins? But we will seal up their hearts, and they shall not hearken. (102) We will relate unto thee some stories of these cities. Their apostles had come unto them with evident miracles, but they were not *disposed* to believe in that which they had before gainsaid. Thus will GOD seal up the hearts of the unbelievers. (103) And we found not in the greater part of them any *observance* of *their* covenant; but we found the greater part of them wicked doers. (104) Then we sent after the *above-named apostles* Moses with our signs unto Pharaoh and his princes, who treated

---

(100) *The stratagem of God.* "Hereby is figuratively expressed the manner of God's dealing with proud and ungrateful men, by suffering them to fill up the measure of their iniquity, without vouchsafing to bring them to a sense of their condition by chastisements and afflictions till they find themselves utterly lost, when they least expect it."—*Sale, Baidháwi.*

(101) *Those who have inherited the earth, &c., i.e.,* the Quráish, who are here warned of the judgments in store for them on account of their unbelief, unless they repent.

But we will seal up, &c. Rodwell rightly connects this with the preceding by the copulative *and* instead of the disjunctive *but.* The passage should therefore read, *We can afflict them for their sins, and seal up their hearts, and* (wherefore) *they shall not hearken.*

(102, 103) These verses give a sort of summary of what has gone before, and would have been more appropriately placed before ver. 60.

(104) *We sent . . . Moses.* The Qurán everywhere presents Moses as the apostle of the Egyptians as well as of the Israelites. He is sent to them to warn them against *idolatry,* and to urge them to the

them unjustly; but behold what was the end of the corrupt doers? (105) And Moses said, O Pharaoh, verily I am an apostle *sent* from the LORD of all creatures. (106) It is just that I should not speak of God other than the truth. Now am I come unto you with an *evident* sign from your LORD: send therefore the children of Israel away with me. Pharaoh answered, If thou comest with a sign, produce it, if thou speakest truth. (107) Wherefore he cast down his rod; and behold, it *became* a visible serpent.

---

worship of the true God. The children of Israel who believe on him are therefore his followers—are true Muslims. See parallel passages in chaps. x. 76-93, and xl. 24-49.

The Moses of the Qurán is a Muhammad in disguise. Muslims believe Moses to have been a black man.

Pharaoh. "Which of the kings of Egypt this Pharaoh of Moses was is uncertain. Not to mention the opinions of the European writers, those of the East generally suppose him to have been al Walíd, who, according to some, was an Arab of the tribe of Ád, or, according to others, the son of Musáb, the son of Riyán, the son of Walíd the Amalekite. There are historians, however, who suppose Kabús, the brother and predecessor of al Walíd, was the prince we are speaking of, and pretend he lived six hundred and twenty years, and reigned four hundred,—which is more reasonable, at least, than the opinion of those who imagine it was his father Musáb, or grandfather Riyán. Abulfida says that Musáb being one hundred and seventy years old, and having no child, while he kept the herds saw a cow calve, and heard her say at the same time, O Musáb, *be not grieved, for thou shalt have a wicked son, who will be at length cast into hell.* And he accordingly had this Walíd, who afterwards coming to be king of Egypt, proved an impious tyrant."—*Sale, Baidháwi, Zamakhsharí.*

Treated them unjustly, i.e., refused to believe the signs of his apostleship.

(107) *A visible serpent.* "The Arab writers tell enormous fables of this serpent or dragon. For they say that he was hairy, and of so prodigious a size, that when he opened his mouth, his jaws were fourscore cubits asunder, and when he laid his lower jaw on the ground, his upper reached to the top of the palace; that Pharaoh seeing this monster make towards him, fled from it, and was so terribly frightened that he befouled himself; and that the whole assembly also betaking themselves to their heels, no less than twenty-five thousand of them lost their lives in the press. They add that Pharaoh upon this adjured Moses by God who had sent him to take away the serpent, and promised he would believe on him and let the Israelites go; but when Moses had done what he requested, he relapsed, and grew as hardened as before."—*Sale, Baidháwi.*

(108) And he drew forth his hand *out of his bosom;* and behold, it *appeared* white unto the spectators.

|| (109) The chiefs of the people of Pharaoh said, This R $\frac{14}{4}$ man is certainly an expert magician : (110) he seeketh to dispossess you of your land. What therefore do ye direct? (111) They answered, Put off him and his brother *by fair promises for some time,* and *in the mean while* send unto the cities persons, (112) who may assemble and bring unto thee every expert magician. (113) So the magicians came unto Pharaoh; (114) *and* they said, Shall we surely receive a reward if we do overcome? (115) He answered, Yea; and ye shall certainly be of those who approach near *unto my throne.* (116) They said, O Moses, either do thou cast down *thy rod first,* or we will cast down *ours. Moses* answered, Do ye cast down *your rods first.* (117) And when they had cast *them* down, they enchanted the eyes of

---

The common view is that it was an ordinary serpent, and that the Egyptians regarded it as having been produced by magic.

(108) *He drew forth his hand, &c.* The Bible nowhere says this miracle was performed before Pharaoh. There seems to have been Jewish tradition to which Muhammad was indebted for his knowledge on this point (see Rodwell's note *in loco*). Sale thinks we may fairly infer from Exod. iv. 8, 9, that both signs were shown to Pharaoh.

(109) *The chiefs of the people.* These chiefs, who symbolise the Arab chiefs of Makkah, are represented as equally guilty with Pharaoh. They continually mock at the miracles or *signs* of Moses and Aaron, and stir up Pharaoh to rebellion against God.

(110) *What . . . do ye direct?* This is a question addressed by Pharaoh to his counsellors.

(113) *Magicians.* " The Arabian writers name several of these magicians, besides their chief priest Simeon, viz., Sadúr and Ghadúr, Jaath and Musfa, Warán and Zamán, each of whom came attended with their disciples, amounting in all to several thousands."—*Sale.*

The *Tafsír-i-Raufi* gives the names of these magicians as follows :—Simeon, Sadúr and Adúr, Hathat and Musfa. They were accompanied by 70,000 followers.

(117) *They enchanted the eyes.* " They provided themselves with a great number of thick ropes and long pieces of wood, which they contrived by some means to move, and make them twist themselves one over the other ; and so imposed on the beholders, who at a distance took them to be true serpents."—*Sale, Baidháwi.*

The *Tafsír-i-Raufi* says they prepared their ropes by rubbing upon

the men *who were present*, and terrified them; and they performed a great enchantment. (118) And we spake by revelation unto Moses, *saying*, Throw down thy rod. And behold, it swallowed up *the rods* which they had *caused falsely to appear* changed *into serpents*. (119) Wherefore the truth was confirmed, and that which they had wrought vanished. (120) And *Pharaoh and his magicians* were overcome there, and were rendered contemptible. (121) And the magicians prostrated themselves, worshipping; (122) *and* they said, We believe in the LORD of all creatures, (123) the LORD of Moses and Aaron. (124) Pharaoh

---

them certain chemicals, filling their sticks with quicksilver, which, under the heat of the sun, or, according to others, the heat of fires previously kindled under the place where they were thrown, made them curl up and intertwine so as to appear at a distance like real serpents. The number of rods and ropes thus changed into the appearance of serpents is said to have been forty thousand.

(118) *Behold, it swallowed up, &c.* "The expositors add, that when this serpent had swallowed up all the rods and cords, he made directly towards the assembly, and put them into so great a terror that they fled, and a considerable number were killed in the crowd: then Moses took it up, and it became a rod in his hand as before. Whereupon the magicians declared that it could be no enchantment, because in such case their rods and cords would not have disappeared."—*Sale, Baidháwi.*

(120) *Were rendered contemptible.* Rodwell translates *drew back humiliated*, which agrees with the Urdú and Persian translations, which have it *they returned disgraced.*

(121) *The magicians prostrated, &c.* "It seems probable that all the magicians were not converted by this miracle, for some writers introduce Sadúr and Ghadúr only acknowledging Moses's miracle to be wrought by the power of God. These two, they say, were brothers, and the sons of a famous magician, then dead ; but on their being sent for to court on this occasion, their mother persuaded them to go to their father's tomb to ask his advice. Being come to the tomb, the father answered their call, and when they had acquainted him with the affair, he told them that they should inform themselves whether the rod of which they spoke became a serpent while its masters slept, or only when they were awake ; for, said he, enchantments have no effect while the enchanter is asleep, and therefore, if it be otherwise in this case, you may be assured that they act by a divine power. These two magicians then, arriving at the capital of Egypt, on inquiry found to their great astonishment that when Moses and Aaron went to rest their rod became a serpent, and guarded them while they slept. And this was the first step towards their conversion."—*Sale, Baidháwi, Tafsír-i-Raufi.*

said, Have ye believed on him before I have given you permission? Verily this is a plot which ye have contrived in the city, that ye might cast forth from thence the inhabitants thereof. But ye shall surely know *that I am your master;* (125) *for* I will cause your hands and your feet to be cut off on the opposite sides, then I will cause you all to be crucified. (126) The *magicians* answered, We shall certainly return unto our LORD *in the next life;* (127) for thou takest vengeance on us only because we have believed in the signs of our LORD when they have come unto us. O LORD, pour on us patience, and cause us to die Muslims.

|| (128) And the chiefs of Pharaoh's people said, Wilt R $\frac{15}{5}$. thou let Moses and his people go, that they may act corruptly in the earth, and leave thee and thy gods? *Pharaoh*

---

(124) *Permission.* Abdul Qádir says Pharaoh professed to be a god, and caused images of himself to be worshipped by the people.

A plot, i.e., "This is a confederacy between you and Moses, entered into before ye left the city to go to the place of appointment, to turn out the Copts, or native Egyptians, and establish the Israelites in their stead."—*Sale, Baidháwi.*

(125) On the punishments said here to have been threatened by Pharaoh, see chap. v. 37, 38, 42-44. There is undoubtedly an anachronism in this passage.

(127) *Cause us to die Muslims.* "Some think these converted magicians were executed accordingly ; but others deny it, and say that the king was not able to put them to death ; insisting on these words of the Qurán (chap. xxviii. 35), *You two, and they who follow you, shall overcome.*"—*Sale, Baidháwi.*

This passage teaches that Islám is the one only true religion, the religion of Moses, and therefore the religion of the Pentateuch. The Qurán here again points to the reasons for its own rejection. See note on chap. ii. 136.

(128) *Leave thee and thy gods.* "Some of the commentators, from certain impious expressions of this prince recorded in the Qurán (chap. xxvi. 28; xxviii. 38), whereby he sets up himself as the only god of his subjects, suppose that he was the object of their worship, and therefore instead of *áliḥataká, thy gods,* read *iláhataka, thy worship.*"

See above, on ver. 124. Pharaoh, says the *Tafsír-i-Raufi,* worshipped the stars, calling the images of himself, used by the people, *little gods,* and himself *the great god.* Much of this kind of comment is due to the manifest inconsistency of the Qurán in representing Pharaoh sometimes as an idolater (note the expression "thy gods," here and chap. x. 79), and at other times as claiming to be the *only*

answered, We will cause their male children to be slain, and we will suffer their females to live; and *by that means we shall prevail over them*. (129) Moses said unto his people, Ask assistance of GOD and suffer patiently: for the earth is God's; he giveth it for an inheritance unto such of his servants as he pleaseth; and the *prosperous end shall be* unto those who fear *him*. (130) They answered, We have been afflicted *by having our male children slain* before thou camest unto us, and also since thou hast come unto us. *Moses* said, Peradventure it may happen that our LORD will destroy your enemy, and will cause you to succeed *him* in the earth, that he may see how ye will act *therein*.

R 16/6.

|| (131) And we formerly punished the people of Pharaoh with dearth and scarcity of fruits, that they might be warned. (132) Yet when good happened unto them,

---

God. This error may have arisen out of a mistaken apprehension of the use of the word *god*. See Exod. vii. 1.

Male children to be slain. This is an anachronism, but the commentators reconcile this statement with history by saying, as given by Sale, "We will continue to make use of the same cruel policy to keep the Israelites in subjection as we have hitherto done." But the form of words in the original obliges us to regard this as a new order, and there is not a word in the Qurán to justify the statement of of Abdul Qádir, that "this practice, which had been ordered before and afterwards discontinued, was here again inaugurated." Certainly there is nothing in history to substantiate such a statement. It is simply a device to reconcile the Qurán with history.

We shall prevail. "The commentators say that Pharaoh came to this resolution because he had either been admonished in a dream, or by the astrologers or divines, that one of that nation should subvert his kingdom."—*Sale, Baidháwi, Jaláluddín.*

(129) *The earth is God's.* The *Tafsír-i-Raufí* says that Moses here predicts that the children of Israel should possess the land of Egypt. See below on ver. 137.

(130) *Your enemy, i.e.,* Pharaoh.

(131) *Death and famine.* The allusion is to the seven years' famine under the Pharaoh who domiciled the children of Israel in Egypt. This Pharaoh is here identified with the Pharaoh of Quránic celebrity! This famine was inflicted as a warning, which, being unheeded, was followed by the plagues of ver. 134.

(132) *Unto them.* The context proves beyond doubt that the persons referred to here are the Egyptians, but the *murmurings* described belong to Israel in the desert.

they said, This *is owing* unto us; but if evil befell them, they attributed *the same* to the ill-luck of Moses, and those who *were* with him. Was not their ill-luck with GOD? But most of them knew it not. (133) And they said *unto Moses,* Whatever sign thou show unto us, to enchant us therewith, we will not believe on thee. (134) Wherefore we sent upon them a flood, and locusts, and lice, and frogs and blood; distinct miracles: but they behaved proudly, and became a wicked people. (135) And when the plague

---

Ill-luck. "The original word properly signifies *to take an ominous and sinister presage* of any future event, from the flight of birds, or the like."—*Sale.*

(133) *We will not believe on thee.* Muhammad undoubtedly thought that Moses was sent to the Egyptians to call them to repentance, as well as to deliver Israel from the hand of Pharaoh. He thought of him as a prophet of Egypt, as he thought of himself as the prophet of Arabia. Moses is here rejected, and the Egyptians refuse to become Muslims. The children of Israel, and all who believe in Moses, he regards in the light of his own followers seeking an asylum from persecution in Abyssinia, and perhaps Madína.

(134) *A flood.* Arnold thinks the allusion must be to the deluge, inasmuch as the drowning in the Red Sea occurred *after* the plagues (Islám and Christianity, p. 140). But the story of Noah, given in this chapter, vers. 60–65, shows that Muhammad did not mean the deluge in speaking *of a flood* here. We must therefore regard this statement as either an addition to the Jewish story or as referring to the drowning in the Red Sea. Historical accuracy is not one of the virtues of the oracle of Islám, as this chapter abundantly illustrates. Muslim commentators, as Baidháwi, &c., understand a deluge to be meant, and describe it as given in the following from Sale's notes on this passage :—" This inundation, they say, was occasioned by unusual rains, which continued eight days together, and the overflowing of the Nile ; and not only covered their lands, but came into their houses, and rose as high as their backs and necks ; but the children of Israel had no rain in their quarters. As there is no mention of any such miraculous inundation in the Mosaic writings, some have imagined this plague to have been either a pestilence or the smallpox, or some other epidemical distemper. For the word *tufán,* which is used in this place, and is generally rendered a *deluge,* may also signify any other universal destruction or mortality."

Lice. "Some will have these insects to have been a larger sort of tick ; others, the young locusts before they have wings."—*Sale, Baidháwi.*

The order of the plagues, so far as mentioned here, is exactly the reverse of that in Exodus, but the order here is recognised as the true one by all Muslim authorities.

(135) *Plague, i.e.,* any one of the plagues already mentioned.

fell on them, they said, O Moses, entreat thy LORD for us, according to that which he hath covenanted with thee; verily if thou take the plague from off us, we will surely believe thee, and we will let the children of Israel go with thee. But when he had taken the plague from off them until the term *which God had granted them* was expired, behold they broke their promise. (136) Wherefore we took vengeance on them, and drowned them in the *Red Sea*; because they charged our signs with falsehood, and neglected them. (137) And we caused the people who had been rendered weak to inherit the eastern parts of the earth and the western parts thereof, which we blessed *with fertility;* and the gracious word of thy LORD was fulfilled on the children of Israel, for that they had endured with patience: and we destroyed the *structures* which Pharaoh and his people had made, and that which they had erected.

RUBA. ‖ (138) And we caused the children of Israel to pass through the sea, and they came unto a people who gave

---

We will believe thee, i.e., we will acknowledge the true God, and accept thee as his prophet; in other words, we will be Muslims. See notes above on vers. 104, 127, and 133.

We will let the children of Israel go with thee, i.e., to their own country. But see on ver. 133.

They broke their promises. If the conjecture mentioned in note on ver. 95 has any truth in it, there is in this and the following verse an implied warning against unbelief.

(136) *Drowned them.* See notes on chap. x. 90-92, and xx. 79-81.

Because, &c. This statement is a direct contradiction of the teaching of Moses. The Egyptians did not deny the miracles of Moses, but "Pharaoh hardened his heart."

(137) *We caused . . . to inherit.* The commentators say the reference is to Syria. If so, *eastern parts* and *western* refer most probably to the lands on the eastern and western sides of the Jordan. The passage in connection with what follows, however, raises the suspicion that Muhammad here intended us to understand that God gave the Israelites the victory over Pharaoh, and so made them masters of the country on both sides of the Red Sea. See also chap. xvii. 106.

The structures. Those mentioned in chap. xxviii. 38, and xl. 38, 39.

(138) *A people.* "These people some will have to be of the tribe

themselves up to *the worship of* their idols, *and* they said, O Moses, make us a god, in like manner as these *people* have gods. Moses answered, Verily ye are an ignorant people: (139) for *the religion* which these follow *will be* destroyed, and that which they do is vain. (140) He said, Shall I seek for you any other god than GOD, since he hath preferred you to the *rest of the* world? (141) And *remember* when we delivered you from the people of Pharaoh, who grievously oppressed you; they slew your male children, and let your females live: therein was a great trial from your LORD.

|| (142) And we appointed unto Moses *a fast of* thirty R $\frac{17}{7}$. nights *before we gave him the law,* and we completed them by *adding of* ten *more;* and the stated time of his LORD was fulfilled in forty nights. And Moses said unto his brother Aaron, Be thou my deputy among my people *during my absence;* and behave uprightly, and follow not

---

of Amalek, whom Moses was commanded to destroy, and others of the tribe of Lakhm. Their idols, it is said, were images of oxen, which gave the first hint to the making of the golden calf."—*Sale, Baidháwi.*

Make us a god. This request being addressed to Moses contradicts the Bible (Exod. xxxii. 1, and Acts vii. 40). The reason for their returning to idolatry was that they had lost confidence in the absent Moses.

As these have, i.e., the Amalekites. The Israelites, however, did not adopt a new form of idolatry, but merely lapsed into that which they had adopted while in Egypt.

(142) *Thirty nights.* "The commentators say that God, having promised Moses to give him the law, directed him to prepare himself for the high favour of speaking with God in person by a fast of thirty days, and that Moses accordingly fasted the whole month of Dhu'l Quada; but not liking the savour of his breath, he rubbed his teeth with a dentifrice, upon which the angels told him that his breath before had the odour of musk (see Prelim. Disc., p. 176), but that his rubbing his teeth had taken it away. Wherefore God ordered him to fast ten days more, which he did; and these were the first ten days of the succeeding month, Dhu'l Hajja. Others, however, suppose that Moses was commanded to fast and pray thirty days only, and that during the other ten God discoursed with him."
—*Sale, Baidháwi, Jaláluddín.*

Nights. The ordinary custom among Muslims is to fast during the day-time, eating only during the night. Concerning the reckon-

the way of the corrupt doers. (143) And when Moses came at our appointed time, and his LORD spake unto him, he said, O LORD, show me *thy glory*, that I may behold thee. *God* answereth, Thou shalt in no wise behold me; but look towards the mountain, and if it stand firm in its place, then thou shalt see me. But when his LORD appeared with glory in the mount, he reduced it to dust. And Moses fell down in a swoon. And when he came to himself he said, Praise be unto thee! I turn unto thee with repentance, and I *am* the first of true believers. (144) *God* said *unto him*, O Moses, I have chosen thee above *all* men, *by honouring thee* with my commissions, and by my speaking *unto thee:* receive therefore that which I have brought thee, and be *one* of those who give thanks. (145) And we wrote for him on the tables an

---

ing *by nights* Savary says :—"The Arabs reckoned by *nights* as we do by *days*. This custom doubtless had its rise from the excessive heat of their climate. They dwell amidst burning sands, and while the sun is above the horizon they usually keep within their tents. When he sets they quit them, and enjoy coolness and a most delightful sky. Night is in a great measure to them that which day is to us. Their poets, therefore, never celebrate the charms of a beautiful day; but these words, *Lailí! Lailí!* O night! O night! are repeated in all their songs."

Be my deputy. Lit., act as my Khalífah. See note on chap. vi. 165.

(143) *His Lord spake.* "Without the mediation of any other, and face to face, as he speaks to the angels."—*Sale, Baidháwi.*

Show me thy glory. The ellipsis should have been *thyself*, not *thy glory*. This request was refused. Even the *glory* of God, as seen on the mountain, which Muslims call al Zabír, caused Moses to swoon and reduced the mountain to dust!

The first of true beliverers. See a similar expression in chap. vi. 14. The meaning here is that Moses was the first true believer among the Israelites, or perhaps Egyptians. The *Tafsír-i-Raufi* paraphrases thus : " *I am the first believer in thy dignity and glory; or this, that I am the first to believe in the impossibility of seeing thee as thou art.*" Moses is called *Kalímulláh*, the *speaker with God*, referring to the circumstance here narrated.

(144) *Receive . . . that which, &c.* The Tauret written on tables of stone. Sale says :—"The Muhammadans have a tradition that Moses asked to see God on the day of Arafát, and that he received the law on the day they slay the victims at the pilgrimage of Makkah, which days are the ninth and tenth of Dhu'l Hajja."

(145) *The tables.* " These tables, according to some, were seven in

admonition concerning every matter, and a decision in every case, *and said,* Receive this with reverence; and command thy people that they live according to the most excellent *precepts* thereof. I will show you the dwelling of the wicked. (146) I will turn aside from my signs those who behave themselves proudly in the earth, without justice: and although they see every sign, yet they shall not believe therein; and although they see the way of righteousness, yet they shall not take that way; but if they see the way of error, they shall take that way. (147) This *shall come to pass* because they accuse our signs of imposture, and neglect the same. But as for them who deny the truth of our signs and the meeting of the life to come, their works shall be vain: shall they be rewarded otherwise than *according to* what they shall have wrought? || (148) And the people of Moses, after his *departure,* took a corporeal calf, *made* of their ornaments, which

R $\frac{18}{8}$

---

number, and according to others ten. Nor are the commentators agreed whether they were cut out of a kind of lote-tree in Paradise called al Sidra, or whether they were chrysolites, emeralds, rubies, or common stone. But they say that they were each ten or twelve cubits long ; for they suppose that not only the ten commandments but the whole law was written thereon : and some add that the letters were cut quite through the tables, so that they might be read on both sides, which is a fable of the Jews."—*Sale, Baidháwi.*

And a decision in every case. These words are omitted in Rodwell's translation, but present in all copies of the Qurán in Arabic I have been able to consult. Evidently Muhammad believed and taught that Moses while in Mount Sinai received not the ten commandments only (Exod. xxxiv. 28, 29 ; xxxi. 18), but also the whole code of laws contained in the Pentateuch.

The dwelling of the wicked, viz., "The desolate habitations of the Egyptians, or those of the impious tribes of Ád and Thamúd, or perhaps hell."—*Sale.*

(146, 147) See notes above on vers. 97-100.

(148) *A corporeal calf.* Rodwell renders the word here translated "corporeal," *ruddy like gold.* The Persian and Urdu translations agree with Sale. See also note on chap. ii. 50.

Ornaments. The *Tafsír-i-Raufí* says this idol was made of the ornaments borrowed from the Egyptians on the eve of their departure (Exod. xii. 35, 36).

Which lowed. See note on chap. ii. 50. This also contradicts Bible history.

lowed. Did they not see that it spake not unto them, neither directed them in the way? *yet* they took it *for their god,* and acted wickedly. (149) But when they repented with sorrow, and saw that they had gone astray, they said, Verily if our LORD have not mercy upon us, and forgive us not, we shall certainly become *of the number* of those who perish. (150) And when Moses returned unto his people, full of wrath and indignation, he said, An evil thing is it that ye have committed after my *departure;* have ye hastened the command of your LORD? And he threw down the tables, and took his brother by the *hair of the* head, and dragged him unto him. *And Aaron* said unto him, Son of my mother, verily the people prevailed against me, and it wanted little but they had slain me: make not *my* enemies therefore to rejoice over me, neither place me with the wicked people. (151) *Moses* said, O LORD, forgive me and my brother, and receive us into thy mercy; for thou art the most merciful of those who exercise mercy.

‖ (152) Verily as for them who took the calf *for their god,* indignation shall overtake them from their LORD, and ignominy in this life: thus will we reward those who

---

(149) *When they repented.* This statement makes the repentance of the Israelites to have taken place during the absence of Moses.

(150) *He threw down the tables,* " which were all broken, and taken up to heaven, except one only; and this, they say, contained the threats and judicial ordinances, and was afterwards put into the ark."—*Sale, Baidháwi.*

Muhammad seems to have been ignorant of the renewal of the tables, described in Exod. xxxiv.

Dragged him. This scene seems to have been entirely due to the imagination of Muhammad. Exod. xxxii. 21-24 teaches no more than that Moses was angry with his brother for having had anything to do with the sin of the multitude.

(151) *Forgive me and my brother.* Forgive me for treating my elder brother with such disrespect, or for breaking the tables, and forgive my brother for whatever fault he committed in connection with the worship of the calf.—*Tafsír-i-Raufí.* This passage disproves the claim of modern Muslims that all the prophets were sinless.

(152) See notes on chap. ii. 53.

imagine falsehood. (153) But unto them who do evil, and afterwards repent, and believe *in God*, verily thy LORD *will* thereafter *be* clement *and* merciful. (154) And when the anger of Moses was appeased, he took the tables; and in what was written thereon was a direction and mercy unto those who feared their LORD. (155) And Moses chose out of his people seventy men, *to go up with him to the mountain* at the time appointed by us: and when a storm of thunder and lightning had taken them away, he said, O LORD, if thou hadst pleased, thou hadst destroyed them before, and me *also;* wilt thou destroy us for that which the foolish *men* among us have committed? This is only thy trial; thou wilt thereby lead into error whom thou pleasest, and thou wilt direct whom thou pleasest. Thou art our protector, therefore forgive us, and be merciful unto us; for thou art the best of those who forgive. (156) And write down for us good in this world, and in the life to come; for unto thee are we directed. *God* answered, I will inflict my punishment on whom I please; and my mercy extendeth over all things; and I will write down *good* unto those who shall fear *me*, (157) and give alms, and who shall believe in our signs; (158) who shall follow the apostle, the illiterate prophet, whom

---

(154) *He took the tables, i.e.*, "the fragments of what was left," say the commentators. The passage plainly says *the tables*, meaning the *whole*, though broken in pieces. See note above on ver. 150.

(155) See notes on chap. ii. 54, and chap. iv. 152. In chap. iv. this sin and its punishment is made to precede the worship of the calf and its judgment.

Thou wilt . . . lead into error, &c. See note on chap. ii. 155, and vi. 125.

(158) *The illiterate prophet.* See Prelim. Disc., pp. 73, 74.

Rodwell thinks Muhammad insincere in making this claim. See his note *in loco*. We need only consider what a man of letters was in Muhammad's time to enable us to decide whether the Qurán justifies this claim of Muhammad or not. To Muslims, however, it is accepted, as doubtless Muhammad intended it should be, as one of the chief arguments to prove the miraculous character of the Qurán. But the manner in which this expression is thrown into this verse and the next raises the conjecture, which with us amounts to an opinion, that this appellation came originally from the Jews, who used it in

they shall find written down with them in the law and the gospel: he will command them that which is just, and will forbid them that which is evil, and will allow them as lawful the good things *which were before forbidden*, and will prohibit those which are bad; and he will ease them of their heavy burden, and of the yokes which were upon them. And those who believe in him, and honour him, and assist him, and follow the light, which hath been sent down with him, *shall be* happy.

R 20/10.

|| (159) Say, O men, Verily I am the messenger of GOD unto you all: unto him *belongeth* the kingdom of heaven and earth; there is no GOD but he; he giveth life, and he causeth to die. Believe therefore in God and his apostle, the illiterate prophet, who believeth in GOD and his word; and follow him, that ye may be *rightly* directed. (160) Of the people of Moses *there is* a party who direct *others* with truth, and act justly according to the same. (161)

---

expressing their contempt for the *Gentile prophet*, the term *Ummí* meaning *Gentile* in the technical sense. Muhammad would readily adopt the name, for reasons already expressed.

Written down with them in the law and the gospel, i.e., "both foretold by name and certain description."—*Sale*. The passages usually quoted by Muslims as referring to their Prophet are Deut. xviii. 15, xxxiii. 2; Ps. l. 2; Isa. xxi. 7, and lxiii. 1–6; Hab. iii. 3; John i. 21, xiv. 16, xvi. 7; and Rev. vi. 4. Muhammad nowhere ventures to quote the Scripture foretelling his advent, except in chap. lxi. 6, where he certainly shows himself to be *illiterate* in respect to the New Testament Scriptures.

Good things . . . and bad. See note on chap. iii. 49, and chap. v. 2–6.

This passage is regarded by Nöeldeke as a Madína revelation, because of the maturity of Islám here presented, and because of the reference to those who "assist" the Prophet, *i.e., the Ansárs*, who were not so called until after the Hijra.

(159) *O men.* Sale understands this to mean all mankind, but it is more natural to understand it as simply addressed to the people of Makkah. See note on chap. ii. 21.

(160) *A party,* viz., "Those Jews who seemed better disposed than the rest of their brethren to receive Muhammad's law, or perhaps such of them as had actually received it. Some imagine they were a Jewish nation dwelling somewhere beyond China, which Muhammad saw the night he made his journey to heaven, and who believed on him."—*Sale, Baidháwi.*

See also notes on chap. vi. 20.

And we divided them into twelve tribes, *as into so many* nations. And we spake by revelation unto Moses when his people asked drink of him, *and we said,* Strike the rock with thy rod; and there gushed thereout twelve fountains, and men knew their *respective* drinking-place. And we caused clouds to overshadow them, and manna and quails to descend upon them, *saying,* Eat of the good things which we have given you for food: and they injured not us, but they injured their own souls. (162) And *call to mind* when it was said unto them, Dwell in this city, and eat *of the provisions* thereof wherever ye will, and say, Forgiveness; and enter the gate worshipping: we will pardon you your sins, *and* will give increase unto the well-doers. (163) But they who were ungodly among them changed the expression into another, which had not been spoken unto them. Wherefore we sent down upon them indignation from heaven, because they transgressed.

(164) And ask them concerning the city, which was situate on the sea, when they transgressed on the Sabbath-day: when their fish came unto them on their Sabbath-day, *appearing* openly *on the water:* but on the day whereon they celebrated no Sabbath, they came not unto them. Thus did we prove them, because they were wicked-doers. (165) And when a party of them said *unto the others,* Why do ye warn a people whom GOD will destroy, or will punish with a grievous punishment? They answered, *This*

---

(161) See notes on chap. ii. 56 and 59. This stone, says Baidháwi, was thrown down from Paradise by Adam. Shuaib having possession of it, gave it with the rod to Moses. The *Tafsir-i-Raufi* says the stone lay hidden in the desert, but spoke to Moses as he passed by, saying, "Take me; I will be of use to thee."
(162, 163) See notes on chap. ii. 57, 58.
(164) *The city.* Ailah or Elath, on the Red Sea. See chap. ii. 64.
(165) *Why do ye warn, &c.?* Commentators differ as to the persons asking this question, some referring it to the pious, others to the unbelievers.
An excuse. "That we have done our duty in dissuading them from their wickedness."—*Sale.* This seems to decide the question as to who asked the question, *Why do ye warn, &c.?*

is an excuse *for us* unto your LORD, and peradventure they will beware. (166) But when they had forgotten the admonitions which had been given them, we delivered those who forbade *them* to do evil; and we inflicted on those who had transgressed a severe punishment, because they had acted wickedly. (167) And when they proudly refused *to desist* from what had been forbidden them, we said unto them, Be ye *transformed into* apes, driven away *from the society* of men. (168) And *remember* when thy LORD declared that he would surely send against *the Jews* until the day of resurrection *some nation* who should afflict them with a grievous oppression; for thy LORD is swift in punishing, and he *is* also ready to forgive, *and* merciful: (169) and we dispersed them among the nations in the earth. *Some* of them are upright persons, and *some* of them are otherwise. And we proved them with prosperity and with adversity, that they might return *from their disobedience;* (170) and a succession *of their posterity* hath succeeded after them, who have inherited the book *of the law,* who receive the temporal *goods* of this world, and say, It will surely be forgiven us: and if a temporal *advantage* like the former be offered them, they accept it *also.* Is it not the covenant of the book *of the law* established with them, that they should not speak of GOD *aught*

(166, 167). See notes on chap. ii. 64, and v. 65.
(168) See note on chap. v. 69. Comp. Deut. xxviii. 49, 50.
(169) *Upright . . . and . . . otherwise.* Comp. chap. iii. 113, 199. This passage is certainly of Madína origin, but revealed soon after the Hijra, when some of the Jews became Muslims. The unbelievers are reminded of the fate of their rebellious forefathers.

(170) *Who receive, &c.* "By accepting of bribes for wresting judgment, and for corrupting the copies of the Pentateuch, and by extorting of usury, &c."—*Sale, Baidháwi.*

Aught but truth. The lying of the Jews alluded to here, say the commentators, was their saying that their sins were all forgiven them; the sins of the night were forgiven in the day, and the sins of the day in the night. See *Tafsír-i-Raufi.*

They diligently read, &c. This passage also shows that the Jews in Muhammad's time were in possession of genuine copies of their Scriptures.

but the truth? Yet they diligently read that which is therein. But the enjoyment of the next life *will be* better for those who fear *God than the wicked gains of these people:* (Do ye not therefore understand?) (171) and for those who hold fast the book *of the law*, and are constant at prayer: for we will by no means suffer the reward of the righteous to perish. (172) And when we shook the mountain *of Sinai* over them, as though it had been a covering, and they imagined, that it was falling upon them; *and we said*, Receive the *law* which we have brought you with reverence; and remember that which is *contained* therein, that ye may take heed.

(173) And when thy LORD drew forth their posterity R $\frac{2\ 2}{1\ 2}$. from the lions of the sons of Adam, and took them to witness against themselves, *saying*, Am not I your LORD? They answered, Yea: we do bear witness. *This was done* lest ye should say at the day of resurrection, Verily we were negligent as to this *matter, because we were not apprised thereof:* (174) or lest ye should say, Verily our fathers were formerly guilty of idolatry, and we are *their* posterity who have succeeded them; wilt thou therefore destroy us for that which vain men have committed? (175) Thus do we explain *our* signs, that they may return *from their vanities.* (176) And relate unto *the Jews* the history of him unto whom we brought our signs, and he

---

(172) *The mountain.* See note on chap. ii. 62. This passage is based on Jewish tradition. See Rodwell *in loco.*

(173) *Thy Lord drew forth, &c.* "The commentators tell us that God stroked Adam's back, and extracted from his loins his whole posterity, which should come into the world until the resurrection, one generation after another; that these men were actually assembled together in the shape of small ants, which were endued with understanding; and that after they had, in the presence of the angels, confessed their dependence on God, they were again caused to return into the loins of their great ancestor."—*Sale, Baidháwi, Jaláluddín, Yahya.*

This transaction is said to have taken place in the valley of Mumán, near Arafát; others say it took place in the plain of Dahia of India. See *Tafsír-i-Raufi in loco.* This passage clearly recognises the doctrine of pre-existence, as held by Origen.

(176) *The history of him.* "Some suppose the person here in-

departed from them; wherefore Satan followed him, and he became *one* of those who were seduced. (177) And if we had pleased, we had surely raised him thereby *unto wisdom;* but he inclined unto the earth, and followed his own desire. Wherefore his likeness as the likeness of a dog, which, if thou drive him away, putteth forth his tongue, or, if thou let him alone, putteth forth his tongue *also.* This is the likeness of the people who accuse our signs of falsehood. Rehearse therefore *this* history *unto them,* that they may consider. (178) Evil is the similitude of those people who accuse our signs of falsehood, and injure their own souls. (179) Whomsoever GOD shall direct, he *will be rightly* directed; and whomsoever he shall lead astray, they shall perish. (180) Moreover we have created for hell many of the genii and of men; they have hearts by which they understand not, and they have eyes by which they see not, and they have ears by which they hear not. These are like the brute beasts; yea, they go more astray; these are the negligent. (181) GOD hath most excellent names; therefore call on him by the same;

---

tended to be a Jewish Rabbi, or one Ummaya Ibn Abu Salab, who read the Scriptures, and found thereby that God would send a prophet about that time, and was in hopes that he might be the man; but when Muhammad declared his mission, believed not on him through envy. But according to the more general opinion, it was Balam, the son of Beor, of the Canaanitish race, well acquainted with part at least of the Scripture, having even been favoured with some revelations from God, who being requested by his nation to curse Moses and the children of Israel, refused it at first, saying, 'How can I curse those who are protected by the angels?' But afterwards he was prevailed on by gifts; and he had no sooner done it, than he began to put out his tongue like a dog, and it hung down upon his breast."—*Sale, Baidhâwi, Jalâluddîn,* &c. Comp. 2 Pet. ii. 5, and Jude ii.

(178) *Who accuse, &c.* See note on chap. iii. 185, and above on ver. 2.

(179, 180) This passage clearly makes God the author of evil. He is said to create genii and men for the express purpose of filling hell with them. Comp. chap. xi. 119. But see notes on chap. iii. 145, 155. The creation of the righteous is mentioned in ver. 182.

(181) *God hath . . . names.* These are ninety-nine in number, and are all to be found in the Qurán. They are repeated by pious Muslims, with the aid of a rosary, as a matter of merit. They are as follows:—The Merciful, the Compassionate, the King, the Most

and withdraw from those who use his name perversely: they shall be rewarded for that which they shall have wrought. (182) And of those whom we have created there are a people who direct *others* with truth, and act justly according thereto.

‖ (183) But those who devise lies against our signs, we will suffer them to fall gradually into ruin, by a *method* which they knew not: (184) and I will grant them to enjoy a long and prosperous life; for my stratagem is effectual. (185) Do they not consider that there is no devil in their companion? He is no other than a public

---

Holy, the Tranquil, the Faithful, the Protector, the Victorious, the Mighty, the Self-Exalted, the Creator, the Maker, the Former, the Forgiver, the Wrathful, the Giver, the Cherisher, the Conqueror, the Knower, the Seizer, the Expander, the Depresser, the Exalter, the Strengthener, the Disgracer, the Hearer, the Seer, the Ruler, the Just, the Benignant, the Informer, the Great, the Pardoner, the Rewarder, the High, the Great, the Rememberer, the Powerful, the Satisfier, the Glorious, the Kind, the Guardian, the Answerer, the All-embracing, the Wise, the All-loving. the Glorious, the Provider, the Strong, the Firm, the Friend, the Praiseworthy, the Beginner, the Reckoner, the Restorer, the Life-giver, the Destroyer, the Living, the Self-subsisting, the Finder, the Glorious, the Unique, the Eternal, the Powerful, the Prevailing, the Leader, the Finisher, the First, the Eternal, the Everlasting, the Innermost, the Revealer, the Governor, the Pure, the Propitious, the Remitter, the Avenger, the Merciful, the King of the Kingdom, the Lord of Glory and Honour, the Equitable, the Assembler, the Rich, the Enricher, the Possessor, the Prohibitor, the Afflicter, the Benefactor, the Light, the Guide, the Creator, the Observer, the Inheritor, the Director, the Patient, the Mild.—See Macbride's *Muhammadan Religion Explained,* pp. 121-123, and *Tafsír-i-Raufi in loco.*

Rewarded. "As did Walíd Ibn al Mughaira, who hearing Muhammad give God the title of al Rahmán, or *the Merciful,* laughed aloud, saying he knew none of that name, except a certain man who dwelt in Yamáma; or as the idolatrous Makkans did, who deduced the names of their idols from those of the true God, deriving, for example, Allát from Allah, al Uzza from al Azíz, *the Mighty,* and Manát from al Mannán, *the Bountiful."—Sale.*

(183) *We will suffer them to fall, &c.* "By flattering them with prosperity in this life, and permitting them to sin in an uninterrupted security, till they find themselves unexpectedly ruined."— *Sale, Baidháwi.*

(185) *Their companion,* viz., "In Muhammad, whom they gave out to be possessed when he went up to Mount Safá, and from thence

preacher. Or do they not contemplate the kingdom of heaven and earth, and the things which GOD hath created; and *consider* that peradventure it may be that their end draweth nigh? And in what new declaration will they believe, after this? (186) He whom GOD shall cause to err shall have no director; and he shall leave them in their impiety, wandering in confusion. (187) They will ask thee concerning the *last* hour, at what time its coming is fixed? Answer, Verily the knowledge thereof is with my LORD; none shall declare the fixed time thereof, except he. *The expectation thereof* is grievous in heaven and on earth: it shall come upon you no otherwise than suddenly. They will ask thee, as though thou wast well acquainted therewith. Answer, Verily the knowledge thereof is with GOD alone: but the greater part of men know it not. (188) Say, I am able neither to procure advantage unto myself, nor to avert mischief *from me*, but as GOD pleaseth. If I knew the secrets *of God*, I should surely enjoy abundance of good, neither should evil befall me. Verily I am no other than a denouncer of threats, and a messenger of good tidings unto people who believe.

---

called to the several families of each respective tribe, in order to warn them of God's vengeance if they continued in their idolatry."—Sale, *Baidháwi*.

The original literally translated, *Do they not consider that there is to their friend naught from the genii?*

A public preacher. This is the character in which Muhammad loved to appear at Makkah. This claim is *now* made in the sense that he is appointed of God to be a warner or preacher, hence the transition from the position of reformer to that of apostle.

Declaration, i.e., the plain revelation of the Qurán.

(186) See note on vers. 179 and 180.

(187) *Grievous in heaven, i.e.,* to angels as well as to men, genii, &c.

The knowledge thereof, &c. Compare Matt. xxiv. 36.

(188) This verse goes against those who attribute to Muhammad the gift of foretelling future events. Much more does it refute the assertions of those who say that Muhammad will intercede for his people on the judgment-day, tradition to the contrary notwithstanding, for no genuine tradition can contradict the uniform teaching of the Qurán. See note on chap. ii. 47, 123, and 254, and vi. 49.

|| (189) It is he who hath created you from one person, and out of him produced his wife, that he might dwell with her: and when he had known her, she carried a light burden *for a time,* wherefore she walked *easily* therewith. But when it became more heavy, she called upon GOD their LORD, *saying,* If thou give us *a child* rightly shaped, we will surely be thankful. (190) Yet when he had given them *a child* rightly shaped, they attributed companions unto him, for that which he had given them. But far be that from GOD which they associated *with him!* (191) Will they associate *with him false gods* which create nothing, but are themselves created; (192) and

R $\frac{24}{14}$.

---

(189) *One person.* This certainly refers to Adam. The story given by Sale below is an invention of the commentators to escape from the conclusion that Adam and Eve became idolaters.

(190) *They attributed companions unto him.* "For the explaining of this whole passage the commentators tell the following story. They say that when Eve was big with her first child, the devil came to her and asked her whether she knew what she carried within her, and which way she should be delivered of it; suggesting that possibly it might be a beast. She, being unable to give an answer to this question, went in a fright to Adam, and acquainted him with the matter, who not knowing what to think of it, grew sad and pensive. Whereupon the devil appeared to her again (or, as others say, to Adam), and pretended that he by his prayers would obtain of God that she might be safely delivered of a son in Adam's likeness, provided they would promise to name him Abdul Hárith, or the *servant of al Hárith* (which was the devil's name among the angels), instead of Abdullah, or *the servant of God,* as Adam had designed. This proposal was agreed to, and accordingly, when the child was born, they gave it that name, upon which it immediately died. And with this Adam and Eve are here taxed as an act of idolatry. The story looks like a *rabbinical* fiction, and seems to have no other foundation than Cain's being called by Moses Obed-adámah, that is, *a tiller of the ground,* which might be translated into Arabic by Abdul Hárith.

"But al Baidháwi, thinking it unlikely that a prophet (as Adam is by the Muhammadans supposed to have been) should be guilty of such an action, imagines the Qurán in this place means Kussai, one of Muhammad's ancestors, and his wife, who begged issue of God, and having four sons granted them, called their names Abd Manáf, Abd Shams, Abdul Uzza, and Abdul Dár, after the names of four principal idols of the Quraish. And the following words also he supposes to relate to their idolatrous posterity."—*Sale, Baidháwi, Yahya.*

can neither give them assistance, nor help themselves? (193) And if ye invite them to the *true* direction, they will not follow you : it will be equal unto you whether ye invite them, or whether ye hold your peace. (194) Verily the *false deities* whom ye invoke besides GOD are servants like unto you. Call therefore upon them, and let them give you an answer, if ye speak truth. (195) Have they feet, to walk with? Or have they hands, to lay hold with? Or have they eyes, to see with? Or have they ears, to hear with? Say, Call upon your companions, and then lay a snare for me, and defer *it* not; (196) for GOD *is* my protector, who sent down the book *of the Qurán;* and he protecteth the righteous. (197) But they whom ye invoke besides him cannot assist you, neither do they help themselves; (198) and if ye call on them to direct you, they will not hear. Thou seest them look towards thee, but they see not. (199) Use indulgence, and command that which is just, and withdraw far from the ignorant. (200) And if an evil suggestion from Satan be suggested unto thee, *to divert thee from thy duty,* have recourse unto GOD: for he heareth *and* knoweth. (201) Verily they who fear *God*, when a temptation from Satan assaileth them, remember *the divine commands*, and behold,

---

(194) *The false deities . . . are servants.* The sun, moon, and stars are here alluded to.

(195) Comp. Isa. xliv. 8-21, and Ps. cxv. 3-8.

Lay a snare for me. This points to a period near the Hijra when the Quraish were ready by any means to destroy their dangerous neighbour. Muhammad expresses confidence in God ; may he not have already seen the way to deliverance in the completed arrangements made for retiring to Madína?

(199) *Use indulgence;* " or, as the words may also be translated, *Take the superabundant overplus,* meaning that Muhammad should accept such voluntary alms from the people as they could spare. But the passage, if taken in this sense, was abrogated by the precept of legal alms, which was given at Madína."—*Sale.*

It is more natural to understand this as an exhortation to Muhammad to be forbearing toward the idolaters of Makkah.

And withdraw. This seems clearly to refer to the Hijra. See chap vi. 106.

(200) See notes on chaps. iv. 116, and vi. 112.

they clearly see *the danger of sin and the wiles of the devil.* (202) But as for the brethren *of the devils,* they shall continue them in error, and afterwards they shall not preserve themselves *therefrom.* (203) And when thou bringest not a verse *of the Qurán* unto them, they say, Hast thou not put it together? Answer, I follow that only which is revealed unto me from my LORD. This *book containeth* evident proofs from your LORD, and *is* a direction and mercy unto people who believe. (204) And when the Qurán is read attend thereto, and keep silence, that ye may obtain mercy. (205) And meditate on thy LORD in thine own mind, with humility and fear, and without loud speaking, evening and morning; and be not *one* of the negligent. (206) Moreover *the angels* who are with my LORD do not proudly disdain his service, but they celebrate his praise and worship him.

---

(202) *The brethren.* Those under the influence of devils.

(203) *Hast thou not put it together? i.e.,* "Hast thou not yet contrived what to say; or canst thou obtain no revelation from God?" —*Sale.*

The garbled stories, learned from Jewish tradition, so plentifully given in this chapter, entirely justify the taunt intended here. See note on ver. 85.

Muhammad's reply is, as usual, a reassertion of his own inspiration.

(204) *Keep silence.* The occasion on which this verse was revealed was as follows:—A young Muslim, standing behind the Prophet, kept repeating in a loud voice the passages of the Qurán which were being read, thus creating confusion in the service. The passage enjoins silence on the part of all Muslims during prayers, except the Imám or leader.

(205) *Evening and morning.* The five times for prayer probably had not yet been fixed. The commentators say these are the most important seasons of prayer.

(206) *Worship him.* This is one of the fifteen places in the Qurán where the reader must, according to some, prostrate himself in reading; according to others, this prostration is meritorious, though not required.

CHAPTER VIII.

ENTITLED SURAT AL ANFÁL (THE SPOILS).

Revealed at Madína.

INTRODUCTION.

THE title of this Sura was taken from the question of the first verse concerning spoils. The chapter, however, has but little to do with this subject, almost the whole of it being taken up with a description of the miraculous character of the battle of Badr, with allusions to events immediately preceding or following it, by which the faithful are confirmed in their confidence in God and Muhammad. Islám is declared to have now received the seal of God to its truth, and consequently all who hereafter may oppose it will merit shame and destruction both in this world and in the world to come.

The confident and often defiant tone, perceptible in this chapter, may be accounted for by the circumstances under which it was written. Muhammad had been successful beyond expectation, and the sometimes despondent Muslims were now exulting over those from whom they had so lately fled in fear. Muhammad, ever ready to use his opportunities, declares this victory to be decisive proof of the divine favour. God had brought it all about that he "might accomplish the thing which was decreed to be done; that he who perisheth hereafter may perish after demonstrative evidence, and that he who liveth may live by the same evidence."

Accordingly the infidels are denounced in no measured terms. Even the proud Quraish are addressed in a patronising manner, and are offered an amnesty on condition of their ceasing to oppose. The hypocrites and hitherto disaffected inhabitants of Madína are reproved and warned, while the duplicity of the Jews is threatened.

There is, however, the anticipation of future trouble. It required no more than the sagacity of a politician to foretell it. The Muslims are therefore urged to prepare for the holy war, and to fight with that assurance which enables one man to face ten of his adversaries. God would be on their side, and the infidels would only rush on to certain destruction.

Nothing could be in stronger contrast than the spirit of this chapter compared with the latter part of chapter iii., written just after the Muslim defeat at Ohod. Such a comparison should make it clear to Muslims that the revelation of the Qurán, instead of being copied from the Preserved Table under the throne of God, was copied from the heart-table of Muhammad himself.

Probable Date of the Revelations.

It is certain that the greater part of this chapter was written immediately after the battle of Badr in A.H. 2. Indeed there is no part of it which may not be referred to this period excepting vers. 73–75, which must be assigned to the earlier months of A.H. 1. Sale mentions the fact that some authorities would place vers. 30–36 among the Makkan revelations, but the evidence seems to me to be against them. This passage might, however, belong to an earlier period than A.H. 2, inasmuch as it relates to the flight from Makkah. Yet the victory of Badr would naturally recall to Muhammad's mind the circumstances of his flight, and thus lead to their mention here.

Principal Subjects.

	VERSES
Spoils belong to God and his Apostle	1
True believers and their future reward	2–4
Muslims reproved for distrusting their Prophet	5, 6
God gives the Muslims either the Quraish or their caravan	7
The victory of Badr a seal to Islám	8
Angelic aid vouchsafed to Muhammad	9
The Muslims refreshed and comforted before the battle	10, 11
The angels enjoined to comfort the faithful by destroying the infidel Quraish	12
Infidels are doomed to punishment here and hereafter	13, 14
Muslims are never to turn their backs on the infidels on pain of hell-fire	15, 16
The victory of Badr a miracle	17, 18
The Quraish are warned against further warfare with the Muslims	19
Muslims exhorted to steadfastness in faith	20, 21
Infidels compared to deaf and dumb brutes	22, 23
Believers are to submit themselves to God and his Apostle	24

	VERSES
They are warned against civil strife, deception, and treachery	25–28
God's favour to true believers	29
Plots against Muhammad frustrated by God	30
The infidels liken the Qurán to fables	31
The Quraish were protected from deserved punishment by Muhammad's presence among them	32, 33
The idolaters of Makkah rebuked and threatened	34–38
An amnesty offered to the Quraish	39
Impenitent idolaters to be extirpated from the earth	40, 41
How the spoils of war are to be divided	42
The Muslims were led by God to fight at Badr to attest the truth of Islám	43, 44
The Muslims encouraged, and the infidels lured to destruction, by each seeing the other to be few in number	45, 46
Believers exhorted to obedience	47, 48
Believers warned against impious vainglory	49
The devil deserts the Quraish at Badr	50
The fate of hypocrites	51–53
Their doom like that of Pharaoh and his people	54–56
The worst of beasts are the infidels	57
Treachery to be met with its like	58–60
God is against the infidels	61
The Muslims excited to war against unbelievers	62
Condition of peace with unbelievers	63
The miracle of Arab union	64
God with the Prophet and the Muslims in warring for the faith	65, 66
Muslims reproved for accepting ransom for the captives taken at Badr	68–70
Captive Quraish exhorted to accept Islám, and warned against deception	71
The brotherhood of the Ansárs and Muháj Jirín	73–75
The hereditary rights of blood-relations re-established	76

Suls.

R $\frac{1}{15}$.

IN THE NAME OF THE MOST MERCIFUL GOD.

‖ (1) THEY will ask thee concerning the spoils: Answer, The *division of the* spoils *belongeth* unto GOD and the

---

(1) *The spoils*, taken at the battle of Badr. "It consisted of 115 camels, 14 horses, a large store of leather (beds and rugs), and much equipage and armour."—*Muir's Life of Mahomet*, vol. iii. p. 111.

Apostle. Therefore fear GOD, and compose the matter amicably among you: and obey GOD and his Apostle, if ye are true believers. (2) Verily the true believers *are those* whose hearts fear when GOD is mentioned, and whose faith increaseth when his signs are rehearsed unto them, and *who* trust in their LORD; (3) who observe the stated times of prayer, and give alms out of that which we have bestowed on them. (4) These are really believers: they shall have *superior* degrees *of felicity* with their LORD, and forgiveness, and an honourable provision. (5) As thy LORD brought thee forth from thy house with truth, and

---

The division, &c. Rodwell translates this passage correctly—*The spoils are God's and the Apostle's.* The ellipsis understood by Sale, however, points to the cause for this revelation. It was due to a dispute between those who pursued the Quraish at Badr and those who remained behind to guard the Prophet and the camp as to the *division* of the spoils. Muhammad silences both parties by telling them the victory was due to neither, but to God, and therefore the spoil was God's and his Apostle's, and that they must await the divine command as to its disposal.—*Idem*, p. 112.

"It is related that Saad Ibn Abi Waqqás, one of the companions, whose brother Omair was slain in this battle, having killed Said Ibn al As, took his sword, and carrying it to Muhammad, desired that he might be permitted to keep it; but the Prophet told him that it was not his to give away, and ordered him to lay it with the other spoils. At this repulse and the loss of his brother Saad was greatly disturbed; but in a very little while this chapter was revealed, and thereupon Muhammad gave him the sword, saying, 'You asked this sword of me when I had no power to dispose of it, but now I have received authority from God to distribute the spoils, you may take it.'"—*Sale, Baidháwi.*

(2–4) See notes on chap. ii. 3–5.

(5) *As thy Lord, &c., i.e.,* from Madína. "The particle *as* having nothing in the following words to answer it, al Baidháwi supposes the connection to be, that the division of the spoils belonged to the Prophet, notwithstanding his followers were averse to it, as they had been averse to the expedition itself."—*Sale.*

Rodwell supplies the word *Remember,* and translates, *Remember how thy Lord, &c.* The Urdu translations agree with Sale.

Part . . . were averse. This passage refers to the following circumstances:—Muhammad having received information of the approach of a caravan of the Quraish under Abu Sufián, went forth with his followers to plunder it. But Abu Sufián being apprised of the Muslim expedition, gave them the slip by turning aside and pursuing his journey by another way. Succours had been called for from Makkah, and 950 armed men, mounted on camels and horses,

part of the believers were averse *to thy directions:* (6) they disputed with thee concerning the truth, after it had been made known unto them; no otherwise than as if they had been led forth to death, and had seen *it with their eyes.* (7) And *call to mind* when GOD promised you one of the two parties, that it should be *delivered* unto you, and ye desired that the *party* which was not furnished with arms should be *delivered* unto you: but GOD purposed to make known the truth in his words, and to cut off the uttermost part of the unbelievers; (8) that he might verify the truth, and destroy falsehood, although

---

had answered the summons, and notwithstanding the safety of the caravan, they determined to advance and punish the Muslims. Muhammad and his people advanced with the expectation of an easy victory and abundant spoil, but learned to their chagrin of Abu Sufián's escape and the near approach of the succours. The question now arose among the disappointed followers whether they should pursue the caravan or follow Muhammad to the battle. By the aid of revelation and the interposition of Abu Baqr, Omar, and others, the disobedient were induced to submit to Muhammad's orders to attack the succours, which resulted in the celebrated battle of Badr. See Sale's note *in loco*, and Muir's *Life of Mahomet*, vol. iii. chap. xii.

(6) *After it had been made known.* Muhammad pretended to have received a promise from Gabriel that he should have either the caravan or victory over the succours. Victory was therefore assumed beforehand, but the smallness of their number made them afraid.

(7) *One of the two parties.* "That is, either the caravan or the succours from Makkah. Father Marracci, mistaking *al 'air* and *al nafir*, which are appellatives, and signify *the caravan* and *the troop* or body of succours, for proper names, has thence coined two families of the Quraish never heard of before, which he calls Airenses and Naphirenses (Marracci in Alc., p. 297)."—*Sale.*

Ye desired, that the caravan, guarded by only forty armed men, should be attacked.

But God proposed, &c. "As if he had said, Your view was only to gain the spoils of the caravan and to avoid danger; but God designed to exalt his true religion by extirpating its adversaries."—*Sale, Baidháwi.*

(8) *That he might verify the truth.* The victory of the Muslims is here declared to be evident proof of the divine mission of Muhammad and the truth of his religion. This claim gave ground to much doubt among the faithful and to scoffs and jeers among unbelievers after the defeat at Ohod. See notes on chap. iii. 121, and verses following.

the wicked were averse *thereto.* (9) When ye asked assistance of your LORD, and he answered you, Verily I will assist you with a thousand angels, following one another *in order.* (10) And this GOD designed only as good tidings for you, and that your hearts might thereby rest secure: for victory *is* from GOD alone; and GOD is mighty *and* wise.

∥ (11) When a sleep fell on you as a security from him, R $\frac{2}{16}$. and he sent down upon you water from heaven, that he

---

(9) *Assistance from your Lord.* "When Muhammad's men saw they could not avoid fighting, they recommended themselves to God's protection; and their Prophet prayed with great earnestness, crying out, 'O God, fulfil that which thou hast promised me: O God, if this party be cut off, thou wilt be no more worshipped on earth.' And he continued to repeat these words till his cloak fell from off his back."—*Sale,* and the *Tafsír-i-Raufi.*

A thousand angels. See notes on chap. iii. 13, and 123-125. In chap. iii. 127, the number of angels is given at 3000. The commentators reconcile the discrepancy by saying that at first 1000 angels appeared, "which," says Sale, "were afterwards reinforced with 3000 more. Wherefore some copies, instead of *a thousand,* read *thousands,* in the plural."

(10) See notes on chap. iii. 126.

(11) *Water from heaven.* The following is Baidháwi's comment as given by Sale:—

"The spot where Muhammad's little army lay was a dry and deep sand, into which their feet sank as they walked, the enemy having the command of the water; and that having fallen asleep, the greater part of them were disturbed with dreams, wherein the devil suggested to them that they could never expect God's assistance in the battle, since they were cut off from the water, and besides suffering the inconveniency of thirst, must be obliged to pray without washing, though they imagined themselves to be the favourites of God, and that they had his Apostle among them. But in the night rain fell so plentifully, that it formed a little brook, and not only supplied them with water for all their uses, but made the sand between them and the infidel army firm enough to bear them; whereupon the diabolical suggestions ceased."

Muir, however, assures us, on the authority of the K. Wáqkídi, that the Muslims had secured "the sole command of the water" previous to the fall of rain and the night's comfortable rest. Most likely the rain was interpreted by the ever-sagacious Prophet as a sign of victory granted from heaven, inasmuch as three blessings had resulted therefrom already—(1) sound sleep, (2) water for ceremonial purification instead of sand, and (3) the sand was made solid, and so their "feet were established."

might thereby purify you, and take from you the abomination of Satan, and that he might confirm your hearts, and establish *your* feet thereby. (12) *Also* when thy LORD spake unto the angels, *saying*, Verily I am with you; wherefore confirm those who believe. I will cast a dread into the hearts of the unbelievers. Therefore strike off *their* heads, and strike off all the ends of their *fingers*. . (13) This *shall they suffer*, because they have resisted GOD and his Apostle: and whosoever shall oppose GOD and his Apostle, verily GOD *will be* severe in punishing *him*. (14) This *shall be your punishment;* taste it therefore: and the infidels shall *also* suffer the torment of *hell*-fire. (15) O true believers, when ye meet the unbelievers marching *in great numbers against you*, turn not *your* backs unto them: (16) for whoso shall turn his back unto them in that day, unless he turneth aside to fight, or retreateth to *another* party *of the faithful*,

---

(12) *Thy Lord spake.* According to Rodwell, the address to the angels ends at "unbelievers," making the following words, "therefore strike," &c., an exhortation to the Muslims. The *Tafsîr-i-Raufi* and *Abdul Qádir* understand these words also to have been addressed to the angels. "The angels did not know," says the *Tafsîr-i-Raufi,* "where to strike a fatal blow;" hence the words, "strike off their heads"—literally *smite their necks*—and the allusion to *the ends of their* fingers is understood to include all the members of the body.

Sale understands the exhortation to be addressed to the Muslims. He says:—"This is the punishment expressly assigned the enemies of the Muhammadan religion, though the Muslims did not inflict it on the prisoners they took at Badr, for which they are reprehended in this chapter." The spirit of the passage is certainly very different from that of chap. ii. 256.

(13) *God will be severe.* The punishment will be severe if taken prisoner in the world, and afterwards in the final destruction of the soul.—*Tafsîr-i-Raufi.*

(14, 15) The *revelation* is here plainly made Muhammad's vehicle for a military harangue. Was Muhammad sincere in uttering such exhortations as the very words of God? Muslims claim complete inspiration for them, and accept Muhammad's claim to have been simply the mouthpiece of Divinity. Are the apologists for Islâm ready to do the same? If not, the only fair inference they can draw is that he was an impostor. Self-deception cannot be pleaded here. There is every sign of intelligent, deliberate policy. He desires to incite his followers to bold, desperate warfare. They have come to believe him to be inspired, and he never scruples to impose on their credulity for the accomplishment of his ambitious purposes.

shall draw on himself the indignation of GOD, and his abode shall be in hell; an ill journey *shall it be thither!* (17) And ye slew not those *who were slain at Badr yourselves,* but GOD slew them. Neither didst thou, *O Muhammad,* cast *the gravel into their eyes,* when thou didst *seem to* cast *it;* but GOD cast *it,* that he might prove the true believers by a gracious trial from himself, for GOD heareth and knoweth. (18) This *was done* that GOD might also weaken the crafty devices of the unbelievers. (19) If ye desire a decision *of the matter between us,* now hath a decision come unto you: and if ye desist *from opposing the Apostle,* it *will be* better for you. But if ye return *to attack him,* we will also return *to his assistance;* and your forces shall not be of advantage unto you at all, although they be numerous; for GOD is with the faithful.

|| (20) O true believers, obey GOD and his Apostle, and turn not back from him, since ye hear *the admonitions of*

R $\frac{3}{17}$.

---

(17) *God slew them.* See note on chap. iii. 13.
God heareth. The commentators say the angelic help at Badr was vouchsafed in answer to Muhammad's prayer.
(19) *Now hath a decision come.* The word translated *decision (al fatah)* means also *victory.* The Quraish had prayed for victory. Taking hold of the curtains of the Kaabah, they said, "O God, grant the victory to the superior army, the party that is most rightly directed, and the most honourable." Muhammad derisively plays on the word rendered victory in their prayer, and says, "Now hath a *decision* come unto you," &c. See *Baidhāwi* in Sale's note here.
(20) *God and his Apostle.* This joining of God and his Apostle, so prevalent in this chapter, savours strongly of blasphemy. True, the union intended is not organic or vital, but official, Muhammad being, as he here pretends, the deputy of God. Nevertheless, the union is of such a character, that in the succeeding clause, in the exhortation "*turn not back from him,*" the pronoun may apply to either God or Muhammad, and, to bring all the circumstances of the dispute about spoils into consideration, I think it must be applied to the latter. The assumption of Muslims that God is the speaker does not seem to me to apply here, for, in the first place, the sin of identifying God with a sinful man (*shirk*) would in that case be removed from the Apostle only to be fastened on God; and, secondly, if God were the speaker, why invariably speak of himself in the *third* person? and finally, the reason given for obedience is "since ye hear," *i.e.,* since ye are obedient unto God, being Muslims or *submitters* of yourselves to God. Surely such an exhortation predicates the Apostle as the exhorter. The commentators say that the expression signifies that

the Qurán. (21) And be not as those who say, We hear, when they do not hear. (22) Verily the worst *sort of* beasts in the sight of GOD are the deaf *and* the dumb, who understand not. (23) If GOD had known any good in them, he would certainly have caused them to hear: and if he had caused them to hear, they would surely have turned back and have retired afar off. (24) O true believers, answer GOD and *his* Apostle when he inviteth you unto that which giveth you life; and know that GOD goeth between a man and his heart, and that before him ye shall be assembled. (25) Beware of sedition; it will not affect those

obedience to the Prophet is obedience to God, and *vice versa.* Certainly this is what Muhammad intended when he thus associated his name with that of God.

(22) Abdul Qádir says this verse means that men who hearken not to God are worse than beasts.

(23) *Caused them to hear.* "That is, to hearken to the remonstrances of the Qurán. Some say that the infidels demanded of Muhammad that he should raise Kusai, one of his ancestors, to life, to bear witness to the truth of his mission, saying he was a man of honour and veracity, and they would believe his testimony: but they are here told that it would have been in vain."—*Sale.*

(24) *That which giveth life, i.e.,* "The knowledge of religion or orthodox doctrine, or crusade. or the declaration of faith in God and his Prophet, or the Qurán—all of which have life-giving power to Muslims."—*Tafsír-i-Raufi.*

God goeth between, &c. "Not only knowing the innermost secrets of his heart, but overruling a man's design, and disposing him either to belief or infidelity."—*Sale.*

(25) *Sedition.* "The original word signifies any epidemical crime, which involves a number of people in its guilt; and the commentators are divided as to its particular meaning in this place."—*Sale.*

The *Tafsír-i-Raufi* says by the word *fitna* is intended the heresy and apostasy of the last times, when Muslims will be indifferent to the commands and prohibitions of their religion, indolent in the crusade for the faith, &c.

Others think the allusion is to the conduct of Abu Lubába at the siege of the Bani Quraidha referred to in note on ver. 27 (see Muir's *Life of Mahomet,* vol. iii. p. 272, note), which, however, is improbable. The most probable allusion. to my mind, is the conduct of those who disputed about the spoils of Badr.

It will not affect, &c., i.e., the result of divisions and internal dissensions must lead to common ruin. Muhammad well understood the importance of unity among the faithful. The success of Islám depended on it. Hence he strains every nerve to bring all classes together by a common submission to himself.

who are ungodly among you particularly, *but all of you in general;* and know that GOD is severe in punishing. (26) And remember when ye were few *and* reputed weak in the land, ye feared lest men should snatch you away; but *God* provided you a place of refuge, and he strengthened you with his assistance, and bestowed on you good things, that ye might give thanks. (27) O true believers, deceive not GOD and *his* apostle; neither violate your faith against your own knowledge. (28) And know that your wealth and your children *are* a temptation *unto you;* and that with GOD is a great reward.

‖ (29) O true believers, if ye fear GOD, he will grant you a distinction, and will expiate your sins from you, and will forgive you; for GOD is endued with great liberality. (30) And *call to mind* when the unbelievers

R $\frac{4}{18}$.

---

(26) This verse is addressed to the Muhájjarín, or those who fled with Muhammad from Makkah to Madína.

(27) *Deceive not God.* "Al Baidháwi mentions an instance of such treacherous dealing in Abu Lubába, who was sent by Muhammad to the tribe of the Quraidha, then besieged by that prophet, for having broken their league with him, and perfidiously gone over to the enemies at the war of the ditch, to persuade them to surrender at the discretion of Saad Ibn Muádh, prince of the tribe of Aus, their confederates, which proposal they had refused. But Abu Lubába's family and effects being in the hands of those of Quraidha, he acted directly contrary to his commission, and instead of persuading them to accept Saad as their judge, when they asked his advice about it, drew his hand across his throat, signifying that he would put them all to death. However, he had no sooner done this than he was sensible of his crime, and going into a mosque tied himself to a pillar, and remained there seven days without meat or drink, till Muhammad forgave him."—*Sale.*

(28) Abdul Qádir says the allusion here is to the *children* of the refugees, still in Makkah, and to the *wealth* acquired by warring against the unbelievers. The former tempted them to lukewarmness in the struggle with the Makkans, and the latter tempted them to concealment and falsehood in reporting the spoil taken by them.

(29) *A distinction, i.e.*, "A direction that you may distinguish between truth and falsehood, or success in battle to distinguish the believers from the infidels, or the like."—*Sale.*

Will expiate your sins. See note on chap. iii. 194.

(30) "When the Makkans heard of the league entered into by Muhammad with those of Madína, being apprehensive of the consequence, they held a council, whereat they say the devil assisted in

plotted against thee, that they might either detain thee *in bonds*, or put to death, or expel thee *the city;* and they plotted *against thee:* but GOD laid a plot *against them;* and GOD is the best layer of plots. (31) And when our signs are repeated unto them, they say, We have heard; if we pleased we could certainly pronounce *a composition* like unto this: this is nothing but fables of the ancients. (32) And when they said, O GOD, if this be the truth from thee, rain down stones upon us from heaven, or inflict on us some *other* grievous punishment. (33) But GOD was

---

the likeness of an old man of Najd. The point under consideration being what they should do with Muhammad, Abu'l Bakhtári was of opinion that he should be imprisoned, and the room walled up, except a little hole, through which he should have necessaries given him till he died. This the devil opposed, saying that he might probably be released by some of his own party. Hásham Ibn Amru was for banishing him, but his advice also the devil rejected, insisting that Muhammad might engage some other tribes in his interest, and make war on them. At length Abu Jahl gave his opinion for putting him to death, and proposed the manner, which was unanimously approved."—*Sale, Baidhāwi.*

God laid a plot. "Revealing their conspiracy to Muhammad, and miraculously assisting him to deceive them and make his escape, and afterwards drawing them to the battle of Badr."—*Sale.*

See note on Prelim. Disc., p. 85.

(31) *If we pleased, we could, &c.* This verse proves very clearly that Muhammad's contemporaries were not convinced of the miraculous character of the Qurán, as claimed by Muhammad. See chaps. ii. 23 and xvii. 90, and notes there. Arnold in his *Islám and Christianity*, pp. 324-328, shows very conclusively that the style of the Qurán was not admitted to be of superior excellence by many competent judges in the early days of Islám. The policy of Muhammad's claim, and therefore of the only miracle or *sign* he could ever point to as testimony to his claim to be a prophet, was exposed a thousand years ago by al Kindí, an Arab Christian scholar in the service of the Khalífah al Mámún, whose work has lately been discovered. He declares it "to be destitute of order, style, elegance, or accuracy of composition or diction," and claims that the poetical works of al Qáis and other contemporaries of Muhammad were superior in every aspect to the Qurán. Having read the Qurán of Musailama the false prophet, he declared it to be superior in style to the work of Muhammad. See also chap. vi. 94, and note there.

Fables of the ancients. See note on chaps. vi. 24 and vii. 203.

(32) *Rain down stones.* Baidháwi ascribes this speech to al Nudhár Ibn al Hárith. Abdul Qádir says it was Abu Láhab.

not *disposed* to punish them, while thou wast with them ; nor was GOD *disposed* to punish them when they asked pardon. (34) But they have nothing *to offer in excuse* why GOD should not punish them, since they hindered *the believers* from *visiting* the holy temple, although they are not the guardians thereof. The guardians thereof are those only who fear *God;* but the greater part of them know it not. (35) And their prayer at the house *of God* is no other than whistling and clapping of the hands. Taste therefore the punishment, for that ye have been unbelievers. (36) They who believe not expend their

---

(33) *While thou wast with them.* The commentators here annotate as follows : "Judgment receded before the footsteps of Muhammad while at Makkah, but now had judgment overtaken them (the Makkans). In like manner, while the sinner remains contrite and repents, he escapes the punishment of his sin, be it ever so great. The prophet said, 'Sinners have refuge in two things : in my person and in repentance.'"—*Tafsir-i-Raufi.*

Nor ... when they asked pardon. "Saying, *God forgive us !* Some of the commentators, however, suppose the persons who asked pardon were certain believers who stayed among the infidels ; and others think the meaning to be that God would not punish them provided they asked pardon."—*Sale.*

(34) *They hindered, &c.* As at Hudaibaya, see Prelim. Disc., p. 89. *The guardians ... are those ... who fear God.* This was said to justify the claim that the Quraish were not the guardians of the Kaabah. They had the hereditary right to the guardianship of the temple, that right having been conceded to the great progenitor of Muhammad himself, Kusai, nearly two centuries before. See Muir's *Life of Mahomet,* vol. i. p. ccii. Muhammad's claim must have been grounded on this' rejection on account of idolatry, and therefore could only apply to those of his fellow-tribesmen who still persisted in their adherence to the old idolatry. For we find this same tribe confirmed in the guardianship of the Kaabah after the conquest of Makkah. See note on chap. iv. 56. Even the Quraish might not guard the temple unless they had within them the fear of God.

(35) *Whistling and clapping.* "It is said that they used to go round the Kaabah naked (see notes on chap. vii. 28-34), both men and women, whistling at the same time through their fingers and clapping their hands. Or, as others say, they made this noise on purpose to disturb Muhammad when at his prayers, pretending to be at prayers also themselves."—*Sale, Baidháwi.*

Taste therefore, now, defeat at Badr and afterwards suffering in exile and imprisonment, and *at last* at the judgment-day taste the fire.—*Tafsir-i-Raufi.*

(36) "The persons particularly meant in this passage were twelve

wealth to obstruct the way of GOD: they shall expend it, but afterwards it shall become *matter of* sighing *and regret* unto them, and at length they shall be overcome; (37) and the unbelievers shall be gathered together into hell; (38) that GOD may distinguish the wicked from the good, and may throw the wicked one upon the other, and may gather them all in a heap, and cast them into hell. These are they who shall perish.

R 5/1.

∥ (39) Say unto the unbelievers, that if they desist *from opposing thee*, what is already past shall be forgiven them; but if they return *to attack thee*, the exemplary punishment of the former *opposers of the prophets* is already past, *and the like shall be inflicted on them*. (40) Therefore fight against them until there be no opposition *in favour of idolatry*, and the religion be wholly GOD'S. If

---

of the Quraish, who gave each of them ten camels every day to be killed for provisions for their army in the expedition of Badr; or, according to others, the owners of the effects brought by the caravan, who gave great part of them to the support of the succours from Makkah. It is also said that Abu Sufián, in the expedition of Ohod, hired two thousand Arabs, who cost him a considerable sum, besides the auxiliaries which he had obtained *gratis*."—*Sale, Baidháwi*.

They shall be overcome. The *Tafsír-i-Raufi* regards this as a prophecy of the conquest of Makkah. The verses following, however, clearly show this statement to be based upon the assurance that God will cause the righteous to triumph. The victory at Badr was looked upon as clearly indicating the Divine favour. It therefore portended the eventual triumph of the Muslims. Such prophecies are of daily occurrence.

(39) *If they return.* This probably refers to the declaration of the Quraish that they would return to avenge the defeat of Badr.

The exemplary punishment, &c. Abdul Qádir translates, "The custom of the former (peoples) has passed before them." There is in the saying a subtle allusion to the defeat of the Quraish at Badr, in accordance with the doom of infidels in former times.

(40) *Fight against them.* See notes on chap. ii. 190-193. Mr. Bosworth Smith (*Mohammed and Mohammedanism*, 2d ed. p. 201) thinks that Muhammad was constrained to draw the sword by force of circumstances and the hatred of his enemies. The "perfect model of the saintly virtues" found in the Makkan prophet is thus suddenly and "by accident" converted into a general, and so we have "the mixed and sullied character of the prophet-soldier Muhammad." It is certain that all the exhortations of the later chapters of the Qurán, like that of the text, are entirely inconsistent with the spirit

they desist, verily GOD seeth that which they do; (41) but if they turn back, know that GOD is your patron; *he is* the best patron, and the best helper.

|| (42) And know that whenever ye gain any *spoils*, a fifth part thereof belongeth unto GOD, and to the Apostle, and *his* kindred, and the orphans, and the poor, and the traveller; if ye believe in GOD, and that which we have sent down unto our servant on the day of distinction, on the day whereon the two armies met: and GOD is almighty. (43) When ye were *encamped* on the hithermost side of the valley, and they were *encamped* on the farther side, and the caravan *was* below you; and if ye had mutually

TENTH SIPARA.

---

of the teaching of the earlier chapters. They are not, however, inconsistent with the spirit of the Arabian Prophet. His savage cruelty and cold-hearted revenge, exhibited in the very beginning of his soldier career, are in too strong contrast with saintly virtues to permit us to believe in the reality of the saint. It was policy rather than saintliness which withheld the command to fight, and when the time came to fight, we find Muhammad leading the fray—not carried along with it by force. See on this point Prelim. Disc., p. 83.

Until there be no opposition, *i.e.*, "Until the infidels cease to oppose."—*Abdul Qádir.* The original reference was to the opposition of the Quraish, but the spirit of the passage makes it apply to all opposers of Islám.

(42) *A fifth part.* "According to this law, a fifth part of the spoils is appropriated to the particular uses here mentioned, and the other four-fifths are to be equally divided among those who were present at the action ; but in what manner or to whom the first fifth is to be distributed, the Muhammadan doctors differ, as we have elsewhere observed (Prelim. Disc., pp. 224–226). Though it be the general opinion that this verse was revealed at Badr, yet there are some who suppose it was revealed in the expedition against the Jewish tribe of Qainuqáa, which happened a little above a month after."—*Sale, Baidháwi.*

Sent down . . . on the day of distinction, *i.e.*, "of the battle of Badr, which is so called because it *distinguished* the true believers from the infidels."—*Sale.* The plain import of the passage is that the law of spoils was given to *Muhammad* at Badr, and therefore the "general opinion" as to the date of revelation is certainly correct.

(43) *The caravan was below you*, *i.e.*, "by the sea-side, making the best of their way to Makkah."—*Sale.*

Ye would certainly have declined, &c. Owing to the superior number of the Quraish. Rodwell translates the clause thus : "Ye would have failed the engagement ;" but this may mean that the Muslims

appointed *to come to a battle,* ye would certainly have declined the appointment; but *ye were brought to an engagement without any previous appointment,* that GOD might accomplish the thing which was *decreed to be* done; (44) that he who perisheth *hereafter* may perish after demonstrative evidence, and that he who liveth may live by *the same* evidence; GOD *both* heareth *and* knoweth. (45) When thy LORD caused *the enemy* to appear unto thee in thy sleep few *in number;* and if he had caused them to appear numerous unto thee, ye would have been disheartened, and would have disputed concerning the matter: but GOD preserved *you from this;* for he knoweth the innermost parts of the breasts *of men.* (46) And when he caused them to appear unto you when ye met *to be*

---

would have been *defeated,* whereas the meaning intended is that they would have been afraid to fight at all.

The thing ... decreed. Lit. *the thing to be done, i.e.,* "By granting a miraculous victory to the faithful, and overwhelming their enemies for the conviction of the latter and the confirmation of the former."—*Sale, Baidháwi.*

(45, 46) On the question of discrepancy between this passage and chap. iii. 13, Sale, on the authority of Baidháwi, Jaláluddín, and Yahya, says—

"This seeming contradictory to a passage in the third chapter, where it is said that the Muslims appeared to the infidels to be twice their own number, the commentators reconcile the matter by telling us that just before the battle began the Prophet's party seemed fewer than they really were, to draw the enemy to an engagement; but that so soon as the armies were fully engaged, they appeared superior, to terrify and dismay their adversaries. It is related that Abu Jahl at first thought them so inconsiderable a handful, that he said one camel would be as much as they could all eat."

The fact upon which this miracle is based is thus given by Muir: "Mahomet had barely arrayed his line of battle when the advanced column of the Coreish appeared over the rising sands in front. Their greatly superior numbers were concealed by the fall of the ground behind, and this imparted confidence to the Muslims."—*Life of Mahomet,* vol. iii. p. 100. Yet all this is represented here as the fulfilment of a prophetic vision, granted to the Prophet on the night preceding the battle, " with which Muhammad had acquainted his companions for their encouragement."—*Sale.* But unfortunately for this vision, we are credibly informed by the historians (Kátib-i-Wáqkídí, &c.) that on the day previous Muhammad, having captured the water-carriers of the Quraish at the well of Badr, had learned from them the approximate number of his enemies.

few in your eyes, and diminished your *numbers* in their eyes; that GOD might accomplish the thing which *was decreed to be* done; and unto GOD shall *all* things return.

‖ (47) O true believers, when ye meet a party *of the infidels,* stand firm, and remember GOD frequently, that ye may prosper: (48) and obey GOD and his Apostle, and be not refractory, lest ye be discouraged, and your success depart from you; but persevere with patience, for GOD *is* with those who persevere. (49) And be not as those who went out of their houses in an insolent manner, and to appear with ostentation unto men, and turned aside from the way of GOD; for GOD comprehendeth that which they do. (50) And *remember* when Satan prepared their works for them, and said, No man shall prevail against you to-

R $\frac{6}{2}$.

---

(47) Here begins a military harangue, characteristic of the prophet-soldier of Madína. Obedience to "God and his Apostle" is urged by every motive of piety and self-interest.

(48) *Lest . . . your success depart.* The quarrel over the distribution of the booty might well awaken fears for the future success of his warfare. Hence the wisdom of his determination to divide the spoils himself as the agent of God to whom they belonged (ver. 1). Whilst admiring the wisdom of the general, will any one believe in the sincerity of the prophet?

(49) *Those who went out, &c.* "These were the Makkans, who, marching to the assistance of the caravan, and being come as far as Juhfa, were there met by a messenger from Abu Sufián, to acquaint them that he thought himself out of danger, and therefore they might return home; upon which Abu Jahl, to give the greater opinion of the courage of himself and his comrades, and of their readiness to assist their friends, swore that they would not return till they had been at Badr, and had there drunk wine and entertained those who should be present and diverted themselves with singing-women. The event of which bravado was very fatal, several of the principal Quraish, and Abu Jahl in particular, losing their lives in the expedition."—*Sale, Baidháwi.*

"Jihád (crusading) is worship, but when done in pride and vainglory it is not acceptable to God."—*Abdul Qádir.*

(50) *Remember when Satan, &c.* "Some understand this passage figuratively of the private instigation of the devil, and of the defeating of his designs, and the hopes with which he had inspired the idolaters. But others take the whole literally, and tell us that when the Quraish on their march bethought themselves of the enmity between them and the tribe of Kanána, who were masters of the country about Badr, that consideration would have prevailed on them to return, had not the devil appeared in the likeness of Suráqah

day; and I will surely be near *to assist* you. But when the two armies appeared in sight of each other, he turned back on his heels, and said, Verily I am clear of you: I certainly see that which ye see not; I fear GOD, for GOD is severe in punishing.

R ⅞.

‖ (51) When the hypocrites, and those in whose hearts *there was* an infirmity, said, Their religion hath deceived these *men:* but whosoever confideth in GOD *cannot be deceived;* for GOD *is* mighty *and* wise. (52) And if thou didst behold when the angels caused the unbelievers to die: they strike their faces and their backs, and *say unto*

Ibn Málik, a principal person of that tribe, and promised them that they should not be molested, and that himself would go with them. But when they came to join battle, and the devil saw the angels descending to the assistance of the Muslims, he retired; and al Hárith Ibn Hásham, who had him then by the hand, asking him whither he was going, and if he intended to betray them at such a juncture, he answered in the words of this passage, 'I am clear of you all, for I see that which ye see not;' meaning the celestial succours. They say further, that when the Quraish, on their return, laid the blame of their overthrow on Suráqah, he swore that he did not so much as know of their march till he heard they were routed: and afterwards, when they embraced Muhammadanism, they were satisfied it was the devil."—*Sale, Baidháwi, Jaláluddín.*

Wáqkidí gives the circumstantial evidence of a witness regarding the devil's behaviour on this occasion, his jumping into the sea, what he said, &c. See Muir's *Life of Mahomet,* vol. iii. p. 125, note.

(51) *Their religion hath deceived these men.* This saying is ascribed by some to the Madína hypocrites, who, seeing the fewness of the Muslims, thought their purpose to attack so large an army a piece of folly, attributable only to the madness of fanaticism. But the fact that the Muslims went forth from Madína to plunder a comparatively defenceless caravan, and not to attack the army of the Quraish, is against this interpretation. Others therefore explain that there were among the Quraish certain persons who were partially persuaded of the truth of Islám, but declined to flee to Madína with other refugees. These went along with the Quraish, intending to go over to the Muslims provided they should be more in number than they, but seeing the Muslims to be few in number, they said *their religion hath deceived them.* See the *Tafsír-i-Raufí in loco.*

(52) *When the angels, &c.* "This passage is generally understood of the angels who slew the infidels at Badr, and who fought (as the commentators pretend) with iron maces, which shot forth flames of fire at every stroke (*Baidháwi, Jaláluddín*). Some, however, imagine that the words hint, at least, at the examination of the sepulchre, which the Muhammadans believe every man must undergo after

them, Taste ye the pain of burning: (53) this *shall ye suffer* for that which your hands have set before you, and because GOD is not unjust towards *his* servants. (54) *These have acted* according to the wont of the people of Pharaoh, and of those before them, who disbelieved in the signs of GOD: therefore GOD took them away in their iniquity; for GOD *is* mighty *and* severe in punishing. (55) This *hath come to pass* because GOD changeth not *his* grace, wherewith he hath favoured any people, until they change that which is in their souls; and for that GOD *both* heareth *and* seeth. (56) According to the wont of the people of Pharaoh, and of those before them, who charged the signs of their LORD with imposture, *have they acted:* wherefore we destroyed them in their sins, and we drowned the people of Pharaoh; for they were all unjust persons. (57) Verily the worst cattle in the sight of GOD are those who are *obstinate* infidels, and will not believe. (58) As to those who enter into a league with thee, and afterwards violate their league at every *convenient* opportunity, and fear not *God;* (59) if thou take them in war, disperse, by *making* them *an example, those who shall come* after them, that they may be warned; (60) or if thou apprehend treachery from any people, throw back *their league* unto

---

death, and will be very terrible to the unbelievers" (Prelim. Disc., p. 127).—*Sale.*
(53) *Which your hands, &c.* See note on chap. ii. 94.
(54–56) See notes on chap. vii. 128–137.
God changeth not his grace. This passage recognises the freedom of the will, and consequently man's responsibility for his sin. Comp. chap. iii. 145, note.
(57) See note on ver. 22. The allusion here is probably to the Jews, either the Bani Qainuqáa or the Bani Quraidha. See Muir's *Life of Mahomet,* vol. iii. p. 135.
(58) *Afterwards violate their league,* "as did the tribe of Quraidha." —*Sale.* So too the *Tafsír-i-Raufi.* See the story of the treachery of this tribe in Muir's *Life of Mahomet,* vol. iii. chap. xvii.
(59) *Making them an example, i.e.,* by slaying them. How well this command was performed let the 800 gory heads of the Bani Quraidha tell.—*Muir's Life of Mahomet,* vol. iii. p. 278.
(60) *If thou apprehend treachery.* The road to covenant-breaking is here made easy. A suspicion of the Prophet or of his successors that the Jews or Christians with whom covenant had been made were

them with like treatment; for GOD loveth not the treacherous.

R ⅜. (61) And think not that the unbelievers have escaped *God's vengeance,* for they shall not weaken *the power of God.* (62) Therefore prepare against them what force ye are able, and troops of horse, whereby ye may strike a terror into the enemy of GOD, and your enemy, and into other *infidels* besides them, whom ye know not, *but* GOD knoweth them. And whatsoever ye shall expend in the defence of the religion of GOD, it shall be repaid unto you, and ye shall not be treated unjustly. (63) And if they incline unto peace, do thou *also* incline thereto; and put thy confidence in GOD, for it is he who heareth *and* knoweth. (64) But if they seek to deceive thee, verily GOD *will be* thy support. It is he who hath strengthened

---

treacherous is made a sufficient ground for breaking that covenant. As an illustration of this principle, see Muhammad's conduct toward the Bani Nadhír, described in Muir's *Life of Mahomet,* vol. iii. p. 209.

Like treatment. Lit. *render them the like.* The drift of this passage is so plainly contrary to the principles of honourable dealing, as to make even the Muslim commentators feel the need of softening the tone of it as far as possible. Baidháwi seems to justify the course here prescribed as fair. Abdul Qádir says the meaning is, that in case of a suspicion of treachery, the correspondence should be conducted with that *caution* which marked their dealings before conditions of peace were made. He concludes his comment here by saying, "There is no immoral teaching here." Yet notwithstanding the pious sentiment which follows at the end of this verse, *God loveth not the treacherous,* we are left with the conviction that counter-treachery is here justified as a means of self-defence. Of course it is only justifiable when used by Muslims.

(61) *Think not.* Sale says, "Some copies read it in the third person, *Let not the unbelievers think,*" &c.

Who have escaped, i.e., from Badr.

(62) *Prepare . . . what force ye are able.* Prepare for the holy war against the infidels. Primarily the allusion was to the Quraish and the treacherous Jews, but now it has a general application. See *Abdul Qádir* and *Tafsír-i-Raufi.*

Troops of horse. Muhammad here encourages the formation of cavalry in his army. To all such he promises repayment. Later on he ordered that the spoil of a horseman should be three times that of a footman. From chap. lix. ver. 6 we learn that Muhammad claimed and appropriated all the spoil of the expedition against the Bani Nadhír, because he alone rode on horseback.

thee with his help, and with *that of* the faithful, and hath united their hearts. If thou hadst expended whatever *riches are* in the earth, thou couldst not have united their hearts, but GOD united them; for he *is* mighty *and* wise.

|| (65) O Prophet, GOD is thy support, and such of the R $\frac{9}{5}$. true believers who followeth thee. (66) O Prophet, stir up the faithful to war: if twenty of you persevere *with constancy*, they shall overcome two hundred, and if there be one hundred of you, they shall overcome a thousand of those who believe not; because they are a people which do not understand. (67) Now hath GOD eased you, for he knew that ye were weak. If there be an hundred of you who persevere *with constancy*, they shall overcome two hundred; and if there be a thousand of you, they shall overcome two thousand, by the permission of GOD; for GOD is with those who persevere. (68) It hath not been *granted* unto any prophet that he should possess captives,

---

(64) *Hath united their hearts.* The *Tafsír-i-Raufí* thinks the allusion here is to the union of the tribes of Aus and Khazraj, who had been deadly enemies for more than a century before. It might, however, refer to union between other tribes as well.

God united them, i.e., by the bonds of Islám. The union of the tribes of Arabia under the banner of Islám is regarded by Muslims as a miracle, and therefore a proof of their Prophet's mission.

(65) "This passage, as some say, was revealed in a plain called al Baida, between Makkah and Madína, during the expedition of Badr; and, as others, in the sixth year of the Prophet's mission, on the occasion of Omar's embracing Muhammadanism."—*Sale.*

(66, 67) These verses were revealed at different times, but belonging to the same subject, have been grouped together by the compilers. Compare with Lev. xxvi. 8 and Josh. xxiii. 10. The *Tafsír-i-Raufí* says both verses were intended to arouse a spirit of fortitude in battle. As a result of the first injunction, that one Muslim should stand against ten infidels, one of the faithful was slain; whereupon that command was abrogated, and the more moderate one given in its place, which is introduced by the words *Now hath God eased you* (from the rigour of the first command), *for he knew that ye were weak.*

By the permission of God. One would naturally conclude that the first command might have stood on this ground.

(68) *Any prophet.* This verse was given to justify the cruelty of Muhammad towards the captives taken at Badr, many of whom were put to death in cold blood. But for the merciful pleading of Abu Baqr, all would have met a similar fate. The apology for this cruelty here given is that all warrior-prophets had been obliged to

until he hath made a great slaughter *of the infidels* in the earth. Ye seek the accidental *goods* of this world, but GOD regardeth the life to come; and GOD *is* mighty *and* wise. (69) Unless a revelation had been previously deli-

---

make "a great slaughter of the infidels" before they could succeed. Those who would paint the character of Muhammad in soft colours are guilty of deliberate misrepresentation. See on this subject Muir's *Life of Mahomet*, vol. iii. pp. 113-118.

A great slaughter. "Because severity ought to be used where circumstances require it, though clemency be more preferable where it may be exercised with safety. While the Muhammadans therefore were weak, and their religion in its infancy, God's pleasure was that the opposers of it should be cut off, as is particularly directed in this chapter. For which reason they are here upbraided with their preferring the lucre of the ransom to their duty."—*Sale.*

Ye seek the . . . goods. It would seem that in the Prophet's opinion the Muslims were not so much actuated by feelings of mercy in pleading for the lives of their Makkan captives as by a desire for the ransom-money.

(69) *Unless a revelation, &c.* Lit. *a writing—kitáb.* Abdul Qádir translates thus: "*Had this not been written in God's decrees,*" viz., that many of the captives would be converted to Islám. Muir says, "It may simply mean, 'Had there not been a previous decree to the contrary, a grievous punishment had overtaken you.'"—*Life of Mahomet,* vol. iii. p. 118, note.

This was a message, leaving it with Muhammad to decide whether the prisoners taken at Badr should be slain, or whether they should be ransomed, on condition that there should be an equal number of the Muslims slain at Ohod. Tradition tells us that Muhammad decided to receive the ransoms on the ground that when the Muslims should be slain, they would inherit Paradise and the crown of martyrdom.—*Muir's Life of Mahomet,* vol. iii. pp. 117, 118.

Sale gives the following, taken from Muslim authorities, who felt constrained to place the responsibility of the vindictive spirit shown by their Prophet towards his enemies to the credit of others :—

"Among the seventy prisoners whom the Muslims took in this battle were al Abbás, one of Muhammad's uncles, and Okail, the son of Abu Tálib and brother of Ali. When they were brought before Muhammad, he asking the advice of his companions what should be done with them, Abu Baqr was for releasing them on their paying ransom, saying that they were near relations to the Prophet, and God might possibly forgive them on their repentance ; but Omar was for striking off their heads, as professed patrons of infidelity. Muhammad did not approve of the latter advice, but observed that Abu Baqr resembled Abraham, who interceded for offenders, and that Omar was like Noah, who prayed for the utter extirpation of the wicked antediluvians ; and thereupon it was agreed to accept a ransom from them and their fellow-captives. Soon after which, Omar, going into the Prophet's tent, found him and Abu Baqr

vered from GOD, verily a severe punishment had been inflicted on you for *the ransom* which ye took *from the captives at Badr.* (70) Eat therefore of what ye have acquired, *that which is* lawful *and* good; for GOD *is* gracious *and* merciful.

‖ (71) O Prophet, say unto the captives who are in your hands, If GOD shall know any good *to be* in your hearts, R 10/6.

---

weeping, and asking them the reason of their tears, Muhammad acquainted him that this verse had been revealed condemning their ill-timed lenity towards their prisoners, and that they had narrowly escaped the Divine vengeance for it, adding, that if God had not passed the matter over, they had certainly been destroyed to a man, excepting only Omar and Saad Ibn Muádh, a person of as great severity, and who was also for putting the prisoners to death." See also note on chap. iii. 140.

It seems that the fierce vindictive spirit apparent in the Qurán at this period was due in some measure at least to the defeat at Ohod. Yet, excepting a few personal enemies of the Prophet, who were summarily executed, all the prisoners were ransomed with the hearty consent of Muhammad himself, who not only needed the ransom price as a compensation to his followers, who were sorely grieved and disappointed at the loss of the caravan they had hoped to capture, but he also hoped for the conversion of some of the captive Quraish. See below on ver. 71. But the battle at Ohod, resulting in the defeat of Muhammad and the slaughter of many of the faithful, not only aroused among the Muslims a bitter desire for vengeance, but required an explanation. Why this defeat? Why were the favourites of Heaven smitten before the infidels? These questions are answered in the latter part of chapter iii. Now, as the number of infidels killed at Badr was raised by the Qurán itself from forty-nine to *seventy* (chap. iii. 140), in order to correspond with the *seventy* Muslims killed at Ohod, it is almost certain that the spirit of the Prophet after Ohod has been, so to speak, forced back upon Badr.

A severe punishment. "That is, had not the ransom been, in strictness, lawful for you to accept, by God's having in general terms allowed you the spoil and the captives, ye had been severely punished. . . . Yet did not this crime go absolutely unpunished neither; for in the battle of Ohod the Muslims lost seventy men, equal to the number of prisoners taken at Badr; which was so ordered by God, as a retaliation or atonement for the same."—*Sale.*

(70) *Eat therefore, i.e.,* "Of the ransom which ye have received of your prisoners. For it seems, on this rebuke, they had some scruple of conscience whether they might convert it to their own use or not." —*Sale, Baidháwi.*

(71) *Say unto the captives.* This was said in the hope that the captive Quraish might yet be induced to profess Islám, and this hope was in some measure realised.

he will give you better than what hath been taken from you; and he will forgive you, for GOD *is* gracious *and merciful*. (72) But if they seek to deceive thee, verily they have deceived GOD; wherefore he hath given *thee* power over them: and GOD *is* knowing *and* wise. (73) Moreover, they who have believed, and have fled their country, and employed their substance and their persons in fighting for the religion of GOD, and they who have given *the Prophet* a refuge *among them*, and have assisted *him*, these *shall be deemed* the one nearest of kin to the

---

He will give you better, &c. "That is, if ye repent and believe, God will make you abundant retribution for the ransom ye have now paid. It is said that this passage was revealed on the particular account of al Abbás, who being obliged by Muhammad, though his uncle, to ransom both himself and his two nephews, Okail and Naufal Ibn al Hárith, complained that he should be reduced to beg alms of the Quraish as long as he lived. Whereupon Muhammad asked him what was become of the gold which he delivered to Omm al Fadhl when he left Makkah, telling her that he knew not what might befall him in the expedition, and therefore, if he lost his life, she might keep it herself for the use of her and her children. Al Abbás demanded who told him this; to which Muhammad replied that God had revealed it to him. And upon this al Abbás immediately professed Islám, declaring that none could know of that affair except God, because he gave her the money at midnight. Some years after, al Abbás reflecting on this passage, confessed it to be fulfilled; for he was then not only possessed of a large substance, but had the custody of the well Zamzam, which, he said, he preferred to all the riches of Makkah."—*Sale, Baidháwi.*

(72) *If they seek to deceive thee.* Of this passage Muir says:—"This is explained to mean 'deceit in not paying the ransom agreed upon;' but it seems an unlikely interpretation, as the ransom was ordinarily paid down on the spot. It may be a significant intimation that those who came over to Islám would be released without ransom;—the deceit contemplated being a treacherous confession of faith followed by desertion to Makkah."—*Life of Mahomet,* vol. iii. p. 119, note.

The same thing is probably intended by the statement of the previous verse, "He will forgive you," &c.

He hath given thee power over them. The prophet-general of Madína speaks in different terms from those of the "warner" of Makkah. Comp. chap. lxxxviii. 21, 22.

(73) *Who . . . have fled, &c.* The Muhájjirín, or refugees, a term at first applicable only to those who fled from Makkah, but afterwards to all who fled to the Prophet's standard.

They who have assisted, i.e., the Ansárs, or Helpers. This term at

other. But they who have believed, but have not fled their country, shall have no *right of* kindred at all with you, until they *also* fly. Yet if they ask assistance of you on account of religion, *it belongeth* unto you *to give them* assistance; except against a people between whom and yourselves *there shall be* a league *subsisting:* and GOD seeth that which ye do. (74) And as to the infidels, let them be *deemed* of kin the one to the other. Unless ye do this, there will be a sedition in the earth, and grievous corruption. (75) But as for them who have believed, and left their country, and have fought for GOD'S true religion, and who have allowed *the Prophet* a retreat *among* them, and have assisted *him*, these are really believers; they shall receive mercy and an honourable provision. (76) And they who have believed since, and have fled their

---

first applied only to those of Madína who identified themselves with Islám, but other people from the neighbouring tribes having put themselves under the leadership of Muhammad, and having helped him repeatedly, the term was applied to all who allied themselves to Muhammad.

Nearest of kin. "And shall consequently inherit one another's substance, preferably to their relations by blood. And this, they say, was practised for some time, the Muhájjirín and Ansárs being judged heirs to one another, exclusive of the deceased's other kindred, till this passage was abrogated by the following :—*Those who are related by blood shall be deemed the nearest of kin to each other."—Sale.*

Abdul Qádir thinks the relationships of Muslims referred to here to pertain to *faith* only and to the future life, and thus reconciles this verse with ver. 76. But there is nothing in the language to warrant such an interpretation. As a matter of policy this law was inaugurated in order to bind the Muslims together in the earlier days of the Hijra, but it could not long bear the pressure of its own weight, and hence was abrogated by the law of ver. 76.

(74) This verse illustrates the political sagacity of Muhammad. He divides all Arabs into two classes, and *unites* all his following, from whatever quarter they might come, against the fragmentary elements of the opposition.

(75) This verse corresponds with ver. 73, except in so far as the change of law required a change in the language. I think it very probable that this verse gives the *revised reading* of ver. 73, and was intended to take its place in the Qurán.

(76) See notes on ver. 73, also notes on chap. iv. 6-13.

country, and have fought with you, these *also* are of you. And those who are related by consanguinity *shall be deemed* the nearest of kin to each other *preferably to strangers* according to the book of GOD: GOD knoweth all things.

CHAPTER IX.

ENTITLED SURAT AL TAUBA (REPENTANCE, IMMUNITY).

Revealed at Madína.

INTRODUCTION.

OF the many titles given to this chapter, those of *Immunity* and *Repentance* are most commonly known. The former title is based on the first verse, the latter on the third verse, or, perhaps better still, upon the spirit of the whole chapter, which is a call to repentance to a multitude of disaffected and lukewarm Muslims and Arabs who declined to accompany Muhammad in his expedition to Tabúq. Sale says :—"It is observable that this chapter alone has not the auspiciatory form, *In the name of the most merciful God*, prefixed to it; the reason of which omission, as some think, was, because these words imply a concession of security, which is utterly taken away by this chapter after a fixed time; wherefore some have called it the chapter of *Punishment;* others say that Muhammad (who died soon after he had received this chapter), having given no direction where it should be placed, nor for the prefixing the Bismillah to it, as had been done to the other chapters, and the argument of this chapter bearing a near resemblance to that of the preceding, his companions differed about it, some saying that both chapters were but one, and together made the seventh of the seven long ones, and others that they were two distinct chapters; whereupon, to accommodate the dispute, they left a space between them, but did not interpose the distinction of the Bismillah.

"It is agreed that this chapter was the last which was revealed, and the only one, as Muhammad declared, which was revealed entire and at once, except the one hundred and tenth.

"Some will have the two last verses to have been revealed at Makkah."

The statement that this chapter was the last revealed is based upon the testimony of tradition, but the internal evidence fixes the date of most of the revelations within the ninth year of the Hijra. With this also Muslim tradition agrees. It would therefore appear that during one whole year no revelation was vouchsafed to Muhammad, which is contrary to other traditions, which assign portions of chapters ii., v., &c., to the time of the farewell pilgrimage in the end of A.H. 10.

The statement that this whole chapter was revealed at one time is also unfounded, as will be seen by reference to the date of the revelations given below.

Probable Date of the Revelations.

Following Noeldeke for the most part, vers. 1-12 belong to the latter part of A.H. 9, when Muhammad sent Ali to Makkah to notify to the tribes assembled there that henceforth the Holy Temple would be closed against idolaters. Vers. 13-16, however, belong to an earlier period, viz., A.H. 8, when Muhammad planned his expedition for the capture of Makkah. To these may be added vers. 17-24, which, however, mark the time when Muhammed first thought of conquering his native city. Some would place vers. 23 and 24 among the revelations enunciated previous to the expedition to Tabúq in A.H. 9.

Vers. 25-27 mention the victory at Hunain (Shawál, A.H. 8), and belong to the period immediately following the siege of Tayif, *i.e.,* Dzu'l Qáada, A.H. 8.

Ver. 28 seems to be connected with vers. 1-12, and therefore belongs to the latter part of A.H. 9.

Vers. 29-128 refer to the events connected with the expedition to Tabúq, which occurred in Rajab of A.H. 9. They were not, however, all enunciated at one time, but partly before the expedition, partly on the march, and partly after the return.

Vers. 29-35 may be referred to the time of arrival at Tabúq, when the Christian prince, John of Aylah, tendered his submission to Muhammad, paying tribute (Jazya).

Vers. 36 and 37, referring to the abolition of the intercalary year and the fixing the time of the pilgrimage in accordance with the changes of the lunar year, must be assigned to the Dzu'l Hajja of A.H. 10.

The remaining verses Noeldeke distributes as follows:—*Previous to the expedition,* vers. 38-41 (of which, according to Ibn Hishám, 924, ver. 41 is the oldest of the whole Sura), and 49-73. *On the march,* vers. 42-48 and 82-97 (of which ver. 85, if it refers to the death of Abdullah Ibn Ubbai, must have been added later on). *After the return*, vers. 74-81 and 98-113, of which vers. 108-111 were enunciated just before the entry into Madína.

Vers. 114-117, if they refer to the visit of Muhammad to the tomb of his mother, Amína Bint Wahb, as many authorities state, must be referred to the latter part of A.H. 6. But if they refer to the death of Abdullah Ibn Ubbai, they belong to a period about two months later than the return from Tabúq. This latter seems to be founded on the best authority.

Vers. 118 and 119 were enunciated about fifty days after the return from Tabúq (see note on ver. 119). The remaining verses, excepting 129 and 130, which are probably of Makkan origin, belong to the time immediately after the return from Tabúq.

Principal Subjects.

	VERSES
Four months' immunity proclaimed to idolaters . . .	1, 2
After four months, all idolaters to be slain, with exception of those with whom treaties have been made . . .	3-5
Ignorant idolaters to be taught the religion of Islám, after which, if they repent, they are to be spared alive .	5, 6
No new league to be made with idolaters	7
Idolaters are not to be trusted	8-10
Penitent idolaters to be regarded as brethren . . .	11
Muslims exhorted to fight against the truce-breakers of Makkah	13-16
All but Muslims to be excluded from the sacred temples .	17, 18
Abbás rebuked for his vainglory	19
The Muhájjirín assigned the first rank among Muslims—their reward	20-22
True believers to refuse friendship with nearest kin if they be infidels	23, 24
The victory of Hunain due to God's help	25-27
Idolaters excluded from the Kaabah	28
The Jews and Christians as well as idolaters to be attacked . .	29
Jews and Christians reproved for applying the epithet "Son of God" to Ezra and Jesus	30
They also worship their priests and monks	31, 32
Islám superior to all other religions	33
Stingy Muslims likened to covetous monks—their punishment	34, 35
Infidels may be attacked in sacred months	36
The sacred months not to be transferred	37
Muslims exhorted to go on expedition to Tabúq by reference to God's help to Muhammad and Abu Baqr in the cave	38-41

	VERSES
The lukewarm Muslims rebuked for wishing to stay at home	42
Muhammad rebuked for excusing some of these from going	43
Willingness to fight for Muhammad, a test of faith	44–46
Seditious Muslims rebuked	47–50
The sure reward of the faithful	51, 52
God refuses the offerings of infidels and hypocrites	53–55
The wealth and prosperity of infidels a sign of their reprobation	55
Half-hearted Muslims reproved	56, 57
Those who had spread libellous reports regarding Muhammad's use of alms rebuked	58, 59
How alms should be expended	60
Grumblers and hypocrites threatened	61–69
They are warned by the example of the wicked in former ages	70
The faithful described—their rewards	71–73
Hypocrites denounced and threatened	74, 75
Prosperity of infidels a prelude to their destruction	76–79
God shall scoff at the scoffers	80
The traducers of the faithful shall never be forgiven	81
Punishment of the "stayers at home"	82–84
Muhammad forbidden to pray at the grave of unbelievers and hypocrites	85
The Prophet not to wonder at the prosperity of the wicked	86–88
Reward of those who assist the Apostle in his wars	89, 90
Hypocritical Arabs of the desert reproved	91
Who may lawfully remain at home in time of war	92, 93
Other hypocrites reproved	94–97
The Baduín, the worst of hypocrites	98, 99
Some of them true believers	100
The reward of the Ansars and Muhájjirín	101
The desert Arabs and some of the people of Madína reproved	102
The penitent confessors in Madína are pardoned	103–106
Others await God's decision in their case	107
Denunciation against those who built a Masjid in opposition to Muhammad and his faithful ones	108–111
True believers are sold to God	112, 113
Muslims not to pray for idolatrous relatives	114
Why Abraham prayed for his idolatrous parents	115
God merciful to the faithful	116–118
The three recreant Ansars pardoned	119

	VERSES
The people of Madina rebuked for want of loyalty to Muhammad	120–122
Some believers excused from going to war	123
True believers to war against neighbouring infidels and hypocrisy	124
Reproof of those who doubt the revelations of God and Muhammad	125–128
The Apostle trusts in the help of God	129, 130

|| (1) A DECLARATION of immunity from GOD and his Apostle unto the idolaters with whom ye have entered into league. (2) Go to and fro in the earth *securely* four months; and know that ye shall not weaken GOD, and

(1) *God and his Apostle.* See note on chap. viii. 20. This formula occurs sixteen times in this chapter.

With whom ye have entered into league. "Some understand this sentence of the *immunity* or *security* therein granted to the infidels for the space of four months; but others think that the words properly signify that Muhammad is here declared by God to be absolutely *free* and *discharged* from all truce or league with them after the expiration of that time; and this last seems to be the truest interpretation.

"Muhammad's thus renouncing all league with those who would not receive him as the Apostle of God or submit to become tributary was the consequence of the great power to which he was now arrived. But the pretext he made use of was the treachery he had met with among the Jewish and idolatrous Arabs—scarce any keeping faith with him except Bani Dhamra, Bani Kinána, and a few others."—*Sale, Jaláluddín, Baidháwi, Yahya.*

This proclamation seals the triumph of Islám over all Arabia. Henceforth there is to be no more compromise with idolaters. They are to be converted to Islám or be destroyed by the sword. Previous treaties of peace are to be respected, though this is due to the clemency of "God and his Apostle," who here declare the Muslims to be free from obligation to observe such treaties. How completely the tables have been turned! The Makkan refugee now dictates laws for all Arabia!

(2) *Four months.* These were, according to some authorities, Shawál, Dhu'l Qáada, Dhu'l Hajja, and Muharram, this revelation having been made in Shawál. Others, computing from Dhu'l Hajja,

that GOD will disgrace the unbelievers. (3) And a declaration from GOD and his Apostle unto the people, on the day of the greater pilgrimage, that GOD is clear of the idolaters, and his Apostle *also*. Wherefore if ye repent, this will be better for you; but if ye turn back, know that ye shall not weaken GOD: and denounce unto those who believe not a painful punishment. (4) Except such of the idolaters with whom ye shall have entered into a

---

when the *proclamation* of this revelation was made, reckon the months to be Dhu'l Hajja, Muharram, Safar and Rabi-ul-auwal. The latter seems to be the sounder opinion.

(3) *The greater pilgrimage.*, viz., "The tenth of Dhu'l Hajja, when they slay the victims at Mína, which day is their great feast, and completes the ceremonies of the pilgrimage. Some suppose the adjective *greater* is added here to distinguish the pilgrimage made at the appointed time from *lesser pilgrimages*, as they may be called, or *visitations* of the Kaabah, which may be performed at any time of the year; or else because the concourse at the pilgrimage this year was greater than ordinary, both Muslims and idolaters being present at it.

"The promulgation of this chapter was committed by Muhammad to Ali, who rode for that purpose on the Prophet's slit-eared camel from Madína to Makkah; and on the day above mentioned, standing up before the whole assembly at al Aqabah, told them that he was the messenger of the Apostle of God unto them. Whereupon they asking him what was his errand, he read twenty or thirty verses of the chapter to them, and then said, 'I am commanded to acquaint you with four things: 1. That no idolater is to come near the temple of Makkah after this year; 2. That no man presume to compass the Kaabah naked for the future (see chap. vii. 27-34). 3. That none but true believers shall enter Paradise; and 4. That public faith is to be kept.'"—*Sale, Baidháwi.*

"There seems a kind of contradiction between the first verse, in which all treaties are cast aside, and the subsequent verse and intimation by Ali that treaties would be respected. Perhaps it was meant that, notwithstanding any treaty, idolaters would be prevented from coming to the pilgrimage, though the treaty would be in other respects observed. Or it may mean that, although Mahomet had permission given him in the first verse to cast aside treaties with idolaters, yet he nevertheless voluntarily engaged to respect those treaties which had been faithfully kept. The latter interpretation is not so suitable as the other to the style of the Coran."—*Muir's Life of Mahomet,* vol. iv. p. 210, note.

(4) *Except such.* The exception is in respect to the *painful punishment* denounced against the unbelievers in the previous verse. So long as the idolaters with whom treaties of peace had already been made

league, and who afterwards shall not fail you in any instance, nor assist any *other* against you. Wherefore perform the covenant *which ye shall have made* with them, until their time *shall be elapsed;* for GOD loveth those who fear *him.* (5) And when the months *wherein ye are* not allowed *to attack them* shall be past, kill the idolaters wheresoever ye shall find them, and take them *prisoners,* and besiege them, and lay wait for them in every convenient place. But if they shall repent, and observe the appointed times of prayer and pay the legal alms, dismiss them freely; for GOD *is* gracious *and* merciful. (6) And if any of the idolaters shall demand protection of thee, grant him protection, that he may hear the word of GOD, and afterwards let him reach the place of his security. This *shalt thou do,* because they are people which know not *the excellency of the religion thou preachest.*

---

should remain faithful to their treaty engagements, they should be exempt from the *punishment* described in the following verse. The spirit of the passage seems clearly to be opposed to that of the first verse. It is probable that several revelations relating to idolaters, and delivered at different times, have been woven together by the compilers of the Qurán. If this view be correct, the first verse was promulgated at a later period than what follows, and we have here an illustration of how the spirit of inspiration subserved the political interests of the Prophet.

(5) *Kill the idolaters.* Compare this passage with chap. iv. 88, 89. *Wherever ye shall find them.* "Either within or without the sacred territory."—*Sale.* This passage, with what follows, is said to abrogate chap. ii. 216.

If they shall repent, &c., i.e., if they shall embrace Islám, not only formally but heartily. They must perform the duties of Islám. "Hence," says Abdul Qádir, "Abu Baqr slew those who declined to give legal alms, as he did the idolaters."

(6) *That he may hear the word of God.* The plain meaning of this passage, according to the *Tafsír-i-Raufi,* is that the ignorant were to be made acquainted with the claims of Islám, *and if then they accepted it,* they were to be allowed to proceed to their homes in peace ; if not, they were to be slain. Sale's paraphrase here seems to me to mistake the purport of the general order to slay all impenitent idolaters, excepting those with whom treaties had been made, and who had observed their treaty obligations. He says, "You shall give him a safe-conduct, that he may return home again securely, in case he shall not think fit to embrace Muhammadanism."

R 2/8. ‖ (7) How shall the idolaters be admitted into a league with GOD and with his Apostle, except those with whom ye entered into a league at the holy temple? So long as they behave with fidelity towards you, do ye *also* behave with fidelity towards them; for GOD loveth those who fear *him*. (8) How *can they be admitted into a league with you*, since, if they prevail against you, they will not regard in you *either* consanguinity or faith? They will please you with their mouths, but their hearts will be averse *from you;* for the greater part of them are wicked doers. (9) They sell the signs of GOD for a small price, and obstruct his way; it is certainly evil which they do. (10) They regard not in a believer *either* consanguinity or faith; and these are the transgressors. (11) Yet if they repent and observe the appointed times of prayer, and give alms, *they shall be deemed* your brethren in religion. We distinctly propound *our* signs unto people who understand.

(7) *Those with whom ye entered into a league*, *i.e.*, the Bani Dhamra and Bani Kináua, mentioned in note to ver. 1.

(8) *How?* This ambiguous interrogative is variously understood. In addition to what is inserted in the text we find the following: "How can they?"—*Rodwell*. "How shall we not smite the infidels?"—*Abdul Qádir.* "How can there be peace?"—*Fatah-ar-Rahmán.* The Persian translation agrees with Sale.

If they prevail. The allusion seems to be clearly to Arab unbelievers. If so, this portion of the chapter must be referred to an earlier date than that claimed for it by some of the commentators. The spirit of the following verse, especially the charge against the unbelievers, that they "sell the signs of God for a small price," points to the Quraish of Makkah in particular, with whom are perhaps associated the disaffected inhabitants of Madína, as especially intended here. With this view agrees the tradition concerning the hypocrisy of Jallás, given in Muir's *Life of Mahomet*, vol. iii. p. 30, note.

(9) Compare chap. ii. 175, 176, and see notes there.

(11) *If they repent and observe, &c.* This passage clearly asserts the necessity of piety in religion as an evidence of true repentance. The *piety* required, however, is simply the *outward* observance of the rites of Islám. The contrast between Islám and Christianity on this point is very marked, and needs only to be emphasised to reveal the difference between the counterfeit and the true. The ring of a genuine coin is unmistakable.

(12) But if they violate their oaths after their league, and revile your religion, oppose the leaders of infidelity (for there is no trust in them), that they may desist *from their treachery.* (13) Will ye not fight against people who have violated their oaths, and conspired to expel the Apostle *of God;* and who of their own accord assaulted you for the first time? Will ye fear them? But it is more just that ye should fear GOD, if ye are true believers. (14) Attack them, *therefore;* GOD shall punish them by your hands, and will cover them with shame, and will give you the victory over them; and he will heal the breasts of the people who believe, (15) and will take away

(12) *Oppose the leaders.* Rodwell translates, "Do battle with the ringleaders." This accords with the Persian and Urdú translations. Muslims are now to take active measures for the suppression of infidelity.

(13) *Will ye not fight, &c.* Sale, on the authority of Baidháwi, paraphrases thus: "As did the Quraish in assisting the tribe of Baqr against those of Khudháah (see Prelim. Disc., p. 93), and laying a design to ruin Muhammad without any just provocation; and, as several of the Jewish tribes did, by aiding the enemy and endeavouring to oblige the Prophet to leave Madína as he had been obliged to leave Makkah."

It seems more natural to regard the *people* here referred to as the inhabitants of Makkah in particular. This is the view of the *Tafsír-i-Raufí.* The passage, then, belongs to a period preceding the capture of Makkah, and was intended to stir up the faithful to make war upon the Quraish, who had violated the treaty made at Hudaibiya. This view accounts for the allusion to the perfidy of those who regard neither religion nor consanguinity in ver. 8.

(14) *By your hands.* This passage seems to teach that Muslim crusade against idolatry was commanded by God as a sovereign act of judgment, just as Moses was commanded to destroy the Canaanites. The Muslim, therefore, uses the same arguments in defence of the former that we do in respect of the conduct of Joshua and the Israelites. See note on chap. ii. 191.

Will heal the breasts, &c. Sale, on the authority of Baidháwi, says the allusion is to "those of Khudháah; or, as others say, certain families of Yaman and Saba, who went to Makkah, and there professed Muhammadanism, but were very injuriously treated by the inhabitants; whereupon they complained to Muhammad, who bid them take comfort, for that joy was approaching."

It seems to me more natural to refer the *healing* to those Muslim who were reluctant to fight against their own kindred at Makkah. This is the class specially exhorted (in vers. 23, 24) to drown all filial and fraternal affection in zeal for God and his Apostle. Love

the indignation of their hearts: for GOD will be turned unto whom he pleaseth; and GOD *is* knowing *and* wise. (16) Did ye imagine that ye should be abandoned, whereas GOD did not yet know those among you who fought *for his religion,* and took not *any* besides GOD, and his Apostle, and the faithful *for their* friends? GOD is well acquainted with that which ye do.

R ⅜. ‖ (17) It is not *fitting* that the idolaters should visit the temples of GOD, being witnesses against their own souls of *their* infidelity. The works of these *men* are vain, and they shall remain in *hell*-fire for ever. (18) But he only shall visit the temples of GOD who believeth in

---

for Islám is to be supreme; natural affection may wound the heart, but God "will heal the breasts of the people who believe."

(15) *Indignation of their hearts.* The meaning of this verse depends on ver. 14. According to the view of the commentators, it would be that God, by avenging the faithful upon their persecutors, would satisfy their desire for revenge. My own interpretation of that verse requires this to mean that by *healing the breasts* of the faithful, their indignation at the idea of warring against friends and relations during even the sacred months would be removed amidst the glories of the victory of Islám. This I think to be the better interpretation.

For God will be turned unto whom he pleaseth. The *Tafsír-i-Raufi* regards this as a prophecy foretelling the conversion of Abu Sufián, Akrama Bin Abu Jahl, &c. The passage, however, points to those who, having been reluctant to fight against their relatives, had become reconciled to the views of the Prophet, which fact is here regarded as a sign of the Divine favour.

(16) *God did not yet know.* Rodwell translates, "As if God did not yet know." The *Tafsír-i-Raufi* paraphrases, "Since God has not yet made known." The passage seems to mean that the sincerity of those who claimed to be Muslims could only be known by a trial of their faith, and that the present defection of some was no reason for supposing that all had been abandoned of God.

God is well acquainted, &c., i.e., he knows who are his true followers and who are hypocrites.

(17) *The temples of God.* Literally, *the masjids of God.* Idolaters are here refused admittance to the mosque as well as to the sacred Kaabah at Makkah, a requirement carefully observed in all Muslim communities.

(18) *He only shall visit, &c.* "These words are to warn the believers from having too great a confidence in their own merits, and

GOD and the last day, and is constant at prayer, and payeth the legal alms, and feareth GOD alone. These perhaps may become of *the number of* those who are rightly directed. (19) Do ye reckon the giving drink to the pilgrims and the visiting of the holy temple *to be actions as meritorious* as *those performed by* him who believeth in GOD and the last day, and fighteth for the religion of GOD? They shall not be held equal with GOD; for GOD directeth not the unrighteous people. (20) They who have believed, and fled their country, and employed their substance and their persons in the defence of GOD'S true religion, shall be in the highest degree *of honour* with GOD; and these are they who shall be happy. (21) Their LORD sendeth them good tidings of mercy from him, and goodwill, and of gardens wherein they shall enjoy lasting pleasure: (22) they shall continue therein for ever; for with GOD is a great reward. (23) O true believers, take not your fathers or your brethren for friends, if they love infidelity

---

likewise to deter the unbelievers; for if the faithful will but *perhaps* be saved, what can the others hope for?"—*Sale, Baidháwi.*

On the ground of this verse Jews and Christians should also be excluded from the mosque, for whilst these perform the duties here required, and though faith in Muhammad as the Apostle of God is not expressly asserted here as one of the requirements, yet the plain intent of the whole is to exclude all except Muslims.

(19) "This passage was revealed on occasion of some words of Abbás, Muhammad's uncle, who, when he was taken prisoner, being bitterly reproached by the Muslims, and particularly by his nephew Ali, answered, "You rip up our ill actions, but take no notice of our good ones; we visit the temple of Makkah, and adorn the Kaabah with hangings, and give drink to the pilgrims, and free captives."—*Sale, Baidháwi.*

(20) This passage looks like a Madína revelation. The praise bestowed upon the Muhájjarín may, however, be retrospective. The revelation was certainly intended to stir up Muslim fanaticism. The spirit of the fanatic (*Gházi*) is the spirit of the true Muslim.

(21) *Gardens, &c.* See note on chap. iii. 15.

(23) *Take not your fathers . . . for friends.* The *Tafsír-i-Raufi* says this passage refers to those who neglected to perform the pilgrimage on account of domestic opposition and hindrance. The spirit of the passage in this place seems rather to point to those who were reluctant to fight against their relations in Makkah. May not that clemency of Muhammad towards its people, when it fell into his

above faith; and whosoever among you shall take them for *his* friends, they will be unjust doers. (24) Say, If your fathers, and your sons, and your brethren, and your wives, and your relations, and *your* substance which ye have acquired, and *your* merchandise which ye apprehend may not be sold off, and *your* dwellings wherein ye delight, be more dear unto you than GOD, and his Apostle, and the advancement of his religion; wait until GOD shall send his command, for GOD directeth not the ungodly people.

R $\frac{4}{10}$. (25) Now hath GOD assisted you in many engagements, and *particularly* at the battle of Hunain, when ye pleased yourselves in your multitude, but it was no manner of advantage unto you, and the earth became too strait

---

hands, be in some measure accounted for on the ground of this known antipathy of his people to slaughter their relatives, and to destroy property in which they had so deep an interest?

(24) *Wait until God shall send his command.* Sale, on the authority of Baidhāwi, says, "Or shall punish you. Some suppose the taking of Makkah to be here intended." This confirms the view that the relations here intended were the relatives of the refugees in Makkah, and points to a time previous to the capture of Makkah as the period in which this passage was revealed.

(25) *God assisted . . . at . . . Hunain.* "This battle was fought in the eighth year of the Hijra, in the valley of Hunain, which lies about three miles from Makkah towards Tayif, between Muhammad, who had an army of twelve thousand men, and the tribes of Hawāzin and Thakīf, whose forces did not exceed four thousand. The Muhammadans, seeing themselves so greatly superior to their enemies, made sure of the victory; a certain person, whom some suppose to have been the Prophet himself, crying out, 'These can never be overcome by so few.' But God was so highly displeased with this confidence, that in the first encounter the Muslims were put to flight, some of them running away quite to Makkah, so that none stood their ground except Muhammad himself and some few of his family; and they say the Prophet's courage was so great, that his uncle al Abbās, and his cousin Abu Sufiān Ibn al Hārith, had much ado to prevent his spurring his mule into the midst of the enemy, by laying hold of the bridle and stirrup. Then he ordered al Abbās, who had the voice of a Stentor, to recall his flying troops; upon which they rallied, and the Prophet throwing a handful of dust against the enemy, they attacked them a second time, and by the Divine assistance gained the victory."—*Sale, Baidhāwi, Jalāluddīn.*

The earth became too straight for you. "Alluding to the narrow and precipitous character of the pass, where their great numbers, of

for you, notwithstanding it was spacious; then did ye retreat and turn your backs. (26) Afterwards GOD sent down his security upon his Apostle and upon the faithful, and sent down troops *of angels*, which ye saw not; and he punished those who disbelieved; and this was the reward of the unbelievers. (27) Nevertheless GOD will hereafter be turned unto whom he pleaseth; for GOD *is* gracious *and* merciful. (28) O true believers, verily the idolaters are unclean; let them not therefore come near unto the holy

---

which they had been vaingloriously proud, only added to the difficulty."—*Muir's Life of Mahomet*, vol. iv. p. 143, note.

(26) *God sent down his security.* "The original word is *Sakínat*, which the commentators interpret in this sense; but it seems rather to signify the *Divine presence*, or Shekinah, appearing to aid the Muslims."—*Sale.* See also note on chap. ii. 248.

Send down troops. Commentators differ as to the number. Some say there were 5000, others 8000 and 16000. Tradition describes the uniform they wore, and declares that they filled the valley like a cloud, and were in multitude like an army of ants. See Sale, and Muir's *Life of Mahomet*, vol. iv. p. 144, note.

Which ye saw not. "As usual, Muhammad's wonderful things are only seen or known to himself. Elisha showed his servants the angels ready to fight, but Muhammad never has a witness. His great witness for the night journey did not see it, but only swore he believed it."—*Brinckman in " Notes on Islám."*

The commentators, however, say that the infidels saw the angelic hosts, and were, of course, reliable witnesses.

He punished those who disbelieved, i.e., the infidels who were defeated, for many were slain, 6000 of their women and children taken captive, 24,000 camels, 4000 ounces of silver, and over 40,000 goats became spoil for the Muslims.—*Tafsír-i-Raufí.*

(27) *Hereafter turned, &c.* "Besides a great number of proselytes who were gained by this battle, Muhammad, on their request, was so generous as to restore the captives (which were no less than six thousand) to their friends, and offered to make amends himself to any of his men who should not be willing to part with his prisoners." —*Sale, Baidháwi.*

This took place some time after the battle on the return of the army from Tayif, and was done as a matter of policy, as all the authorities show. See Muir's *Life of Mahomet*, vol. iv. pp. 142, 148, 149. Yet this matter is here described as the subject of prophecy. Surely it did not now require much prophetic foresight to foretell the conversion of at least some of the unfortunate Hawázin.

(28) *The idolaters are unclean.* This verse seems to be connected with those at the beginning of the chapter. Muhammad is now

temple after this year. And if ye fear want, *by the cutting off trade and communication with them,* GOD will enrich you of his abundance, if he pleaseth; for GOD *is* knowing *and* wise. (29) Fight against them who believe not in GOD nor the last day, and forbid not that which GOD and

---

master of Arabia. The idolaters are now to be converted by force. Exclusion from the sacred precincts of the ancient pantheon is now visited upon them, accompanied with the command to the Muslims to slay them wherever they find them, unless they confess Islám. The purity of the Muslims was not affected by contact with idolatry in visiting the idol temple at Makkah (for such it was until captured by Muhammad), so long as Islám was too weak to abolish it. Now that Muhammad is victorious, the spirit of his inspiration suddenly informs him that idolaters are unclean, and that Muslims may not perform the rites of the pilgrimage with them. Muhammad was not, however, in any way inconsistent with the principle that seems to have guided him everywhere—that everything was right that could in any way advance the cause of Islám. He was therefore right in becoming almost a Jew in hope of winning them. This failing, he was justified in patronising an idol temple and idolatrous rites in order to win over the Arabs. On the same principle he could condone assassination, sanction the plunder of caravans and the murder of defenceless merchants, even in the sacred months, and could on the same principle deny having any complicity in it. He could for the same reason witness the massacre of 800 Jewish prisoners, and spare, with a show of magnanimity, his bitterest enemies on the capture of Makkah. All was right—all was commanded of God, that promoted his selfish ambition, in the advancement of his political and prophetic or politico-prophetical pretensions. He had unhesitatingly adopted the pernicious rule that evil may be done in order to the accomplishment of a good end—that the end sanctifies the means.

After this year, i.e., the ninth year A.H. "In consequence of this prohibition, neither Jews nor Christians, nor those of any other religion, are suffered to come near Makkah to this day."—*Sale.*

God will enrich you. "This promise, says al Baidháwi, was fulfilled by God's sending plenty of rain, and disposing the inhabitants of Tabála and Jurásh, two towns in Yaman, to embrace Islám, who thereupon brought sufficient provisions to Muhammad's men; and also by the subsequent coming in of the Arabs from all quarters to him."—*Sale.*

(29) *Fight against them, &c.* "That is, those who have not a just and true faith in these matters, but either believe a plurality of gods, or deny the eternity of hell-torments, or the delights of Paradise as described in the Qurán. For, as it appears by the following words, the Jews and Christians are the persons here chiefly meant."—*Sale.*

The *Tafsír-i-Raufi* says the passage alludes to "the Jews, who

his Apostle have forbidden, and profess not the true religion, of those unto whom the scriptures have been delivered, until they pay tribute by right of subjection, and they be reduced low.

‖ (30) The Jews say, Ezra is the son of GOD; and the R $\frac{5}{11}$.

---

allegorise (in respect to the Godhead), and the Christians, who acknowledge a Trinity; the Jews, who deny eating and drinking in Paradise, and the Christians, who declare the enjoyments of heaven to be spiritual."

Profess not the true religion, &c. It is here implied that Islám was the religion of Jewish prophets and of Jesus, from which Jews and Christians have departed. The Qurán, by this claim so often repeated, challenges investigation, and thereby points to the evidence of its own imposture. See notes on chap. ii. 136.

Until they pay tribute, &c. "This I think the true meaning of the words *an yadin*, which literally signify *by* or *out of hand*, and are variously interpreted; some supposing they mean that the tribute is to be paid *readily*, or by their *own hands* and not by another; or that tribute is to be exacted of the *rich* only, or those who are able to pay it, and not of the poor; or else that it is to be taken as a *favour* that the Muhammadans are satisfied with so small an imposition, &c. That the Jews and Christians are, according to this law, to be admitted to protection on payment of tribute, there is no doubt, though the Muhammadan doctors differ as to those of other religions. It is said that Omar at first refused to accept tribute from a Magian, till Abdul Rahmán Ibn Auf assured him that Muhammad himself had granted protection to a Magian, and ordered that the professors of that religion should be included among *the people of the book*, or those who found their religion on some book which they suppose to be of Divine origin. And it is the more received opinion that these three religions only ought to be tolerated on the condition of paying tribute: others, however, admit the Sabians also. Abu Hanífa supposed people of any religion might be suffered, except the idolatrous Arabs; and Málik excepted only apostates from Muhammadanism. The least tribute that can be taken from every such person is generally agreed to be a *dinár*, or about ten shillings a year; nor can he be obliged to pay more, unless he consent to it: and this, they say, ought to be laid as well on the poor as on the rich. But Abu Hanífa decided that the rich should pay forty-eight *dirhams* (twenty, and sometimes twenty-five of which made a *dinár*) a year; one in middling circumstances half that sum; and a poor man, who was able to get his living, a quarter of it; but that he who was not able to support himself should pay nothing."—*Sale, Baidháwi.*

(30) *Ezra is the son of God.* "This grievous charge against the Jews the commentators endeavour to support by telling us that it is meant of some ancient heterodox Jews or else of some Jews of

Christians say, Christ is the Son of GOD. This is their saying in their mouths; they imitate the saying of those who were unbelievers in former times. May GOD resist them. How are they infatuated! (31) They take their priests and their monks for *their* lords, besides GOD, and Christ

---

Madína, who said so for no other reason than for that the law being utterly lost and forgotten during the Babylonish captivity, Ezra having been raised to life after he had been dead one hundred years (chap. ii. 259, note), dictated the whole anew unto the scribes out of his own memory; at which they greatly marvelled, and declared that he could not have done it unless he were the son of God. Al Baidháwi adds, that the imputation must be true, because this verse was read to the Jews, and they did not contradict it, which they were ready enough to do in other instances. That Ezra did thus restore not only the Pentateuch, but also the other books of the Old Testament, by Divine revelation, was the opinion of several of the Christian fathers, who are quoted by Dr. Prideaux, and of some other writers, which they seem to have first borrowed from a passage in that very ancient apocryphal book called in our English Bible the *Second Book of* Esdras (chap. xiv. 20, &c.) Dr. Prideaux tells us that herein the fathers attributed more to Ezra than the Jews themselves, who suppose that he only collected and set forth a correct edition of the Scriptures, which he laboured much in, and went a great way in the perfecting of it. It is not improbable, however, that the fiction came originally from the Jews, though they be now of another opinion, and I cannot fix it upon them by any direct proof. For, not to insist upon the testimony of the Muhammadans (which yet I cannot but think of some little weight in a point of this nature), it is allowed by the most sagacious critics that the Second Book of Ezra was written by a Christian indeed, but yet one who had been bred a Jew, and was intimately acquainted with the fables of the Rabbins; and the story itself is perfectly in the taste and way of thinking of those men."—*Sale, Baidháwi.*

Rodwell regards this charge against the Jews as purely the invention of Muhammad.

May God resist them. The spirit of this passage is in marked contrast with the allusions made to the "people of the book" in the earlier chapters of the Qurán. Compare chap. v. 85, and note there.

The whole passage points to the latter years of the Prophet's life, when he began to realise that the Christian power of Heracleus was likely to oppose the strongest barrier to his ambitious projects.

(31) *Priests . . . for their lords.* An inference from the use of the title *Rabbi*, coupled with the reverence accorded to the ordained ministry. See note on chap. iii. 63. The charge here made, that Christians worshipped their priests and monks as they did Christ and God, is scarcely true. It is also noteworthy that the Messiah is here deliberately denied all divine honours, and that the depre-

the son of Mary; although they are commanded to worship one GOD only: there is no GOD but he; far be that from him which they associate *with him!* (32) They seek to extinguish the light of GOD with their mouths; but GOD willeth no other than to perfect his light, although the infidels be averse *thereto.*

(33) It is he who hath sent his Apostle with the direction and true religion, that he may cause it to appear superior to every *other* religion, although the idolaters be averse *thereto.* (34) O true believers, verily many of the priests and monks devour the substance of GOD in vanity, and obstruct the way of GOD. But unto those who trea-

NISF.

---

catory formula, "far be it from him," &c., is the same as that used in reproaching the idolatrous Arabs for their service to heathen gods. Whatever phrases, therefore, we find in the Qurán expressive of Messianic dignity must be attributed to the ignorance of the Prophet as to their real import. See notes on chaps. ii. 86 and iii. 39.

(32) *The light of God, i.e.,* the Qurán, or the Divine Unity, or the prophetic office of Muhammad, &c.—*Tafsír-i-Raufi.*

(33) *Superior to every other religion.* Rodwell translates more correctly, "victorious over every other religion." This was true of the religions of Arabia, to which the expression must primarily be referred, but it is not true of the religions of the world, Islám at present being almost everywhere subject to or dependent for existence on Christian rule.

Christian apologists for Islám, in their endeavour to draw a favourable comparison between Islám and Christianity, are in the habit of ignoring the fact that what is good and true in Islám is very much more clearly revealed in the Old and New Testament Scriptures, while at the same time they carefully set aside the peculiar doctrines of Christianity: the new birth, the atonement of Christ, the graces of the Holy Spirit, and the holy character essential to the Christian life. By such a process black may be made to appear white, and *vice versa.* See R. Bosworth Smith's *Mohammed and Mohammedanism,* pp. 338, 339. This writer's statement that Islám is "the religion of stability," a religion dwelling on the "inherent dignity" of human nature, "the religion of the best parts of Asia and Africa," with the implication that Christianity is unsuited to the stable races, is contradicted by the history of the Church and of her missions.

(34) *Monks devour, &c.* "By taking bribes, says Baidháwi, meaning, probably, the money they took for dispensing with the commands of God, and by way of commutation."—*Sale.* It more probably refers to the fact that these classes were supported by the people.

Obstruct the way of God, i.e., by preventing their followers from becoming Muslims.

sure up gold and silver, and employ it not for the advancement of GOD's true religion, denounce a grievous punishment. (35) On the day *of judgment their treasures* shall be intensely heated in the fire of hell, and their foreheads, and their sides, and their backs shall be stigmatised therewith; *and their tormentors shall say*, This is what ye have treasured up for your souls; taste therefore that which ye have treasured up. (36) Moreover, the *complete* number of months with GOD is twelve months, *which were ordained* in the book of GOD on the day whereon he created the heavens and the earth: of these, four are sacred. This is the right religion; therefore deal not unjustly with yourselves therein. But attack the idolaters in all *the months*, as they attack you in all; and know that GOD is with those who fear *him*. (37) Verily the transferring *of a sacred month*

Those who treasure up, &c. This refers to all men, being suggested by the conduct of the priests and monks. The exigencies of Islám required that all Muslims should be willing to give freely of their substance for the support of religion. Hence the dreadful denunciation of the next verse, pointing at once to the fate of Christian monks and Muslim misers.

(35) This verse describes the fate not only of miserly Muslims, but also that of the Christian priests and monks of ver. 31. "Thus," says Muir in his *Life of Mahomet*, vol. iv. p. 212, "with threats of abasement and with bitter curses, Mahomet parted finally from the Jews and Christians, whom he had so long deceived with vain professions of attachment to their Scriptures, and from whose teaching he had borrowed all that was most valuable in his own system. Having reached the pinnacle of prosperity and power, he cast contemptuously aside the supports to which in no small measure he owed his elevation."

(36) *The complete number of months.* "According to this passage, the intercalation of a month every third or second year, which the Arabs had learned of the Jews, in order to reduce their lunar years to solar years, is absolutely unlawful, For by this means they fixed the time of the pilgrimage and of the feast of Ramadhán to certain seasons of the year, which ought to be ambulatory."—*Sale.* See also Prelim. Disc., pp. 229, 230, and chap. ii. 185, note.

The book of God, viz., the Preserved Table.—*Sale.*

Four are sacred. See Prelim. Disc., p. 228.

Attack the idolaters in all. "For it is not reasonable that you should observe the sacred months with regard to those who do not acknowledge them to be sacred, but make war against you therein." —*Sale.* See notes on chap. ii. 191, 193.

to another month is an additional infidelity. The unbelievers are led into an error thereby: they allow a *month* to be violated one year, and declare it sacred *another* year, that they may agree in the number of *months* which GOD hath commanded to be kept sacred; and they allow that which GOD hath forbidden. The evil of their actions hath been prepared for them; for GOD directeth not the unbelieving people.

|| (38) O true believers, what ailed you, that when it was said unto you, Go forth *to fight* for the religion of GOD, ye inclined heavily towards the earth? Do ye prefer the present life to that which is to come? But the provision of this life, in *respect of* that which is to come, is but slender. (39) Unless ye go forth *when ye are summoned to war, God* will punish you with a grievous punishment; and he will place another people in your stead, and ye shall not hurt him at all; for GOD is almighty. (40) If

R $\frac{6}{12}$.

---

(37) *An additional infidelity.* "This was an invention or innovation of the idolatrous Arabs, whereby they avoided keeping a sacred month, when it suited not their conveniency, by keeping a profane month in its stead, transferring, for example, the observance of *Muharram* to the succeeding month *Safar*. The first man who put this in practice, they say, was Junáda Ibn Auf, of the tribe of Kinánà. These ordinances relating to the months were promulgated by Muhammad himself at the pilgrimage of *valediction*."—*Sale.*

They . . . declare it sacred another year, &c. "As did Junáda, who made public proclamation at the assembly of pilgrims that their gods had allowed *Muharram* to be profane, whereupon they observed it not; but the next year he told them that the gods had ordered it to be kept sacred."—*Sale, Baidháwi.*

(38) *What ailed you,* viz., "In the expedition of Tabúq, a town situate about half-way between Madina and Damascus, which Muhammad undertook against the Greeks, with an army of thirty thousand men, in the ninth year of the Hijra. On this expedition the Muslims set out with great unwillingness, because it was undertaken in the midst of the summer heats, and at a time of great drought and scarcity, whereby the soldiers suffered so much, that this army was called the *distressed army;* besides, their fruits were just ripe, and they had much rather have stayed to have gathered them."—*Sale, Jaláluddín, Baidháwi.*

(39) *Another people in your stead.* See chap. v. 59, and notes there.

ye assist not *the Prophet,* verily GOD *will assist him, as he* assisted him formerly, when the unbelievers drove him out *of Makkah,* the second of two when they *were* both in the cave: when he said unto his companion, Be not grieved, for GOD is with us. And GOD sent down his security upon him, and strengthened him with armies *of angels,* whom ye saw not. And he made the word of those who believed not to be abased, and the word of GOD was exalted; for GOD *is* mighty *and* wise. (41) Go forth *to battle,* both light and heavy, and employ your substance and your persons for the advancement of GOD's religion. This will be better for you, if ye know it. (42) If it had been a near advantage, and a moderate journey, they had surely followed thee; but the way seemed tedious unto them: and yet they will swear by GOD, *saying,* If we had been able, we had surely gone forth with you. They

---

(40) *The unbelievers, i.e.,* the people or chiefs of Makkah, who compelled his flight to Madína.

The second of two. "That is, having only Ábu Baqr with him."—*Sale.* See Prelim. Disc., pp. 86, 87.

His security. See note on ver. 26.

Armies of angels. The allusion is to the angelic hosts, whose help he pretended to have received at the battle of Badr, at the Ditch, and at Hunain. If these angels are here intended, then the statement that they were not seen by the Muslims does not accord with the statements of chap. iii. 13, 123, and chap. viii. 44, 45.

(41) *Light and heavy.* Savary translates *young and old.* The *Tafsir-i-Raufi* comments as follows: "Go forth on horseback and on foot, in health or sickness, young and old, poor and rich, without preparation and with preparation, the virgin and the married woman."

The advancement of God's religion. The faithful are now to hold their all in readiness to promote the cause of Islám by the sword. The outlook is not now upon unbelieving Arabia, as in chap. ii. 190 and 244, but upon the unbelieving world. The expedition to Tabúq was the beginning of a struggle which was only accomplished in part by the conquest of Constantinople; and yet this was far from realising, the ambitious purpose of the Prophet of Arabia.

(42) *A near advantage, &c.* "That is, had there been no difficulties to surmount in the expedition to Tabúq, and the march thither had been short and easy, so that the plunder might have cost them little or no trouble, they would not have been so backward."—*Sale.*

They will swear, &c. This verse, with those following to ver. 48, are said by the commentators to have been revealed during the

destroy their own souls; for GOD knoweth that they are liars.

|| (43) GOD forgive thee! why didst thou give them R. $\frac{7}{13}$. leave *to stay at home,* until they who speak the truth, *when they excuse themselves,* had become manifested unto thee, and thou hadst known the liars? (44) They who believe in GOD and the last day will not ask leave of thee to be excused from employing their substance and their persons for the advancement of GOD's true religion; and GOD knoweth those who fear *him.* (45) Verily they only will ask leave of thee *to stay behind* who believe not in GOD and the last day, and whose hearts doubt *concerning the faith;* wherefore they are tossed to and fro in their doubting. (46) If they had been willing to go forth *with thee,*

---

march to Tabúq, and the statement of the text is regarded as a prophecy, which was, of course, fulfilled on the return of the army to Madína. Granting the claim that the passage was revealed on the way to Tabúq, the character of this prophecy may be determined from the statement of ver. 48, where these same hypocrites are said to have "sought to raise sedition" *on a previous occasion.* It is, however, almost certain, from the statement of ver. 47, that the passage was enunciated after the return, and delivered as a rebuke to the hypocrites and others affected by their indifference.

(43) *God forgive thee.* Muhammad is here "reprehended for having excused some of his followers from going on this expedition, as Abdullah Ibn Ubbai and his hypocritical adherents, and three of the Ansárs."—*Sale.*

The *Tafsír-i-Itaufi* regards this as a benediction, which in no way implies that the Prophet had sinned, and illustrates it by reference to the Oriental custom of pronouncing a benediction on the watercarrier, "The Lord pardon thee;" to which he replies, "The Lord have mercy on thee." Here, the commentators says, no charge of sinfulness is intended, and so when God speaks to the Prophet, saying, "God forgive thee," no crime is laid to his charge! The fact is overlooked that the *custom* alluded to could only exist among sinful men, ever needing God's mercy and pardon. The passage certainly implies the sinfulness of Muhammad. The doctrine of Muslims that the prophets were sinless cannot even bear the light of the Qurán, which clearly charges sin against all the great prophets (nabi ul ázim) excepting Jesus. See chap. ii. 253.

Until . . . thou hadst known. "Contrast to Christ, 'knowing their thoughts,' and Peter discovering the lies of Ananias and his wife."—*Brinckman's "Notes on Islám."*

(44–46) These verses teach that all interests of private individuals must yield to the interests of Islám. Failure here is a sure sign of

they had certainly prepared for that *purpose* a provision *of arms and necessaries:* but GOD was averse to their going forth; wherefore he rendered them slothful, and it was said *unto them,* Sit ye still with those who sit still. (47) If they had gone forth with you, they had only been a burden unto you, and had run to and fro between you, stirring you up to sedition; and *there would have been some among you who would have given ear unto them:* and GOD knoweth the wicked. (48) They formerly sought to raise a sedition, and they disturbed thy affairs, until the truth came, and the decree of GOD was made manifest; although they were adverse thereto. (49) There is of them who saith *unto thee,* Give me leave *to stay behind,* and expose me not to temptation. Have they not fallen into temptation *at home?* But hell will surely encompass the unbelievers. (50) If good happen unto thee, it grieveth them: but if a misfortune befall thee, they say, We ordered our business before, and they turn their backs, and rejoice *at thy mishap.* (51) Say, Nothing shall befall us but what GOD hath decreed for us; he is our patron,

---

infidelity. Another point worthy of notice is that man's free agency and God's sovereignty are both clearly recognised in this passage.

Sit . . . with those who sit still, i.e., with those who are incapable of active service, as the women and children, the aged and infirm.

(48) *Formerly sought to raise a sedition.* As at Ohod. See notes on chap. iii. 156–160.

(49) *Expose me not to temptation.* "By obliging me to go, against my will, on an expedition the hardships of which may tempt me to rebel or to desert. It is related that one Jadd Ibn Qais said that the Ansárs well knew he was much given to women, and he dared not trust himself with the Greek girls; wherefore he desired he might be left behind, and he would assist them with his purse."—*Sale, Baidháwi.*

Have they not fallen, &c., i.e., by falling into the sin of cowardice and infidelity.

(50) *It grieveth them.* For envy, or because they are unable to share the booty.

We ordered our business before, i.e., "We took care to keep out of harm's way by staying at home."—*Sale.*

(51) *What God hath decreed.* Literally, *What God hath written,* meaning what God hath determined from eternity, and recorded on the Preserved Table. On the question of Muhammad's fatalism see notes on chap. iii. 145 and 155.

and on GOD let the faithful trust. (52) Say, Do ye expect *any other should befall* us than one of the two most excellent things, *either victory or martyrdom?* But we expect concerning you that GOD inflict a punishment on you, *either* from himself or by our hands. Wait, therefore, *to see what will be the end of both;* for we will wait for you. (53) Say, Expend *your money in pious uses, either* voluntarily or by constraint, it shall not be accepted of you, because ye are wicked people. (54) And nothing hindereth their contributions from being accepted of them, but that they believe not in GOD and his Apostle, and perform not the *duty of* prayer otherwise than sluggishly, and expend not *their money for God's service* otherwise than unwillingly.

|| (55) Let not therefore their riches or their children R $\frac{8}{14}$. cause thee to marvel. Verily GOD intendeth only to punish them by these things in this world, and that their souls may depart while they are unbelievers. (56) They

---

(52) *The two most excellent things.* This passage illustrates the confidence Muhammad had in the success of Islám, whilst it shows the strong spirit of fanaticism already fixed in the minds of the Muslims. To fight for Islám was to conquer or to gain admission to Paradise. An army made up of men holding such a faith could hardly fail of success. War and bloodshed thus sanctified are the very antipodes of the peace and benevolence of the Gospel.

We will wait for you. The threat contained in this verse shows the changed attitude of Muhammad towards the disaffected. Compare chap. ii. 108. Either God would punish them by a judgment from heaven, as he had punished Ád and Thamúd (Prelim. Disc., pp. 20–22), or they would be punished by the faithful by Divine command. The facility with which Muhammad could produce such commands was, no doubt, well understood by the hypocrites, so that these words would convey to their minds a very distinct threat of assault.

(53, 54) The distinction between true Muslims and merely nominal adherents is here clearly defined. The former were those who had consecrated all to Islám, and held themselves ready to obey every command of the Prophet with unquestioning obedience. Their bodies, souls, time, strength, property, all was devoted to their religion. The unpardonable sin was want of devotion to Muhammad and his cause. The property of hypocrites could not be accepted except as the lawful booty of the faithful.

(55) Comp. with chap. iii. 179.

swear by God that they are of you; yet they are not of you, but are people who stand in fear. (57) If they find a place of refuge, or caves, or a retreating hole, they surely turn towards the same, and in a headstrong manner haste *thereto.* (58) There is of them also who spreadeth ill reports of thee, in relation to *thy distribution of* the alms: yet if they receive *part* thereof they are well pleased; but if they receive not *a part* thereof, behold they are angry. (59) But if they had been pleased with that which GOD and his Apostle had given them, and had said, GOD is our support; GOD will give unto us of his abundance, and his Prophet *also;* verily unto GOD do we make our supplications: *it would have been more decent.* (60) Alms *are to be distributed* only unto the poor and the needy, and those

---

(56) *People who stand in fear.* "Hypocritically concealing their infidelity, lest ye should chastise them, as ye have done the professed infidels and apostates; and yet ready to avow their infidelity when they think they may do it with safety."—*Sale.*

(58, 59) *Them also who spread ill reports of thee, &c.* "This person was Abu'l Jawádh, the hypocrite, who said Muhammad gave them away among the keepers of sheep only; or, as others suppose, Ibn Dhu'l Khuwaisarah, who found fault with the Prophet's distribution of the spoils taken at Hunain, because he gave them all among the Makkans, to reconcile and gain them over to his religion and interest."—*Sale, Abdul Qádir.*

Complaints among the Muslims frequently grew out of the claim of Muhammad that the booty was God's (see chap. viii. 1), and that the distribution of it depended upon His will as revealed by the Apostle. So long as the division was equal, no objection, so far as we know, was ever raised. Dissatisfaction on this point arose out of Muhammad's purpose to gain influence by means of rich presents bestowed out of the common heap, as at Hunain, alluded to above. Yet we find the Prophet deliberately associating God with himself in carrying out this very worldly policy by appealing to one of the lowest passions of depraved human nature.

If, as seems certain, the allusion is to the trouble at Hunain, God is here also made a partner in appeasing the covetous Muslim Bedouins by a promise of increased booty in future expeditions (see above in ver. 27). This is styled in the next verse (59) the *abundance of God and his Prophet,* which the faithful receive in answer to their prayers. Was there no consciousness of deception and imposture in this affair?

(60) This verse abrogates chap. ii. 214 on the subject of almsgiving. See Prelim. Disc., pp. 172-175.

The poor and the needy. "The commentators make a distinction

who are employed in *collecting and distributing* the same, and unto those whose hearts *are* reconciled, and for *the redemption of* captives, and unto those who are in debt *and insolvent*, and for the advancement of GOD's religion, and unto the traveller. *This is* an ordinance from GOD; and GOD *is* knowing *and* wise. (61) There are some of them who injure the Prophet, and say, He is an ear. Answer, He is an ear of good unto you; he believeth in GOD, and giveth credit to the faithful, (62) and *is* a mercy

between these two words in the original, *fakír* and *miskín;* one, they say, signifies him who is utterly destitute both of money and means of livelihood ; the other, one who is in want indeed, but is able to get something towards his own support. But to which of the two words either of these different significations properly belongs the critics differ."—*Sale.*

Those whose hearts are reconciled. These were the Arab chiefs upon whom Muhammad lavished expensive presents in order to secure their allegiance to Islám. See the matter fully described in Muir's *Life of Mahomet*, vol. iv. pp. 152–155.

Sale's note here is as follows :—"Those who were lately enemies to the faithful, but have now embraced Muhammadanism and entered into amity with them. For Muhammad, to gain their hearts and confirm them in his religion, made large presents to the chief of the Quraish out of the spoils at Hunain, as has been just now mentioned. But this law, they say, became of no obligation when the Muhammadan faith was established, and stood not in need of such methods for its support."

(61) *He is an ear.* Rodwell translates "He is *all* ear." Sale paraphrases thus : "He hears everything that we say, and gives credit to all the stories that are carried to him." This seems to express blameworthiness on the part of the Prophet. The *Tafsír-i-Raufi* understands these words to express the feelings of the Prophet's enemies, who, taking advantage of his simplicity, spoke evil of him behind his back, in the assurance that, if reported, he would credit their hypocritical professions of friendship. This view accords with the verses following.

An ear of good, i.e., "Giving credit to nothing that may do you hurt."—*Sale.*

Giveth credit to the faithful. It is here intimated that the Prophet was aware of the evil-speaking of his enemies, and that he did not credit the declarations of loyalty made by the unbelievers.

That Muhammad deserved the title here given him is abundantly exhibited by the numerous passages of the Qurán specially written to refute the sayings of his foes, or to record the lessons in Jewish history and tradition he had learned from friends. To use a modern expression, " he was thoroughly wide-awake." He understood his followers and divined the purposes of his enemies, because he *heard* them

unto such of you who believe. But they who injure the Apostle of GOD shall suffer a painful punishment. (63) They swear unto you by GOD, that they may please you; but it is more just that they should please GOD and his Apostle, if they are true believers. (64) Do they not know that he who opposeth GOD and his Apostle shall without doubt *be punished with* the fire of hell, *and* shall remain therein for ever? This will be great ignominy. (65) The hypocrites are apprehensive lest a Sura should be revealed concerning them, to declare unto them that which *is* in

---

express their feelings, carefully treasuring all in his memory until such time as he had determined on to reveal his knowledge, while assuming the outward garb of one inspired, and pretending to have received his knowledge by revelation, declaring it as coming from God himself. Comp. note on chap. ii. 145.

(63, 64) *God and his Apostle.* The chief duty of a Muslim is here declared to be to *please God and his Apostle,* for to *oppose God and his Apostle* is sure to end in the punishment of *the fire of hell.* A Muslim sees nothing in this passage derogatory to Muhammad's character, because he believes that he was truly a prophet of God, and therefore judges that to oppose the Prophet is to oppose God. How our Christian apologists for Muhammad can exonerate their hero here we cannot imagine. Was he a prophet? Did he originate the language of this passage in his own mind, or did he receive it, as he pretended, directly from God, so that he was merely the mouthpiece of God? We are not aware that any of these admirers of Muhammad hold opinions consistent with such a claim. But if he be the author of the Qurán, and if he be not a prophet, how can he be exonerated from blasphemy and imposture in the use of such language as this? We should indeed like to hear what they have to say in defence of this very characteristic feature of the revelations of the Qurán. See also chap. viii. 20.

(65) *The hypocrites are apprehensive lest a Sura.* This passage illustrates Muhammad's method of procedure. The *hypocrites* had already abundant experience as to the correspondence between the wishes and designs of the Prophet and the Suras of his Qurán. They had seen this fact illustrated in bloody characters in the case of their Jewish neighbours, in characters of a different hue in the matter of the distribution of the spoils, and the numerous interferences of the inspiring angel in settlement of grave matters pertaining to the Prophet's harem. No wonder they should be "apprehensive lest a Sura should be revealed concerning them." No wonder that, as a result of such apprehension, hypocrisy soon became lost in zeal for the cause of the Prophet. On the word *sura,* see introduction to chap. i.

their hearts. Say *unto them,* Scoff ye; *but* GOD will surely bring to light that which ye fear *should be discovered.*

|| (66) And if thou ask them *the reason of this scoffing,* SULA. they say, Verily we were only engaged in discourse, and jesting *among ourselves.* Say, Do ye scoff at GOD and his signs, and at his Apostle? (67) Offer not an excuse: now are ye become infidels, after your faith. If we forgive a part of you, we will punish a part, for that they have been wicked doers.

|| (68) Hypocritical men and women are the one of R $\frac{9}{15}$. them of the other: they command that which is evil, and forbid that which is just, and shut their hands *from giving alms.* They have forgotten GOD, wherefore he hath forgotten them: verily the hypocrites are those who act wickedly. (69) GOD denounceth unto the hypocrites, both men and women, and to the unbelievers, the fire of hell; they shall remain therein *for ever:* this will be their sufficient *reward;* GOD hath cursed them, and they shall endure a lasting torment. (70) As they who have

---

(66) *Jesting.* "It is related that in the expedition of Tabúq, a company of hypocrites, passing near Muhammad, said to one another, 'Behold that man! he would take the strongholds of Syria: away! away!' which being told the Prophet, he called them to him, and asked them why they had said so; whereto they replied with an oath, that they were not talking of what related to him or his companions, but were only diverting themselves with indifferent discourse, to beguile the tediousness of the way."—*Sale, Baidháwi.*

Such stories have every appearance of being invented to account for the text. Hypocrites were not in the habit of going on distant expeditions; and, at this date in the career of the Prophet, they would not have ventured to jest at his expense, and that in his hearing. The passage must be assigned to an earlier date.

(68) *One of them from the other.* Rodwell translates this idiom, and renders it "imitate one another." *Who act wickedly, i.e.,* they opposed Muhammad's pretensions, and declined to spend money for his wars. As to moral conduct, we have every reason to believe them to have been better than the Muslims. But with these morality had already become identical with adhesion to Islám.

(69) *God denounceth . . . the fire of hell.* Of the seven apartments of hell, the lowest is assigned to the hypocrites. See Prelim. Disc., p. 148.

(70) This description of the hypocrites points to the days of their prosperity and power, and confirms what was said under ver. 66.

been before you, *so are ye*. They were superior to you in strength, and had more abundance of wealth and of children, and they enjoyed their portion *in this world;* and ye also enjoy your portion *here*, as they who have preceded you enjoyed their portion. And ye engage yourselves in vain discourses, like unto those wherein they engaged themselves. The works of these are vain *both* in this world and in that which is to come; and these are they who perish. (71) Have they not been acquainted with the history of those who have been before them? of the people of Noah, and of Ád, and of Thamúd, and of the people of Abraham, and of the inhabitants of Madian, and of the *cities which were* overthrown. Their apostles came unto them with evident demonstrations, and GOD was not disposed to treat them unjustly; but they dealt unjustly with their own souls. (72) And the faithful men and the faithful women are friends one to another: they command that which is just, and they forbid that which is evil; and they are constant at prayer, and pay their appointed alms; and they obey GOD and his Apostle: unto these will GOD be merciful; for he *is* mighty *and* wise. (73) GOD promiseth unto the true believers, both men and women, gardens through which rivers flow, wherein they shall remain for ever; and delicious dwellings in the gardens of perpetual abode: but

---

(71) *The people of Noah, &c.* See notes on chap. vii. 60–86. *The cities . . . overthrown,* namely, "Sodom and Gomorrah, and the other cities which shared their fate, and are thence called *Al Mutikifát,* or *the subverted."—Sale.*

(73) *Both men and women.* See note on chap. iv. 123.

Gardens. "Lit. *gardens* of Eden; but the commentators do not take the word Eden in the sense which it bears in Hebrew, as has been elsewhere observed." See Prelim. Disc., p. 155.—*Sale.*

"In Hebrew it signifies *a place of delight.* In the Arabic it means *a place fit for the pasturing of flocks."—Savary.*

But good-will from God, &c. The commentators have very little to say on this passage—one of the few passages suggesting a higher joy in heaven than the satisfaction of carnal appetites. The very exceptions of the Qurán prove the rule that the heaven of Islám is one of carnal joy. See notes on chaps. ii. 25 and iii. 15.

good-will from GOD *shall be their* most excellent *reward.* This *will be* great felicity.

∥ (74) O Prophet, wage war against the unbelievers R $\frac{10}{16}$.

---

(74) *Wage war against the unbelievers, &c.* Mr. Bosworth Smith in his *Mohammed and Mohammedanism,* pp. 137-142, admits a change of practice on the part of Muhammad in respect to his opponents: "The free toleration of the purer among the creeds around him, which the Prophet had at first enjoined, gradually changes into intolerance. Persecuted no longer, Mohammed becomes a persecutor himself; with the Koran in one hand, the scymiter in the other, he goes forth to offer to the nations the threefold alternative of conversion, tribute, death." This, however, along with his being "guilty more than once of conniving at the assassination of inveterate opponents, and the massacre of the Bani Koraitza," is excused partly on the ground that, believing himself to be inspired, he "found an ample precedent for the act in the slaughter of the Midianites by Moses or the Canaanites by Joshua," and partly on the ground of his being an Oriental, who must therefore be judged by a lower standard of morality. In Mr. Smith's estimation these are apparently but a few slight blemishes in an otherwise estimable character. In opposition to Gibbon, he lauds the magnanimity of Muhammad on his capture of Makkah. "If ever he had worn a mask at all, he would now at all events have thrown it off; if lower aims had gradually sapped the higher, or his moderation had been directed, as Gibbon supposes, by his selfish interests, we should now have seen the effect; now would have been the moment to gratify his ambition, to satiate his lust, to glut his revenge. Is there anything of the kind? Read the account of the entry of Mohammed into Mecca, side by side with that of Marius or Sulla into Rome. Compare all the attendant circumstances, the outrages that preceded, and the use made by each of his recovered power, and we shall then be in a position better to appreciate the magnanimity and moderation of the Prophet of Arabia."

I have thus quoted at length, because this is perhaps the strongest plea for Muhammad's sincerity and magnanimity to be found in the English language. It is made to cover a multitude of Muhammad's sins. And yet I am persuaded that Gibbon's estimate of his character is the fairest. It must never be forgotten that this so-called magnanimity was avowedly exceptional. It was contrary to numerous threats made by the Prophet in previous years. It was in striking contrast with the spirit shown at Badr and Ohod, and yet was in equally striking accord with his treatment of the Bani Hawázin after the battle of Hunain. There were indeed important reasons for the clemency shown towards the people of Makkah. Not to mention the fact that hundreds of the Muslims, like the Prophet himself, were bound to the Makkans by ties of relationship, there were many secret disciples in Makkah. Besides, there is very good reason to believe that both Abbás and Abu Sufián were in collusion with Muhammad, and that the city was really surrendered by them

CHAP. IX.]　　　　　(302)　　　　　[SIPARA X.

and the hypocrites, and be severe unto them; for their dwelling shall be hell: an unhappy journey *shall it be thither!* (75) They swear by GOD that they said not *what they are charged with:* yet they spake the word of infidelity, and became unbelievers after they had embraced Islám. And they designed that which they could not effect; and they did not disapprove *the design for any other reason* than because GOD and his Apostle had enriched them of his bounty. If they repent, it will be better for them; but if they relapse, GOD will punish them with a grievous torment in this world and in the next; and they shall have no portion on earth, nor any

to Muhammad, with the express understanding that violence should not be permitted. Then policy would dictate clemency, inasmuch as the powerful tribes which, a few days later, well-nigh defeated him at Hunain, would have gained much by any impolitic severity towards the people of the holy city. Muhammad's treatment of the inhabitants of Makkah, therefore, rather argues in favour of his wisdom and prudence than of his forbearance and clemency. The passage under consideration, written at least a year after the capture of Makkah, testifies to the intolerant temper of Muhammad. He had now secured the power to do what he always desired to do, and there was no reason for concealing the real hatred with which he regarded every rival religion. Indeed, the mainspring of his whole prophetic career was *policy.* He was as magnanimous as he was cruel whenever the interest of his prophetico-political pretensions required it.

(75) *They spake the word of infidelity.* "It is related that al Jallás Ibn Suwaid, hearing some passages of this chapter which sharply reprehended those who refused to go on the above-mentioned expedition of Tabúq, declared that if what Muhammad said of his brethren was true, they were worse than asses. Which coming to the Prophet's ear, he sent for him, and he denied the words upon oath. But on the immediate revelation of this passage, he confessed his fault, and his repentance was accepted."—*Sale, Baidháwi.*

They designed, &c. "The commentators tell us that fifteen men conspired to kill Muhammad on his return from Tabúq, by pushing him from his camel into a precipice as he rode by night over the highest part of al Aqabah. But when they were going to execute their design, Hudhaifah, who followed and drove the Prophet's camel, which was led by Ammár Ibn Yasir, hearing the tread of camels and the clashing of arms, gave the alarm, upon which they fled. Some however suppose the design here meant was a plot to expel Muhammad from Madína."—*Sale, Baidháwi.*

Had enriched them. "For Muhammad's residing at Madína was of great advantage to the place, the inhabitants being generally poor,

protector. (76) There are some of them who made a covenant with GOD, *saying*, Verily if he give us of his abundance, we will give alms, and become righteous people. (77) Yet when they had given unto him of his abundance, they became covetous thereof, and turned back, and retired afar off. (78) Wherefore he hath caused hypocrisy to succeed in their hearts, until the day whereon they shall meet him; for that they failed to perform unto GOD that which they had promised him, and for that they prevaricated. (79) Do they not know that GOD knoweth

and in want of most conveniences of life; but on the Prophet's coming among them, they became possessed of large herds of cattle, and money also. Al Baidháwi says that the above-named al Jallás, in particular, having a servant killed, received, by Muhammad's order, no less than ten thousand *dirhems*, or about three hundred pounds, as a fine for the redemption of his blood."—*Sale*.

The predatory expeditions of the Muslims, the plunder of numerous caravans, and the successful wars waged against the wealthy Jewish tribes in the vicinity of Madína, must have resulted in changing the condition of the people from poverty to wealth. Let it be observed that the Qurán here justifies all the means adopted by "his Apostle" for the acquisition of this wealth. It was, in the strictest and most direct sense of the words, a gift from God and Muhammad.

(76) *If he give . . . we will give, &c.* "An instance of this is given in Thálabah Ibn Hátib, who came to Muhammad, and desired him to beg of God that he would bestow riches on him. The Prophet at first advised him rather to be thankful for the little he had than to covet more, which might become a temptation to him; but on Thálabah's repeated request and solemn promise that he would make a good use of his riches, he was at length prevailed on, and preferred the petition to God. Thálabah in a short time grew vastly rich, which Muhammad being acquainted with, sent two collectors to gather the alms; other people readily paid them, but when they came to Thálabah, and read the injunction to him out of the Qurán, he told them that it was not alms, but tribute, or next kin to tribute, and bid them go back till he had better considered of it. Upon which this passage was revealed; and when Thálabah came afterwards and brought his alms, Muhammad told him that God had commanded him not to accept it, and threw dust on his head, saying, 'This is what thou hast deserved.' He then offered his alms to Abu Baqr, who refused to accept them, as did Omar some years after, when he was Khalífah."—*Sale*.

I confess this story sounds exceedingly like an invention of the commentators. Its spirit accords better with a later period in the history of the Khalífahs. It is given, however, on the authority of Baidháwi.

(79) This verse clearly teaches that God is omniscient—that all things are open to the gaze of his all-seeing eye.

whatever they conceal, and their private discourses; and that GOD is the knower of secrets? (80) They who traduce such of the believers as are liberal in *giving* alms *beyond what they are obliged,* and those who find nothing *to give* but *what they gain by* their industry, and therefore scoff at them: GOD shall scoff at them, and they shall suffer a grievous punishment. (81) Ask forgiveness for them, or do not ask forgiveness for them; *it will be equal.* If thou ask forgiveness for them seventy times, GOD will by no means forgive them. This *is the divine pleasure,* for

---

(80) *They who traduce . . . believers.* "Al Baidháwi relates that Muhammad, exhorting his followers to voluntary alms, among others, Abd-ur-Rahmán Ibn Auf gave four thousand *dirhems*, which was one-half of what he had; Asim Ibn Adda gave a hundred beasts' loads of dates ; and Abu Ukail a *saá*, which is no more than a sixtieth part of a load, of the same fruit, but was the half of what he had earned by a night's hard work. This Muhammad accepted : whereupon the hypocrites said that Abd-ur-Rahmán and Asim gave what they did out of ostentation, and that God and his Apostle might well have excused Abu Ukail's mite ; which occasioned this passage.

"I suppose this collection was made to defray the charge of the expedition of Tabúq, towards which, as another writer tells us, Abu Baqr contributed all that he had, and Othmán very largely, viz., as it is said, three hundred camels for slaughter, and a thousand *dinárs* of gold."—*Sale, Tafsír-i-Raufi.*

(81) *God will by no means forgive them.* "In the last sickness of Abdullah Ibn Ubbái, the hypocrite (who died in the ninth year of the Hijra), his son, named also Abdullah, came and asked Muhammad to beg pardon of God for him, which he did, and thereupon the former part of this verse was revealed. But the Prophet, not taking that for a repulse, said he would *pray seventy times* for him ; upon which the latter part of the verse was revealed, declaring it would be absolutely in vain. It may be observed that the numbers *seven,* and *seventy,* and *seven hundred,* are frequently used by the Eastern writers, to signify not so many precisely, but only an indefinite number, either greater or lesser, several examples of which are to be met with in the Scriptures."—*Sale, Baidháwi.*

If we are to credit this story, as all Muslims do, it very well illustrates Muhammad's character as an intercessor on behalf of sinners. He may *intercede,* but there is no certainty he will be heard. According to this story, he does not even know that he will not be heard. Of course the reply of the Muslim is, that his office as intercessor only begins with the judgment-day, and that *then* it will be effectual. But then it will only be of avail in the case of Muslims who are now assured salvation on the ground of their

that they believe not in GOD and his Apostle; and GOD directeth not the ungodly people.

∥ (82) They who were left at home *in the expedition* R $\frac{11}{17}$. *of Tabúq* were glad of their staying behind the Apostle of GOD, and were unwilling to employ their substance and their persons for the advancement of GOD'S true religion; and they said, Go not forth in the heat. Say, The fire of hell will be hotter; if they understood *this*. (83) Wherefore let them laugh little and weep much, as a reward for that which they have done. (84) If GOD bring thee back unto some of them, and they ask thee leave to go forth *to war with thee*, say, Ye shall not go forth with me for the future, neither shall ye fight an enemy with me; ye were pleased with sitting *at home*

---

being Muslims. They therefore require no intercessor. There can be no doubt that the doctrine of Muhammad's intercession is at variance with the teaching of the Qurán. Nevertheless, the faith of Muslims is not only that Muhammad will intercede for them at the judgment-day, but that a multitude of saints can intercede for them even now. This faith testifies against the Qurán, and, so far, attests the doctrine of salvation by atonement and Christ's intercession as taught in the Bible. Muslims feel their need of an intercessor. The Qurán gives them none, whereupon they constitute Muhammad and a host of saints their intercessors.

It is probable that the story given by Sale misrepresents the feelings of Muhammad toward Abdullah Ibn Ubbái at the time of his death. "Muhammad prayed over his corpse, thereby professing to recognise Abdullah as having been a faithful Moslem; he walked behind the bier to the grave, and waited there till the ceremonies of the funeral were ended."—*Muir's Life of Mahomet*, vol. iv. p. 200.

(82) *They who were left behind*, *i.e.*, the hypocrites, under the leadership of Abdullah Ibn Ubbái.

Go forth in the heat. "This they spoke in a scoffing manner to one another, because, as has been observed, the expedition of Tabúq was undertaken in a very hot and dry season."—*Sale*.

(84) *And they ask thee.* "That is, if thou return in safety to Madína to the hypocrites, who are here called some of them who stayed behind, because they were not all hypocrites. The whole number is said to have been twelve."—*Sale, Baidháwi*.

A careful perusal of this whole passage will convince almost any one but a Muslim that this revelation was delivered after the return from Tabúq to Madína. Note the passive forms in the verses preceding this. Here, however, the revelation purports to have emanated while still absent on the expedition. The resolution of

the first time; sit ye *at home* therefore with those who stay behind. (85) Neither do thou ever pray over any of them who shall die, neither stand at his grave, for that they believed not in GOD and his Apostle, and die in their wickedness. (86) Let not their riches or their children cause thee to marvel; for GOD intendeth only to punish them therewith in this world, and that their souls may depart while they are infidels. (87) When a Sura is sent down, *wherein it is said,* Believe in GOD, and go forth to

---

the Prophet concerning the disaffected is here presented as a revelation from God.

With those who stay behind, viz., the women and children, the sick and infirm.

(85) *Neither do thou ever pray over any of them.* "This passage was also revealed on account of Abdullah Ibn Ubbai. In his last illness he desired to see Muhammad, and, when he was come, asked him to beg forgiveness of God for him, and requested that his corpse might be wrapped up in the garment that was next his body (which might have the same efficacy with the habit of a Franciscan), and that he would pray over him when dead. Accordingly, when he was dead, the Prophet sent his shirt, or inner vestment, to shroud the corpse, and was going to pray over it, but was forbidden by these words. Some say they were not revealed till he had actually prayed for him."—*Sale, Baidháwi.*

But see note above on ver. 81. This command is rigidly observed by all Muslims. All who profess belief "in God and his Apostle" are regarded as orthodox, notwithstanding their immoral character. But those who reject Islám, however holy their lives, are so wicked that even the vilest Muslim may not sully his character for piety by being present at his burial. The words "neither stand at his grave" are understood to prohibit all attendance at the funerals of unbelievers.

Observe that Muhammad practised the old heathen Arab custom of praying for the dead, a practice still current among Muslims, but limited by this verse to prayers for the faithful. The practice is utterly at variance with the teaching of the Qurán and the principles of Islám, but having the example of the Prophet, Muslims feel justified in the practice, as they do in kissing the black stone at Makkah. See note on chap. ii. 196.

(86) *To punish them therewith, i.e.,* by inflicting upon them the care and anxiety which their riches and children bring with them.—*Tafsír-i-Raufi.*

A better interpretation would be that by these very blessings the infidels are wedded to their infidelity, and their final condemnation thereby ensured.

(87) *A Sura.* See introduction to chap. i., and note above on ver. 65. The word here is used as equivalent to any portion of the Qurán containing a message or revelation for the people.

war with his Apostle; those who are in plentiful circumstances among them ask leave of thee *to stay behind*, and say, Suffer us to be *of the number* of those who sit *at home*. (88) They are well pleased to be with those who stay behind, and their hearts are sealed up; wherefore they do not understand. (89) But the Apostle, and those who have believed with him, expose their fortunes and their lives *for God's service;* they shall enjoy the good things *of either life*, and they shall be happy. (90) GOD hath prepared for them gardens through which rivers flow; they shall remain therein *for ever*. This will be great felicity.

‖ (91) And certain Arabs of the desert came to excuse themselves, *praying* that they might be permitted *to stay behind;* and they sat *at home* who had renounced GOD and his Apostle. But a painful punishment shall be inflicted on such of them as believe not. (92) In those who are weak, or are afflicted with sickness, or in those who find not wherewith to contribute *to the war*, it shall be no crime *if they stay at home*, provided they behave themselves faithfully towards GOD and his Apostle. There is no room *to lay blame* on the righteous; for GOD *is* gracious *and* merciful: (93) nor on those unto whom,

---

Suffer us, &c. See above on vers. 82–84.

(90) *They shall remain, &c.* Warring for the faith is here made the reason and ground of salvation, being the test of faith and obedience.

(91) *Certain Arabs of the desert.* "These were the tribes of Asad and Ghatfán, who excused themselves on account of the necessities of their families, which their industry only maintained. But some write they were the family of Amar Ibn al Tufail, who said that if they went with the army, the tribe of Tay would take advantage of their absence, and fall upon their wives and children, and their cattle."—*Sale, Baidháwi.*

(92) This verse defines the classes of Muslims exempt from military service in a holy war or crusade.

Weak, by reason of age or health.

Who find not wherewith to contribute, on account of "their extreme poverty," as those of Juhaina, Muzaina, and Banu Udhra."—*Sale.*

Provided they behave themselves, &c., i.e., do not show contempt for their undertakings, and thus sympathise with their enemies.

when they came unto thee *requesting* that thou wouldest supply them with necessaries for travelling, thou didst answer, I find not wherewith to supply you, returned, their eyes shedding tears for grief that they found not wherewith to contribute *to the expedition.* (94) But there is reason *to blame* those who ask leave of thee *to sit at home,* when they are rich. They are pleased to be with those who stay behind, and GOD hath sealed up their hearts, wherefore they do not understand.

Eleventh Sipara.

|| (95) They will excuse themselves unto you when ye are returned unto them. Say, Excuse not yourselves; we will by no means believe you: GOD hath acquainted us with your behaviour; and GOD will observe his actions, and his Apostle *also:* and hereafter shall ye be brought before him who knoweth that which is hidden and that which is manifest, and he will declare unto you that which ye have done. (96) They will swear unto you by

---

(93) *Eyes shedding tears, &c.* "The persons here intended were seven men of the Ansárs, who came to Muhammad and begged he would give them some patched boots and soled shoes, it being impossible for them to march so far barefoot in such a season; but he told them he could not supply them; whereupon they went away weeping. Some however say these were the Banu Mukrán, and others Abu Musa and his companions."—*Sale, Baidháwi.*

These are honoured in Muslim tradition as *The Weepers* (Al Bakkáím). Compare Judges ii. 1, 5.

(95) *God hath acquainted us.* We are here informed by the author of the Qurán that this revelation was delivered during the expedition to Tabúq, or at least before its return to Madína. Now granting that Muhammad was a prophet indeed, as Muslims do, there is nothing in the statement of the text derogatory to such a character. But those who claim that Muhammad was not an impostor, while denying his prophetic claims, find themselves in trouble here. For if he had no revelation, as is here claimed, how vindicate his honesty and truthfulness? Could he be deluded into a belief like this without being a madman? We think not. Such a plea of madness, if set up in any court of justice, would undoubtedly be set aside as simply incredible. The position of Christian apologists for Islám is unreasonable. If Muhammad were a prophet—and if sincere and honest, as is claimed, he must have been a prophet—the apologists should profess Islám without delay. But if he were not a prophet, he must have been an impostor of no ordinary character.

(96) *They will swear, &c.* The statements of this and the follow-

GOD, when ye are returned unto them, that ye may let them alone. Let them alone, therefore, for they are an abomination, and their dwelling *shall be* hell, a reward for that which they have deserved. (97) They will swear unto you, that ye may be well pleased with them; but if ye be well pleased with them, verily GOD will not be well pleased with people who prevaricate. (98) The Arabs of the desert are more obstinate in *their* unbelief and hypocrisy, and it is easier for them to be ignorant of the ordinances of that which GOD hath sent down unto his Apostle; and GOD *is* knowing *and* wise. (99) Of the Arabs of the desert there is who reckoneth that which he expendeth *for the service of God to be as* tribute, and waiteth that some change *of fortune may befall* you. A change for evil *shall happen* unto them; for GOD *both* heareth *and* knoweth. (100) And of the Arabs of the

---

ing verses purport to be prophecies, which were literally fulfilled shortly after their enunciation. From a Muslim standpoint they are prophecies, but from a Christian standpoint, and from the standpoint of the Christian apologists of Muhammad, they must be regarded as deliberate forgeries, perpetrated by Muhammad on his return from Tabúq or thereabout. As to the matter of the prophecies, there is nothing in them which Muhammad could not have devised or foreseen, even before his return from Tabúq.

(98) *The Arabs of the desert are more obstinate, &c.* "Because of their wild way of life, the hardness of their hearts, their not frequenting people of knowledge, and the few opportunities they have of being instructed."—*Sale, Baidháwi.*

(99) *There is who reckoneth . . . as tribute, i.e.*, "or a contribution exacted by force, the payment of which he can in no wise avoid."—*Sale.*

Waiteth some change, &c. "Hoping that some reverse may afford a convenient opportunity of throwing off the burden."—*Sale.*

The character here given to the Bedouins was substantiated by their universal rebellion on the death of Muhammad. See Muir's *Life of Mahomet*, vol. iv. p. 300.

According to Burckhardt and Palgrave, they still show the same instability, except as they become adherents to the Waháby faith, which Burckhardt calls "the Protestantism, or even Puritanism, of the Muhammadans," whose principle is, "The Korán, and nothing but the Korán."—*Notes on the Bedouins and Wahábys*, vol. i. p. 102.

(100) *Of the Arabs . . . there is who believeth, &c.* "The Arabs meant in the former of these two passages are said to have been the

desert there is who believeth in GOD and in the last day, and esteemeth that which he layeth out *for the service of God* to be the *means of* bringing him near unto GOD and the prayers of the Apostle. Is it not unto them *the means of* a near approach ? GOD shall lead them into his mercy ; for GOD *is* gracious *and* merciful.

|| (101) *As for* the leaders *and* the first of the Muhájjirín and the Ansárs, and those who have followed them in well-doing, GOD is well pleased with them, and they are well pleased in him: and he hath prepared for them gardens watered by rivers; they shall remain therein for ever. This shall be great felicity. (102) And of the Arabs of the desert who *dwell* round about you, *there are* hypocritical persons; and of the inhabitants of Madína *there are some* who are obstinate in hypocrisy. Thou knowest them not, *O Prophet, but* we know them: we

---

tribes of Asad, Ghatfán, and Banu Tamím ; and those intended in the latter, Abdullah, surnamed Dhu'l Bajádín, and his people."—*Sale, Baidháwi.*

That which he layeth out, &c. Expenditure in the holy cause of Islám is here declared to be the ground of acceptance with God. The prayers of the Apostle can only be obtained by loyalty to the same cause. Apparently allusion is made to the prohibition of ver. 85.

(101) *The Muhájjirín and the Ansárs.* "The Muhájjirín, or *refugees,* were those of Makkah who fled thence on account of their religion ; and the Ansárs, or *helpers,* were those of Madína, who received Muhammad and his followers into their protection, and assisted them against their enemies. By the leaders of the Muhájjirín are meant those who believed on Muhammad before the Hijra, or early enough to pray towards Jerusalem, from which the Qiblah was changed to the temple of Makkah in the second year of the Hijra, or else such of them as were present at the battle of Badr. The leaders of the Ansárs were those who took the oath of fidelity to him at al Aqabah, either the first or the second time."—*Sale, Baidháwi.*

(102) *Hypocritical persons, i.e.,* the tribes of Juhaina, Muzaina, Aslam, Ashja, and Ghafár, who dwelt in the neighbourhood of Madína.—*Sale, Baidháwi.*

Thou knowest them not. Many passages like this illustrate Muhammad's marvellous subtlety. If he knew them, he thus endeavoured to conceal the fact. If he did not know them, he would reach them by bringing them under the omniscient eye of God.

will surely punish them twice; afterwards shall they be sent to a grievous torment. (103) And others have acknowledged their crimes. They have mixed a good action with another *which is* bad: peradventure GOD will be turned unto them; for GOD *is* gracious *and* merciful. (104) Take alms of their substance, that thou mayest cleanse them and purify them thereby; and pray for them, for thy prayers shall be a security *of mind* unto them; and GOD *both* heareth *and* knoweth. (105) Do they not know that GOD accepteth repentance from his servants and accepteth alms, and that GOD is easy to be

---

We will punish them twice. "Either by exposing them to public shame and putting them to death; or by either of those punishments and the torment of the sepulchre; or else by exacting alms of them by way of fine, and giving them corporal punishment."—*Sale, Baidháwi.*

(103) *Others have acknowledged their crimes.* "Making no hypocritical excuses for them. These were certain men who, having stayed at home instead of accompanying Muhammad to Tabúq, as soon as they heard the severe reprehensions and threats of this chapter against those who had stayed behind, bound themselves to the pillars of the mosque, and swore that they would not loose themselves till they were loosed by the Prophet. But when he entered the mosque to pray, and was informed of the matter, he also swore that he would not loose them without a particular command from God; whereupon this passage was revealed, and they were accordingly dismissed."—*Sale, Baidháwi.*

Another which is bad. "Though they were backward in going to war, and held with the hypocrites, yet they confessed their crime and repented."—*Sale.*

(104) *Take alms, &c.* "When these persons were loosed, they prayed Muhammad to take their substance, for the sake of which they had stayed at home, as alms, to cleanse them from their transgression; but he told them he had no orders to accept anything from them: upon which this verse was sent down, allowing him to take their alms."—*Sale, Baidháwi.*

Compare Luke xi. 41, where the idea seems to be that the presence in the treasure-house of those things required to be given in alms is defiling to the whole. Here the idea of giving a certain sum in alms in order to expiate crime is certainly intended, and it is here taught that alms confer holiness upon the giver, which accords with a tradition as follows:—"Verily the shade of a believer, and his place of asylum and cause of rest and redemption on the day of resurrection, are from his alms, given in the road to God."—*Mishqát al Musábih*, vol. i. p. 453.

reconciled *and* merciful? (106) Say *unto them*, Work *as ye will;* but GOD will behold your work, and his Apostle *also*, and the true believers; and ye shall be brought before him who knoweth that which is kept secret, and that which is made public; and he will declare unto you whatever ye have done. (107) And *there are* others *who* wait with suspense the decree of GOD, whether he will punish them, or whether he will be turned unto them; but GOD *is* knowing *and* wise. (108) *There are some* who have built a temple to hurt *the faithful*, and to *propagate* infidelity, and to *foment* division among the true believers, and for a lurking-place for him who hath fought against GOD and his Apostle in time past; and they swear, *saying*, Verily, we intended no other than *to do* for the best;

---

(106) *Work*, i.e., see that your works correspond with your profession of repentance.

(107) *Others who wait.* "This verse refers to Káb Ibn Málik, a poet, who had done good service to Mahomet, and to two other believers who had incurred his special displeasure. They had no pretext to offer for their absence from the army, and their bad example had encouraged the hesitating and disaffected citizens in their neglect of the Prophet's summons. These could not with any show of justice be reprimanded or punished if the far more serious offence of those three, his professed followers, were passed over. A ban was therefore placed upon them. They were cut off from all intercourse with the people, and even with their own wives and families. Fifty days passed thus miserably, and the lives of the three men became a burden to them. At length the heart of Mahomet relented, and by the delivery of the revelation (recorded in vers. 118 and 119 below) he received them back into his favour." —*Muir's Life of Mahomet*, vol. iv. p. 197.

(108) *Who have built a temple.* "When Banu Ámru Ibn Auf had built the temple or mosque of Qubá, which will be mentioned by and by, they asked Muhammad to come and pray in it, and he complied with their request. This exciting the envy of their brethren, Banu Ganím Ibn Auf, they also built a mosque, intending that the Imám or priest who should officiate there should be Abu Amír, a Christian monk; but he dying in Syria, they came to Muhammad and desired he would consecrate, as it were, their mosque by praying in it. The Prophet accordingly prepared himself to go with them, but was forbidden by the immediate revelation of this passage, discovering their hypocrisy and ill design: whereupon he sent Málik Ibn al Dukhshum, Maan Ibn Addi, Amír Ibn al Saqan, and al Wahsha, the Ethiopian, to demolish and burn it;

but GOD is witness that they do certainly lie. (109) Stand not *up to pray* therein for ever. *There is* a temple founded on piety, from the first day *of its building.* It is more just that thou stand *up to pray* therein : therein *are* men who

which they performed, and made it a dunghill. According to another account, this mosque was built a little before the expedition of Tabúq, with a design to hinder Muhammad's men from engaging therein ; and when he was asked to pray there, he answered that he was just setting out on a journey, but that when he came back, with God's leave, he would do what they desired ; but when they applied to him again, on his return, this passage was revealed."—*Sale, Jaláluddín.*

A lurking-place for him, &c. "That is, Ábu Amír, the monk, who was a declared enemy to Muhammad, having threatened him at Ohod, that no party should appear in the field against him but he would make one of them ; and, to be as good as his word, he continued to oppose him till the battle of Hunain, at which he was present ; and being put to flight with those of Hawázín, he retreated into Syria, designing to obtain a supply of troops from the Grecian emperor to renew the war ; but he died at Kinnisrín. Others say that this monk was a confederate at the war of the ditch, and that he fled thence into Syria."—*Sale, Jaláluddín.*

(109) *A temple founded on piety,* viz., "that of Qubá, a place about two miles from Madína, where Muhammad rested four days before he entered that city, in his flight from Makkah, and where he laid the foundation of a mosque, which was afterwards built by Banu Amru Ibn Auf. But according to a different tradition, the mosque here meant was that which Muhammad built at Madína."

Men who love to be purified. " Al Baidháwi says that Muhammad, walking once with the Muhájjarín to Qubá, found the Ansárs sitting at the mosque door, and asked them whether they were believers, and, on their being silent, repeated the question ; whereupon Omar answered that they were believers ; and Muhammad demanding whether they acquiesced in the judgment Omar had made of them, they said yes. He then asked them whether they would be patient in adversity and thankful in prosperity, to which they answering in the affirmative, he swore by the Lord of the Kaabah that they were true believers. Afterwards he examined them as to their manner of performing the legal washings, and particularly what they did after easing themselves. They told him that in such a case they used three stones, and after that washed with water ; upon which he repeated these words of the Qurán to them."—*Sale.*

The purity and holiness required by the Qurán is invariably of this character. The traditions relating to purification are simply abominable, and yet they were scrupulously taught to every Muslim woman and to every youth, the Mullah gravely introducing the subject by the statement that *there is no shame in religion.* Thus by striving after ceremonial cleanliness the very fountain of moral purity is polluted.

love to be purified, for GOD loveth the clean. (110) Whether therefore is he better who hath founded his building on the fear of GOD and *his* good-will, or he who hath founded his building on the brink of a bank of earth which is washed away by waters, so that it falleth with him into the fire of hell? GOD directeth not the ungodly people. (111) Their building which they have built will not cease *to be an occasion of* doubting in their hearts, until their hearts be cut in pieces; and GOD *is* knowing *and* wise.

|| (112) Verily GOD hath purchased of the true believers their souls and their substance, *promising* them the enjoyment of Paradise *on condition that* they fight for the cause of GOD: whether they slay or be slain, the promise for the same is assuredly due by the law, and the gospel, and the Qurán; and who performeth his contract more faithfully than GOD? Rejoice therefore in the contract which ye have made. This shall be great happiness. (113) The penitent, *and* those who serve *God* and praise *him, and* who fast, and bow down, and worship, *and* who command that which is just and forbid that which is evil, and keep the ordinances of GOD, *shall likewise be rewarded with Paradise:* wherefore bear good tidings unto the faithful.

---

(110) Compare with the simile used by our Lord in Matt. vii. 24-27.

(111) *Until their hearts be cut in pieces.* "Some interpret these words of their being deprived of their judgment and understanding, and others of the punishment they are to expect, either of death in this world, or of the rack of the sepulchre, or the pains of hell."—*Sale.*

Others refer it to the bitter pangs of conscience. See Rodwell's note *in loco.*

(112) *God hath purchased . . . their souls, i.e.,* "He has been pleased to grant them the joys of Paradise for their meritorious works."—*Tafsír-i-Raufi.*

It would appear that there is a double purchase—the believer's purchase of Paradise by works of merit and God's purchase of believers by the allurements of Paradise. The salvation of a soul here is dependent on its readiness "to fight for the cause of God."

The promise for the same, &c. "God hath purchased the souls of believers; in return they are to enjoy Paradise if they fight for God.

(114) It is not *allowed* unto the Prophet, nor those who are true believers, that they pray for idolaters, although they be of kin, after it is become known unto them that they are inhabitants of hell. (115) Neither did Abraham ask forgiveness for his father, otherwise than in pursuance of a promise which he had promised unto him; but when it became known unto him that he was an enemy unto GOD, he declared himself clear of him. Verily Abraham

---

Conquered or slain, this is promised in the law, the gospel, and the Korán. This verse is perhaps the greatest untruth in the whole of the Korán."—*Brinckman's "Notes on Islám."*

Certainly the statement recorded in this verse has no foundation in truth. The teaching is diametrically opposed to all the doctrine of the Bible. The passage, however, illustrates the ignorance of Muhammad as to Biblical teaching and his unscrupulous habit of bolstering up the doctrines of his Qurán by assertions contrary to truth. Worse than this, these are all put into the mouth of the God of truth.

(114) *It is not allowed . . . to pray for idolaters.* "This passage was revealed, as some think, on account of Abu Tálib, Muhammad's uncle and great benefactor, who, on his deathbed, being pressed by his nephew to speak a word which might enable him to plead his cause before God, that is, to profess Islám, absolutely refused. Muhammad, however, told him that he would not cease to pray for him till he should be forbidden by God—which he was by these words. Others suppose the occasion to have been Muhammad's visiting his mother Amína's sepulchre at al Abwá, soon after the taking of Makkah; for they say that while he stood at the tomb he burst into tears, and said, 'I asked leave of God to visit my mother's tomb, and he granted it me; but when I asked leave to pray for her, it was denied me.'"—*Sale, Baidháwi.*

After it is become known. "By their dying infidels. For otherwise it is not only lawful but commendable to pray for unbelievers, while there are hopes of their conversion."—*Sale.*

The passage clearly teaches that Muslims are permitted to pray for departed friends, provided they were not idolaters. What advantages can accrue to the dead from these prayers is not clear. The Muslim doctors say it secures a mitigation of the punishment of the grave and of the pains to be inflicted on the judgment-day. It has been made the basis of as profitable a business to the Muslim priests as ever Purgatory brought to the priests of Rome.

(115) *A promise,* viz., "To pray that God would dispose his heart to repentance. Some suppose this was a promise made to Abraham by his father, that he would believe in God. For the words may be taken either way."—*Sale.*

Clear of him. "Desisting to pray for him, when he was assured by inspiration that he was not to be converted; or after he actually died an infidel."—*Sale.*

See notes on chap. vi. 77-84.

was pitiful and compassionate. (116) Nor is GOD *disposed* to lead people into error after that he hath directed them, until that which they ought to avoid is become known unto them; for GOD knoweth all things. (117) Verily unto GOD *belongeth* the kingdom of heaven and of earth; he giveth life and he causeth to die; and ye have no patron or helper besides GOD. (118) GOD is reconciled unto the Prophet, and unto the Muhájjirín and the Ansárs, who followed him in the hour of distress, after that it had wanted little but that the hearts of a part of them had swerved *from their duty:* afterwards was he turned unto them, for he *was* compassionate *and* merciful towards

---

Abraham was pitiful, &c. It is here suggested that Abraham's condition and feeling was like that of Muhammad. The passage seems to teach that Abraham's pity and compassion were chiefly manifest before the command of God came forbidding their exercise.

(116) *Nor is God to lead people into error, i.e.,* "To consider or punish them as transgressors. This passage was revealed to excuse those who had prayed for such of their friends as had died idolaters before it was forbidden, or else to excuse certain people who had ignorantly prayed towards the first Qibla, and drank wine, &c."— *Sale.*

Sin, according to most Muslim authorities, is a *conscious act committed against known law,* wherefore sins of ignorance are not numbered in the catalogue of crimes. The "leading into error" mentioned seems to be equivalent to a retributive giving over to reprobation.

(118) *God is reconciled to the Prophet,* &c. "Having forgiven the crime they committed, in giving the hypocrites leave to be absent from the expedition to Tabúq, or for the other sins which they might, through inadvertence, have been guilty of. For the best men have need of repentance."—*Sale, Baidháwi.*

This passage declares Muhammad to have been in fault in permitting those to remain at home who had requested permission to do so. This passage is contrary to the Muslim belief that Muhammad was always inspired. For if so, how err in the matter here reproved? It also animadverts the doctrine of Muhammad's being absolutely sinless. See note on chap. ii. 253.

The hour of distress, viz., "In the expedition of Tabúq, wherein Muhammad's men were driven to such extremities that, besides what they endured by reason of the excessive heat, ten men were obliged to ride by turns on one camel, and provisions and water were so scarce that two men divided a date between them, and they were obliged to drink the water out of the camels' stomachs."—*Sale, Baidháwi.*

them. (119) And *he is* also *reconciled* unto the three who were left behind, so that the earth became too strait for them, notwithstanding its spaciousness, and their souls became straitened within them, and they considered that there was no refuge from GOD, otherwise than *by having recourse* unto him. Then was he turned unto them that they might repent, for GOD *is* easy to be reconciled *and* merciful.

‖ (120) O true believers, fear GOD and be with the sincere. (121) There was no *reason* why the inhabitants of Madína, and the Arabs of the desert who dwell around them, should stay behind the Apostle of GOD, or should prefer themselves before him. This *is unreasonable*, because they are not distressed either by thirst, or labour, or hunger, for the defence of GOD'S true religion; neither do they stir a step which may irritate the unbelievers; neither do they receive from the enemy any damage, but a good

R $\frac{15}{4}$.

---

(119) *The three who were left behind.* "Or, as it may be translated, *who were left in suspense*, whether they should be pardoned or not. These were three Ansárs, named Qáb Ibn Málik, Halál Ibn Umaiya, and Marára Ibn Rabí, who went not with Muhammad to Tabúq, and were therefore, on his return, secluded from the fellowship of the other Muslims, the Prophet forbidding any to salute them or to hold discourse with them; under which interdiction they continued fifty days, till, on their sincere repentance, they were at length discharged from it by the revelation of this passage."—*Sale.*

See note on ver. 106 above.

God is easy to be reconciled. It was Muhammad who was not easy to be reconciled, and yet he deliberately ascribes all he had done to God. Is it possible to believe him sincere in this business? If so, there is no apparent alternative but to regard him as being given over to believe a lie.

(121) *Should prefer themselves before him.* "By not caring to share with him the dangers and fatigues of war. Al Baidháwi tells us, that after Muhammad had set out for Tabúq, one Abu Khaithama, sitting in his garden, where his wife, a very beautiful woman, had spread a mat for him in the shade, and had set new dates and fresh water before him, after a little reflection, cried out, ' This is not well, that I should thus take my ease and pleasure while the Apostle of God is exposed to the scorching of the sunbeams and the inclemencies of the air;' and immediately mounting his camel, took his sword and lance, and went to join the army."—*Sale.*

A good work is written down, &c., i.e., though they sit idly by, so far as the warfare is concerned, yet they receive benefit through the

work is written down unto them for the same; for GOD suffereth not the reward of the righteous to perish. (122) And they contribute not any sum either small or great, nor do they pass a valley; but it is written down unto them that GOD may reward them with a recompense exceeding that which they have wrought. (123) The believers are not *obliged* to go forth *to war* altogether: if a part of every band of them go not forth, *it is* that they may diligently instruct themselves in *their* religion, and may admonish their people when they return unto them, that they may take heed to themselves.

‖ (124) O true believers, wage war against such of the infidels as are near you; and let them find severity in

---

plunder of the infidels, in which they have some participation. The reason for this proceeding is given in the next verse.

(123) *Not obliged to go forth.* "That is, if some of every tribe or town be left behind, the end of their being so left is that they may apply themselves to study, and attain a more exact knowledge of the several points of their religion, so as to be able to instruct such as, by reason of their continual employment in the wars, have no other means of information. They say that after the preceding passages were revealed, reprehending those who had stayed at home during the expedition of Tabúq, every man went to war, so that the study of religion, which is rather more necessary for the defence and propagation of the faith than even arms themselves, became wholly laid aside and neglected; to prevent which for the future a convenient number are hereby directed to be left behind, that they may have leisure to prosecute their studies."—*Sale.*

(124) *Wage war against . . . the infidels.* Arabia now lay at the feet of Muhammad; even foreign conquest had been undertaken with success. For this reason the command to wage war for the faith against all, both far away and near at hand, is now promulgated. The principle of chap. ii. 256 had long since been abandoned, and while the Muslims had hardly grasped the plan of the Prophet during his lifetime, yet the doctrine of a universal conquest of the world for Islám was clearly set forth in the Qurán. Comp. chap. ii. 193, 215, and 244, and notes there.

Such . . . as are near. "Either of your kindred or neighbours; for these claim your pity and care in the first place, and their conversion ought first to be endeavoured. The persons particularly meant in this passage are supposed to have been the Jews of the tribes of Quraidha and Nadhír, and those of Khaibar; or else the Greeks of Syria."—*Sale, Baidháwi.*

It seems best to apply this injunction to the infidels still to be

you: and know that GOD is with those who fear *him*. (125) Whenever a Sura is sent down, there are some of them who say, Which of you hath this caused to increase in faith? It will increase the faith of those who believe, and they shall rejoice: (126) but unto those in whose hearts there is an infirmity it will add *further* doubt unto their *present* doubt; and they shall die in their infidelity. (127) Do they not see that they are tried every year once or twice? yet they repent not, neither are they warned. (128) And whenever a Sura is sent down, they look at one another, *saying*, Doth any one see you? then do they turn aside. GOD shall turn aside their hearts *from the truth;* because they are a people who do not understand. (129) Now hath an apostle come unto you of our own nation, an excellent *person:* it is *grievous* unto him that ye commit wickedness; *he is* careful over you, *and* compassionate and merciful towards the believers.

---

found in Arabia, and especially to the disaffected citizens of Madína, who were now to be dealt with in a different spirit from that shown while Muhammad had reason to fear them.

Let them find severity. Compare this with chap. iii. 160, and see notes there.

(125) The commentators say "the hypocrites were usually known when a crusade was proclaimed," *i.e.*, by their unwillingness to go to the war. A readiness to fight in the cause of Islám had now become the test of faith.

(127) *Tried every year, i.e.*, " by various kinds of trials, or by being called forth to war, and by being made witnesses of God's miraculous protection of the faithful."—*Sale.*

(128) *They look at one another.* "They wink at one another to rise and leave the Prophet's presence, if they think they can do it without being observed, to avoid hearing the severe and deserved reproofs which they apprehend in every new revelation. The persons intended are the hypocritical Muslims."—*Sale.*

(129) *An apostle . . . of our own nation.* See note on chap. iii. 165. This encomium, self-invented, and put into the mouth of God, is hardly consistent with the character of Muhammad as described by the apologists. Perhaps some one of them will undertake to show us how this comports with a character for honest sincerity and prophetic purity.

It is grievous to him that ye commit wickedness. The wickedness grievous to the Arabian Prophet was indifference to his wishes and

(130) If they turn back, say, GOD is my support; there is no GOD but he. On him do I trust; and he is the LORD of the magnificent throne.

---

want of zeal in the crusade against the infidels. It is notable that he was never grieved at the assassination of Káb and the plunder of the Quraish at Nakhla during the sacred months, or the slaughter of eight hundred helpless prisoners in cold blood.

CHAPTER X.

ENTITLED SURAT AL YUNAS (JONAH).

Revealed at Makkah.

INTRODUCTION.

THIS chapter is so called on account of the mention of the Prophet Jonah in ver. 98. It is undoubtedly of Makkan origin. There are some, however, who would assign vers. 41 and 94, or vers. 94-97, or 41-109, or even the whole Sura, to Madína. The only ground for such an opinion seems to be the reference made to the Jews in various parts of the chapter, which Jews are supposed to be of Madína. But, granting that the Jews referred to belonged to Madína, it does not follow that the chapter belongs to Madína, for history proves that for some time previous to the Hijra, Muhammad had intercourse with many of the people of Madína, some of whom were no doubt Jews. A tradition tells of Jews going to Makkah to question the Prophet, which, though in great measure apocryphal, must have had some foundation in fact. However this may be, Muhammad's familiarity with Jewish history and tradition shows that he had Jews among his friends and acquaintance. Certainly the matter of this chapter, as well as the style and animus of discourse, points to Makkah.

Date of the Revelations.

Little can be said as to the date of the revelations. The allusion to the famine in ver. 22 points to a period not far removed from the Hijra; and if what has been said of Muhammad's intercourse with the Jews of Madína be well founded, that fact points to the same period.

Principal Subjects.

	VERSES
The Makkans charge their Prophet with sorcery because he is a man from among them	1, 2
The Creator and Ruler of the universe the only true God	3
Believers rewarded at death for good deeds	4

	VERSES
Unbelievers punished after death	4
God's works are signs to all men	5, 6
Rewards and punishments of the faithful and the unbelieving	7–11
God's purpose in prospering the wicked	12
Men pray to God in affliction, but forget Him with the return of prosperity	13
The people of Makkah warned by the example of former generations	14, 15
The Quraish desire a different Qurán—Muhammad protests his inability to alter it	16–18
Idolaters trust intercessors who can neither profit nor harm them	19
All men originally professed one religion	20
The people demand of Muhammad a sign	21
When men despise the judgments of God he threatens greater suffering	22
Unbelievers remember God in distress by land and sea, but forget Him when delivered	23, 24
Life likened to water which sustains vegetable life	25
Paradise for Muslims and hell for the infidels	26–28
Idolaters will be deserted by their gods in the judgment-day	29–31
Idolaters exhorted to worship him whom they recognise as their Creator, Preserver, and Governor	32–37
The Qurán no forgery; it confirms the former Scriptures	38
Those who charge Muhammad with imposture challenged to produce a chapter like it	39, 40
Some believe in the Qurán, others reject it	41
The unbelieving Quraish declared to be reprobate	42–47
An apostle is sent to every nation	48
Unbelievers mock at the threatenings of their prophet	49
Every nation has its fixed period of existence	50
Infidels will believe when their punishment comes upon them	51–55
God is the Author of life and death	56, 57
The Qurán an admonition and direction to the unbelievers	58, 59
Lawful food not to be prohibited	60, 61
Muhammad ever under Divine guidance	62
The blessedness of those who believe and fear God	63–65
Unbelievers cannot harm the Prophet	66–68
Those rebuked who say that God hath begotten children	69–71
Muhammad likened to Noah and other prophets	72–75
Moses and Aaron sent to Pharaoh and his princes	76
They are rejected as sorcerers and perverters of the national religion	77–82

	VERSES
A few of the people only believe on them	83
Moses and Aaron with the believers put their trust in God	84–86
The Israelites commanded to be constant in prayer to God	87
Moses's prayer, that God would destroy the Egyptians, is heard	88, 89
Pharaoh and his people drowned in the sea	90
He repents and is raised out of the sea for a sign to the people	90–92
The Israelites are provided with a habitation and blessing	93
Jews and Christians appealed to in confirmation of the statements of the Qurán	94, 95
No kind of miracle will suffice to make the reprobate believe	96–98
Infidels do not believe on Muhammad because God does not permit them to do so	99–103
The people of Makkah exhorted to accept the true orthodox faith	104–107
Muhammad not responsible for the faith or unbelief of the people	108
The Prophet exhorted to be patient	109

IN THE NAME OF THE MOST MERCIFUL GOD.

|| (1) AL. R. These are the signs of the wise book. (2) Is it a strange thing unto the men *of Makkah*, that we have revealed *our will* unto a man from among them, *saying*, Denounce threats unto men *if they believe not;* and bear good tidings unto those who believe, that on the merit of their sincerity they have an interest with their LORD? The unbelievers say, This is manifest sorcery. (3) Verily your LORD is GOD, who hath created the heavens and the earth in six days; and then ascended

THIRD MUNZIL.

R 1/6.

---

(1) A. L. R. See Prelim. Disc., pp. 100–102.

(2) *A man from among them.* "And not one of the most powerful among them neither; so that the Quraish said it was a wonder God could find out no other messenger than the orphan pupil of Abu Tálib."—*Sale, Baidháwi.*

This is manifest sorcery. "Meaning the Qurán. According to the reading of some copies, the words may be rendered, 'This man (*i.e.*, Muhammad) is no other than a manifest sorcerer.'"—*Sale.*

(3) *In six days.* See note on chap. vii. 55.

his throne, to take on himself the government of *all* things. There is no intercessor, but by his permission. This is GOD, your LORD; therefore serve him. Will ye not consider? (4) Unto him shall ye all return *according to* the certain promise of GOD; for he produceth a creature and then causeth it to return again: that he may reward those who believe and do that which is right, with equity. But as for the unbelievers, they shall drink boiling water, and *they shall suffer* a grievous punishment for that they have disbelieved. (5) It is he who hath ordained the sun to shine *by day*, and the moon for a light *by night;* and had appointed her stations, that ye might know the number of years, and the computation *of time*. GOD hath not created this, but with truth. He explaineth *his* signs unto people who understand. (6) Moreover in the vicissitudes of night and day, and whatever GOD hath created in heaven and earth, are surely signs unto men who fear *him*. (7) Verily they who hope not to meet us *at the last day*, and delight in this present life, and rest securely in the same, and who are negligent of our signs: (8) their dwelling shall be *hell-*fire, for that which they have deserved. (9) But as to those who believe, and work righteousness, their LORD will direct them because of their faith; they shall have rivers flowing through gardens of pleasure. (10) Their prayer therein *shall be* Praise be unto thee, O GOD! and their salutation therein *shall be* Peace! (11)

No intercessor, but &c. "These words were revealed to refute the foolish opinion of the idolatrous Makkans, who imagined their idols were intercessors with God for them."—*Sale*. See notes on chap. ii. 47, 123, 254; vi. 50.

(4) *Boiling water.* See chap. ii. 38.

(5) *But with truth, i.e.*, to manifest the truth of the Divine unity. The Makkan preacher here sets forth God the Creator as the true object of worship.

(7) *Who hope not to meet us, i.e.*, the Quraish, who strenuously denied the doctrine of bodily resurrection.

(9) *Believe and work righteousness.* See note on chap. ii. 25, 223; and chap. iii. 15.

(10) *Their salutation.* "Either the mutual salutation of the blessed to one another, or that of the angels to the blessed."—*Sale.*

and the end of their prayer *shall be*, Praise be unto GOD, the LORD of all creatures!

|| (12) If GOD should cause evil to hasten unto men, R $\frac{2}{7}$. according to their desire of hastening good, verily their end had been decreed. Wherefore we suffer those we hope not to meet us *at the resurrection* to wander amazedly in their error. (13) When evil befalleth a man, he prayeth unto us *lying* on his side, or sitting, or standing; but when we deliver him from his affliction, he continueth *his former course of life*, as though he had not called upon us *to defend him* against the evil which had befallen him. Thus was that which the transgressors committed prepared for them. (14) We have formerly destroyed the generations *who were* before you, O men of *Makkah*, when they had acted unjustly, and our apostles had come unto them with evident *miracles* and they would not believe. Thus do we reward the wicked people. (15) Afterwards did we cause you to succeed them in the earth, that we might see how ye would act. (16) When our evident signs are recited unto them, they who hope not to meet us *at the resurrection*, say, Bring a different Qurán from this; or make some change therein. Answer, It is not *fit* for me that I should change it at my pleasure: I follow that only which is revealed unto me. Verily I fear, if I should be disobedient unto my LORD, the punishment of the great day. (17) Say, if GOD had so pleased, I had not read it unto you, neither had I taught you the same.

---

(11) Compare the Revelation, chap. iv. 8, and v. 11-13.
(13) See notes on chap. ii. 15, 16.
(13) *Prayeth . . . on his side or sitting, &c.*, *i.e.*, "in all postures and at all times."—*Sale*. The *Tafsír-i-Raufi* informs us that allusion is here made to the great famine which visited Makkah shortly before the Hijra. See below on ver. 23.
(15) The allusion is to the prosperity succeeding the famine referred to in note on preceding verse.
(16) *Bring a different Qurán*, *i.e.*, instead of denouncing threatenings against us, bring us a message of mercy.—*Tafsír-i-Raufi*.
Not fit that I should change it. "The changes or abrogations of the Koran do not contradict this verse, as Muhammad says God is the Author of them."—*Brinckman's "Notes on Islám."*

I have already dwelt among you to the age *of forty years*, before *I received it*. Do ye not therefore understand? (18) And who is more unjust than he who deviseth a lie against GOD, or accuseth his signs of falsehood? Surely the wicked shall not prosper. (19) They worship besides GOD that which can neither hurt them or profit them, and they say, These are our intercessors with GOD. Answer, Will ye tell GOD that which he knoweth not, neither in

---

(17) *To the age.* Rodwell translates literally "for years." Sale's addition "of forty years" is, however, correct. "For so old was Muhammad before he took upon him to be a prophet; during which time his fellow-citizens well knew that he had not applied himself to learning of any sort, nor frequented learned men, nor had ever exercised himself in composing verses or orations, whereby he might acquire the art of rhetoric or elegance of speech (Prelim. Disc., p. 73). A flagrant proof, says al Baidháwi, that this book could be taught him by none but God."

This view, however, does not agree with what is recorded of his previous career. Is it likely that he should have been trained in the same household with Ali, who knew both how to read and write, and not have received similar instruction? Could he have conducted an important mercantile business for years without some knowledge of letters? That he could read and write in later years is certain. Tradition tells us he said to Muáwia, one of his secretaries, "Draw the ب straight, divide the س properly," &c., and that in his last moments he called for writing materials. The question arises, When did he acquire this art? The commentators say that God gave him the power, as he did his inspiration, and they quote chap. xcvi. 4, one of the earliest verses of the Qurán, in proof. Certainly that verse seems to teach clearly that he could write as well as read, though it by no means teaches that he had not received the knowledge of both beforehand, or that he did not receive it in the ordinary way. His use of amanuenses does not militate against his knowledge of the art of writing, for such use of amanuenses was common in that age, even among the most learned. But still there remains the testimony of many traditions and the almost universal belief of Muhammadans. How account for this? I am inclined to think it originated with a misunderstanding of Muhammad's repeated claim that he was the "Illiterate Prophet," or rather the "Prophet of the Illiterate," the term "illiterate" being generally applied by the Jews to the Arabs. See notes on chap. v. 85, 86. This misunderstanding turned out to the furtherance of Muhammad's claims, inasmuch as the miracle of the matchless style of the Qurán was enhanced by the consideration that the Prophet was illiterate. On the whole, we think there is very good reason for believing Muhammad to have been acquainted with the art of both reading and writing from an early period in his life.

(19) *These are our intercessors.* See Prelim. Disc., p. 36.

heaven nor in earth? Praise be unto him! and far be that from him which they associate *with him!* (20) Men were professors of one religion only, but they dissented *therefrom;* and if a decree had not previously issued from thy LORD *deferring their punishment,* verily the *matter* had been decided between them, concerning which they disagreed. (21) They say, Unless a sign be sent down unto him from his LORD *we will not believe.* Answer, Verily that which is hidden *is known* only unto GOD: wait, therefore, *the pleasure of God;* and I also will wait with you.

|| (22) And when we caused the men *of Makkah* to taste R $\frac{3}{8}$. mercy, after an affliction which had befallen them, behold, they *devised* a stratagem against our signs. Say *unto them,* GOD is more swift in *executing* a stratagem *than ye.* Verily our messengers write down that which

---

That which he knoweth not, viz., "That he hath equals or companions either in heaven or on earth, since he acknowledgeth none."—*Sale.*

(20) *One religion only.* "That is to say, the true religion, or Islám, which was generally professed, as some say, till Abel was murdered, or, as others, till the days of Noah. Some suppose the first ages after the Flood are here intended; others, the state of religion in Arabia from the time of Abraham to that of Amru Ibn Luhai, the great introducer of idolatry into that country."—*Sale.*

(21) *Unless a sign be sent, &c.* This verse shows that as yet Muhammad wrought no miracle; but he seems to have expected to receive the power to do so. At least this seems to be the best interpretation of the following sentence:—"Wait, therefore, and I also will wait with you."

(22) *After an affliction.* This affliction is described by the commentators as a famine, yet there is no tradition giving any satisfactory account of it. The repeated references to it in the Qurán prove that some kind of affliction did occur, which Muhammad declared to be due to the Divine vengeance against the wickedness of the Quraish. See chaps. vii. 95, and xxiii. 77-79. See Muir's *Life of Mahomet,* vol. ii. p. 227. Sale, on the authority of Baidháwi says, "That they were afflicted with a dearth for seven years, so that they were very near perishing; but no sooner relieved by God's sending them plenty, than they began again to charge Muhammad with imposture, and to ridicule his revelations."

Our messengers, i.e., "guardian angels."—*Sale.* "The two recording angels called the *Mua'qqibát,* or the angels who continually succeed each other, who record the good and evil actions of a man, one standing at his right hand and another on his left."—*Hughes, Notes on Muhammadanism,* p. 82.

ye deceitfully devise. (23) It is he who hath given you conveniences for travelling by land and by sea; so that ye be in ships, which sail with them, with a favourable wind, and they rejoice therein. *And when* a tempestuous wind overtaketh them, and waves come upon them from every side, and they think themselves encompassed *with inevitable dangers*, they call upon GOD, exhibiting the pure religion unto him, *and saying*, Verily if thou deliver us from this *peril*, we will be of those who give thanks. (24) But when he hath delivered them, behold, they behave themselves insolently in the earth, without justice. O men, verily the violence which ye commit against your own souls *is for the* enjoyment of this present life only; afterwards unto us shall ye return, and we will declare unto you that which ye have done. (25) Verily the likeness of this present life is no other than as water, which we send down from heaven, and wherewith the productions of the earth are mixed, of which men eat, and cattle *also*, until the earth receive its vesture, and be adorned *with various plants:* the inhabitants thereof imagine that they have power over the same; *but* our command cometh unto it by night or by day, and we render it *as though it had been* mowen, as though it had not yesterday abounded *with fruits*. Thus do we explain *our* signs unto people who consider. (26) GOD inviteth unto the dwelling of peace, and directeth whom he pleaseth into the right way. (27) They who do right shall *receive* a most excellent *reward*, and a superabundant addition; neither blackness

---

(23) *Exhibiting the pure religion.* "That is, applying themselves to God only, and neglecting their idols; their fears directing them in such an extremity to ask help of him only who could give it."—*Sale.*
Compare with this verse Psalm cvii. 23-31.
(26) *Dwelling of peace* = Paradise; and *right way* = Islám. See chap. vi. 126, 127.
(27) *Superabundant addition.* "For their reward will vastly exceed the merit of their good works. Al Ghazáli supposes this *additional recompense* will be the beatific vision."—*Sale.* Prelim. Disc., p. 159.
Neither blackness. See Prelim. Disc., p. 149.

nor shame shall cover their faces. These *shall be* the inhabitants of Paradise; they shall continue therein *for ever*. (28) But they who commit evil *shall* receive the reward of evil, equal thereunto, and they shall be covered with shame (*for* they shall have no protector against GOD); as though their faces were covered with the profound darkness of the night. These shall be the inhabitants of *hell*-fire: they shall remain therein *for ever*. (29) On the day *of the resurrection* we will gather them altogether; then will we say unto the idolaters, *Get ye* to your place, ye and your companions: and we will separate them from one another; and their companions will say *unto them*, Ye do not worship us; (30) and GOD is a sufficient witness between us and you; neither did we mind your worshipping *of us*. (31) There shall every soul experience that which it shall have sent before it; and they shall be brought before GOD their true LORD; and the *false deities* which they vainly imagined shall disappear from before them.

NISF.

‖ (32) Say, Who provideth you food from heaven and R 4/9.

---

(28) *Equal thereunto,* "*i.e.*, though the blessed will be rewarded beyond their deserts, yet God will not punish any beyond their demerits, but treat them with the exactest justice."—*Sale.*

But what kind of justice is that which rewards beyond merit? See ver. 27. Is not this view of God's justice accountable for the perverted ideas of justice prevalent in Muslim countries, where the most trifling services are reckoned as deserving munificent rewards?

(29) *Companions, i.e.,* idols or inferior deities worshipped by the Quraish.

Ye do not worship us. "But ye really worshipped your own lusts, and were seduced to idolatry, not by us, but by your own superstitious fancies. It is pretended that God will, at the last day, enable the idols to speak, and that they will thus reproach their worshippers, instead of interceding for them, as they hoped. Some suppose the angels, who were also objects of the worship of the pagan Arabs, are particularly intended in this place."—*Sale.*

(31) *Every soul shall experience.* "Some copies, instead of *tablu,* read *tatlu, i.e., shall follow* or *meditate upon.*"—*Sale.*

That which it shall have sent before it. See note on chap. ii. 94.

(32–37) This passage contains very cogent reasoning against the idolaters, and very justly represents their folly in worshipping inferior deities, while regarding God as the source of all their blessings,

earth? or who hath the absolute power over the hearing
and the sight? and who bringeth forth the living from
the dead, and bringeth forth the dead from the living?
and who governeth *all* things? They will surely answer,
GOD. Say, Will ye not therefore fear *him?* (33) This is
therefore GOD your true LORD: and what *remaineth there*
after truth except error? How therefore are ye turned
aside *from the truth?* (34) Thus is the word of thy LORD
verified upon them who do wickedly; that they believe
not. (35) Say, Is there any of your companions who
produceth a creature, and then causeth it to return *unto
himself?* Say, GOD produceth a creature, and then causeth
it to return *unto himself.* How therefore are ye turned
aside *from his worship?* (36) Say, Is there any of your
companions who directeth unto the truth? Say, GOD
directeth unto the truth. Whether is he, therefore, who
directeth unto the truth more worthy to be followed, or
he who directeth not, unless he be directed? What aileth
you therefore, that ye judge as ye do? (37) And the
greater part of them follow an *uncertain* opinion only; but
a *mere* opinion attaineth not unto any truth. Verily GOD
knoweth that which they do. (38) This Qurán could not
have been composed by *any* except GOD; but *it is* a confirmation of that which was *revealed* before it, and an

---

and fleeing to him in every time of trouble. These teachings
account for much of the success of Islám as a missionary religion.
Its pure monotheism stands out in strong contrast with the polytheism of the idolaters.

(38) *The Qurán could not have been composed by any except God.*
"No reason is given why none other but God could have composed
it. In the next verse Muhammad declares the interpretation of the
Koran had not come to the people he reproves: if, then, they did
not understand it, how could they judge if it was miraculous?
If it was 'dark sentences to them,' their saying was true that the
verses were meaningless, jangling rhymes."—*Brinckman's* "*Notes on
Islam.*" See also notes on chaps. ii. 23, and vi. 93.

A confirmation of that which was revealed before it. This passage
explicitly declares the former Scriptures to be the Word of God. It
also claims that the Qurán explains these Scriptures. If, therefore, it
fails to fulfil its own claims, it thereby proves itself a forgery.

explanation of the scripture; there is no doubt thereof; *sent down* from the LORD of all creatures. (39) Will they say, *Muhammad* hath forged it? Answer, Bring therefore a chapter like unto it; and call whom you may *to your assistance*, besides GOD, if ye speak truth. (40) But they have charged that with falsehood, the knowledge whereof they do not comprehend, neither hath the interpretation thereof come unto them. In the same manner did those who were before them accuse *their prophets* of imposture; but behold, what was the end of the unjust! (41) There are some of them who believe therein; and there are some of them who believe not therein: and thy LORD well knoweth the corrupt doers.

|| (42) If they accuse thee of imposture, say, I have R $\frac{5}{10}$. my work and ye have your work; ye shall be clear of that which I do, and I will be clear of that which ye do. (43) There are some of them who hearken unto thee; but wilt thou make the deaf to hear, although they do not understand? (44) And there are some of them who look at thee; but wilt thou direct the blind, although they see not? (45) Verily GOD will not deal unjustly with men

---

(39) *Will they say Muhammad hath forged it?* The charge of imposture is as old as Muhammad's prophetic claims. In reply he gave no better proof of his sincerity than that of this verse. On this claim see chaps. ii. 23 and vi. 93.

(40) *In the same manner, &c.* Muhammad here likens himself to the former prophets. But unfortunately for the likeness, it is not true. The former prophets, as a class, were not charged with imposture.

(41) *Some . . . who believe, &c., i.e.,* "There are some of them who are inwardly well satisfied of the truth of thy doctrine, though they are so wicked as to oppose it; and there are others of them who believe it not, through prejudice and want of consideration. Or the passage may be understood in the future tense, of some who should afterwards believe and repent, and of others who should die infidels." —*Sale, Baidhàwi.*

(42) See note on chap. iii. 185.

(44) *Although they see not.* "These words were revealed on account of certain Makkans, who seemed to attend while Muhammad read the Qurán to them or instructed them in any point of religion, but yet were as far from being convinced or edified, as if they had not heard him at all."—*Sale.*

in any respect: but men deal unjustly with their own souls. (46) On a certain day he will gather them together, as though they had not tarried above an hour of a day; they shall know one another. Then shall they perish who have denied the meeting of GOD; and were not *rightly* directed. (47) Whether we cause thee to see a part of *the punishment* wherewith we have threatened them, or whether we cause thee to die *before thou see it;* unto us shall they return: then *shall* GOD *be* witness of that which they do. (48) Unto every nation *hath* an apostle *been sent;* and when their apostle came, *the matter* was decided between them with equity; and they were not treated unjustly. (49) *The unbelievers* say, When *will* this threatening *be made good*, if ye speak truth? (50) Answer, I am able neither to procure advantage unto myself, nor to avert mischief *from me*, but as GOD pleaseth. Unto every nation is fixed term *decreed;* when their term therefore is expired, they shall not have respite for an hour, neither shall *their punishment* be anticipated. (51) Say, Tell me, if the punishment of GOD overtake you by night or by day, what *part* thereof will the ungodly

---

(45) *Men deal unjustly, &c.* "For God deprives them not of their senses or understanding; but they corrupt and make an ill use of them."—*Sale.*

(46) *As though they had not tarried, &c.* This passage, which alludes to the resurrection, teaches that death is a sleep from which men shall awaken as though they had slept but an hour.

They shall know one another, "as if it were but a little while since they parted. But this will happen during the first moments only of the resurrection, for afterwards the terror of the day will disturb and take from them all knowledge of one another."—*Sale.*

(48) See notes on chap. vi. 41. This idea was borrowed from the Jews.

With equity. "By delivering the Prophet and those who believed on him, and destroying the obstinate infidels."—*Sale.*

How far this is from the truth the reader need not be told.

(50) *When their term is expired, &c.* The doctrine of the decrees as here set forth carries with it a strong bent towards fatalism. But see note on chap. iii. 145.

Their punishment. This insertion is an error. The word *it*, meaning *the fixed time*, would convey the meaning of the original.

(51) *By night or by day, i.e.*, sudden and unexpected. The infi-

wish to be hastened? (52) When it falleth *on you*, do ye then believe it? Now *do ye believe, and wish it far from you*, when as ye formerly desired it should be hastened? (53) Then shall it be said unto the wicked, Taste the punishment of eternity ; would ye receive *other* than the reward of that which ye have wrought? (54) They will desire to know of thee whether this be true. Answer, Yea, by my LORD, it is certainly true; neither shall ye weaken *God's power so as to escape it*.

|| (55) Verily, if every soul which hath acted wickedly had whatever is on the earth, it would *willingly* redeem itself therewith *at the last day*. Yet they will conceal *their* repentance, after they shall have seen the punishment ; and *the matter* shall be decided between them with equity, and they shall not be unjustly treated. (56) Doth not whatsoever is in heaven and on earth *belong* unto GOD? Is not the promise of GOD true ? But the greater part of them know *it* not. (57) He giveth life, and he causeth to die ; and unto him shall ye *all* return. (58) O men, now hath an admonition come unto you from your LORD, and a remedy for the *doubts* which are in *your* breasts; and a direction and mercy unto the true believers. (59) Say, Through the grace of GOD and his mercy ; therein therefore let them rejoice ; this will be better than what they heap together *of worldly riches*.

R $\frac{6}{11}$.

---

dels had said they did not believe in the threatened judgments of Muhammad's revelation, and had defiantly declared their wish for it to come upon them at once."—*Tafsír-i-Raufi.*

(55) *They will conceal their repentance.* "To hide their shame and regret, or because their surprise and astonishment will deprive them of the use of speech. Some, however, understand the verb which is here rendered *will conceal* in the contrary signification, which it sometimes bears ; and then it must be translated, 'They will openly declare their repentance,' &c."—*Sale, Jaláluddín, Baidháwi.*

Rodwell translates, "they will proclaim their repentance."

(57) This is said in proof of the doctrine of the resurrection and judgment which the Quraish so strenuously rejected.

(58) *An admonition, i.e.*, the Qurán. How it could be "a remedy for the doubts" of the Quraish is not very evident, seeing "the interpretation" had not yet come to them. See ver. 38.

CHAP. X.]   (334)   [SIPARA XI.

(60) Say, Tell me, of that which GOD hath sent down unto you for food, have ye declared *part to be* lawful, and *other part to be* unlawful? Say, Hath GOD permitted you to *make this distinction?* or do ye devise *a lie* concerning GOD? (61) But what will be the opinion of those who devise a lie concerning GOD on the day of the resurrection? Verily GOD is endued with beneficence towards mankind; but the greater part of them do not give thanks.

R 7/12.

|| (62) Thou shalt be *engaged* in no business, neither shalt thou be *employed* in meditating on *any passage* of the Qurán; nor shall ye do any action, but we will be witnesses over you, when ye are employed therein. Nor is so much as the weight of an ant hidden from thy LORD in earth or in heaven: neither *is there anything* lesser than that, or greater, but it is *written* in the Perspicuous Book. (63) Are not the friends of GOD *the persons* on whom no fear shall come, and who shall not be grieved? (64) They who believe and fear *God*, (65) shall receive good tidings in this life and in that which is to come. There is no change in the words of GOD. This *shall be* great felicity. (66) Let not their discourse grieve thee; for all might *belongeth* unto GOD: he *both* heareth *and* knoweth. (67) Is not whoever *dwelleth* in heaven and on earth *subject* unto GOD? What therefore do they follow who invoke idols besides GOD? They follow nothing but a *vain*

---

(60) *Food . . . lawful and unlawful.* See chap. vi. 118, 119.

(61) *Tafsír-i-Raufi* paraphrases as follows: "And thou, O my beloved, art not in any condition, nor readest thou aught of the divine Qurán; nor do ye, O men, any work, but we are present with you in the day ye begin it."

This is one of the few passages of the Qurán which teach the omnipresence of God.

Weight of an ant. See chap. iv. 39, and note there.

Perspicuous Book. "The Preserved Table whereon God's decrees are recorded."—*Sale.*

(65) *No change in the words of God, i.e.,* his promises are sure.

(66) *Their discourse,* viz., "the impious and rebellious talk of the infidels."—*Sale.*

opinion; and they only utter lies. (68) It is he who hath ordained the night for you, that you may take your rest therein, and the clear day *for labour:* verily herein are signs unto people who hearken. (69) They say, GOD hath begotten children: GOD forbid! He is self-sufficient. Unto him *belongeth* whatsoever is in heaven and on earth: ye have no demonstrative proof of this. Do ye speak of GOD that which ye know not? (70) Say, Verily, they who imagine a lie concerning GOD shall not prosper. (71) *They may enjoy* a provision in this world; but afterwards unto us shall they return, and we will then cause them to taste a grievous punishment, for that they were unbelievers.

|| (72) Rehearse unto them the history of Noah, when he said unto his people, O my people, if my standing forth *among you,* and my warning *you* of the signs of GOD, be grievous unto you, in GOD do I put my trust. Therefore lay your design *against me,* and assemble your false gods; but let not your design be *carried on* by you *in* the dark: then come forth against me, and delay not. (73) And if ye turn aside *from my admonitions,* I ask not any reward of you *for the same;* I expect my reward from GOD alone, and I am commanded to be *one* of those who are resigned *unto him.* (74) But they accused him of imposture, wherefore we delivered him, and those who *were* with him in the ark, and we caused them to survive *the flood,* but we drowned those who charged our signs with falsehood. Behold, therefore, what was the end of those who were warned *by Noah.* (75) Then did we send, after him,

SULS.

R $\frac{8}{13}$.

---

(69) *God hath begotten children.* This is said of the Quraish. Compare chap. vi. 101. The opinion of the idolaters here combated no doubt exercised an influence in leading Muhammad to reject the doctrine of the sonship of Christ.

(71) *A provision in this world.* Alluding to the prosperity of the infidel Quraish.

(72) *The history of Noah.* See chap. vii. 60.

(73) *I ask not any reward from you.* "Therefore, ye cannot excuse yourselves by saying that I am burdensome to you."—*Sale.*

(75) *Then did we send . . . apostles.* "As Húd, Sálih, Abraham,

apostles unto their *respective* people, and they came unto them with evident demonstrations: yet they were not *disposed* to believe in that which they had before rejected as false. Thus do we seal up the hearts of the transgressors. (76) Then did we send, after them, Moses and Aaron unto Pharaoh and his princes with our signs: but they behaved proudly, and were a wicked people. (77) And when the truth from us had come unto them, they said, Verily this is manifest sorcery. (78) Moses said *unto them*, Do ye speak *this* of the truth, after it hath come unto you? Is this sorcery? but sorcerers shall not prosper. (79) They said, Art thou come unto us to turn us aside from that *religion* which we found our fathers practise, and that ye two may have the command in the land? But we do not believe you. (80) And Pharaoh said, Bring unto me every expert magician. And when the magicians were come, Moses said unto them, Cast down that which ye are about to cast down. (81) And when they had cast down *their rods and cords*, Moses said *unto them*, The enchantment which ye have performed shall GOD surely render vain; for GOD prospereth not the work of the wicked doers; (82) and GOD will verify the truth of his words, although the wicked be adverse *thereto*.

R $\frac{9}{14}$.

‖ (83) And there believed not *any* on Moses, except a generation of his people, for fear of Pharaoh and of his

---

Lot, and Shuaib, to those of Ád, Thamúd, Babel, Sodom, and Midian."—*Sale*.

(76) *Moses and Aaron, &c.* See notes on chap. vii. 104, &c.

(77) *Sorcery*. According to the Qurán, the charges made against the former prophets were of a kind with those made by the Quraish against Muhammad. This constant effort of Muhammad, everywhere visible in the Qurán, does not well accord with the conduct of the prophets to whom he likened himself.

(79) *To turn us aside, &c.* Here again the Qurán contradicts Holy Writ. Moses and Aaron are nowhere in the Bible set forth as apostles sent for the conversion of the Egyptians to the true faith. Nor is there any reason to believe that Pharaoh regarded Moses and Aaron as usurpers striving to obtain "the command of the land."

(83) *Except a generation*. "For when he first began to preach, a few of the younger Israelites only believed in him; the others not

princes, lest he should afflict them. And Pharaoh was lifted up with pride in the earth, and was surely *one* of the transgressors. (84) And Moses said, O my people, if ye believe in GOD, put your trust in him, if ye be resigned *to his will*. (85) They answered, We put our trust in GOD: O LORD, suffer us not to be afflicted by unjust people; (86) but deliver us, through thy mercy, from the unbelieving people. (87) And we spake by inspiration unto Moses and his brother, *saying*, Provide habitations for your people in Egypt, and make your houses a place of worship, and be constant at prayer; and bear good news unto the true believers. (88) And Moses said, O LORD, verily thou hast given unto Pharaoh and his people *pompous* ornaments and riches in this present life, O LORD, that they may be seduced from thy way: O LORD, bring their riches to nought, and harden their hearts; that they may not believe, until they see *their* grievous punishment.

---

giving ear to him for fear of the king. But some suppose the pronoun *his* refers to Pharaoh, and that these were certain Egyptians who, together with his wife Asia, believed in Moses."—*Sale, Baidháwi.*

The allusion may be to the magicians, who are said to have been converted to the faith of Moses and Aaron. See chap. vii. 121-127. Arnold thinks the allusion is to the Israelites (*Islám and Christianity,* p. 139). The succeeding verses seem to justify this view.

(87) *Make your houses a place of worship.* "So Jaláluddín expounds the original word Qibla, which properly signifies that place or quarter towards which one prays. Wherefore al Zamakhsharí supposes that the Israelites are here ordered to dispose their oratories in such a manner that, when they prayed, their faces might be turned towards Makkah, which he imagines was the Qibla of Moses, as it is that of the Muhammadans. The former commentator adds that Pharaoh had forbidden the Israelites to pray to God, for which reason they were obliged to perform that duty privately in their houses."—*Sale.*

It is more likely that the allusion is to the Passover feast. Abdul Qádir says that the Israelites were made to occupy a special quarter of the city so as to escape the judgments about to come on Pharaoh.

(88) *Pompous ornaments.* "As magnificent apparel, chariots, and the like."—*Sale.*

Harden their hearts. This statement also contradicts the Pentateuch.

Your petition is heard. "The pronoun is in the dual number; the antecedent being Moses and Aaron. The commentators say that, in consequence of this prayer, all the treasures of Egypt were turned into stones."—*Sale, Jaláluddín.*

(89) *God* said, Your petition is heard; be ye upright, therefore, and follow not the way of those who are ignorant. (90) And we caused the children of Israel to pass through the sea: and Pharaoh and his army followed them in a violent and hostile manner; until, when he was drowning, he said, I believe that there is no GOD but he on whom the children of Israel believe; and I am *one* of the resigned. (91) Now *dost thou believe*, when thou hast been hitherto rebellious, and one of the wicked doers? (92) This day will we raise thy body *from the bottom of the sea*, that thou mayest be a sign unto those who shall be after thee; and verily a great number of men are negligent of our signs.

‖ (93) And we prepared for the children of Israel an established dwelling *in the land of Canaan*, and we provided good things for their sustenance; and they differed not *in point of religion* until knowledge had come unto them; verily thy LORD will judge between them on the

---

Be ye upright. "Or, as al Baidháwi interprets it, Be ye constant and steady in preaching to the people. The Muhammadans pretend that Moses continued in Egypt no less than forty years after he had first published his mission, which cannot be reconciled to Scripture." —*Sale*.

(90) *I am one of the resigned.* "These words, it is said, Pharaoh repeated often in his extremity that he might be heard. But his repentance came too late; for Gabriel soon stopped his mouth with mud lest he should obtain mercy, reproaching him at the same time in the words which follow."—*Sale*.

This is a vague rendering of the Jewish legend that Pharaoh repented and was forgiven, and that he was raised from the dead, in accordance with Exod. ix. 15, 16. See Rodwell *in loco*, and Arnold's *Islám and Christianity*, p. 140.

(92) *We will raise thy body.* "Some of the children of Israel doubting whether Pharaoh was really drowned, Gabriel, by God's command, caused his naked corpse to swim to shore that they might see it (cf. Exod. xiv. 30). The word here translated *body*, signifying also a *coat of mail*, some imagine the meaning to be that his corpse floated armed with his coat of mail, which they tell us was of gold, by which they knew that it was he."—*Sale*.

(93) *Until knowledge, &c., i.e.,* "until the law had been revealed and published by Moses."—*Sale*. It seems to me the *knowledge* intended here is that of the Qurán, and the allusion is to the rejection of Muhammad by the Jews, though some were questioning whether he were not a prophet, and perhaps even believing him to be such. See Muir's *Life of Mahomet*, vol. ii. p. 183.

day of resurrection concerning that wherein they disagreed. (94) If thou art in doubt concerning *any part of* that which we have set down unto thee, ask them who have read the book *of the law* before thee. Now hath the truth come unto thee from thy LORD; be not therefore *one* of those who doubt; (95) neither be thou *one* of those who charge the signs of GOD with falsehood, lest thou become *one* of those who perish. (96) Verily those against whom the word of thy LORD is decreed shall not believe, (97) although there come unto them every *kind of* miracle, until they see the grievous punishment *prepared for them.* (98) And if *it were* not *so*, some city, *among the many which have been destroyed*, would have believed; and the faith of its *inhabitants* would have been of advantage unto them; *but none of them believed, before the execution of their sentence*, except the people of Jonas. When they believed, we delivered them from the punishment of shame in this world, and suffered them to enjoy

---

(94) *If thou art in doubt . . . ask, &c.* "That is, concerning the truth of the histories which are here related. The commentators doubt whether the person here spoken be Muhammad himself, or his auditor."—*Sale.*

This passage clearly confirms the Scriptures current in the days of Muhammad. See note on chap. vi. 93.

(98) *Except the people of Jonas*, viz., "the inhabitants of Ninive, which stood on or near the place where al Mausal now stands. This people having corrupted themselves with idolatry, Jonas, the son of Mattai (or Amittai, which the Muhammadans suppose to be the name of his mother), an Israelite of the tribe of Benjamin, was sent by God to preach to and reclaim them. When he first began to exhort them to repentance, instead of hearkening to him, they used him very ill, so that he was obliged to leave the city, threatening them, at his departure, that they should be destroyed within three days, or, as others say, within forty. But when the time drew near, and they saw the heavens overcast with a black cloud, which shot forth fire and filled the air with smoke, and hung directly over their city, they were in a terrible consternation, and getting into the fields with their families and cattle, they put on sackcloth and humbled themselves before God, calling aloud for pardon, and sincerely repenting of their past wickedness. Whereupon God was pleased to forgive them, and the storm blew over."—*Sale, Baidháwi, Jaláluddín.*

their lives and possessions for a time. (99) But if thy LORD had pleased, verily all who are in the earth would have believed in general. Wilt thou therefore forcibly compel men to be true believers? (100) No soul can believe but by the permission of GOD; and he shall pour out *his* indignation on those who will not understand. (101) Say, Consider whatever is in heaven and on earth: but signs are of no avail, neither preachers unto people who will not believe. (102) Do they therefore expect any other than *some terrible judgment,* like unto the judgments *which have fallen* on those who have gone before them? Say, Wait ye *the issue;* and I also will wait with you; (103) then will we deliver our apostles and those who believe. Thus is it a justice due from us that we should deliver the true believers.

‖ (104) Say, O men *of Makkah,* if ye be in doubt concerning my religion, verily I worship not the *idols* which ye worship, besides GOD; but I worship GOD, who will

---

For a time. Sale says, "Until they died in the ordinary course of nature." It is better to understand it of the continued duration of the city. See Jonah iii. 10.

(99) *If thy Lord had pleased, &c.* The Prophet was very desirous all should believe on Islám, but God revealed this verse to show that the question of faith depends on his will.—*Tafsír-i-Raufí.*

Forcibly compel, &c. Brinckman says this verse "distinctly forbids Muhammad to use force for Islám, and contradicts at least thirty other verses of the Korán."—*Notes on Islám,* p. 110. But the commentators say this verse is abrogated by "the sword verse." See chap. iv. 88 and chap. ix. 5. Both parties seem to have missed the sense of the verse. The meaning evidently is that the *Prophet can do nothing,* since "none can believe but by the permission of God."

(100) *No soul can believe, &c. . . . and he shall pour, &c.* The free agency of the unbeliever is not recognised here. The infidel is such because God is not pleased he should believe (ver. 99), and because he is an infidel, God will "pour out his indignation" on him.

(104–109) These verses contain Muhammad's confession of faith at Makkah. They are at once a defence of his opposition to the national idolatry and an exhortation to his countrymen to believe in the true God. Muhammad is no guardian, but only a preacher of the true religion. God is the judge, and will decide between the Prophet and the unbelievers. Some, however, regard the last sentence of ver. 108 as abrogated by the command to convert by the sword. See *Tafsír-i-Raufí in loco.*

cause you to die: and I am commanded to be *one* of the true believers. (105) And *it was said unto me,* Set thy face towards the *true* religion, *and be* orthodox; and by no means be *one* of those who attribute companions *unto God;* (106) neither invoke, besides GOD, that which can neither profit thee nor hurt thee: for if thou do, thou *wilt* then certainly *become one* of the unjust. (107) If GOD afflict thee with hurt, there is none who can relieve thee from it except he; and if he willeth thee any good, there is none who can keep back his bounty: he will confer it on such of his servants as he pleaseth; and he *is* gracious and merciful. (108) Say, O men, now hath the truth come unto you from your LORD. He therefore who shall be directed, will be directed to *the advantage of* his own soul; but he who shall err, will err only against the same. I am no guardian over you. (109) Do thou, *O Prophet,* follow that which is revealed unto thee: and persevere with patience until GOD shall judge; for he is the best judge.

CHAPTER XI.

ENTITLED SURAT AL HÚD.

Revealed at Makkah.

INTRODUCTION.

I HAVE not been able to find any better reason for the name of this chapter than that given by Sale: that the story of that prophet is repeated in it.

There is much in this chapter of a like character with the seventh chapter. Its several parts are closely connected together, and present what may be called an elaborate vindication of Muhammad's claim to be a prophet. The Quraish had rejected him as an impostor, and had styled his Qurán a forgery. Accordingly he falls back upon the example of former prophets, and threatens the infidels with that Divine wrath which had invariably destroyed the unbelievers who had rejected his predecessors in this holy office.

In respect to the histories of the prophets given in this chapter, there is one feature worthy of very special attention, as it bears directly on the question of Muhammad's sincerity and honesty as a religious teacher: it is *the Muhammadan colouring of the history of these prophets*. They were all, like Muhammad, sent to reclaim their people from idolatry. Like him, they were all rejected by the great majority of the people, only a few poor, despised persons professing faith in their prophet's message. Like him, they were all charged with imposture, and their messages were characterised as forgeries. This conduct was invariably followed by Divine retribution, the prophets and their followers being miraculously delivered from wicked hands.

The whole chapter marks a period of sharp and bitter opposition on the part of Muhammad's townsmen. It is probable that this fact, as well as the sharp epileptic paroxysms with which these revelations are said to have been accompanied, caused Muhammad to designate "Húd and its Sisters" as the "*Terrific Suras.*" "The

'*Sisters*' are variously given as Suras xi., xxi., lvi., lxix., lxxvii., lxxviii., lxxxi., and ci.; all Meccan, and some of them very early Suras."—*Muir's Life of Mahomet*, vol. ii. p. 88.

Probable Date of the Revelations.

As to the date of composition, little can be said that is satisfactory beyond the fact that it belongs to a period of Muhammad's prophetic career at Makkah when the opposition of the Quraish was very fierce. A part of the chapter would seem to indicate the period immediately preceding the Ban of the Húshimites, say B.H. 4 (see note on ver. 91), but the greater part must be referred to a period succeeding that event (see notes on vers. 37 and 55).

Principal Subjects.

	VERSES
The Qurán a revelation from God	1, 2
Muhammad a warner and a preacher of goodness	3–5
Infidels cannot hide their sin from God	6
God the Creator and Preserver of all creatures	7, 8
The resurrection rejected by the infidels as sorcery	8
They scoff at threatened punishment	9
Mercy and judgment alike disregarded by infidels	10, 11
Those who persevere in good works shall be rewarded	12
The unbelievers demand a sign from heaven	13
Muhammad charged with forging the Qurán	14
He challenges the infidels to produce ten chapters like it, or to become Muslims	14, 15
The miserable fate of those who live for this present world	16, 17
Moses and the Jews attest the truth of the Qurán	18
The maligners of prophets shall be cursed	19–23
The blessed portion of believers	24
Similitudes of believers and unbelievers	25

The History of Noah:—

He is sent as a public preacher	26, 27
The chiefs of his people reject him as a liar	28
Noah protests his integrity—Refuses to drive away his poor followers—Deprecates being thought a seer or an angel	29–32
His people challenge him to bring on the threatened judgment	33
Noah declares that God destroys and saves whom he pleaseth	34, 35
Noah's people declare his message a forgery	36

	VERSES
God tells Noah that no more of his people will believe on him	37
He is commanded to make an ark	38
Noah builds the ark and is derided by the people	39
Embarks with his followers and one pair each of the animals	40, 41
Noah in vain entreats his unbelieving son to embark	42, 43
The waters abate and the ark rests on Al Júdi	44
Noah pleads with God for his son	45
God reproves him for his intercession for his son	46
Noah repents and asks pardon for his fault	47
He descends from the ark	48
This history a secret revealed to Muhammad	49

The History of Húd:—

He is sent to call Ád from idolatry	50–52
The Ádites reject him as a liar	53
Húd protests his integrity, and declares his trust in God to save him from their plots	54–57
God delivers Húd and his followers	58
The Ádites reject their messenger and are destroyed	59, 60

The History of Sálih:—

He is sent to call the Thamúdites from idolatry	61
They reject his message	62
Sálih protests his integrity, and gives them a she-camel as a sign from God	63, 64
They kill the camel, and are threatened with destruction	65
Sálih and his followers are saved from destruction	66
The Thamúdites are miserably destroyed	67, 68

The History of Abraham and Lot:—

God's messengers sent to Abraham—He entertains them	69
He is filled with fear because they refuse to eat his meat	70
The angels quiet his fears and tell him they are sent to the people of Lot	70, 71
Sarah receives the promise of Isaac and Jacob	71–73
Abraham intercedes for the people of Lot	74
The angels refuse his request	75
Lot is anxious for the safety of his angel visitors	76
The Sodomites attack his house	77–79
The angels warn Lot to leave the city and inform him of the destruction impending over his people and his wife	80
The cities are overthrown and the people killed by a shower of bricks	81, 82

The History of Shuaib:—

He is sent to call the Midianites from idolatry . .	83
He reproaches them for dishonest weights and measures	84–86
The people reject him, refusing to leave their idols .	87
Shuaib protests his integrity, and exhorts them to flee the fate of the people of Noah, Húd, Sálih, and Lot	88–90
The people threaten to stone him	91
Shuaib threatens them with Divine judgment . .	92–94
God destroys the infidels, but saves Shuaib and his followers	95, 96

The History of Moses:—

He is sent with signs to Pharaoh and his princes .	97
They reject him, and are consigned to hell-fire . .	98–100
Exhortation and warning drawn from the fate of these cities	101–105
The condition of the righteous and wicked in judgment .	106–109
Muhammad not to doubt about the religion of the Quarish	110
The Quarish doubt the Qurán as the Jews did the Pentateuch	111
God will punish their evil deeds	112
Muhammad exhorted to be steadfast	113, 114
An exhortation to prayer	115
God just in destroying the unbelieving cities . . .	116–118
The unbelievers predestinated to damnation . . .	119
The whole history of the prophets related to Muhammad	120
Unbelievers threatened	121, 122
Muhammad exhorted to put his trust in God . . .	123

IN THE NAME OF THE MOST MERCIFUL GOD.

|| (1) A. L. R. (2) *This* book, the verses whereof are R ⅟· guarded against corruption, and are also distinctly ex-

---

(1) *A. L. R.* See Prelim. Disc., pp. 100–102.
(2) *Guarded against corruption.* "According to the various senses which the verb *uhkimat* in the original may bear, the commentators suggest as many different interpretations. Some suppose the meaning to be, according to our version, that the Qurán is not liable to be corrupted, as the law and the gospel have been in the opinion of the Muhammadans; others, that every verse in this particular chapter

plained, *is a revelation* from the wise, the knowing *God*: (3) that ye serve not *any other* GOD (verily I am a denouncer *of threats*, and a bearer of good tidings unto you from him); (4) and that ye ask pardon of your LORD, and then be turned unto him. He will cause you to enjoy a plentiful provision, until a prefixed time; and unto every one that hath merit *by good works* will he give his abundant *reward*. But if ye turn back, verily I fear for you the punishment of the great day: (5) unto GOD shall ye return; and he is almighty. (6) Do they not double *the folds of* their breasts, that they may conceal *their designs* from him? When they cover themselves with their garments, doth not he know that which they conceal and that which they discover? For he knoweth the innermost parts of the breasts *of men*.

---

is in full force, and not one of them abrogated; others, that the verses of the Qurán are disposed in a clear and perspicuous method, or contain evident and demonstrative arguments; and others, that they comprise judicial declarations to regulate both faith and practice."—*Sale, Baidháwi, Jaláluddín, Zamakhshari.* See also Prelim. Disc., sect. iii.

Distinctly explained. "The signification of the verb *fussilat*, which is here used, being also ambiguous, the meaning of this passage is supposed to be, either that the verses are distinctly proposed or expressed in a clear manner; or that the subject-matter of the whole may be distinguished or divided into laws, monitions, and examples; or else that the verses were revealed by parcels."—*Sale.*

(3) *A denouncer, &c.* The usual title claimed at Makkah, and probably assumed along with the prophetic office.

(4) The condition of salvation is here declared to be repentance and good works. See notes on chap. iii. 31.

(6) *Double . . . their breasts.* "Or, as it may be translated, 'Do they not turn away their breasts?'"—*Sale.* Rodwell has it, "Do they not doubly fold up their breasts?"

He knoweth the innermost parts. "This passage was occasioned by the words of the idolaters, who said to one another, 'When we let down our curtains (such as the women use in the East to screen themselves from the sight of the men, when they happen to be in the room), and wrap ourselves up in our garments, and fold up our breasts, to conceal our malice against Muhammad, how should he come to the knowledge of it?' Some suppose this passage relates to certain hypocritical Muslims; but this opinion is generally rejected, because this verse was revealed at Makkah, and the birth of hypocrisy among the Muhammadans happened not till after the Hijra."—*Sale.*

|| (7) There is no *creature* which creepeth on the earth but GOD *provideth* its food; and he knoweth the place of its retreat, and where it is laid up. The whole *is written* in the perspicuous book *of his decrees*. (8) It is he who hath created the heavens and the earth in six days (but his throne was above the waters *before the creation thereof*), that he might prove you, *and see* which of you would excel in works. If thou say, Ye shall surely be raised again after death; the unbelievers will say, This is nothing but manifest sorcery. (9) And verily if we defer their punishment unto a determined season, they will say, What hindereth it *from falling on us?* Will it not come upon them on a day, wherein there shall be none to avert *it* from them; and that which they scoffed at shall encompass them?

|| (10) Verily, if we cause man to taste mercy from us, and afterwards take it away from him, he *will* surely *become* desperate and ungrateful. (11) And if we cause him to taste favour after an affliction had befallen him, he will surely say, The evils *which I suffered* are passed from me, and he *will become* joyful and insolent: (12) except those who persevere with patience and do that which is right; they shall *receive* pardon and a great reward. (13) Per-

---

(7) This passage also teaches the omniscience of God, and also the doctrine of a particular providence. Everything is a matter of eternal decree.

(8) *Six days.* See chaps. vii. 55, and x. 3.

His throne was, &c. "For the Muhammadans suppose this throne, and the waters whereon it stands, which waters they imagine are supported by a spirit or wind, were, with some other things, created before the heavens and earth. This fancy they borrowed from the Jews, who also say that the throne of glory then stood in the air, and was borne on the face of the waters by the breath of God's mouth" (*Rashi* ad Gen. i. 2).—*Sale.*

Manifest sorcery. See note on chap. x. 77.

(11) *After an affliction.* The allusion is to the famine which befell Makkah, see chap. x. 22 and note. The effect of the withdrawal of mercy is to make the unbeliever "cast aside all hope of Divine favour, for want of patience and God" (*Sale*); but the restoration of Divine favour has no other effect than to make them "joyful and insolent."

adventure thou wilt omit *to publish* part of that which hath been revealed unto thee, and thy breast will become straitened, lest they say, Unless a treasure be sent down unto him, or an angel come with him, *to bear witness unto him, we will not believe.* Verily thou art a preacher *only;* and GOD is the governor of all things. (14) Will they say, He hath forged *the Qurán?* Answer, Bring therefore ten chapters like unto it, forged *by yourselves;* and call on whomsoever ye may *to assist you,* except GOD, if ye speak truth. (15) But if they *whom ye call to your assistance* hear you not; know that *this book* hath been revealed by the knowledge of GOD only, and that there is no GOD but he. *Will* ye therefore *become* Muslims? (16) Whoso chooseth the present life and the pomp thereof, unto them will we give *the recompense of* their works therein, and the same shall not be diminished unto them. (17) These are they for whom no *other reward* is *prepared* in the next life except the fire *of hell:* that which they have done in *this life* shall perish, and that which they have wrought *shall be* vain. (18) Shall he therefore *be compared with them* who followeth the evident declaration of his LORD,

---

(13) *That which hath been revealed unto thee.* Godfrey Higgins, whom our Indian Mussalmáns are so fond of quoting, since his apology has become known through Sayad Ahmad's garbled translation, thinks Muhammad imagined himself to be inspired, as did "Johanna Southcote, Baron Swedenborg, &c."—*Apology for Mohamed,* p. 83.

Unless a treasure, &c. See notes on chap. vi. 34-36.

A preacher only. See notes on chaps. ii. 119, iii. 184, and vi. 109.

(14) *He hath forged.* See chap. x. 39.

"This was the number which he first challenged them to compose; but they not being able to do it, he made the matter still easier, challenging them to produce a single chapter only, comparable to the Qurán in doctrine and eloquence."—*Sale.*

See also on chap. ii. 23.

Rodwell thinks the challenge in such passages is not to produce a book which shall equal the Qurán in point of poetry or rhetoric, but "in the importance of its subject-matter, with reference to the Divine unity, the future retribution," &c. All Muslim authorities, so far as I know, include the rhetoric and poetry among the incomparable excellences.

and whom a witness from him attendeth, preceded by the book of Moses, *which was revealed for* a guide, and *out of mercy to mankind?* These believe in the *Qurán;* but whosoever of the confederate *infidels* believeth not therein, is threatened the fire *of hell, which threat shall certainly be executed:* be not therefore in a doubt concerning it; for it is the truth from thy LORD: but the greater part of men will not believe. (19) Who is more unjust than he who imagineth a lie concerning GOD? They shall be set before the LORD *at the day of judgment,* and the witnesses shall say, These are they who devised lies against their LORD. Shall not the curse of GOD *fall* on the unjust; (20) who turn *men* aside from the way of GOD, and seek to render it crooked, and who believe not in the life to come? (21) These were not able to prevail *against God* on earth, *so as to escape punishment;* neither had they any protectors besides GOD: their punishment shall be doubled unto them. They could not hear, neither did they see. (22) These are they who have lost their souls; and the *idols* which they falsely imagined have abandoned them. (23) There is no doubt but they shall be most miserable in the world to come. (24) But as for those who believe and do good works, and humble themselves before their LORD,

---

(18) *A witness.* Various opinions obtain as to who this witness was. Some say the Qurán is meant. Others say Gabriel or an angel. Others will have it to be the Light of Muhammad, which impartial spectators always beheld in the countenance of the prophet. —*Tafsír-i-Raufi.*

The book of Moses. The Pentateuch is here again referred to in such a way as to show that Muhammad regarded the copies current in his day as genuine.

These believe, i.e., those who possess the book of Moses. No doubt Muhammad was confirmed in his prophetic claims by the flattery of some Jewish followers. *His own doubts* seem to be expressed in what follows: "Be not therefore in doubt concerning it;" and yet they are only expressed to be refuted by this testimony.

It is the truth from thy Lord. This passage with verse below, if it may be applied to Muhammad, assert his sincerity in his own claims as strongly as any in the Qurán.

(19) *The witnesses.* "That is, the angels and prophets, and their own members."—*Sale.*

they shall be the inhabitants of Paradise; they shall remain therein *for ever*. (25) The similitude of the two parties is as the blind and the deaf, and *as* he who seeth and heareth: shall they be compared as equal? Will ye not therefore consider?

R 3/3.

‖ (26) We formerly sent Noah unto his people; *and he said*, Verily I am a public preacher unto you; (27) that ye worship GOD alone; verily I fear for you the punishment of the terrible day. (28) But the chiefs of the people, who believed not, answered, We see thee *to be* no other than a man, like unto us; and we do not see that any follow thee, except those who are the most abject among us, *who have believed on thee* by a rash judgment; neither do we perceive any excellence in you above us: but we esteem you to be liars. (29) *Noah* said, O my people, tell me; if I have *received* an evident declaration from my LORD, and he hath bestowed on me mercy from himself, which is hidden from you, do we compel you to *receive* the same, in case ye be averse thereto? (30) O my people, I ask not of you riches, for *my preaching unto you*: my reward is with GOD alone. I will not drive away those who have believed: verily they shall meet their LORD *at the resurrection;* but I perceive that ye are

---

(25) *The two parties.* "Believers and unbelievers."—*Sale.* Muir thinks there is an allusion to the confederates of Makkah and the believers of Madína. See *Life of Mahomet*, vol. ii. p. 225 note.

(26) *We sent Noah, &c.* See notes on chap. vii. 60.

(28) *We see thee, &c.* This is what the chiefs of the Quraish said to Muhammad. See note on chap. x. 77.

A rash judgment. "For want of mature consideration, and moved by the first impulse of their fancy."—*Sale.*

(29) *Do we compel you, &c.* Muhammad had not yet conceived the idea of using the force of the sword to make converts. Moral suasion is the instrument now used. If the infidels choose the fire of hell, it is no concern of the prophets. He is not responsible. He is only a preacher of good news and a warner.

(30) *I will not drive away, &c.* "For this they asked him to do, because they were poor mean people. The same thing the Quraish demanded of Muhammad, but he was forbidden to comply with their request" (see chap. vi. 51).—*Sale.*

ignorant men. (31) O my people, who shall assist me against GOD, if I drive them away? Will ye not therefore consider? (32) I say not unto you, The treasures of GOD are in my power; neither *do I say*, I know the secrets *of God:* neither do I say, Verily I am an angel; neither do I say of those whom your eyes do contemn, GOD will by no means bestow good on them: (GOD best knoweth that which is in their souls;) for then should I certainly be *one* of the unjust. (33) They answered, O Noah, thou hast already disputed with us, and hast multiplied disputes with us; now therefore do thou bring that *punishment* upon us wherewith thou hast threatened us, if thou speakest truth. (34) *Noah* said, Verily GOD alone shall bring it upon you, if he pleaseth; and ye shall not prevail against him, *so as to escape the same.* (35) Neither shall my counsel profit you, although I endeavour to counsel you aright, if GOD shall please to lead you into error. He is your LORD, and unto him shall ye return. (36) Will the *Makkans* say, *Muhammad* hath forged *the Qurán?* Answer, If I have forged it, on me *be* my guilt; and let me be clear of that which ye are guilty of.

|| (37) And it was revealed unto Noah, *saying,* Verily R ¼. none of thy people shall believe, except he who hath

---

(31) See notes on chap. vi. 51.
(32) See notes on chap. vi. 49. A comparison of these two passages shows with what facility Muhammad placed the account of his own persecutions in the mouths of former prophets. Here Noah utters the very words Muhammad utters!
(35) *If God shall please to lead you into error.* See notes on chap. x. 99, 100.
(36) The italics of the text seem to me certainly to be misplaced. Rodwell and Palmer have fallen into the same error. The passage is identical in meaning with that of ver. 14 and x. 39. But here these words are put in the mouths *of the chiefs of the people of Noah*, and the reply protesting sincerity is that *of Noah* himself. Both the preceding and succeeding contexts require this interpretation.
Understood in this light, the passage is most damaging to the claims of Muhammad for sincerity.
(37) *None ... shall believe, &c.* If this statement reflects the feeling of Muhammad, as I believe it does, the chapter must be referred to that period of Muhammad's career at Makkah when he

already believed; be not therefore grieved for that which they are doing. (38) But make an ark in our presence, *according to the form and dimensions* which we have revealed *unto thee;* and speak not unto me in behalf of those who have acted unjustly, for they *are doomed to be* drowned. (39) And he built the ark; and so often as a company of his people passed by him they derided him; *but* he said, Though ye scoff at us *now*, we will scoff at you

---

despaired of his people believing on him, probably some time after the ban against the Hashimites.

(39) *They derided him.* "For building a vessel in an inland country, and so far from the sea; and for that he was turned carpenter, after he had set up for a prophet."—*Sale, Baidháwi.*

(40) *Heaven poured forth.* "Or, as the original literally signifies, *boiled over;* which is consonant to what the Rabbins say, that the waters of the deluge were boiling hot.

This oven was, as some say, at Kufa, in a spot whereon a mosque now stands; or, as others rather think, in a certain place in India, or else at Aín Warda, in Mesopotamia; and its exudation was the sign by which Noah knew the flood was coming. Some pretend that it was the same oven which Eve made use of to bake her bread in, being of a form different from those we use, having the mouth in the upper part, and that it descended from patriarch to patriarch, till it came to Noah (*vide* D'Herbelot, *Bibl. Orient.* art. *Noah*). It is remarkable that Muhammad, in all probability, borrowed this circumstance from the Persian Magi, who also fancied that the first waters of the deluge gushed out of the oven of a certain old woman named Zala Kufa (*vide* Hyde, *De Rel. Vet. Persar.*, and Lord's *Account of the Relig. of the Persees*, p. 9).

"But the word *tannúr*, which is here translated *oven*, also signifying the *superficies of the earth*, or *a place whence waters spring forth*, or *where they are collected*, some suppose it means no more in this passage than the spot or fissure whence the first eruption of waters brake forth."—*Sale, Baidháwi, Jalàluddín.*

One pair. "Or, as the words may also be rendered, and some commentators think they ought, *two pair*, that is, two males and two females of each species; wherein they partly agree with divers Jewish and Christian writers (Aben Ezra, Origen, &c.), who from the Hebrew expression, *seven and seven*, and *two and two, the male and his female* (Gen. vii. 2), suppose there went into the ark fourteen pair of every clean, and two pair of every unclean species. There is a tradition that God gathered together unto Noah all sorts of beasts, birds, and other animals (it being indeed difficult to conceive how he should come by them all without some supernatural assistance), and that, as he laid hold on them, his right hand constantly fell on the male and his left on the female."—*Sale, Jalàluddín.*

Except him, &c. "This was an unbelieving son of Noah, named Canaan or Yam; though others say he was not the son of Noah, but

hereafter as ye scoff at us; (40) and ye shall surely know on whom a punishment shall be inflicted, which shall cover him with shame, and on whom a lasting punishment shall fall. *Thus were they employed* until our sentence was put in execution and the oven poured forth *water. And* we said *unto Noah,* Carry into *the ark* of every *species of animals* one pair; and thy family (except him on whom a previous sentence *of destruction* hath passed), and those who believe. But there believed not with him except a few. (41) And *Noah* said, Embark thereon, in the name of GOD, while it moveth forward and while it standeth

---

his grandson by his son Ham, or his wife's son by another husband; nay, some pretend he was related to him no farther than by having been educated and brought up in his house. The best commentators add that Noah's wife, named Wáila, who was an infidel, was also comprehended in this exception, and perished with her son."—*Sale, Baidháwi, Jaláluddín, Zamakhshari.*

Much of this is Muslim invention, a kind of improvement on the Jewish tradition alluded to in the text. The whole passage is a clear contradiction of the Bible, which the Qurán professes to attest.

Those who believe. "Noah's family being mentioned before, it is supposed that by these words are intended the other believers, who were his proselytes, but not of his family; whence the common opinion among Muhammadans of a greater number than eight being saved in the ark seems to have taken its rise."—*Sale, Baidháwi.*

See also notes on chap. vii. 60.

Except a few, viz., "his other wife, who was a true believer, his three sons, Shem, Ham, and Japhet, and their wives, and seventy-two persons more."

See note on chap. vii. 65.

(41) *While it standeth still.* "That is, omit no opportunity of getting on board. According to a different reading, the latter words may be rendered, *who shall cause it to move forward and to stop,* as there shall be occasion. The commentators tell us that the ark moved forwards or stood still as Noah would have it, on his pronouncing only the words, *In the name of God.*

It is to be observed that the more judicious commentators make the dimensions of the ark to be the same with those assigned by Moses, notwithstanding others have enlarged them extravagantly, as some Christian writers (Origen, *Contr. Cels.* lib. 4) have also done. They likewise tell us that Noah was two years in building the ark, which was framed of Indian plane-trees; that it was divided into three stories, of which the lower was designed for the beasts, the middle one for the men and women, and the upper for the birds; and that the men were separated from the women by the body of Adam, which Noah had taken into the Ark. This last is a tradition of the

still; for my LORD *is* gracious *and* merciful. (42) And *the ark* swam with them between waves like mountains; and Noah called unto his son, who was separated *from him, saying,* Embark with us, my son, and stay not with the unbelievers. (43) He answered, I will get on a mountain, which will secure me from the water. *Noah* replied, There is no security this day from the decree of GOD, except for him on whom he shall have mercy. And a wave passed between them, and he became *one* of those who were drowned. (44) And it was said, O earth, swallow up thy waters, and thou, O heaven, withhold *thy rain.* And *immediately* the water abated, and the decree was fulfilled, and *the ark* rested on *the mountain* Al Júdi; and it was said, Away with the ungodly people!

Eastern Christians (Jacob. Edessenus, apud *Barcepham de Parad.*, part l. chap. 14. *Vide* etiam Eliezer, pirke chap. 23), some of whom pretended that the matrimonial duty was superseded and suspended during the time Noah and his family were in the ark (Ambros, *De Noa et Arca,* chap. 21), though Ham has been accused of not observing continency on that occasion, his wife, it seems, bringing forth Canaan in the very ark (*vide* Heidegger, *Hist. Patriarchar.*, vol. i. p. 409)."—*Sale, Baidháwi, Yahya.*

(42) *Noah called unto his son.* See note above on ver. 40.

(44) *Al Júdi.* "This mountain is one of those which divide Armenia on the south from Mesopotamia and that part of Assyria which is inhabited by the Kurds, from whom the mountains took the name of Kardu, or Gardu, by the Greeks turned into Gordyæi, and other names (see Bochart, *Phaleg.*, l. i. c. 3). Mount al Júdi (which name seems to be a corruption, though it be constantly so written by the Arabs, for Jordi or Giordi) is also called Thamánin, probably from a town at the foot of it (D'Herbelot, *Bibl. Orient.*, pp. 404, 676), so named from the number of persons saved in the ark, the word *thamánin* signifying *eighty,* and overlooks the country of Diyár Rabíah, near the cities of Mausal, Furdu, and Jazírat Ibn Omar, which last place one affirms to be but four miles from the place of the ark, and says that a Muhammadan temple was built there with the remains of that vessel by the Khalífah Omar Ibn Abdulazíz, whom he by mistake calls Omar Ibn al Khattáb.

"The tradition which affirms the ark to have rested on these mountains must have been very ancient, since it is the tradition of the Chaldeans themselves (Berosus, apud *Joseph. Antiq.*, l. xiv. p. 135); the Chaldee paraphrasts consent to their opinion (*Onkelos et Jonathan* in Gen. viii. 4), which obtained very much formerly, especially among the Eastern Christians. To confirm it, we are told that the remainders of the ark were to be seen on the Gordyæan moun-

|| (45) And *Noah* called upon his LORD, and said, O LORD, ʀᴜʙᴀ. verily my son is of my family, and thy promise is true, for thou art the most just of those who exercise judgment. (46) *God* answered, O Noah, verily he is not of thy family; this *intercession of thine for him* is not a righteous work. Ask not of me therefore that wherein thou hast no knowledge; I admonish thee that thou become not *one* of the ignorant. (47) *Noah* said, O LORD, I have recourse unto thee *for the assistance of thy grace*, that I ask not of thee that wherein I have no knowledge; and unless thou for-

---

tains. Berosus and Abydenus both declare there was such a report in their time, the first observing that several of the inhabitants thereabouts scraped the pitch off the planks as a rarity, and carried it about them for an amulet; and the latter saying that they used the wood of the vessel against many diseases with wonderful success. The relics of the ark were also to be seen here in the time of Epiphanius, if we may believe him (Epiph., *Hæres.*, 18); and we are told the Emperor Heraclius went from the town of Thamánin up to the mountain al Júdi, and saw the place of the ark (Elmacin, l. i. c. 1). There was also formerly a famous monastery, called *the Monastery of the Ark*, upon some of these mountains, where the Nestorians used to celebrate a feast-day on the spot where they supposed the ark rested; but in the year of Christ 776 that monastery was destroyed by lightning, with the church and a numerous congregation in it. Since which time it seems the credit of this tradition hath declined, and given place to another, which obtains at present, and according to which the ark rested on Mount Masis in Armenia, called by the Turks Aghir-dagh, or *the heavy* or *great mountain*, and situate about twelve leagues south-east of Erivan."—*Sale.*

(45) *Thy promise is true.* "Noah here challenges God's promise that he would save his family."—*Sale.*

(46) *He is not of thy family.* "Being cut off on account of his infidelity."—*Sale.*

The *Tafsír-i-Raufi* expresses the opinion of some that Noah did not know his son was an infidel, and that had he known it, he would not have interceded for him.

This is quite in accordance with the intercession claimed for the prophets; *they may intercede for their true followers only.* Their intercession is of no avail to save the unbelieving, as illustrated by the case mentioned in the text.

This whole story is contrary to the teaching of the Bible.

A righteous work. "According to a different reading, this passage may be rendered, *for he hath acted unrighteously.*"—*Sale.* The reading of the text is certainly correct, as is evident from the succeeding context.

give me and be merciful unto me, I shall be *one* of those who perish. (48) It was said *unto him*, O Noah, come down from the *ark*, with peace from us, and blessings upon thee, and upon a part of those who are with thee; but as for a part *of them*, we will suffer them to enjoy *the provision of this world*, and afterwards shall a grievous punishment from us be inflicted on them *in the life to come*. (49) This is a secret history which we reveal unto thee; thou didst not know it, neither did thy people before this. Wherefore persevere with patience, for the *prosperous* issue shall attend the pious.

R 5/5.

|| (50) And unto *the tribe of* Ád *we sent* their brother Húd. He said, O my people, worship GOD; ye have no GOD besides him; ye only imagine falsehood *in setting up idols and intercessors of your own making*. (51) O my people, I ask not of you for this *my preaching* any recompense; my recompense *do I expect* from him only who hath created me. Will ye not therefore understand? (52) O my people, ask pardon of your LORD, and be turned unto him;

---

(47) *Unless thou forgive me.* This is another passage proving that the prophets are not sinless, as is claimed by Muslims.

(48) *Come down from the ark.* "The Muhammadans say that Noah went into the ark on the tenth of Rajab, and came out of it the tenth of al Muharram, which therefore became a fast. So that the whole time of Noah's being in the ark according to them was six months."—*Sale, Baidháwi.*

A part . . . with thee, i.e., those who continued in the faith of Noah.

A part of them. "That is, such of his posterity as should depart from the true faith and fall into idolatry."—*Sale.* This is hardly satisfactory. Those *with* Noah are here divided into two parts—one of which is to receive a blessing, the other a curse. The allusion is no doubt to Canaan. See Gen. ix. 20-25.

(49) *A secret history.* Of this passage Arnold (*Islám and Christianity,* p. 331) says: "The Koran, in describing the Flood, professes to *reveal* an unheard-of secret." But the purport of the passage is that this secret has been revealed to Muhammad and his people, the Arabs. As yet Muhammad regards himself as the Apostle of God to the Arabs, as Moses had been to the Egyptians. The idea of a universal Islám had not yet been conceived.

(50) See notes on chap. vii. 66.

he will send the heaven to pour forth rain plentifully upon you, and he will increase your strength by *giving* unto you *further* strength; therefore turn not aside to commit evil. (53) They answered, O Húd, thou hast brought us no proof *of what thou sayest;* therefore we will not leave our gods for thy saying, neither do we believe thee. (54) We say no other than that some of our gods have afflicted thee with evil. He replied, Verily I call GOD to witness, and do ye also bear witness that I am clear of that which ye associate *with God* besides him. (55) Do ye all therefore *join to* devise a plot against me, and tarry not; (56) for I put my confidence in GOD, my LORD and your LORD. There is no beast but he holdeth *it* by its forelock; verily my LORD *proceedeth* in the right way. (57) But if ye turn back, I have already declared unto you that with which I was sent unto you; and my LORD shall substitute another nation in your stead, and ye shall not hurt him at all, for my LORD *is* guardian over all things. (58) And when our sentence came *to be put in execution,* we delivered Húd and those who had believed with him through our mercy; and we delivered them from a grievous punishment. (59)

---

(52) *He will send the heaven, &c.* "For the Ádites were grievously distressed by a drouth for three years."—*Sale.* See chap. vii. 71, and note there.

(53) The Ádites present the same objections to their prophet that the Quraish offered to Muhammad, and the answers of Húd are verbatim the answers of Muhammad. This remark applies to the whole catalogue of prophets and peoples given in the Qurán. It is hard to believe that Muhammad was unconscious of manipulation here.

(54) *With evil.* "Or madness having deprived thee of thy reason, for the indignities thou hast offered them."—*Sale.*

(55) *Do ye . . . devise a plot.* Taking this language with that in ver. 57, *My Lord shall substitute another nation in your stead,* as expressive of Muhammad's own saying to the Quraish (see note on ver. 53), it would be a fair inference to fix the date of this revelation at the period when Muhammad began to court the favour of the inhabitants of Madína, *i.e.,* about one year previous to the Hijra.

(56) *By its forelock.* "That is, he exerciseth an absolute power over it, a creature held in this manner being supposed to be reduced to the lowest subjection."—*Sale.*

(58) *Those who believed.* Baidháwi says, "they were in number four thousand."—*Sale.*

And this *tribe of* Ád wittingly rejected the signs of their
LORD, and were disobedient unto his messengers, and they
followed the command of every rebellious perverse person.
(60) Wherefore they were followed in this world by a
curse, and they *shall be followed by the same* on the day of
resurrection. Did not Ád disbelieve in their LORD? Was
it not *said*, Away with Ád, the people of Húd?

R ⅝. ‖ (61) And unto *the tribe of* Thamúd *we sent* their
brother Sálih. He said *unto them*, O my people, worship
GOD; ye have no GOD besides him. It is he who hath
produced you out of the earth, and hath given you an
habitation therein. Ask pardon of him, therefore, and be
turned unto him; for my LORD is near *and* ready to
answer. (62) They answered, O Sálih, thou wast *a person*
on whom we placed our hopes before this. Dost thou
forbid us to worship that which our fathers worshipped?
But we are certainly in doubt concerning *the religion* to
which thou dost invite us, *as* justly to be suspected. (63)
Sálih said, O my people, tell me; if I have received an
evident declaration from my LORD, and he hath bestowed
on me mercy from himself; who will protect me from *the
vengeance of* GOD if I be disobedient unto him? For ye
shall not add unto me other than loss. (64) And *he said*,
O my people, this she-camel of GOD *is* a sign unto you;
therefore dismiss her freely, that she may feed in GOD'S
earth, and do her no harm, lest a swift punishment seize
you. (65) Yet they killed her; and *Sálih* said, Enjoy
yourselves in your dwellings for three days, *after which ye
shall be destroyed.* This is an infallible prediction. (66)
And when our decree came *to be executed*, we delivered
Sálih and those who believed with him, through our

---

(61) *Thamúd.* See note on chap. vii. 14.

(62) *On whom we placed our hopes.* "Designing to have made thee
our prince, because of the singular prudence and other good qualities
which we observed in thee; but thy dissenting from us in point of
religious worship has frustrated those hopes."—*Sale, Baidháwi.*

(65) *Three days,* viz., "Wednesday, Thursday, and Friday."—*Sale,*
see also note on chap. vii. 79.

mercy, from the disgrace of that day; for thy LORD is the strong, the mighty God. (67) But a terrible noise *from heaven* assailed those who had acted unjustly; and in the morning they were found in their houses lying *dead and* prostrate, (68) as though they had never dwelt therein. Did not Thamúd disbelieve in their LORD? Was not Thamúd *cast* far away?

|| (69) Our messengers also came formerly unto Abraham R 7. with good tidings: they said, Peace *be upon thee.* And he answered, *And on you be* peace! And he tarried not, but brought a roasted calf. (70) And when he saw that their hands did not touch the *meat,* he misliked them, and entertained a fear of them. *But* they said, Fear not; for we are sent unto the people of Lot. (71) And his wife *Sarah was* standing by, and she laughed; and we promised her Isaac, and after Isaac, Jacob. (72) She said, Alas!

---

(69) *Our messengers.* "These were the angels who were sent to acquaint Abraham with the promise of Isaac, and to destroy Sodom and Gomorrah. Some of the commentators pretend they were twelve, or nine, or ten in number; but others, agreeable to Scripture, say they were but three, viz., Gabriel, Michael, and Israfíl."—*Sale, Jaláluddín.* See Gen. xviii.

(70) *When he saw that their hands, &c.* Their refusal to eat was regarded by Abraham as a declaration of want of friendship, custom requiring guests to eat in token of friendship.—*Tafsír-i-Raufí.*

Entertained a fear, &c. "Apprehending that they had some ill design against him because they would not eat with him."—*Sale.*

Fear not. "Being angels, whose nature needs not the support of food." This passage is a direct contradiction of Gen. xviii. 8. The Rabbins say the angels pretended to eat. See *Rodwell in loco.*

(71) *And she laughed.* "The commentators are so little acquainted with Scripture, that, not knowing the true occasion of Sarah's laughter, they strain their inventions to give some reason for it. One says that she laughed at the angels discovering themselves, and ridding Abraham and herself of their apprehensions; and another, that it was at the approaching destruction of the Sodomites (a very probable motive in one of her sex). Some, however, interpret the original word differently, and will have it that she did not *laugh,* but that *her courses,* which had stopped for several years, *came upon her* at this time, as a previous sign of her future conception."—*Sale, Baidháwi, Jaláluddín, &c.*

Isaac and Jacob. The references to this promised child are frequently connected with Jacob in such a way as to leave the impression that in Muhammad's mind Isaac and Jacob were brothers,

shall I bear a son, who am old; this my husband also being advanced in years? Verily this *would be* a wonderful thing. (73) *The angels* answered, Dost thou wonder at the *effect of the* command of GOD? The mercy of God and his blessings be upon you, the family of the house: for he *is* praiseworthy, *and* to be glorified. (74) And when his apprehension had departed from Abraham, and the good tidings *of Isaac's birth* had come unto him, he disputed with us concerning the people of Lot; for Abraham was a pitiful, compassionate, and devout *person*. (75) *The angels said unto him*, O Abraham, abstain from this; for now is the command of thy LORD come *to put their sentence in execution,* and an inevitable punishment is ready to fall upon them. (76) And when our messengers came unto Lot, he was troubled for them, and his arm was straightened concerning them; and he said, This is a grievous day. (77) And his people came unto him, rush-

---

born of Sarah. See chaps. xix. 50, and xxi. 72. *Ishmael is nowhere mentioned as the child of promise.* Every reference to him in the Qurán speaks of him as simply *a prophet.* The explanation doubtless is that these references, occurring in Makkan or very early Madína Suras, the spirit of inspiration derived its knowledge mostly from Jewish tradition. The Jews had not yet been rejected. The Arabs were not yet regarded as the chosen people of God.

(72) *Advanced in years.* "Al Baidháwi writes that Sarah was then ninety or ninety-nine years old, and Abraham a hundred and twenty."—*Sale.*

(73) *The house.* "Or the stock whence all the prophets were to proceed for the future. Or the expression may perhaps refer to Abraham and Ishmael's building the Kaabah, which is often called by way of excellence *the house.*"—*Sale.*

(74) *He disputed with us.* "That is, he interceded with us for them. Jaláluddín, instead of the numbers mentioned by Moses, says that Abraham first asked whether God would destroy those cities if three hundred righteous persons were found therein, and so fell successively to two hundred, forty, fourteen, and at last came to one; but there was not one righteous person to be found among them, except only Lot and his family."—*Sale.*

Cf. Gen. xviii. 23–33.

(76) *He was troubled for them.* "Because they appeared in the shape of beautiful young men, which must needs tempt those of Sodom to abuse them. He knew himself unable to protect them against the insults of his townsmen."—*Sale, Jaláluddín, Baidháwi.*

ing upon him, and they had formerly been guilty of wickedness. *Lot* said *unto them*, O my people, these my daughters are more lawful for you: therefore fear GOD, and put me not to shame by *wronging* my guests. Is there not a man of prudence among you? (78) They answered, Thou knowest that we have no need of thy daughters; and thou well knowest what we would have. (79) He said, If I had strength sufficient to *oppose* you, or I could have recourse unto a powerful support, *I would certainly do it.* (80) *The angels* said, O Lot, verily we are the messengers of thy LORD; they shall by no means come in unto thee. Go forth, therefore, with thy family, in some part of the night, and let not any of you turn back; but as for thy wife, that shall happen unto her which shall happen unto them. Verily the prediction *of their punishment* shall be *fulfilled* in the morning: is not the morning near? (81) And when our command came, we turned those *cities* upside down, and we rained upon them

---

(80) *They shall by no means come in unto thee.* "Al Baidhāwi says that Lot shut his door, and argued the matter with the riotous assembly from behind it; but at length they endeavoured to get over the wall; whereupon Gabriel, seeing his distress, struck them on the face with one of his wings and blinded them, so that they moved off crying out for help, and saying that Lot had magicians in his house."—*Sale.*

As for thy wife. "This seems to be the true sense of the passage; but according to a different reading of the vowel, some interpret it, *Except thy wife;* the meaning being that Lot is here commanded to take his family with him *except his wife.* Wherefore the commentators cannot agree whether Lot's wife went forth with him or not; some denying it, and pretending that she was left behind and perished in the common destruction; and others affirming it, and saying that when she heard the noise of the storm and overthrow of the cities, she turned back lamenting their fate, and was immediately struck down and killed by one of the stones mentioned a little lower. A punishment she justly merited for her infidelity and disobedience to her husband."—*Sale.*

For the name of Lot's wife, see note on lxvi. 10. See also note on chap. vii. 84.

(81) *We turned those cities upside down.* "For they tell us that Gabriel thrust his wing under them, and lifted them up so high, that the inhabitants of the lower heaven heard the barking of the dogs and the crowing of the cocks; and then, inverting them, threw them down to the earth."—*Sale, Jalāluddīn, Baidhāwi.*

stones of baked clay, one following another, (82) and being marked from thy LORD; and they *are* not far distant from those who act unjustly.

NISF.

R ⅜.

‖ (83) And unto Madian *we sent* their brother Shuaib: he said, O my people, worship GOD: ye have no GOD but him: and diminish not measure and weight. Verily I see you *to be* in a happy condition; but I fear for you the punishment of the day which will encompass *the ungodly.* (84) O my people, give full measure and just weight; and diminish not unto men *aught* of their matters; neither commit injustice in the earth, acting corruptly. (85) The residue *which shall remain unto you as the gift* of GOD, *after ye shall have done justice to others,* will be better for you *than wealth gotten by fraud,* if ye be true believers. (86) I am no guardian over you. (87) They answered, O Shuaib, do thy prayers enjoin thee that we should leave the *gods* which our fathers worshipped, or that we should not do what we please with our substance? Thou *only,* it

---

Stones of baked clay. Some commentators say these bricks were burned in hell.—*Sale.*

(82) *Being marked.* "That is, as some suppose, streaked with white and red, or having some other peculiar mark to distinguish them from ordinary stones. But the common opinion is that each stone had the name of the person who was to be killed by it written thereon. The army of Abraha al Ashram was also destroyed by the same kind of stones."—*Sale, Jaláluddín, Baidháwi.*

Who act unjustly. "This is a kind of threat to other wicked persons, and particularly to the infidels of Makkah, who deserved and might justly apprehend the same punishment."—*Sale.*

The story of the destruction of Sodom as here given is another instance in which the Qurán contradicts the Bible while professing to attest its truth.

(83) *Madian.* See note on chap. vii. 86.

A happy condition. "That is, enjoying plenty of all things, and therefore having the less occasion to defraud one another, and being the more strongly bound to be thankful and obedient unto God."—*Sale.*

(86) These are the very words used by Muhammad to the Quraish. See chap. x. 108.

(87) *That we should not do what we please, &c.* "For this liberty, they imagined, was taken from them by his prohibition of false weights and measures, or to diminish or adulterate their coin."—*Sale, Baidháwi.*

seems, art the wise *person*, and fit to direct. (88) He said, O my people, tell me: if I have received an evident declaration from my LORD, and he hath bestowed on me an excellent provision, and I will not consent unto you in that which I forbid you; do I seek *any other* than *your* reformation, to the utmost of my power? My support is from GOD alone: on him do I trust, and unto him do I turn me. (89) O my people, let not *your* opposing of me draw on you *a vengeance* like unto that which fell on the people of Noah, or the people of Húd, or the people of Sálih: neither *was* the people of Lot far distant from you. (90) Ask pardon, therefore, of your LORD; and be turned unto him: for my LORD is merciful *and* loving. (91) They answered, O Shuaib, we understand not much of what thou sayest, and we see thee to be a *man* of no power among us: if it had not been *for the sake of* thy family, we had surely stoned thee, neither couldst thou have prevailed against us. (92) *Shuaib* said, O my people, is my family more worthy in your opinion than GOD? and do ye cast him behind you with neglect? Verily my LORD comprehendeth that which ye do. (93) O my people, do ye work according to your condition; I will

(89) *Far distant from you.* "For Sodom and Gomorrah were situate not a great way from you, and their destruction happened not many ages ago; neither did they deserve it on account of their obstinacy and wickedness much more than yourselves."—*Sale.*

(91) *A man of no power.* "The Arabic word *dhaif, weak*, signifying also, in the Himyaritic dialect, *blind*, some suppose that Shuaib was so, and that the Midianites objected that to him, as a defect which disqualified him for the prophetic office."—*Sale.*

Thy family, i.e., "For the respect we bear to thy family and relations, whom we honour as being of our religion, and not for any apprehension we have of their power to assist you against us. The original word, here translated *family*, signifies any number from three to seven or ten, but not more."—*Sale, Baidháwi, Jaláluddín.*

Muhammad here again puts the words of the Quraish into the mouths of the Midianites. He was under the protection of the Háshimites, or of the household of Abu Tálib. The revelation must have been announced before the ban against the Háshimites.

(93) Compare with chap. vi. 135, to see how Muhammad's replies to the Quraish are put into the mouths of other prophets. See note on ver. 53 above.

surely work *according to my duty. And* ye shall certainly know on whom will be inflicted a punishment which shall cover him with shame, and who is a liar. (94) Wait, therefore, *the event;* for I also will wait *it* with you. (95) Wherefore, when our decree came *to be executed,* we delivered Shuaib and those who believed with him, through our mercy; and a terrible noise *from heaven* assailed those who had acted unjustly; and in the morning they were found in their houses lying *dead and* prostrate, (96) as though they had never dwelt therein. Was not Madian removed *from off the earth,* as Thamúd had been removed?

‖ (97) And we formerly sent Moses with our signs and manifest power unto Pharaoh and his princes; (98) but they followed the command of Pharaoh, although the command of Pharaoh did not direct *them* aright. (99) *Pharaoh* shall precede his on the day of resurrection, and he shall lead them into *hell*-fire; an unhappy way *shall it be* which *they* shall be led. (100) They were followed in this *life* by a curse, and on the day of resurrection miserable *shall be* the gift which shall be given *them.* (101) This is *a part* of the histories of the cities, which we rehearse unto thee. Of them there are *some* standing, and *others which are* utterly demolished. (102) And we treated them not unjustly, but they dealt unjustly with their own souls; and their gods which they invoked, besides GOD, were of no advantage unto them at all when the decree of thy LORD came *to be executed on them,* neither were they any other than a detriment unto them. (103) And thus *was* the punishment of my LORD *inflicted,* when he punished the cities which were unjust; for his punishment is grievous and severe. (104) Verily herein is a sign unto him who feareth the punishment of the last

---

(97) *Pharaoh and his princes.* See notes on chap. vii. 104-136.
(99) Compare with chap. x. 90.
(101) *Utterly demolished.* "Literally, *mown down;* the sentence presenting the different images of corn standing and cut down, which is also often used by the sacred writers."—*Sale.*

day: that *shall be a* day, whereon *all* men shall be assembled, and that *shall be* a day whereon witness shall be borne; (105) we defer it not, but to a determined time. (106) When *that day* shall come, no soul shall speak *to excuse itself or to intercede for another* but by the permission of *God.* Of them, *one shall be* miserable and *another shall be* happy. (107) And they who shall be miserable shall be *thrown* into *hell-*fire; (108) there shall they wail and bemoan *themselves:* they shall remain therein so long as the heavens and the earth shall endure, except what thy LORD shall please *to remit of their sentence;* for thy LORD effecteth that which he pleaseth. (109) But they who shall be happy *shall be admitted* into Paradise; they shall remain therein so long as the heavens and the earth endure: besides what thy LORD shall please *to add unto their bliss;* a bounty which shall not be interrupted. (110) Be not therefore in doubt concerning that which these men worship: they worship no other than what their fathers worshipped before *them;* and we will surely give them their full portion, not in the least diminished.

|| (111) We formerly gave unto Moses the book *of the law,* and disputes arose *among his people* concerning it: and unless a previous decree had proceeded from thy

R $\frac{10}{10}$.

---

(108) *Wail and bemoan.* "The two words in the original signify, properly, the vehement drawing in and expiration of one's breath, which is usual to persons in great pain and anguish; and particularly the reciprocation of the voice of an ass when he brays."—*Sale.*

So long as the heavens and the earth shall endure. "This is not to be strictly understood, as if either the punishment of the damned should have an end or the heavens and the earth should endure for ever, the expression being only used by way of image or comparison, which needs not agree in every point with the thing signified. Some, however, think the future heavens and earth, into which the present shall be changed, are here meant."—*Sale, Baidháwi.*

Except what thy Lord shall please to remit. See Prelim. Disc., pp. 149, 150.

(110) *We will surely give them their full portion.* The logical inference from all that is taught in this chapter, and especially in the examples given, is that the Quraish would reject Muhammad, and be ignominiously destroyed. This verse sets the seal to this threat. Muslims are, however, obliged to admit that, with a few exceptions, the "people of Muhammad" are reckoned true believers.

LORD *to bear with them during this life, the matter* had been surely decided between them. And *thy people are also* jealous *and* in doubt concerning the *Qurán.* (112) But unto every one of them will thy LORD render *the reward of* their works; for he well knoweth that which they do. (113) Be thou steadfast, therefore, as thou hast been commanded; and *let him also be steadfast* who shall be converted with thee; and transgress not, for he seeth that which ye do. (114) And incline not unto those who act unjustly, lest the fire *of hell* touch you: for ye have no protectors except GOD; neither shall ye be assisted *against him.* (115) Pray regularly morning and evening; and in the former part of the night, for good *works* drive away evil. This is an admonition unto those who consider: (116) wherefore persevere with patience; for GOD suffereth not the reward of the righteous to perish. (117) Were such of the generations before you endued with understanding and virtue who forbade the acting corruptly in the earth, any more than a few only of those whom we delivered; but they who were unjust followed *the delights* which they enjoyed *in this world,* and were

---

(111) *Thy people are . . . in doubt, &c.* This verse "disproves the miracle of the Qurán. A miracle requires to be so convincing that none who see it can doubt that it is a miracle. Christ did miracles; the fact of them was not doubted by those who saw them done, though the unbelievers and jealous said Satan was the doer of them. If the doubts here referred to are regarding the *meaning* of the Koran, then it is not an easy, light-giving book, as it is said to be."—*Brinckman's "Notes on Islám."*

(115) *Morning and evening.* "Literally in the extremities of the day."—*Sale.*

The former part of the night. "That is, after sunset and before supper, when the Muhammadans say their fourth prayer, called by them *Salát al maghrab,* or the evening prayer."—*Sale, Baidháwi.*

(117) *Which they enjoyed.* "Making it their sole business to please their luxurious desires and appetites, and placing their whole felicity therein."—*Sale.*

Were wicked doers. "Al Baidháwi says that this passage gives the reason why the nations were destroyed of old, viz., for their violence and injustice, their following their own lusts, and for their idolatry and unbelief."—*Sale.*

wicked doers: (118) and thy LORD was not *of such a disposition* as to destroy the cities unjustly, while their inhabitants behaved themselves uprightly. (119) And if thy LORD pleased, he would have made *all* men of one religion; but they shall not cease to differ among themselves, unless those on whom thy LORD shall have mercy: and unto this hath he created them; for the word of thy LORD shall be fulfilled *when he said*, Verily I will fill hell altogether with genii and men. (120) The whole *which we have related* of the histories of *our* apostles do we relate unto thee, that we may confirm thy heart thereby; and herein is the truth come unto thee, and an admonition and a warning unto the true believers. (121) Say unto those who believe not, Act ye according to your condition; we surely will act *according to our duty:* (122) and wait *the issue; for* we certainly wait *it also.* (123) Unto GOD *is known* that which is secret in heaven and earth; and unto him shall the whole matter be referred. Therefore worship him and put thy trust in him; for thy LORD is not regardless of that which ye do.

---

(118) *Unjustly.* "Or, as Baidháwi explains it, for their idolatry only, when they observed justice in other respects."—*Sale.* The meaning, however, is that God never destroys a people without a good reason—and such a good reason is idolatry, as is evident from all the examples given in this chapter.

(119) *I will fill hell, &c.* See notes on chap. vii. 179-183.

(121) See above on ver. 93.

(123) *Thy Lord is not regardless of that which ye do.* Muhammad attributed his grey hairs to this chapter and its sisters. See Muir's *Life of Mahomet,* vol. iv. p. 255.

CHAPTER XII.

ENTITLED SURAT AL YUSUF (JOSEPH).

Revealed at Makkah.

INTRODUCTION.

THIS chapter purports to give an inspired account of the life of the patriarch Joseph. It differs from every other chapter of the Qurán, in that it deals with only one subject. Baidháwi, says Sale, tells us that it was occasioned in the following manner:—

"The Quraish, thinking to puzzle Muhammad, at the instigation and by the direction of certain Jewish Rabbins, demanded of him how Jacob's family happened to go down into Egypt, and that he would relate to them the history of Joseph, with all its circumstances;" whereupon he pretended to have received this chapter from heaven.

Jaláluddín-us-Syutí, in his *Itqán*, says this chapter was given by Muhammad to those Madínese converted at Makkah before the Hijra. Weil conjectures that it was especially prepared with reference to the Hijra. This conjecture has, however, but little in its favour. Certain it is that the chapter belongs to Makkah. Much intercourse with the Jews at Madína would have improved the general historical character of the record.

The story related here bears every mark of having been received at second hand from persons themselves ignorant of the history of Joseph, except as recounted from hearsay among ignorant people. Muhammad's informants had probably learned the story from popular Jewish tradition, which seems to have been garbled and improved upon by the Prophet himself. Certainly no part of the Qurán more clearly reveals the hand of the forger. The whole chapter is a miserable travesty of the Mosaic account of Joseph. In almost every instance the facts of the original story are misrepresented, misplaced, and garbled, while the additions are often wanting the poor authority of the Rabbins. Nevertheless, this story is not only related as coming from God, but also as attesting the Divine character of the Qurán. It is significant that this chapter was rejected by the Ajáredites and Maimúnians as apocryphal and spurious.

Probable Date of the Revelations.

There are those (as Jaláluddín-us-Sayutí) who would assign vers. 1–3 to Madína, but the generally received opinion, as stated above, is that the whole chapter belongs to Makkah. The spirit shown in vers. 105, 110, towards the unbelieving Quraish, along with the general character of the chapter, based as it is upon information drawn from Jewish sources, point to the years immediately preceding the Hijra as the period to which it belongs. Muir, in his *Chronological List of Suras*, places it just before chap. xi. See *Life of Mahomet*, vol. ii. Appendix.

Principal Subjects.

	VERSES
The Prophet acquainted by inspiration with the history of Joseph	1–3
Joseph tells his father of his vision of the stars	4
Jacob warns Joseph against the jealousy of his brethren	5
Jacob understands the dream to signify Joseph's future prophetic character	6
Joseph's story a sign of God's providence	7
Joseph's brethren are jealous of him and of Benjamin	8
They counsel together to kill or to expatriate him	9
One of them advises their putting him into a well	10
They beg their father to send Joseph with them	11, 12
Jacob hesitates through fear that Joseph may be devoured by a wolf	13
Joseph's brethren, receiving their father's consent, take him with them and put him in a well	14, 15
God sends a revelation to Joseph in the well	15
The brethren bring to Jacob the report that Joseph had been devoured by a wolf	16, 17
Jacob does not believe the story of his sons	18
Certain travellers finding Joseph carry him into bondage	19, 20
An Egyptian purchases Joseph and proposes to adopt him	21
God bestows on him wisdom and knowledge	22
The Egyptian's wife endeavours to seduce Joseph	23
By God's grace he was preserved from her enticements	24
She accuses Joseph of an attempt to dishonour her	25

	VERSES
The rent in his garment testifies Joseph's innocence	26, 27
Potipher believes Joseph and condemns his wife	28, 29
The sin of Potipher's wife becomes known in the city	30
The wives of other noblemen, seeing Joseph's beauty, call him an angel	31
Potipher's wife declares her purpose to imprison Joseph unless he yield to her solicitations	32
Joseph seeks protection from God	33
God hears his prayer and turns aside their snares	34
Joseph imprisoned notwithstanding his innocence	35
He undertakes to interpret the dreams of two of the king's servants who were also imprisoned with him	36, 37
Joseph preaches the Divine unity to his fellow-prisoners	38, 40
He interprets the dreams of the two servants	41
Joseph asks to be remembered to the king, but is forgotten	42
The dreams of the king of Egypt	43
The king's interpreters fail to interpret the king's dream	44
Joseph remembers and interprets the king's dream	45–49
The king calls Joseph out of prison	50
The women of the palace acknowledge their sin in endeavouring to entice Joseph to unlawful love	51
Joseph vindicated, yet professes his proneness to sin	52, 53
The king restores Joseph	54
Joseph made king's treasurer at his own request	55–57
His brethren come to him, but do not recognise him	58
Joseph requires his brethren to bring to him their brother Benjamin	59–61
Their money returned in their sacks to induce their return	62
Jacob reluctantly permits Benjamin to go to Egypt with his brethren	63–66
Jacob counsels their entering the city by several gates	67
This counsel of no avail against God's decree	68
Joseph, receiving Benjamin, makes himself known to him	69
He, by guile, brings his brethren under charge of theft	70–76
He insists on retaining Benjamin instead of a substitute	77, 79
After consultation, Benjamin's brethren all return to Jacob but one	80–82
Jacob refuses to credit their story, yet puts his trust in God	83
Jacob grieves for Joseph, and yet tells of his hope	84–86
Jacob sends his sons to inquire after Joseph	87
Joseph makes himself known to his brethren	88–90
He pardons his brethren and sends his inner garment to his father to restore his sight	91–93
Jacob foretells the finding of Joseph, and receives his sight	94–97

	VERSES
He asks pardon for his wicked sons	98, 99
Joseph receives his parents unto him in Egypt . . .	100
Jacob and his sons and wife all do obeisance to Joseph .	101
Joseph praises God for his mercies and professes the Muslim faith	102
The infidels will not believe the signs of the Qurán . .	103-107
The Makkan idolaters invited to the true faith . . .	108
God's apostles in all ages have been but men . . .	109
Unbelievers invariably punished for rejecting the messengers of God	109, 110
The Qurán no forgery, but a confirmation of the writings of former prophets	111

IN THE NAME OF THE MOST MERCIFUL GOD.

‖ (1) A. L. R. (2) These are the signs of the perspicuous R $\frac{1}{13}$ book, which we have sent down in the Arabic tongue, that, peradventure, ye might understand. (3) We relate unto thee a most excellent history, by revealing unto thee this Qurán, whereas thou wast before *one* of the negligent.

(1) *A. L. R.* See Prelim. Disc., pp. 100–102.

(2) *Arabic tongue.* The *Tafsír-i-Raufi* informs us that the reason why the Qurán was revealed in Arabic was because the Arabs would not have understood its meaning had it been revealed in any other. This is certainly a very natural reason. One would think that for a similar reason a translation of the Qurán might be used by nations not understanding Arabic, and that Muslims would not object to the translations of the former Scriptures.

(3) *A most excellent history.* "One of the best methods of convincing a Moslem of the inferiority of the Koran to the Bible would be to read the story of Joseph to him out of each book. In the Koran a beautiful and touching tale is mangled and spoiled."— *Brinckman's* "*Notes on Islam*," p. 112.

This Qurán. "Or this particular chapter; for the word Qurán, as has been elsewhere observed (Prelim. Disc., p. 96), probably signifying no more than a 'reading' or 'lecture,' is often used to denote, not only the whole volume, but any distinct chapter or section of it."—*Sale.*

It is better to understand the word here to be applied to the whole sum of revelation enunciated by Muhammad. The idea seems to be that Muhammad would not have known this "excellent history" but for the Qurán, which contained it.

Thou wast before . . . negligent, i.e., "so far from being acquainted with the story, that it never so much as entered into thy thoughts:

(4) When Joseph said unto his father, O my father, verily I saw *in my dream* eleven stars, and the sun and the moon; I saw them make obeisance unto me: (5) *Jacob* said, O my child, tell not thy vision to thy brethren, lest they devise some plot against thee; for the devil is a professed enemy unto man; (6) and thus, *according to thy dream*, shall thy LORD choose thee, and teach thee the interpretation of *dark* sayings, and he shall accomplish his favour upon thee and upon the family of Jacob, as he hath formerly accomplished it upon thy fathers Abraham and Isaac; for thy LORD *is* knowing *and* wise. (7) Surely in *the history of* Joseph and his brethren there are signs *of God's providence* to the inquisitive; (8) when they said *to*

---

a certain argument, says al Baidháwi, that it must have been revealed to him from heaven."—*Sale.*

Arnold says, "The 'Sura of Joseph,' composed by Mohammed in Mecca before his flight, is given as a direct and immediate revelation from heaven, and appealed to as a proof of his divine mission, though it contains incontrovertible proof of having been partially borrowed from the Bible, and still more largely from Rabbinical tradition. Here was no delusion, no Satanic inspiration, which could have been mistaken for Divine revelation, but a wilful fraud and a palpable deception."—*Islám and Christianity*, p. 75.

(4) *His father*, "who was Jacob, the son of Isaac, and the son of Abraham."—*Sale, Baidháwi.*

Eleven stars. "The commentators give us the names of these stars (which I think it needless to trouble the reader with), as Muhammad repeated them, at the request of a Jew, who thought to entrap him by the question."—*Sale, Baidháwi, Jaláluddín, &c.*

(5) *Tell not thy vision.* A contradiction of the Bible. Comp. Gen. xxxvii. 5, 10.

Some plot. "For they say, Jacob, judging that Joseph's dream portended his advancement above the rest of the family, justly apprehended his brethren's envy might tempt them to do him some mischief."—*Sale.*

This also contradicts the Bible story, which nowhere intimates that Jacob suspected any evil design against Joseph.

(6) *Interpretation of dark sayings.* "That is, of dreams; or, as others suppose, of the profound passages of Scripture, and all difficulties respecting either religion or justice."—*Sale, Tafsír-i-Raufi.*

This is also contrary to the Bible account.

(7) *The inquisitive.* Rodwell translates this "Inquirers," which corresponds with the Urdú translations. The persons referred to were certain Quraish, who, at the suggestion of the Jews, had asked

one another, Joseph and his brother are dearer to our father than we, who are the greater number: our father certainly maketh a wrong judgment. (9) *Wherefore* slay Joseph, or drive him into some *distant or desert part of the earth*, and the face of your father shall be cleared towards you; and ye shall afterwards be people of integrity. (10) One of them spoke and said: Slay not Joseph, but throw him to the bottom of the well; and some travellers will take him up, if ye do *this*. (11) They said *unto Jacob*, O father, why dost thou not intrust Joseph with us, since we are sincere *well-wishers* unto him? (12) Send him with us to-morrow *into the field*, that he may divert himself and sport, and we will be his guardians.

|| (13) *Jacob* answered, It grieveth me that ye take him away; and I fear lest the wolf devour him while ye are negligent of him. (14) They said, Surely if the wolf devour him, when there are so many of us, we shall

Suls.

R $\frac{2}{12}$.

Muhammad how Jacob's family happened to go into Egypt, and that he would relate to them the story of Joseph, whereupon this chapter was revealed.

(8) *His brother*, Benjamin.
(9) *Cleared towards you*, i.e., "He will settle his love wholly upon you, and ye will have no rival in his favour."—*Sale*.
(10) *One of them*. "This person, as some say, was Judah, the most prudent and noble-minded of them all; or, according to others, Reuben, whom the Muhammadan writers call Rublí. And both these opinions are supported by the account of Moses, who tells us that Reuben advised them not to kill Joseph, but to throw him into a pit, privately intending to release him; and that afterwards Judah, in Reuben's absence, persuaded them not to let him die in a pit, but to sell him to the Ishmaelites (Gen. xxxvii. 21, 22, 26, 27)."—*Sale*.

Note that all this is here represented as having taken place *before* Joseph was sent to them in the wilderness.

(12) *And sport*. "Some copies read, in the first person plural, *that we may divert ourselves*. &c."—*Sale*.

The Bible tells us that Jacob sent Joseph of his own accord, and that he sent him, not *with* his brothers, but to search for them in Shechem, and to bring him news of his sons and the flock. The whole passage, here, presumes Joseph to have been but a mere child.

(13) *I fear lest the wolf devour him*. "The reason why Jacob feared this beast in particular, as the commentators say, was either because the land was full of wolves, or else because Jacob had dreamed he saw Joseph devoured by one of these creatures."—*Sale, Baidháwi, Jaláluddín, Zamakhsharí.*

be weak indeed. (15) And when they had carried him with them, and agreed to set him at the bottom of the well, *they executed their design:* and we sent a revelation unto him, *saying,* Thou shalt *hereafter* declare this their action unto them; and they shall not perceive *thee to be Joseph.* (16) And they came to their father at even, weeping, (17) *and* said, Father, we went and ran races with one another, and we left Joseph with our baggage, and the wolf hath devoured him; but thou wilt not believe us although we speak the truth. (18) And they produced his inner garment *stained* with false blood.

This, with what follows in vers. 14, 15, also contradicts the Bible.

(15) *The well.* "This well, say some, was a certain well near Jerusalem, or not far from the river Jordan; but others call it the well of Egypt or Midian. The commentators tell us that, when the sons of Jacob had gotten Joseph with them in the field, they began to abuse and beat him so unmercifully, that they had killed him had not Judah, on his crying out for help, insisted on the promise they had made not to kill him, but to cast him into the well. Whereupon they let him down a little way; but, as he held by the sides of the well, they bound him, and took off his inner garment, designing to stain it with blood, to deceive their father. Joseph begged hard to have his garment returned him, but to no purpose, his brothers telling him, with a sneer, that the eleven stars and the sun and the moon might clothe him and keep him company. When they had let him down half-way, they let him fall thence to the bottom, and there being water in the well (though the Scripture says the contrary), he was obliged to get upon a stone, on which, as he stood weeping, the Angel Gabriel came to him with the revelation mentioned immediately."—*Sale, Baidháwi, Jaláluddín, and Zamakhshari.*

The commentators have added many particulars to the account given in the Qurán, which they have learned from Jewish sources.

A revelation to him. "Joseph being then but seventeen years old, al Baidháwi observes that herein he resembled John the Baptist and Jesus, who were also favoured with the Divine communication very early. The commentators pretend that Gabriel also clothed him in the well with a garment of silk of paradise. For they say that when Abraham was thrown into the fire by Nimrod, he was stripped; and that Gabriel brought this garment and put it on him; and that from Abraham it descended to Jacob, who folded it up and put it into an amulet, which he hung about Joseph's neck, whence Gabriel drew it out."—*Sale, Baidháwi, &c.*

(17) *Ran races.* "These races they used by way of exercise; and the commentators generally understand here that kind of race wherein they also showed their dexterity in throwing darts, which is still used in the East."—*Sale.*

Jacob answered, Nay, but ye yourselves have contrived the thing for your own sakes: however patience is most becoming, and GOD's assistance is to be implored *to enable me to support the misfortune* which ye relate. (19) And certain travellers came, and sent one to draw water for them; and he let down his bucket, and said, Good news! this is a youth. And they concealed him, *that they might sell him* as a piece of merchandise; but GOD knew that which they did. (20) And they sold him for a mean price, for a few pence, and valued him lightly.

(18) *Yourselves have contrived, &c.* "This Jacob had reason to suspect, because, when the garment was brought to him, he observed that, though it was bloody, yet it was not torn."—*Sale, Baidháwi.*

According to the Bible, Jacob said, "Without doubt Joseph is rent in pieces" (Gen. xxxvii. 33).

(19) *Certain travellers,* viz., "a caravan or company travelling from Midian to Egypt, who rested near the well three days after Joseph had been thrown into it."—*Sale.*

To draw water. The Bible says the well was dry (Gen. xxxvii. 24).

He let down. "The commentators are so exact as to give us the name of this man, who, as they pretend, was Málik Ibn Dhúr, of the tribe of Khudháah."—*Sale, Baidháwi.*

Let down his bucket. "And Joseph, making use of the opportunity, took hold of the cord, and was drawn up by the man."—*Sale.*

Good news! "The original words are *Yá bushrá,* the latter of which some take for the proper name of the water-drawer's companion, whom he called to his assistance; and then they must be translated O Bushra."—*Sale.*

They concealed him. "The expositors are not agreed whether the pronoun 'they' relates to Málik and his companions or to Joseph's brethren. They who espouse the former opinion say that those who came to draw water concealed the manner of their coming by him from the rest of the caravan, that they might keep him to themselves, pretending that some people of the place had given him to them to sell for them in Egypt. And they who prefer the latter opinion tell us that Judah carried victuals to Joseph every day while he was in the well, but not finding him there on the fourth day, he acquainted his brothers with it; whereupon they all went to the caravan and claimed Joseph as their slave, he not daring to discover that he was their brother, lest something worse should befall him; and at length they agreed to sell him to them."—*Sale, Baidháwi.*

The only fair interpretation of this passage is that the travellers hid him and sold him as a slave. The adverse opinion of the commentators is due to their desire to make the account tally with the story of Moses.

(20) *A mean price.* "Namely, twenty or twenty-two *dirhems,* and those not of full weight neither; for having weighed one ounce of silver only, the remainder was paid by tale, which is the most un-

‖ (21) And the Egyptian who bought him said to his wife, Use him honourably; peradventure he may be serviceable to us, or we may adopt him for our son. Thus did we prepare an establishment for Joseph in the earth, and we taught him the interpretation of *dark* sayings; for GOD is well able to effect his purpose, but the greater part of men do not understand. (22) And when he had attained his age of strength, we bestowed on him wisdom and knowledge; for thus do we recompense the righteous. (23) And she in whose house he was desired him to lie with her; and she shut the doors and said, Come hither. He answered, GOD forbid! verily my lord hath made my dwelling *with him* easy; and the ungrateful shall not prosper. (24) But she resolved within herself *to enjoy* him, and he would have resolved *to enjoy* her, had he not

---

fair way of payment."—*Sale, Baidhāwi.* Compare with Gen. xxxvii. 28-36.

(21) *The Egyptian.* "His name was Kitfír or Itfír (a corruption of Potipher); and he was a man of great consideration, being superintendent of the royal treasury. The commentators say that Joseph came into his service at seventeen, and lived with him thirteen years; and that he was made prime minister in the thirty-third year of his age, and died at one hundred and twenty. They who suppose Joseph was twice sold differ as to the price the Egyptian paid for him, some saying it was twenty dinárs of gold, a pair of shoes, and two white garments; and others, that it was a large quantity of silver or of gold."—*Sale.*

This person is usually called Azíz or Azíz-i-misr by the commentators and Muslim writers in India.

His wife. "Some call her Raïl, but the name she is best known by is that of Zulaikha."—*Sale.*

We may adopt him. "Kitfír having no children. It is said that Joseph gained his master's good opinion so suddenly by his countenance, which Kitfír, who, they pretend, had great skill in physiognomy, judged to indicate his prudence and other good qualities."—*Sale.*

Dark sayings. See note on ver. 6.

(23) *My lord,* viz., "Kitfír. But others understand it to be spoken of God."—*Sale.*

(24) *He would have resolved, &c.* This contradicts Gen. xxxix. 9; but the story is founded on Jewish tradition, as given in the Babylon Talmud, chap. Nashim, p. 36.

The evident demonstration, &c. "That is, had he not seriously considered the filthiness of whoredom, and the great guilt thereof. Some, however, suppose that the words mean some miraculous voice or apparition, sent by God to divert Joseph from executing the

seen the evident demonstration of his LORD. So we turned away evil and filthiness from him, because he was one of our sincere servants. (25) And they ran *to get one before the other* to the door, and she rent his inner garment behind. And they met her lord at the door. She said, What *shall be* the reward of him who seeketh *to commit* evil in thy family but imprisonment and a painful punishment? (26) And Joseph said, She asked me to lie with her. And a witness of her family bore witness, *saying*, If his garment be rent before, she speaketh truth, and he is a liar;

‖ (27) But if his garment be rent behind, she lieth, and R $\frac{4}{14}$. he is a speaker of truth. (28) And when *her husband* saw that his garment was torn behind, he said, This is a cunning contrivance of your *sex;* for surely your cunning is great. (29) O Joseph, take no further notice of this *affair:* and thou, *O woman*, ask pardon for thy crime, for

---

criminal thoughts which began to possess him. For they say that he was so far tempted with his mistress's beauty and enticing behaviour, that he sat in her lap, and even began to undress himself, when a voice called to him, and bid him beware of her; but he taking no notice of this admonition, though it was repeated three times, at length the Angel Gabriel, or, as others will have it, the figure of his master, appeared to him; but the more general opinion is that it was the apparition of his father Jacob, who bit his fingers' ends, or, as some write, struck him on the breast, whereupon his lubricity passed out at the ends of his fingers.

"For this fable, so injurious to the character of Joseph, the Muhammadans are obliged to their old friends the Jews, who imagine that he had a design to lie with his mistress, from these words of Moses: 'And it came to pass . . . that Joseph went into the house to do his business, &c."—*Sale, Baidháwi, Jaláluddín, &c.*

(25) *They ran.* "He flying from her, and she running after to detain him."—*Sale.*

She rent his garment behind. "Gen. xl. 15 reads, 'He left his garment in her hand . . . and got him out.' The whole garment was left, not torn. Her lord did not *meet them at the door;* ver. 16 (of Gen.) says she laid up the garment by her till her lord came home."—*Brinckman's Notes on Islám*, p. 114.

(26) *A witness of her family*, viz., "a cousin of hers, who was then a child in the cradle."—*Sale, Baidháwi, &c.*

(28, 29) *This is a cunning contrivance, &c.* This decidedly contradicts Gen. xxxix. 19 and 20, where it is said that Potipher believed his wife's story, and in great wrath put Joseph in prison.

thou art a guilty person. (30) And certain women said *publicly* in the city, The nobleman's wife asked her servant to lie with her; he hath inflamed her breast with his love; and we perceive her *to be* in manifest error. (31) And when she heard of their subtle behaviour, she sent unto them and prepared a banquet for them, and she gave to each of them a knife; and she said *unto Joseph*, Come forth unto them. And when they saw him they praised him greatly, and they cut their own hands, and said, O GOD! this is not a mortal; he is no other than an angel,

---

(30) *Certain women.* "These women, whose tongues were so free with Zulaikha's character on this occasion, were five in number, and the wives of so many of the king's chief officers, viz., his chamberlain, his butler, his baker, his jailer, and his herdsman."—*Sale, Baidháwi.*

(31) *She sent unto them.* "The number of all the women invited was forty, and among them were the five ladies above mentioned."—*Sale, Baidháwi.*

Savary says, "The Egyptian women frequently visit and give entertainments to each other. Men are excluded. Only the slaves necessary to wait on the company are admitted. The pleasures of the table are succeeded by music and dancing. They are passionately fond of both. The *Almé*, that is to say, *the learned women*, are the delight of these entertainments. They sing verses in praise of guests, and conclude with love-songs. They afterwards exhibit voluptuous dances, the licentiousness of which is often carried to excess."

They praised him greatly. "The old Latin translators have strangely mistaken the sense of the original word *akbarnáho*, which they render *menstruatæ sunt;* and then rebuke Muhammad for the indecency, crying out demurely in the margin, *O fœdum et obscœnum prophetam!* Erpenius thinks that there is not the least trace of such a meaning in the word; but he is mistaken, for the verb *kabara* in the fourth conjugation, which is here used, has that import, though the subjoining of the pronoun to it here (which possibly the Latin translators did not observe) absolutely overthrows that interpretation."—*Sale.*

Cut their own hands. "Through extreme surprise at the wonderful beauty of Joseph; which surprise Zulaikha foreseeing, put knives into their hands on purpose that this accident might happen. Some writers observed, on occasion of this passage, that it is customary in the East for lovers to testify the violence of their passion by cutting themselves, as a sign that they would spend their blood in the service of the person beloved; which is true enough, but I do not find that any of the commentators suppose these Egyptian ladies had any such design."

The *Tafsír-i-Raufí* says they were beside themselves, and went on cutting their hands without feeling any pain.

deserving the highest respect. (32) And *his mistress* said, This is he for whose sake ye blamed me; I asked him to lie with me, but he constantly refused. But if he do not perform that which I command him, he shall surely be cast into prison, and he shall be made *one* of the contemptible. (33) *Joseph* said, O LORD, a prison is more eligible unto me than *the crime* to which they invite me; but unless thou turn aside their snares from me, I shall youthfully incline unto them, and I shall become *one* of the foolish. (34) Wherefore his LORD heard him, and turned aside their snare from him, for he *both* heareth *and* knoweth. (35) And it seemed good unto them, *even* after they had seen the signs *of innocency*, to imprison him for a time.

|| (36) And there entered into the prison with him two R $\frac{5}{15}$. *of the king's* servants. One of them said, It seemed to me *in my dream* that I pressed wine *out of grapes*. And the other said, It seemed unto me *in my dream* that I carried bread on my head, whereof the birds did eat. Declare unto us the interpretation of *our dreams*, for we perceive that thou art a beneficent person. (37) *Joseph* answered, No food wherewith ye may be nourished shall come

---

(32-34) The spirit of these verses is not only opposed to the history of Joseph as given in the Bible, but is unworthy of a book claiming to be inspired. ' The conduct attributed to Potipher is contrary to reason and common sense.

(35) *It seemed good unto them, &c.* "That is to Kitfír and his friends. The occasion of Joseph's imprisonment is said to be, either that they suspected him to be guilty notwithstanding the proofs which had been given of his innocence; or else that Zulaikha desired it, feigning, to deceive her husband, that she wanted to have Joseph removed from her sight till she could conquer her passion by time, though her real design was to force him to compliance."—*Sale, Baidháwi, &c.*

This is evidently said to account for the imprisonment of Joseph. The excellency of the style and matter of the Qurán are hardly perceptible here.

(36) *Two of the king's servants,* viz., "his chief butler and baker, who were accused of a design to poison him."—*Sale.*

One of them, viz., the butler.

(37) *No food, &c.* "The meaning of this passage seems to be,

unto you, but I will declare unto you the interpretation thereof before it come unto you. This *knowledge is a part* of that which my LORD hath taught me; for I have left the religion of people who believe not in GOD, and who deny the life to come, (38) and I follow the religion of my fathers, Abraham, and Isaac, and Jacob. It is not *lawful* for us to associate anything with GOD. This *knowledge of the divine unity hath been given us* of the bounty of GOD towards us and towards mankind; but the greater part of men are not thankful. (39) O my fellow-prisoners, are sundry lords better or the only true and mighty GOD? (40) Ye worship not, besides him other than the names which ye have named, ye and your fathers, concerning which GOD hath sent down no authoritative proof: yet judgment *belongeth* unto GOD alone, *who* hath commanded that ye worship none besides him. This is the right religion; but the greater part of men know *it* not. (41) O my fellow-prisoners, verily the one of you shall serve wine unto his lord *as formerly;* but the other shall be crucified, and the birds shall eat from off his head. The matter is decreed concerning which ye seek to be informed. (42) And *Joseph* said unto him whom he judged to be the person who should escape of the two, Remember me in the presence of thy lord. But the devil caused him to forget

---

either that Joseph, to show he used no arts of divination or astrology, promises to interpret their dreams to them immediately, even before they should eat a single meal; or else he here offers to prophesy to them beforehand the quantity of the victuals which should be brought them, as a test of his skill."—*Sale.*

I have left the religion, &c. Muhammad here puts his own thoughts and sayings into the mouth of Joseph.

(38) *I follow the religion.* It is noticeable the Qurán here omits the name of Ishmael, showing how closely Muhammad followed the tradition of the Jews.

(40) *The names.* See note on chap. vii. 72.

(42) *The devil caused him to forget.* "According to the explication of some, who take the pronoun *him* to relate to Joseph, this passage may be rendered, 'But the devil caused him (*i.e.,* Joseph) to forget to make his application unto his Lord;' and to beg the good offices

to make mention of *Joseph* unto his lord, wherefore he remained in the prison some years.

|| (43) And the king *of Egypt* said, Verily, I saw *in my dream* seven fat kine, which seven lean kine devoured, and seven green ears *of corn*, and other *seven* withered *ears*. O nobles, expound my vision unto me, if ye be *able to* interpret a vision. (44) They answered, *They are* confused dreams, neither are we skilled in the interpretation of *such kind of* dreams. (45) And *Joseph's fellow-prisoner* who had been delivered, said (for he remembered *Joseph* after a certain space of time), I will declare unto you the interpretation thereof; wherefore let me go *unto the person who will interpret it unto me.* (46) *And he went to the prison, and said,* O Joseph, thou man of veracity, teach us *the interpretation* of seven fat kine, which seven lean kine devoured; and of seven green ears *of corn*, and other *seven* withered *ears, which the king saw in his dream;* that I may return unto the men *who have sent me,* that peradventure they may understand *the same.* (47) *Joseph* answered, Ye shall sow seven years as usual; and *the corn*

R $\frac{6}{16}$.

---

of his fellow-prisoner for his deliverance, instead of relying on God alone, as it became a prophet especially to have done."—*Sale.*

Rodwell shows that the passage is derived from Jewish tradition.

Some years. "The original word signifying any number from three to nine or ten, the common opinion is that Joseph remained in prison seven years, though some say he was confined no less than twelve years."—*Sale, Baidháwi, Jaláluddín.*

The period was *two* years. See Gen. xli. 1.

(43) *The king of Egypt.* "This prince, as the Oriental writers generally agree, was Riyán, the son of al Walíd, the Amalekite (Prelim. Disc., p. 24), who was converted by Joseph to the worship of the true God, and died in the lifetime of that prophet. But some pretend that the Pharaoh of Joseph and of Moses were one and the same person, and that he lived (or rather reigned) four hundred years."

It can scarcely be disputed that the Qurán teaches that the Pharaohs of Joseph and of Moses are the same.

(47) The account here given of the interpretation of the king's dreams is also contrary to the story of Moses. Here it is said the butler asks Joseph the interpretation of the dreams, he yet being in prison. The Bible says that Joseph explained the dream to Pharaoh himself (Gen. xli. 15–37).

which ye shall reap do ye leave in its ear, except a little whereof ye may eat. (48) Then shall there come after this seven grievous *years of famine*, which shall consume what ye shall have laid up as a provision for the same, except a little which ye shall have kept. (49) Then shall there come after this a year wherein men shall have plenty of rain, and wherein they shall press *wine and oil*.

R $\frac{7}{1}$. || (50) And *when the chief butler had reported this*, the king said, Bring him unto me. And when the messenger came unto *Joseph*, he said, Return unto thy lord, and ask of him what was the intent of the women who cut their hands; for my LORD well knoweth the snare which they laid *for me*. (51) *And when the women were assembled before the king*, he said *unto them*, What was your design

---

Leave in its ear. Baidháwi says in order "to preserve it from the weevil."—*Sale.*

(49) *Plenty of rain.* "Notwithstanding what some ancient authors write to the contrary (Plato in *Timæo*, *Pomp. Mela.*), it often rains in winter in the Lower Egypt, and even snow has been observed to fall at Alexandria, contrary to the express assertion of Seneca (*Nat. Quæst.*, l. 4). In the Upper Egypt, indeed, towards the cataracts of the Nile, it rains very seldom (Greave's *Descrip. of the Pyramids*, p. 74, &c.) Some, however, suppose that the rains here mentioned are intended of those which should fall in Ethiopia and occasion the swelling of the Nile, the great cause of the fertility of Egypt; or else of those which should fall in the neighbouring countries, which were also afflicted with famine during the same time."—*Sale.*

The statement of the text is certainly a mistake, testifying to the fallibility of the Prophet.

(50) *Return unto thy lord, &c.* This passage seems to say that Potipher, the lord of Joseph, was identical with the king of Egypt. Rodwell's translation gives this meaning. See Rodwell, v. 51.

The women who cut their hands. "Joseph, it seems, cared not to get out of prison till his innocence was publicly known and declared. It is observed by the commentators that Joseph does not bid the messenger move the king to inform himself of the truth of the affair, but bids him directly to ask the king, to incite him to make the proper inquiry with the greater earnestness. They also observe that Joseph takes care not to mention his mistress, out of respect and gratitude for the favours he had received while in her house."

(51) *What was your design.* Note that the five women who came to Zulaikha's feast are here charged with the same crime as she. Sacred writ knows nothing of this.

when ye solicited Joseph to unlawful love? They answered, GOD be praised! we know not any ill of him. The nobleman's wife said, Now is the truth become manifest: I solicited him to lie with me; and he is *one* of those who speak truth. (52) *And when Joseph was acquainted therewith he said,* This *discovery hath been made* that *my* lord might know that I was not unfaithful unto him in *his* absence, and that GOD directeth not the plot of the deceivers.

‖ (53) Neither do I *absolutely* justify myself: since every soul is prone unto evil, except those on whom my LORD shall show mercy; for my LORD *is* gracious *and* merciful. (54) And the king said, Bring him unto me: I will take him into my own peculiar service. And when *Joseph was brought unto the king, and* he had discoursed with him, he said, Thou art this day firmly established

---

Now is the truth become manifest. There seems to be here a clear contradiction of ver. 28 and onward. There Zulaikha's guilt was manifested not only to her husband, whom I believe to be the king or prince mentioned here, but was spread abroad throughout the whole city. Here, however, she is made to confess the crime for the *first time,* and Joseph is made to express satisfaction at a confession which at last sets him in a right light before his lord.

(52) *That my lord might know, &c.* This verse also confirms the view expressed above, ver. 50, that Joseph's *lord* and the *king* are the same.

(53) *Neither do I justify myself.* "According to a tradition of Ibn Abbás, Joseph had no sooner spoken the foregoing words asserting his innocency, than Gabriel said to him, 'What! not when thou wast deliberating to lie with her?' Upon which Joseph confessed his frailty."—*Sale, Baidháwi.*

See also note on ver. 24.

(54) *Bring him unto me, &c.* Joseph is here said to have been released from prison *after* the interpretation of the dreams. Gen. xli. 14 says he was released *before.*

Thou art this day, &c. "The commentators say that Joseph being taken out of prison, after he had washed and changed his clothes, was introduced to the king, whom he saluted in the Hebrew tongue, and on the king's asking what language that was, he answered that it was the language of his fathers. This prince, they say, understood no less than seventy languages, in every one of which he discoursed with Joseph, who answered him in the same; at which the king, greatly marvelling, desired him to relate his dream, which he did, describing the most minute circumstances: whereupon the king placed Joseph by him on his throne, and made him his Wazir or

with us, *and shalt be* intrusted *with our affairs.* (55) *Joseph* answered, Set me over the storehouses of the land; for I *will be* a skilful keeper *thereof.* (56) Thus did we establish Joseph in the land, that he might provide himself a dwelling therein where he pleased. We bestow our mercy on whom we please, and we suffer not the reward of the righteous to perish; (57) and certainly the reward of the next life is better for those who believe and fear *God.*

R $\frac{8}{2}$. ‖ (58) Moreover, Joseph's brethren came, and went in unto him; and he knew them, but they knew not him.

---

chief minister. Some say that his master Kitfír dying about this time, he not only succeeded him in his place, but, by the king's command, married the widow, his late mistress, whom he found to be a virgin, and who bare him Ephraim and Manasses. So that, according to this tradition, she was the same woman who is called Asenath by Moses. This supposed marriage, which authorised their amours, probably encouraged the Muhammadan divines to make use of the loves of Joseph and Zulaikha as an allegorical emblem of the spiritual love between the Creator and the creature, God and the soul, just as the Christians apply the Song of Solomon to the same mystical purpose." *Vide* D'Herbelot, *Bibl. Orient.,* art. *Jousouf.*—*Sale, Baidháwi.*

This is the popular Muhammadan view, crystallised in the celebrated poem "Yusuf and Zulaikha." The mystical use of the story alluded to by Sale is only prevalent among the Súfí sect of Muslims, who, being Pantheists, apply it very differently from the way Christians interpret and apply the Song of Solomon.

(55) *Joseph's reputation for modesty* suffers sadly at the hands of the Qurán. His character stands out in a very different light in Genesis.

(58) *Joseph's brethren came.* "Joseph, being made Wazír, governed with great wisdom; for he not only caused justice to be impartially administered, and encouraged the people to industry and the improvement of agriculture during the seven years of plenty, but began and perfected several works of great benefit; the natives at this day ascribing to the patriarch Joseph almost all the ancient works of public utility throughout the kingdom, as particularly the rendering the province of al Faiyúm from a standing pool or marsh the most fertile and best-cultivated land in all Egypt. When the years of famine came, the effects of which were felt not only in Egypt, but in Syria and the neighbouring countries, the inhabitants were obliged to apply to Joseph for corn, which he sold to them first for their money, jewels, and ornaments, then for their cattle and lands, and at length for their persons; so that all the Egyptians in general be-

(59) And when he had furnished them with their provisions, he said, Bring unto me your brother, *the son* of your father; do ye not see that I give full measure, and that I am the most hospitable receiver of guests? (60) But if ye bring him not unto me, there shall be no *corn* measured unto you from me, neither shall ye approach *my presence*. (61) They answered, We will endeavour to obtain him of his father, and we will certainly perform *what thou requirest*. And (62) *Joseph* said to his servants, Put their money *which they have paid for their corn* into their sacks, that they may perceive it when they shall be returned to

---

came slaves to the king, though Joseph, by his consent, soon released them, and returned them their substance. The dearth being felt in the land of Canaan, Jacob sent all his sons, except only Benjamin, into Egypt for corn. On their arrival, Joseph (who well knew them) asked them who they were, saying he suspected them to be spies; but they told him they came only to buy provisions, and that they were all the sons of an ancient man, named Jacob, who was also a prophet. Joseph then asked how many brothers there were of them; they answered, Twelve; but that one of them had been lost in a desert. Upon which he inquired for the eleventh brother, there being no more than ten of them present. They said he was a lad, and with their father, whose fondness for him would not suffer him to accompany them in their journey. At length Joseph asked them who they had to vouch for their veracity; but they told him they knew no man who could vouch for them in Egypt. Then, replied he, one of you shall stay behind with me as a pledge, and the others may return home with their provisions; and when ye come again, ye shall bring your younger brother with you, that I may know ye have told me the truth. Whereupon, it being in vain to dispute the matter, they cast lots who should stay behind, and the lot fell upon Simeon. When they departed, Joseph gave each of them a camel, and another for their brother."—*Sale, Baidháwi.*

This comment shows how the commentators have supplémented the Qurán by reference to the Old Testament Scriptures. A strong argument against the Qurán may be drawn from this very use of the Old Testament Scriptures by Muslim commentators, thus attesting the credibility of the book, which is contradicted by the very Qurán they would illustrate by reference to it.

(62) *Their money.* "The original word signifying not only money, but also goods bartered or given in exchange for other merchandise, some commentators tell us that they paid for their corn, not in money, but in shoes and dressed skins."—*Sale, Baidháwi.*

There can be no doubt about the word meaning *money* here, for how could shoes and skins be put into the grain bags so as not to be discovered until their return?

their family, peradventure they will come back *unto us*. (63) And when they were returned unto their father they said, O father, it is forbidden to measure out *corn* unto us *any more unless we carry our brother Benjamin with us:* wherefore send our brother with us and we shall have *corn* measured unto us; and we will certainly guard him *from any mischance*. (64) *Jacob* answered, Shall I trust him with you *with any better success* than I trusted your brother *Joseph* with you heretofore? But GOD is the best guardian, and he is the most merciful of those that show mercy. (65) And when they opened their provision, they found their money had been returned unto them; *and* they said, O father, what do we desire *further?* this our money hath been returned unto us; we will therefore *return, and* provide corn for our family; we will take care of our brother; and we shall receive a camel's burden more *than we did the last time*. This is a small quantity. (66) *Jacob* said, I will by no means send him with you, until ye give me a solemn promise, *and swear* by GOD that ye will certainly bring him back unto me, unless ye be encompassed *by some inevitable impediment*. And when they had given him their solemn promise, he said, GOD is witness of what we say. (67) And he said, My sons, enter not *into the city* by one *and the same* gate,

---

(65) *O father, &c.* Gen. xlii. 25–35 represents this matter very differently. 1. The discovery of a portion of the returned money occurred on the journey. 2. A similar discovery as to the rest of the purchase-money occurred on the opening of the sacks at Jacob's dwelling. 3. Instead of joy, *all* were filled with fear.

This is a small quantity. "The meaning may be, either that the corn they now brought was not sufficient for the support of their families, so that it was necessary for them to take another journey, or else that a camel's load more or less was but a trifle to the king of Egypt. Some suppose these to be the words of Jacob, declaring it was too mean a consideration to induce him to part with his son." —*Sale.*

(66) This also contradicts Gen. xlii. 36–xliii. 14.

(67) *Enter not by one gate.* This, says the *Tafsír-i-Raufí*, was to prevent their appearing in such number and grandeur as to excite the suspicion of the Egyptians. There seems to be a hint here to

but enter by different gates. But *this precaution* will be of no advantage unto you against *the decree of* GOD; for judgment belongeth unto GOD alone: in him do I put my trust, and in him let those confide who *seek in whom to put their trust.* (68) And when they entered *the city,* as their father had commanded them, it was of no advantage unto them against *the decree of* GOD, *and the same served* only *to satisfy* the desire of Jacob's soul, which he had charged *them to perform:* for he was endued with knowledge of that which we had taught him; but the greater part of men do not understand.

|| (69) And when they entered into the presence of R $\frac{9}{3}$. Joseph, he received his brother *Benjamin* as his guest, *and* said, Verily I am thy brother, be not therefore afflicted for that which they have committed *against us.* (70) And when he had furnished them with their provisions, he put *his* cup in his brother *Benjamin's* sack. Then a crier cried *after them, saying,* O company of travellers, ye are surely thieves. (71) They said (and turned back unto them), What *is it* that ye miss? (72) They answered, We miss

---

Joseph's charge against them that they were *spies* in the land. The text is found verbatim in Midr. Rabba on Genesis, par. 91.

(69) *I am thy brother.* "It is related that Joseph, having invited his brethren to an entertainment, ordered them to be placed two and two together, by which means Benjamin, the eleventh, was obliged to sit alone, and bursting into tears, said, 'If my brother Joseph were alive, he would have sat with me.' Whereupon Joseph ordered him to be seated at the same table with himself, and when the entertainment was over, dismissed the rest, ordering that they should be lodged two and two in a house, but kept Benjamin in his own apartment, where he passed the night. The next day Joseph asked him whether he would accept of himself for his brother in the room of him whom he had lost, to which Benjamin replied, 'Who can find a brother comparable unto thee? yet thou art not the son of Jacob and Rachel.' And upon this Joseph discovered himself to him."—*Sale, Baidhâwi.*

This contradiction of Gen. xlv. 1 is also drawn from Rabbinical sources. See reference in Rodwell.

(70) *His cup.* "Some imagine this to be a measure holding a saá (or about a gallon), wherein they used to measure corn or give water to the beasts. But others take it to be a drinking-cup of silver or gold."—*Sale.*

the prince's cup; and unto him who shall produce it *shall be given* a camel's load *of corn,* and I *will be* surety for the same. (73) *Joseph's brethren* replied, By GOD, ye do well know that we come not to act corruptly in the land, neither are we thieves. (74) *The Egyptians* said, What shall be the reward of him *who shall appear to have stolen the cup,* if ye be *found* liars? (75) *Joseph's brethren* answered, As to the reward of him in whose sack it shall be found, let him become *a bondman in* satisfaction of the same: thus do we reward the unjust *who are guilty of theft.* (76) Then he began by their sacks, before *he searched* the sack of his brother; and he drew out *the cup* from his brother's sack. Thus did we furnish Joseph with a stratagem. It was not *lawful* for him to take his brother *for a bondman* by the law of the king *of Egypt,* had not GOD pleased *to allow it, according to the offer of his brethren.* We exalt to degrees *of knowledge and honour* whom we please; and *there is one who is* knowing above all those who are endued with knowledge. (77) *His brethren* said, If *Benjamin* be guilty of theft, his brother *Joseph* hath been also guilty of theft heretofore. But Joseph

---

(73) *Ye do well know, &c.* "Both by our behaviour among you, and our bringing again our money, which was returned to us without our knowledge."—*Sale.*

(75) *Thus do we reward the unjust.* "This was the method of punishing theft used by Jacob and his family; for among the Egyptians it was punished in another manner."—*Sale.*

(76) *Then he began, &c.* "Some suppose this search was made by the person whom Jacob sent after them; others, by Joseph himself when they were brought back to the city."—*Sale.*

It was not lawful, &c. "For there the thief was not reduced to servitude, but was scourged, and obliged to restore the double of what he had stolen."—*Sale, Baidháwi, Jaláluddin.*

(77) *His brother Joseph hath been also guilty, &c.* "The occasion of this suspicion, it is said, was, that Joseph having been brought up by his father's sister, she became so fond of him, that when he grew up, and Jacob designed to take him from her, she contrived the following stratagem to keep him. Having a girdle which had once belonged to Abraham, she girt it about the child, and then pretending she had lost it, caused strict search to be made for it; and it being at length found on Joseph, he was adjudged, according to the above-mentioned law of the family, to be delivered to her as her

concealed these things in his mind, and did not discover them unto them: *and* he said *within himself,* Ye are in a worse condition *than us two;* and GOD best knoweth what ye discourse about. (78) They said *unto Joseph,* Noble *lord,* verily this *lad* hath an aged father; wherefore take one of us in his stead; for we perceive that thou art a beneficent person. (79) *Joseph* answered, GOD forbid that we should take *any other* than him with whom we found our goods; for then should we certainly *be* unjust.

|| (80) And when they despaired of *obtaining Benjamin,* they retired to confer privately together. *And* the elder of them said, Do ye not know that your father hath received a solemn promise from you, in the name of GOD, and how perfidiously ye behaved heretofore towards Joseph? Wherefore I will by no means depart the land *of Egypt* until my father give me leave *to return unto him,* or GOD maketh known his will to me; for he is the best judge. (81) Return ye to your father and say, O father, verily thy son hath committed theft; we bear witness of no more than what we know, and we could not guard against what we did not foresee: (82) and do thou

R $\tfrac{10}{4}$.

---

property. Some, however, say that Joseph actually stole an idol of gold, which belonged to his mother's father, and destroyed it; a story probably taken from Rachel's stealing the images of Laban: and others tell us that he once stole a goat or a hen to give to a poor man."—*Sale, Baidháwi, Jalaluddín.*

Rodwell thinks this portion of the chapter is founded upon some such tradition as Midr. Rabba., par. 92. See Rodwell *in loco.*

God best knoweth what ye discourse. According to the *Tafsír-i-Raufí,* some authorities say that one of Joseph's brethren became quite violent, whereupon Joseph descended from the throne and threw him down, saying, "O ye Canaanites, ye boast yourselves and think none can conquer you." Thus they account for the humble tone of their address in ver. 78.

(80) *The elder,* viz., "Reuben. But some think Simeon or Judah to be here meant; and instead of *the elder,* interpret it *the most prudent of them."—Sale.*

These various explanations of the word *kabíra* would never have been heard of but for the desire to reconcile the passage with Gen. xliv. 16-18. See above on ver. 58.

(81) *Return ye to your father.* There is here probably a confused reference to the imprisonment of Simeon (Gen. xlii. 24).

inquire in the city where we have been, and of the company of merchants with whom we are arrived, and *thou wilt find* that we speak the truth. (83) *And when they were returned, and had spoken thus to their father,* he said, Nay, but rather ye yourselves have contrived the thing for your own sakes, but patience *is* most proper *for me;* peradventure GOD will restore them all unto me; for he *is* knowing *and* wise. (84) And he turned from them and said, Oh how I am grieved for Joseph! And his eyes become white with mourning, he being oppressed with deep sorrow. (85) *His sons* said, By GOD, thou wilt not cease to remember Joseph until thou be brought to death's door, or thou be actually destroyed *by excessive affliction.* (86) He answered, I only represent my grief, which I am not able to contain, and my sorrow unto GOD; but I know *by revelation* from GOD that which ye know not. (87) O my sons, go and make inquiry after Joseph and his brother; and despair not of the mercy of GOD; for none despaireth of God's mercy except the unbelieving people. (88) *Wherefore Joseph's brethren returned into Egypt;* and when they came into

---

(83) *Ye yourselves have contrived the thing.* See the same words in ver. 18 above.

God will restore them all unto me, i.e., Joseph, Benjamin, and "the elder" brother, who, according to the commentators, should be Judah. See *Tafsîr-i-Raufi.*

(84) *His eyes became white.* "That is, the pupils lost their deep blackness and became of a pearl colour (as happens in suffusions), by his continual weeping; which very much weakened his sight, or, as some pretend, made him quite blind."—*Sale, Baidháwi.*

(85) This passage is probably based on Gen. xliii. 2–9.

(86) *But I know, &c.,* viz., "that Joseph is yet alive; of which some tell us he was assured by the angel of death in a dream, though others suppose he depended on the completion of Joseph's dream, which must have been frustrated had he died before his brethren had bowed down before him."—*Sale, Baidháwi.*

It is difficult to reconcile this interpretation with that of ver. 84, though, in consideration of what follows (ver. 97), we must regard it as correct.

(87) *Joseph and his brethren.* This passage contradicts the whole spirit of the Bible story of Joseph.

his presence they said, Noble *lord,* the famine is felt by us and our family, and we are come with a small sum of money; yet give unto us full measure, and bestow *corn* upon us *as* alms, for GOD rewardeth the almsgivers. (89) *Joseph* said *unto them,* Do ye know what ye did unto Joseph and his brother, when ye were ignorant *of the consequences thereof?* (90) They answered, Art thou really Joseph? He replied, I am Joseph, and this is my brother. Now hath GOD been gracious unto us. For whoso feareth *God* and persevereth with patience *shall at length find relief,* since GOD will not suffer the reward of the righteous to perish. (91) They said, By GOD, now hath GOD chosen thee above us, and we have surely been sinners. (92) *Joseph* answered, Let there be no reproach *cast* on you this day. God forgiveth you, for he is the most merciful of those who show mercy. (93) Depart ye with this my inner garment, and throw it on my father's face, and he

---

(88) *With a small sum.* "Their money being clipped and adulterated. Some, however, imagine they did not bring money, but goods to barter, such as wool and butter, or other commodities of small value."—*Sale, Baidhâwi.*

(89) *Do ye know, &c.* "The injury they did Benjamin was the separating him from his brother; after which they kept him in so great subjection that he durst not speak to them but with the utmost submission. Some say that these words were occasioned by a letter which Joseph's brethren delivered to him from their father, requesting the releasement of Benjamin, and by the representing his extreme affliction at the loss of him and his brother. The commentators observe that Joseph, to excuse his brethren's behaviour towards him, attributes it to their ignorance and the heat of youth."—*Sale, Baidhâwi.*

(90) *Art thou really Joseph?* "They say that this question was not the effect of a bare suspicion that he was Joseph, but that they actually knew him, either by his face and behaviour, or by his fore-teeth, which he showed in smiling, or else by putting off his *tiara,* and discovering a whitish mole on his forehead."—*Sale, Baidhâwi.*

It is quite in accordance with this whole chapter that this passage should contradict Moses. And yet this is the "Perspicuous Book" (ver. 1), a "confirmation of those Scriptures which have been revealed before it" (ver. 111, the last verse).

(93) *My inner garment.* "Which the commentators generally suppose to be the same garment with which Gabriel invested him in the well; which having originally come from Paradise, had pre-

shall recover his sight; and *then* come unto me with all your family.

‖ (94) And when the company of travellers was departed *from Egypt on their journey towards Canaan,* their father said *unto those who were about him,* Verily I perceive the smell of Joseph, although ye think that I dote. (95) They answered, By GOD thou art in thy old mistake. (96) But when the messenger of good tidings was come *with Joseph's inner garment,* he threw it over his face, and he recovered his eyesight. (97) *And Jacob* said, Did I not tell you that I knew from GOD that which ye knew not? (98) They answered, O father, ask pardon of our sins for us, for we have surely been sinners. (99) He replied, I will surely ask pardon for you of my LORD, for he *is* gracious *and* merciful. (100) And when *Jacob and his family arrived in Egypt, and* were introduced unto Joseph, he received his parents unto him, and said, Enter ye into Egypt, by

---

served the odour of that place, and was of so great virtue as to cure any distemper in the person who was touched with it."—*Sale, Baidháwi.*

He shall recover his sight. "This is most likely derived from Gen. xlvi. 4, God telling Jacob to go to Egypt, and 'Joseph shall put his hands upon thine eyes.' Jacob's eyes were dim, but not quite blind."—*Brinckman's Notes on Islám,* p. 115.

(94) *The smell of Joseph.* "This was the odour of the garment above mentioned, brought by the wind to Jacob, who smelt it, as is pretended, at the distance of eighty parasangs, or, as others will have, three or eight days' journey off."—*Sale, Baidháwi, Jaláluddín.*

Compare Gen. xxvii. 27.

(95) *Thy old mistake.* "Being led into this imagination by the excessive love of Joseph."—*Sale.*

(96) *The messenger,* viz., "Judah, who, as he had formerly grieved his father by bringing him Joseph's coat stained with blood, now rejoiced him as much by being the bearer of this vest and the news of Joseph's prosperity."—*Sale, Jaláluddín.*

(99) *My Lord.* "Deferring it, as some fancy, till he should see Joseph and have his consent."—*Sale.*

According to Muslim teaching, God cannot pardon a sin against a man without that man's consent. See note on chap. xiv. 11.

(100) *His parents,* viz., "his father and Leah his mother's sister, whom he looked on as his mother after Rachel's death." (See Gen. xxxvii. 10. "Al Baidháwi tells us that Joseph sent carriages and provisions for his father and family, and that he and the king

GOD's favour, in full security. (101) And he raised his parents to the seat of state, and they, *together with his brethren,* fell down and did obeisance unto him. And he said, O my father, this is the interpretation of my vision *which I saw* heretofore; now hath my LORD rendered it true. And he hath surely been gracious unto me, since he took me forth from the prison, and hath brought you hither from the desert, after that the devil had sown discord between me and my brethren; for my LORD is gracious unto whom he pleaseth, and he *is* the knowing, the wise *God.* (102) O LORD, thou hast given me *a part* of the kingdom, and hast taught me the interpretation of *dark* sayings. The Creator of heaven and earth! thou art my protector in this world, and in that which is to come; make me to die a Muslim, and join me with the righteous. (103) This is a secret history which we reveal unto thee,

---

of Egypt went forth to meet them. He adds that the number of the children of Israel who entered Egypt with him was seventy-two, and that when they were led out thence by Moses they were increased to six hundred thousand five hundred and seventy men and upwards, besides the old people and children."—*Sale, Baidháwi, Jaláluddín.*

(101) *He raised his parents, &c.* The basis of this statement may be Gen. xlvii. 11.

This is the interpretation. That Joseph made this statement is contrary to the Bible. The proud, self-satisfied spirit here attributed to Joseph is in entire keeping with the morality of Islám, but a travesty of the Bible account of Joseph.

(102) *Make me to die a Muslim.* "The Muhammadan authors write that Jacob dwelt in Egypt twenty-four years, and at his death ordered his body to be buried in Palestine by his father, which Joseph took care to perform; and then returning into Egypt, died twenty-three years after. They add that such high disputes arose among the Egyptians concerning his burial, that they had like to have come to blows; but at length they agreed to put his body into a marble coffin, and to sink it in the Nile, out of a superstitious imagination that it might help the regular increase of the river, and deliver them from famine for the future; but when Moses led the Israelites out of Egypt, he took up the coffin, and carried Joseph's bones with him into Canaan, where he buried them by his ancestors."
—*Sale, Baidháwi.*

(103) *This is a secret history which we reveal unto thee, &c.* I cannot conceive of Muhammad's making this statement, except as a deli-

O Muhammad, although thou wast not present with the *brethren of Joseph* when they concerted their design and contrived a plot *against him*. But the greater part of men, although they earnestly desire it, will not believe. (104) Thou shalt not demand of them any reward for *thy publishing the Qurán;* it is no other than an admonition unto all creatures.

|| (105) And how many signs soever *there be of the being, unity, and providence of God* in the heavens and the earth, they will pass by them, and will retire afar off from them. (106) And the greater part of them believe not in GOD, without being also guilty of idolatry. (107) Do they not believe that some overwhelming *affliction* shall fall on them as a punishment from GOD, or that the hour *of judgment* shall overtake them suddenly, when they consider not *its approach?* (108) Say *unto those of Makkah*, This is my way; I invite *you* unto GOD by an evident demonstration, *both* I and he who followeth me; and praise be unto God, I am not an idolater. (109) We sent not *any apostles* before thee, except men, unto whom we revealed *our will, and whom we chose* out of those who dwelt in cities. Will they not go through the earth, and see what

---

berate assertion of what he knew to be false. See Arnold's view in note on ver. 3 above.

Muir, in his *Life of Mahomet*, vol. ii. p. 189, puts this matter mildly as follows:—"It is possible that the convictions of Mahomet may have become so blended with his grand object and course of action, that the very *study* of the Coran and effort to compose it were regarded as his best season of devotion. But the stealthy and disingenuous manner in which he now availed himself of Jewish information, producing the result not only as original, but *as evidence of inspiration* (see Sura xxxviii. 70, xxviii. 45-47, xii. 102, &c.), begins to furnish proof of an active, though it may have been unconscious, course of dissimulation and falsehood, to be palliated only by the miserable apology of a pious end."

(106) *Idolatry.* "For this crime Muhammad charges not only on the idolatrous Makkans, but also on the Jews and Christians, as has been already observed more than once."—*Sale.*

It is not likely that Christians are referred to here, as there is scarcely any allusion to them in the Makkan Suras. See Muir's *Life of Mahomet*, vol. ii. p. 189.

(109) *Who dwelt in cities.* "And not of the inhabitants of the

hath been the end of those who have preceded them? But the dwelling of the next life shall surely be better for those who fear *God*. Will they not therefore understand? (110) *Their predecessors were borne with for a time*, until, when *our* apostles despaired *of their conversion*, and they thought that they were liars, our help came unto them, and we delivered whom we pleased; but our vengeance was not turned away from the wicked people. (111) Verily in the histories of *the prophets and their people* there is an instructive example unto those who are endued with understanding. *The Qurán* is not a new invented fiction, but a confirmation of *those scriptures* which *have been revealed* before it, and a distinct explication of everything *necessary in respect either to faith or practice*, and a direction and mercy unto people who believe.

---

deserts; because the former are more knowing and compassionate, and the latter more ignorant and hard-hearted."—*Sale, Baidháwi.*

(111) *The Qurán . . . a confirmation, &c.* This passage certainly attests the former Scriptures then extant as credible, and claims to explain more clearly than there revealed the meaning of them. Surely this one chapter proves not only how untrue this statement is, but how false that other that "the Qurán is not a new invented fiction."

CHAPTER XIII.

ENTITLED SURAT AL RAAD (THUNDER).

Revealed at Makkah.

INTRODUCTION.

THE name of this chapter occurs in ver. 14. All of the best authorities agree that this chapter originated at Makkah. Most of the Muslim commentators make vers. 14, 29-31, to allude to events which occurred at Madína late in the life of the Prophet, and a few writers, says Noeldeke, have thought the whole chapter should be referred to Madína. However, the interpretations given by these commentators are based entirely upon the words of these passages, and, in the absence of better evidence, must be regarded as widely mistaken.

The internal evidence of the chapter is decidedly in favour of referring the origin of the whole to Makkah, excepting perhaps ver. 41.

The contents of the chapter relate entirely to Muhammad's disputes with the infidel Quraish. A remarkable feature of it is its many apologies for Muhammad's failure to perform the miracles demanded by the unbelievers. On this account the author of the Notes on the Roman Urdu Qurán remarks that "this chapter should have been entitled the Chapter of Apologies."

Probable date of the Revelations.

We have already shown that this chapter, excepting ver. 41, must be referred to Makkah. As to the date of composition, the earlier verses of the chapter might be assigned to almost any period in the career of the Makkan preacher; but the latter part of the chapter must be referred to the latter part of his ministry at Makkah. This is evident from the allusion to the "adversity" of the Makkans in ver. 31, the belief of certain Jews in ver. 36, and the obstinate unbelief and opposition of the Quraish in vers. 30 and 42. If we take the allusion in vers. 36 and 37 to be to the lapse of Muhammad in his temporary compromise with idolatry about six years before the Hijra, and if we refer the statements of ver. 42 to the persecutions which arose on Muhammad's recovery from the lapse, and which culminated in the ban against the Háshimites, this portion of the chapter may be referred to the period intervening between the years 6 and 4 B.H.

Principal Subjects.

	VERSES
The infidels reject the Qurán	1
God manifests himself to man in his works	2–4
The unbelievers deny the resurrection	5
Their punishment	6
Threatened judgments sure to come to pass	7
Unbelievers demand a sign	8
God is omniscient	9–12
God's purposes are unchangeable	12
Thunder and lightning manifest God as the true object of worship	13, 14
Idolaters invoke their gods in vain	15
All nature worships the Creator	16, 17
The separation of infidels from true believers typified in the flowing stream and the melting metal	18
True believers described	19–22
Their reward	23, 24
The end of the infidels	25
Abundance of wealth no sign of God's favour	26
The infidels demand a sign from heaven	27
God directs true believers	28
Muhammad sent to an unbelieving people	29
Signs unavailing to make infidels true believers	30
God will punish the unbelievers	31, 32
Idolaters are reprobate	33, 34
Paradise described	35
Certain Jews acknowledge Muhammad to be a prophet	36
Muhammad exhorted to make no compromise with idolatry	36, 37
Wives and children no hindrance to the prophetic office	38
God is lord of his own book	39
Muhammad a preacher only	40
God's judgments sure to come to pass	41
The plots of God's enemies not hidden from him	42
God attests the claims of his Prophet	43

IN THE NAME OF THE MOST MERCIFUL GOD.

‖ (1) A. L. M. R. These are the signs of the book *of the Qurán;* and that which hath been sent down unto thee from thy LORD is the truth; but the greater part of men will not believe. (2) *It is* GOD who hath raised the heavens without visible pillars; *and* then ascended his throne, and compelled the sun and the moon to perform their services: every *of the heavenly bodies* runneth an appointed course. He ordereth *all* things. He showeth *his* signs distinctly, that ye may be assured ye must meet your LORD *at the last day.* (3) *It is* he who hath stretched forth the earth, and placed therein steadfast mountains and rivers; and hath ordained therein of every fruit two *different* kinds. He causeth the night to cover the day. Herein are certain signs upon people who consider. (4) And in the earth are tracts *of land of different natures, though* bordering on each other; and also vineyards, and seeds, and palm-trees springing several from the same root, and singly from distinct roots. They are watered with the same water, yet we render some of them more excellent than others to eat. Herein are surely signs upon people who understand. (5) If thou dost wonder *at the infidels denying the resurrection,* surely wonderful is their saying, After we shall have been *reduced to* dust, shall we *be restored* in a new creature? (6) These are they who believe not in

---

(1) "The meaning of these letters is unknown. Of several conjectural explications which are given of them, the following is one: 'I am the most wise and knowing God.'"—*Sale.*

The truth. See note on chap. iii. 3.

(2) The popular Arab notions as to astronomy are represented here. The Creator of the heavens, with the luminaries thereof, is the true God. His works testify of his eternal power and godhead.

(3) *To different kinds, e.g.,* "sweet and sour, black and white, small and large."—*Sale, Jaláluddín.*

The original word is *zaujain,* meaning *pairs.*

(4) *Tracts of land, &c.* "Some being fruitful and others barren, some plain and other mountainous, &c."—*Sale, Jaláluddín.*

their LORD; these *shall have* collars on their necks, and these *shall be* the inhabitants of *hell*-fire: therein shall they abide for ever. (7) They will ask of thee to hasten evil rather than good: although there have already been examples *of the divine vengeance* before them. Thy LORD is surely endued with indulgence towards men, notwithstanding their iniquity; but thy LORD is also severe in punishing. (8) The infidels say, Unless a sign be sent down unto him from his LORD, *we will not believe.* Thou art *commissioned to be* a preacher only, *and not a worker of miracles;* and unto every people *hath* a director *been appointed.*

---

(6) *Collars.* "The 'collar' here mentioned is an engine something like a pillory, but light enough for the criminal to walk about with. Besides the hole to fix it on the neck, there is another for one of the hands, which is thereby fastened to the neck. And in this manner the Muhammadans suppose the reprobates will appear at the day of judgment. Some understand this passage figuratively, of the infidels being bound in the chains of error and obstinacy."—*Sale, Baidháwi.*

See also chap. v. 69, and note there.

(7) *To hasten evil.* "Provoking and daring thee to call down the Divine vengeance on them for their impenitency."—*Sale.* Rather daring Muhammad to bring down the wrath threatened against them for rejecting his prophetic claims.

(8) It is a fair inference from this verse that Muhammad wrought no miracles, not only because they were asked for, but because he here disclaims being a worker of miracles. "Thou art a preacher only."

The explanation of the commentators (see *Tafsír-i-Hussaini*) that God gave his prophets miracles suited to the age in which they lived, *e.g.*, to Moses it was given to excel in jugglery, to Jesus to excel in the curing art, &c., is very puerile indeed, and predicates excessive ignorance as to the nature of the miracles wrought by these prophets. The author of the Notes on the Roman Urdu Qurán may well ask what the plagues of Egypt had to do with jugglery, or what Christ's walking on the waves, or his raising the dead, or his feeding the five thousand, had to do with the art of medicine; or what evidence is there that the age of Muhammad was marked by anything peculiar in the style or beauty of its literary productions, that the beauty and style of the Qurán should be regarded as a miracle peculiarly suited to that time? The fact is, the passage before us clearly proves that the miracle of the Qurán was never recognised by any of Muhammad's contemporaries outside the pale of Islám.

‖ (9) GOD knoweth what every female beareth *in her womb*, and what the wombs want or exceed *of their due time or number of young*. With him is everything *regulated* according to a *determined* measure. (10) *He* knoweth that which is hidden and that which is revealed. *He is* the great, the most high. (11) He among you who concealeth *his* words, and he who proclaimeth them in public; he also who seeketh to hide himself in the night, and he who goeth forth openly in the day, is equal *in respect to the knowledge of God*. (12) Each of them hath *angels* mutually succeeding each other, before him and behind him; they watch him by the command of GOD. Verily GOD will not change *his grace* which is in men until they change the *disposition* in their souls *by sin*. When GOD willeth evil on a people there shall be none to avert it, neither shall they have any protector beside him. (13) *It is* he who causeth the lightning to appear unto you, to *strike* fear, and *to raise* hope, and who formeth the pregnant clouds. (14) The thunder celebrateth his praise, and the angels *also*, for fear of him. He sendeth his thunder-

---

(12) *They watch him, &c.* See Prelim. Disc., p. 119.

(13) *And to raise hope.* "Thunder and lightning being the sign of approaching rain, a great blessing in the Eastern countries more especially."—*Sale.*

(14) *Thunder celebrateth his praise.* "Or causeth those who hear it to praise him. Some commentators tell us that by the word *thunder* in this place is meant the angel who presides over the clouds, and drives them forward with twisted sheets of fire."—*Sale, Baidháwi.*

While they dispute concerning God. "This passage was revealed on the following occasion. Amar Ibn al Tufail and Arbád Ibn Rábiah, the brother of Labíd, went to Muhammad with an intent to kill him; and Amar began to dispute with him concerning the chief points of his doctrine, while Arbád, taking a compass, went behind him to despatch him with his sword; but the Prophet perceiving his design, implored God's protection; whereupon Arbád was immediately struck dead by thunder, and Amar was struck with a pestilential boil, of which he died in a short time in a miserable condition.

Jaláluddín, however, tells another story, saying that Muhammad having sent one to invite a certain man to embrace his religion, the person but this question to the missionary, 'Who is this apostle, and

bolts, and striketh therewith whom he pleaseth, while they dispute concerning GOD; for he is mighty in power. (15) *It is* he *who* ought of right to be invoked; and the *idols* which they invoke besides him, shall not hear them at all, otherwise than as he *is heard* who stretcheth forth his hands to the water that it may ascend to his mouth when it cannot ascend *thither:* the supplication of the unbelievers is utterly erroneous. (16) Whatsoever is in heaven and on earth worshippeth GOD, voluntarily or of force; and their shadows *also,* morning and evening. (17) Say, Who is the LORD of heaven and earth? Answer, GOD. Say, Have ye, therefore, taken *unto yourselves* protectors beside him, who are unable either to help or to *defend* themselves from hurt? Say, Shall the blind and the seeing be esteemed equal? or shall darkness and light be accounted the same? or have they attributed companions unto GOD. who have created as he hath created, so that their creation bear any resemblance unto his? Say, GOD is the creator of all things; he is the one, the victorious *God.* (18) He causeth water to descend from heaven, and the brooks flow according to their *respective* measure, and the floods bear the floating froth: and from *the metals* which they melt in the fire, seeking *to cast* ornaments or vessels *for use, there ariseth* a scum like unto it. Thus GOD setteth forth truth and vanity. But the scum is thrown off, and that which is useful to mankind remaineth on the earth. Thus doth

---

what is God? Is he of gold, or of silver, or of brass?' Upon which a thunderbolt struck off his skull and killed him."—*Sale.*

This story is manifestly a pure fiction, constructed by the commentators out of the materials found in this passage. If true, the passage would have to be assigned to the year A.H. 9 or 10 at Madína, whereas the internal evidence fixes it, beyond all reasonable dispute, at Makkah before the Hijra.

(16) *Voluntarily or of force.* "The infidels and devils themselves being constrained to humble themselves before him, though against their will, when they are delivered up to punishment."—*Sale.*

Morning and evening. When the shadows are longest, and appear prostrate in the posture of adoration.

(17-22) This is one of the best passages of the Qurán, and points to the best days of the preacher of Makkah.

GOD put forth parables. Unto those who obey their LORD *shall be given* the most excellent *reward;* but those who obey him not, although they were possessed of whatever is in the whole earth and as much more, they would give it *all* for their ransom. These will be brought to a terrible account: their abode *shall be* hell; an unhappy couch *shall it be!*

NISF.

R 3/8.

|| (19) Shall he, therefore, who knoweth that what hath been sent down unto thee from thy LORD is truth be *rewarded* as he who is blind? The prudent only will consider; (20) who fulfil the covenant of GOD, and break not *their* contract; (21) and who join that which GOD hath commanded to be joined, and *who* fear their LORD, and dread an ill account; (22) and who persevere out of a *sincere* desire to please their LORD, and observe the stated times of prayer, and give alms out of what we have bestowed on them, in secret and openly, and who turn away evil with good: the reward of these *shall be* paradise, (23) gardens of eternal abode, which they shall enter, and *also* whoever shall have acted uprightly, of their fathers, and their wives, and their posterity: and the

---

(21) *Who join, &c.* "By believing in all the prophets without exception, and joining thereto the continual practice of their duty, both towards God and man."—*Sale, Jaláluddín.*

(23) *Their wives.* This is one of five passages in the Qurán distinctly asserting that women as well as men shall enter the joys of the Muslim Paradise. The other passages are chaps. ix. 73, xxxvi. 56, xl. 8, xliii. 70.

"Gibbon characteristically observes that 'Mahomet has not specified the male companions of the female elect, lest he should either alarm the jealousy of their former husbands, or disturb their felicity by the suspicion of an everlasting marriage.' The remark, made in raillery, is pregnant with reason, and aims a fatal blow (if any were needed) at the Paradise of Islám. Faithful women will renew their youth in heaven as well as faithful men; why should not their good works merit an equal and analogous reward? But Mahomet shrunk from this legitimate conclusion."—*Muir's Life of Mahomet,* vol. ii. p. 143.

The expression *gardens of eternal abode* is translated by Rodwell "gardens of Eden." But the commentators do not take the word Eden in the sense which it bears in Hebrew. See note on chap. ix. 73.

angels shall go in unto them by every gate, (24) *saying*, Peace be upon you, because ye have endured with patience: how excellent a reward is paradise! (25) But as for those who violate the covenant of GOD after the establishment thereof, and *who* cut in sunder. that which GOD hath commanded to be joined, and act corruptly in the earth, on them shall a curse *fall*, and they shall have a miserable dwelling *in hell*. (26) GOD giveth provision in abundance unto whom he pleaseth, and is sparing *unto whom he pleaseth*. *Those of Makkah* rejoice in the present life, although the present life, in respect of the future, is but a *precarious* provision.

‖ (27) The infidels say, Unless a sign be sent down unto him from his LORD, *we will not believe*. Answer, Verily, GOD will lead into error whom he pleaseth, and will direct unto himself him who repenteth, (28) *and* those who believe, and whose hearts rest securely in the meditation of GOD; shall not *men's* hearts rest securely in the meditation of GOD? They who believe and do that which is right *shall enjoy* blessedness and *partake of* a happy resurrection. (29) Thus have we sent thee to a nation which *other* nations have preceded *unto whom prophets have likewise been sent*, that thou mayest rehearse unto them that which we have revealed unto thee, even while they believe not in the merciful *God*. Say *unto them*, He is my LORD; there is no GOD but he: in him do I trust, and unto him must I return. (30) Though a Qurán *were*

R $\frac{4}{10}$.

---

(24) *Cut in sunder, &c.*, *i.e.*, by dislocating the faith of all the prophets.—*Tafsír-i-Raufí.* This is just what Muhammad and his followers have done.

(27) *The infidels say, &c.* See notes on ver. 8 above.

(28) *They who believe, &c.*, *i.e.*, who believe in Islám and perform the duties required by it.

(29) *Say unto them, &c.* This, says the *Tafsír-i-Raufí*, was said in reply to the Quraish at the treaty made at Hadaibiya. Muhammad had directed the treaty to be headed by the words "Bismillah ir Rahmán-ar-Rahím," when the Quraish asked, "Who is Rahmán?" The story is apparently a pure invention to explain the allusion of the text.

revealed by which mountains should be removed, or the earth cleaved in sunder, or the dead be caused to speak, *it would be in vain.* But the matter *belongeth* wholly unto GOD. Do not, therefore, the believers know, that if GOD pleased, he would certainly direct all men? (31) Adversity shall not cease to afflict the unbelievers for that which they have committed, or to sit down near their habitations, until GOD's promise come; for GOD is not contrary to the promise.

|| (32) Apostles before thee have been laughed to scorn; and I permitted the infidels to enjoy a long and happy life; but afterwards I punished them; and how *severe* was the punishment which I *inflicted on them!* (33) Who is it, therefore, that standeth over every soul, *to observe* that

---

(30) *By which mountains, &c.* "These are miracles which the Quraish required of Muhammad, demanding that he would, by the power of his Qurán, either remove the mountains from about Makkah, that they might have delicious gardens in their room; or that he would oblige the wind to transport them, with their merchandise, to Syria (according to which tradition, the words here translated 'or the earth cleaved in sunder,' should be rendered 'or the earth be travelled over' in an instant); or else raise to life Kusai Ibn Kaláb, and others of their ancestors, to bear witness to him; whereupon this passage was revealed."—*Sale.* See also chap. viii. 23, and note.

(31) *Their habitations.* "It is supposed by some that these words are spoken to Muhammad, and then they must be translated in the second person, 'Nor shalt thou cease to sit down,' &c. For they say this verse relates to the idolaters of Makkah, who were afflicted with a series of misfortunes for their ill-usage of the Prophet, and were also continually annoyed and harassed by his parties, which frequently plundered their caravans and drove off their cattle, himself sitting down with his whole army near the city in the expedition of al Hudaibiya."—*Sale, Baidháwi.*

Until God's promise come, i.e., "till death and the day of judgment overtake them; or, according to the exposition in the preceding note, until the taking of Makkah."—*Sale, Baidháwi.*

The interpretation making this verse refer to the expedition to Hudaibiya is founded upon the imagination of the commentators. It is certainly better to regard the passage as Makkan, and to make the verse allude to some calamity—perhaps the famine of chap. xi. 11—which had overtaken the people, and which Muhammad used to give point to his threatenings.

which it committeth? They attribute companions unto GOD. Say, Name them: will ye declare unto him that which he knoweth not in the earth? or *will ye name them in outward speech only*? But the deceitful procedure of the infidels was prepared for them, and they are turned aside from the *right* path; for he whom GOD shall cause to err shall have no director. (34) They shall suffer a punishment in this life, but the punishment of the next shall be more grievous; and there shall be none to protect them against GOD. (35) *This is* the description of paradise which is promised to the pious. It is watered by rivers; its food is perpetual, and its shade *also:* this shall be the reward of those who fear *God.* But the reward of the infidels shall be *hell-*fire.' (36) Those to whom we have given the scriptures, rejoice at what hath been revealed unto thee. Yet *there are* some of the con-

---

(33) *Outward speech only.* "That is, calling them the companions of God, without being able to assign any reason, or give any proof why they deserve to be sharers in the honour and worship due from mankind to him."—*Sale, Baidháwi.*

Whom God shall cause to err, &c. The idea is that God having given them over to final destruction, they have become judicially blind, and are therefore hopelessly lost. This points to the latter years of Muhammad's career as preacher at Makkah.

(36) *Those . . . rejoice, &c.*, viz., "the first proselytes to Muhammadanism from Judaism and Christianity; or the Jews and Christians in general, who were pleased to find the Qurán so consonant to their own Scriptures." See also notes on chaps. iii. 199, and vi. 20.

"The confidence with which Mahomet refers to the testimony of the Jews and of their Scripture is very remarkable. It leaves us no room to doubt that some amongst the Jews, possessed probably of an imperfect and superficial acquaintance with their own books and traditions, encouraged Mahomet in the idea that he might be, or positively affirmed that he was, 'that prophet whom the Lord their God should raise up unto them of their brethren.'"—*Muir's Life of Mahomet,* vol. ii. pp. 183, 184. Compare chaps. xxxiv. 6, x. 93, vi. 20, xxviii. 52, and xvii. 108.

The confederates who deny. "That is, such of them as had entered into a confederacy to oppose Muhammad, as did Káb Ibn al Ashraf, and the Jews who followed him, and Sayad al Najráni, al Akib, and several other Christians, who denied such parts of the Qurán as contradicted their corrupt doctrines and traditions."—*Sale.*

federates who deny part thereof. Say *unto them*, Verily I am commanded to worship GOD alone; and to him give no companion: upon him do I call, and unto him shall I return. (37) To this purpose have we sent down *the Qurán, a rule of* judgment, in the Arabic language. And verily, if thou follow their desires, after the knowledge which hath been given thee, there shall be none to defend or protect thee against GOD.

$_1$R$_2^6$.   ‖ (38) We have formerly sent apostles before thee, and bestowed on them wives and children; and no apostle had *the power* to come with a sign, unless by the permission of GOD. Every age hath its book *of revelation*. (39) GOD shall abolish and shall confirm *what he pleaseth*. With him is the original of the book. (40) Moreover, whether we cause thee to see any part of that *punishment* wherewith we have threatened them, or whether we cause thee to die *before it be inflicted on them*, verily unto thee *belongeth* preaching *only*, but unto us inquisition. (41) Do they not see that we come into *their* land, and straiten

---

(37) *If thou follow their desires, &c.* This probably refers to Muhammad's temporary lapse in making a compromise with idolatry. For an account of it see Muir's *Life of Mahomet*, vol. ii. chap. v.

(38) *Wives and children.* "As we have on thee. This passage was revealed in answer to the reproaches which were cast on Muhammad on account of the great number of his wives. For the Jews said that if he was a true prophet his care and attention would be employed about something else than women and the getting of children. It may be observed that it is a maxim of the Jews that nothing is more repugnant to prophecy than carnality" (Maimon., *More Nev.*, part ii. c. 36, &c.—*Sale, Jaláluddín, Yahya.*

Every age hath its book. See chap. ii. 4, note.

(39) *Abolish, &c.* See notes on chap. ii. 105.

The original book. "Literally, *the mother of the book*, by which is meant *the Preserved Table*, from which all the written revelations which have been from time to time published to mankind, according to the several dispensations, are transcripts."—*Sale.*

(40) *Unto thee belongeth preaching only.* See above on ver. 8.

(41) *We came into their land, &c.* This passage is of Madína origin, and refers to the encroachments of the Muslims on their idolatrous neighbours. It is probably an addition, made either by Muhammad himself or by the compilers after his death.

the borders thereof *by the conquests of the true believers?* When GOD judgeth, there is none to reverse his judgment; and he *will be* swift in taking an account. (42) Their predecessors formerly devised subtle plots *against their prophets,* but God is master of every subtle device. He knoweth that which every soul deserveth; and the infidels shall surely know whose will be the reward of Paradise. (43) The unbelievers will say, Thou art not sent *of God.* Answer, GOD is a sufficient witness between me and you, and he who understandeth the scriptures.

---

(43) *Thou art not sent.* "The persons intended in this passage, it is said, were the Jewish doctors."—*Sale, Baidháwi.*

He who understandeth the Scriptures. See notes on chap. vi. 20 and above on ver. 36.

END OF VOL. II.

www.ingramcontent.com/pod-product-compliance
Lightning Source LLC
Chambersburg PA
CBHW050850300426
44111CB00010B/1200